Pilgrims, Patrons, and Place

ASIAN RELIGIONS AND SOCIETY SERIES

A Buddha Dharma Kyokai Foundation Book on Buddhism and Comparative Religion

General Editor: Neil McMullin

Edited by Phyllis Granoff and Koichi Shinohara

Editorial Assistant: Jack Laughlin

Pilgrims, Patrons, and Place: Localizing Sanctity in Asian Religions

UBCPress · Vancouver · Toronto

09 08 07 06 05 04 03 5 4 3 2 1

Printed in Canada on acid-free paper

National Library of Canada Cataloguing in Publication Data

Main entry under title:

Pilgrims, patrons, and place : localizing sanctity in Asian religions / Phyllis Granoff and Koichi Shinohara, editors.

(Asian religions and society series, ISSN 1705-4761)
Includes bibliographical references and index.
ISBN 0-7748-1038-6

1. Sacred space – Asia. 2. Asia – Religious life and customs. I. Granoff, P.E. (Phyllis Emily), 1947- II. Shinohara, Koichi, 1941- III. Series.

BL1033.P54 2003 291.3'5'095 C2003-910156-8

This book has been published with the help of a grant from the Buddha Dharma Kyokai Foundation of Canada.

UBC Press gratefully acknowledges the financial support for our publishing program of the Government of Canada through the Book Publishing Industry Development Program (BPIDP), and of the Canada Council for the Arts, and the British Columbia Arts Council.

Book layout and production by Kaleidoscope
Toronto, Canada, www.kveinc.com

All photographs are by the authors unless otherwise indicated.

UBC Press
The University of British Columbia
2029 West Mall
Vancouver, BC V6T 1Z2
604-822-5959 / Fax: 604-822-6083
www.ubcpress.ca

Contents

Contributors

Véronique Bouillier, Directeur de recherches, CNRS, Paris

Robert L. Brown, Department of Art History, University of California at Los Angeles

Winand M. Callewaert, Department of Oriental Studies, University of Leuven

André Couture, Faculté de Théologie, Université Laval

Louis Gabaude, École Française d'Extrême-Orient, Thailand

Phyllis Granoff, Department of Religious Studies, McMaster University

K.I. Koppedrayer, Department of Religion and Culture, Wilfrid Laurier University

Jack Laughlin, Department of Religious Studies, University of Sudbury

Françoise Mallison, Directeur d'Études, École pratique des Hautes Études, Sorbonne

Heidi Pauwels, Department of Asian Languages and Literatures, University of Washington

Koichi Shinohara, Department of Religious Studies, McMaster University

Franciscus Verellen, École Française d'Extrême-Orient and Institute of Chinese Studies, The Chinese University of Hong Kong

Acknowledgements

The editors thank the BDK Foundation, Canada, for their generous support towards the preparation of this volume for publication and for the conference at which these essays were originally presented. We also thank the Social Sciences and Humanities Research Council Canada for their support of the conference.

All photographs are by the authors unless otherwise indicated.

Introduction

Pilgrims, Patrons, and Place: Localizing Sanctity in Asian Religions

PHYLLIS GRANOFF AND KOICHI SHINOHARA

The essays in this volume were originally presented at a conference, Sacred Space and Sacred Biography in Asian Religious Traditions, held in June 1998 at McMaster University and the University of Toronto. The conference was funded by a grant from the Social Sciences and Humanities Research Council of Canada and the Yehan Numata Foundation. A quick perusal of the table of contents makes immediately clear what was one of the most challenging and rewarding features of the conference: its intellectual range and diversity. The essays span a broad geographical area that includes India, Nepal, Thailand, Indonesia, and China. They discuss Buddhism, Jainism, Hinduism, and Taoism, and they explore issues from the classical and medieval periods and the contemporary world. Several examine Asian religions that have been little studied either in Europe or in North America – the Nath Yogīs of Nepal, the Jakhs of Saurashtra, and the sixteenth-century Vaiṣṇava movement of Assam – and which are not often represented in standard works on South Asian religions. The contributors' perspectives are as diverse as their subject matter – anthropologist, art historian, Sinologist, Indologist, or Buddhologist – we each bring to our essays a particular way of seeing and thinking about our material. Nonetheless, from our intensive discussions together we became aware of many common concerns.

Many essays emphasize that sacred places may have a plurality of meanings in a religious community; holy sites may be sanctified in a number of ways – by the presence of certain marvellous natural features thought to yield substances conducive to salvation; by the presence of certain man-made or divinely made objects, things that a saint has used, for example. They may also be sanctified by the deeds of a saint, and it is here that most obviously sacred place and sacred biography intersect. Such multiple layers of meaning may not always be immediately obvious; in one case, we learn how the description of the construction of a sacred city shows remarkable parallels to rituals for the construction of a much earlier sacred space, an impermanent sacrificial altar. This understanding adds layers of meaning to the sacred city, meanings that might have otherwise remained undetected.

A number of essays reveal that sacred places often transcended the immediate and the local and were situated in a time that is cosmic in scale and in realms that lie beyond the terrestrial. In some cases, we note a tension between the strictly local and that which lay beyond it, as a local group in its hagiographies recounted miracles done outside the local territory and sought its legitimation not from local rulers but from the outside world. Sacred sites and the cults associated with them often seemed to be precariously balanced between the specific and the denial of that specificity, whether that was done by situating the sacred place in a cosmic framework, or as we see in one essay, by the enactment of rituals in which a local group must move outside its territory to worship at another sacred place.

Other essays highlight the visionary aspects of sacred place. Access to sacred space is often gained through a religious vision; a revelation may also initiate the recognition of a system of sacred places. The visionary nature may well be related to the paradoxical nature that we noted above; sacred place is both fixed on the ordinary map and beyond all time and space, existing in some heavenly or other-worldly sphere. This, in turn, could have practical repercussions for religious groups who sought to legitimate themselves by reference to sacred place and who argued with each other over the control of holy sites. If they failed to win, a group could deny that a particular holy site was indeed rooted in a specific geographical place and tied to that place. Instead, the holy site could become a visionary place reached by those unable to dominate the place in reality, but who could see it vividly in meditation.

Visions were not limited to cases in which holy places had become contested space. As they spread out from their homeland, missionary religions were faced with the challenge of creating new sacred places. One strategy they used was to deny the specificity of the place that had been the original homeland by creating elaborate visionary geographies in which the new homeland had as much a claim as did the original one. In more than one case, visionary sacred place was associated with other religious concerns – for example, the preservation of the true beliefs in a time of declining virtue. As a cosmic rather than a local site, the sacred place became a shrine to the preserved teaching even at the moment when the world is destroyed. Such eschatological concerns were apparent in early medieval China and in early and medieval India.

Religious groups were not the only ones interested in sacred sites. Political leaders could use patronage of a sacred site to legitimate their much more secular concerns. Of the many dramas enacted on the stage of sacred place, the contests between secular and religious authority, between the erudite learning of the established upper classes and the deep faith of the dispossessed, are discussed in several of the essays.

We would like to introduce the reader to the essays in this collection by highlighting their treatment of some of these general themes.

In his essay, "The Twenty-four Dioceses and Zhang Daoling: The Spatio-Liturgical Organization of Early Heavenly Master Taoism," Franciscus Verellen presents a detailed study of a remarkable use of 'sacred space' in early Taoism. Heavenly Master Taoism developed a system of Twenty-four Dioceses, which as Verellen states, provided the 'basic framework for ordering the spiritual space administered' by the community. The area of these Twenty-four Dioceses corresponds to Sichuan in present-day China. These dioceses were at once specific places on earth and projections of astrological phenomena on earth. They were thus local sites and heavenly sites at the same time. Verellen carefully describes the multiple meanings that the dioceses had for the religious group. They were the seats of administration and the sanctuaries where the rituals of the group were carried out, and they were imbued with sanctity in a number of different ways. Some of them were thought to contain the magical substances, the metals and minerals required for Taoist cultivation. Others were associated with events in the biography of the founder. Still others had been connected with earlier cults. A diocese was thus at once an administrative centre, an earthly counterpart of cosmological entities, a source of wonder-working substances, and the locus of important events in the biography of the important figures of the sect. Verellen also discusses the ways in which the dioceses, by keeping census records of the local population, encroached on civil authority.

This study of the Twenty-four Dioceses highlights one of the common themes in this collection: The dioceses are said to have been created in heaven and then transmitted to Zhang Daoling in a revelation that took place in AD 142 or 143. Finite sacred space thus exists beyond its terrestrial boundaries; the recognition of its earthly counterpart depends upon supernatural revelation. The Twenty-four Dioceses are also connected with eschatological beliefs. Those who participated in the liturgical agenda of the dioceses were to be the survivors of the great cataclysm that would end the world. The power of the dioceses to ensure survival at the end of the world was intimately related not to their nature as earthly sites, but to their many correspondences with heavenly phenomena. Another issue that emerges is the problem that a religious community encountered when it moved from its central location. Verellen discusses how the dioceses, though rooted in a given locale, could be transplanted elsewhere; 'movable' and 'adjunct' dioceses were created to cope with new conditions. The rootedness of sacred space and the necessity to uproot it reappear as a theme in many of the essays.

Koichi Shinohara, in 'The Story of the Buddha's Begging Bowl: Imagining a Biography and Sacred Places,' considers many of these themes. This essay, in particular, discusses the dilemma that Buddhists outside the homeland of Buddhism faced. If holy sites were primarily sanctified by the presence of the Buddha himself, did that mean that as the religion spread there were to be no easily accessible holy places for the new believers? Shinohara describes how Chinese Buddhists coped with this problem. Drawing on strategies that had probably been developed within India in regions like Gandhāra, which was also far from Buddhism's original seat, Chinese Buddhists constructed new holy sites. They did so in a number of ways; instead of sanctifying a site by the presence of the historical Buddha, the new Buddhists relied on an expanded Buddha biography, which told of past Buddhas or past lives of the historical Buddha. They were one step into a process of transcending the local and the here and now; time was now cosmic time, and Shinohara shows how local holy sites became transformed into cosmic space. He reviews a number of accounts that reveal yet another strategy used to create new holy places – the use of portable objects sanctified by the touch of the Buddha that could be taken to Buddhism's new territories. The bowl of the Buddha was one such important cultic object in Gandhāra, as is evidenced by the accounts of Chinese pilgrims to the region and by its depiction in extant sculpted reliefs from Gandhāra.

In addition, Shinohara discusses a remarkable vision of an early medieval Chinese monk. At the end of his life, the *vinaya* master

Daoxuan had a vision in which gods revealed to him a number of extraordinary things. One of their revelations involved the bowl of the Buddha. But this was no ordinary bowl. It replicated itself, levitated, and emitted light. It was no longer just the bowl of the historical Buddha; it was now the bowl of all the Buddhas in the entire universe. In addition, this sacred object was transported from its location on earth and enshrined in a *stūpa* or relic mound in the heavenly realm. Transcending both time and space, it became associated with the preservation of the true religion at a time of declining virtue and increasing chaos. 'Relocalization' of the sacred by means of a portable sacred object in Daoxuan's vision turned into something we might call the 'translocalization' of a sacred object. The specifics of time and place no longer mattered. The bowl of the historical Buddha had become the bowl used by all of the past Buddhas in the universe; it would also be used by the future Buddha. It was no longer in India, nor even in Gandhāra or China. It existed in heaven in elaborate structures created for it by gods and other supernatural beings. Sacred place became increasingly an imagined realm, made known by visions and supernatural revelations. The problem of creating new sacred space was solved by denying the specificity of place. Sacred space was no longer any place on earth, and all terrestrial places could share equally in the vision of the new cosmic place.

Louis Gabaude, in his essay 'Where Ascetics Get Comfort and Recluses Go Public: Museums for Buddhist Saints in Thailand,' looks at a striking modern transformation of the cult of objects connected with saints in Buddhism. Based on his visit to some twenty-five sites in northeastern and northern Thailand, which contain some kind of building dedicated to a saint, Gabaude introduces us to a new kind of *stūpa* or reliquary mound. This is the museum, in which are housed objects connected with the saint during his lifetime. These museums usually contain an image of the saint, either of bronze or wax or resin; the saint's relics; objects that he used; and occasionally books written by the saint or amulets either produced or consecrated by the saint. Gabaude describes for us the transformation of the traditional relic mound, from a closed structure housing relics kept away from the public into a museum where the relics are on constant public display. Gabaude's 'museums' are indeed the opposite of Daoxuan's *stūpas,* located in far-off heavenly realms, accessible now only to religious visions. The tourism they attract, however, suggests the power to draw the faithful of objects that were associated with a saint. The attraction of the Buddha's bowl at Gandhāra and the logic behind the emphasis on portable objects as bearers of sanctity are undeniably clear. Gabaude's analysis of the growth of saints' 'museums' in Thailand today also alerts us to the complexity of monastic politics in the spread of saints' cults and the making of holy sites.

In 'Paradise Found, Paradise Lost: Harirām Vyās's Love for Vrindāban and What Hagiographers Made of It,' Heidi Pauwels studies the 'intersection of sacred biography, sacred place, and community formation' in the Braj area of North India in the late fifteenth and early sixteenth centuries. Vaiṣṇava groups in this period were preoccupied with 'rediscovering' the sites associated with the life of Kṛṣṇa. Pauwels discusses the ways in which Harirām Vyās, one of the pioneer 'discoverers,' sang of Vrindāban, and examines later sectarian appropriations of both Harirām Vyās and the Vrindāban he loved. For Harirām Vyās, sacred space transcended the strictly local and mundane. Vyās discovers in Vrindāban the heavenly abode of Kṛṣṇa and the divine sites of his play, his līlā. Vrindāban exists in a cosmic time for Vyās; it is the source of all creation, prior to and constitutive of both time and place. Vrindāban's essence is captured in religious visions. Despite this emphasis on the transcendent nature of Vrindāban as sacred space, Vyās is aware of Vrindāban as a contested space that is very much the focus of worldly desires. Vyās repeatedly decries the despoliation of his sacred land; he cries out against those who would use Vrindāban for worldly gain. Vrindāban is also the focus of intense competition; Vyās is aware of these competing claims but his response transcends immediate sectarian rivalries. To Vyās, anyone who has absolute devotion to Kṛṣṇa and to Vrindāban, regardless of sectarian affiliation, belongs to the community of true believers. Pauwels traces the appropriation of Vyās by later sectarian authors and the growing interest in their writings in Vrindāban as contested space. Vrindāban is increasingly the stage for sectarian debates. Nonetheless, Vrindāban remains throughout these changes and for all these writers both the local site for which rival groups may compete, and the heavenly realm, to which all may have access in a special kind of seeing gained through devotion.

In 'Pilgrimage as Revelation: Śaṅkaradeva's Journey to Jagannātha Purī,' Phyllis Granoff addresses the themes of sectarian competition for terrestrial sacred space and visionary seeing. Śaṅkaradeva (AD 1449–1568) was the founder of a Vaiṣṇava movement in Assam. As we see in Pauwels' essay, the sixteenth century was a fertile period for the growth of Vaiṣṇava sects. Numerous Vaiṣṇava groups were in the process of settling in the reclaimed holy site of Vrindāban. An equally important Vaiṣṇava place of pilgrimage, at least for Northeastern India, was the temple of Jagannātha at Purī in Orissa. The temple, probably of the twelfth century, had become intimately associated with royal power in Orissa, but it nonetheless remained a religious centre for Vaiṣṇavas from all over the northeast, and indeed elsewhere in India. Like Vrindāban, its religious and economic importance made it a stage for sectarian competition.

Vaiṣṇavism in Northeastern India for the period can be roughly divided into three groups. In addition to Śaṅkaradeva's Vaiṣṇavism in Assam, there was an indigenous Vaiṣṇava movement within Orissa itself, which was an esoteric religious movement greatly influenced by Tantric practices. But the main Vaiṣṇava sect was the ecstatic religion of the Bengali saint Caitanya (AD 1485–1533), which quickly spread throughout North India. The followers of Caitanya competed for control of holy places in Vrindāban and at Purī. Biographies of the Oriya Vaiṣṇava poet-saints confirm the evidence of the Assamese biographies of Śaṅkaradeva, which depict Caitanya and his followers as well-established at Purī and somewhat jealous of their control over the site. Nonetheless, so great was the lure of Purī and so important the legitimization to be gained from Lord Jagannātha, that we find Śaṅkaradeva in his biographies setting out on a pilgrimage from his native Assam to the temple in Orissa.

At first glance it might seem that Śaṅkaradeva faced the opposite problem from that faced by the medieval Chinese Buddhists discussed by Shinohara. For the Chinese Buddhist, the problem was to make China, so far from the original homeland of Buddhism, into a legitimate Buddhist land with specially sanctified sites. The biographies of Śaṅkaradeva concede that the temple of Jagannātha in Orissa was the centre of Vaiṣṇava religious activity; their challenge was to find a role for Śaṅkaradeva at the temple where the Bengalis were already entrenched. Granoff discusses the strategy they used; it is a strategy we have in fact seen the medieval Chinese Buddhists employ. The sacred site is displaced from its actual physical location and transported into a visionary world. Śaṅkaradeva does reach Purī, but the gods in the temple, in fact, come to him. It requires dreams and visionary sight, however, for Śaṅkaradeva and his devotees to see them. The presence of the gods in Śaṅkaradeva's lodging turns the lodging into the true temple. Śaṅkaradeva and his followers make other 'visionary' pilgrimages; they see the holy city of Dvārakā, which had been submerged in the ocean, rise from the sea and Śaṅkaradeva enthroned there as Lord Kṛṣṇa. Granoff also discusses a problem that was perhaps unique to the Hindu context, and that is the problem of the god as pilgrim. Śaṅkaradeva, like Caitanya, was regarded by his followers as a divine incarnation. Why would God ever need to travel to find God? This question, too, is answered by displacement and visionary transposition of the holy site.

Śaṅkaradeva was not the only medieval Indian saint to visit Dvārakā. In 'The "Early Hindi" Hagiographies of Anantadās,' Winand Callewaert introduces us to Pīpā, whose unusual career was recounted in verses by another devotee, Anantadās, probably around 1600. Like the visit of Śaṅkaradeva, Pīpā's visit is to more than just the physical city of Dvārakā. As Callewaert tells us, Pīpā's visit to Dvārakā is also the occasion for him to reveal himself as divine to the people. Callewaert fleshes out our understanding of the religious conditions in sixteenth-century North India. Harirām Vyās and those who later appropriated him as their own were only a sample of the many saints who journeyed across the Indian sacred landscape, often from pilgrimage centre to pilgrimage centre, or from city to city, where they gathered their followers and engaged in debates with their rivals. Callewaert has led the scholarly efforts in editing the texts that are attributed to these poet-saints and in reconstructing their history by closely examining the manuscript evidence – essentially oral texts, the study of which raises many issues, as Pauwels also notes. After a brief selection of verses dealing with other saints, Callewaert discusses in some detail the *parcāi* of Pīpā.

The holy city of Dvārakā, site of one of Śaṅkaradeva's visions and of the revelation of Pīpā's divinity, is the subject of André Couture's essay, 'Dvārakā: The Making of a Sacred Place.' He begins by asking us to broaden our definition of sacred place. We have seen the dioceses of Heavenly Master Taoism, administrative units, magical landscapes, and temples; the supernatural *stūpas* or reliquaries housing the Buddha's begging bowl; the heavenly gardens of Vrindāban, where Kṛṣṇa had sported; and the great temple of Jagannāth at Purī. These are all places that are eternal, either because they correspond to eternal entities in heaven, or because they are indeed the supramundane world that has somehow descended onto the terrestrial place. Dvārakā seems to be the unthinkable: as a holy site that is temporary, it is doomed to perish. Couture gives us a detailed description of Dvārakā in the *Harivaṃśa,* which is regarded as a supplement to the great Sanskrit epic, the *Mahābhārata.* He explains the genesis of the notion of an impermanent sacred space in the Vedic fire altar of earliest Indian ritual. The fire altar has the shape of a bird, and when the city of Dvārakā is fully formed, it comes down to earth as a bird.

Couture argues that Dvārakā should be understood as an extension of the divine body. According to the doctrine of *avatāras* or incarnation, Kṛṣṇa comes to earth to complete a designated task. When the task is done, he must return to heaven. Dvārakā, the locus of the exercise of his divine power, similarly has a limited duration on earth. Couture addresses themes that come up in the other essays, such as the heavenly origins of the holy site. Even more intriguing, perhaps, is the fact that its main architectural structure, the *sabhā* or assembly hall, can be regarded as the eternal presence of the true religion, *dharma.* Eschatological themes such as the destruction of the holy site and the notion of a holy place in which the true religion may be embodied in a physical object cannot fail to remind us of the Heavenly Master Dioceses or Daoxuan's *stūpas.*

In 'Place in the Sacred Biography at Borobudur,' Robert Brown asks us to re-examine our understanding of the concept of 'sacred place.' Borobudur in Central Java is the site of a massive stone Buddhist monument, which scholars have called a *stūpa,* but which is more like a terraced mountain. It was built in the ninth century. The terraces are covered with stone-carved reliefs, some of which illustrate the *Karmavibhaṅga,* a Buddhist text on the law of karma. Other reliefs depict the biography of the Buddha, both from the *jātakas,* which are stories of his past lives, and from the *Lalitavistara,* which describes his historical life. Still other reliefs depict the pilgrimage of Sudhana, in search of transcendent wisdom, a journey described in vivid and visionary language in the *Gaṇḍavyūha.* Borobudur itself is a sacred space; as a *stūpa,* it embodies the presence of the Buddha. It is a unique monument, and scholars have long debated its many possible layers of meaning. But this is not the 'sacred space' that Brown describes; Brown looks at the individual reliefs to see how the artist created a space within a given scene that was different from other narrative space. He suggests that artists had a number of means at their disposal and that the artists at Borobudur used several key techniques. They relied on hierarchy, for example, to indicate the importance of a personage. In the relief, an important individual is placed higher than subsidiary figures; seating the figure on a raised platform thus marks the space around it as sacred space, space occupied by a figure worthy of devotion. Similarly, the presence of retainers and of special architectural structures creates and marks the 'sacred space' of the relief. If Verellen had listed for us the ways in which geographical space can be 'marked' as sacred through 'recognizable objects, structures, activities, and sensations,' Brown does the same for the reliefs at Borobudur. He also raises another important issue that formed a leitmotif of the conference, how sacred space is treated by religions that have left their original homeland. He argues that the sacred space created by the Borobudur reliefs reflects a local understanding of society and human activity that is not simply derived from a rote understanding of imported Indian texts.

Differing patterns of sacred space, created this time not by art but by ritual performance, is one of the themes of Véronique Bouillier's essay, 'Ratannāth's Travels.' The Kānphaṭā Yogīs, followers of yogic practices attributed to the eleventh- or twelfth-century Nāth Yogī Gorakhnāth, established one of their monasteries in the Dang Valley in Nepal. They credit the founding of their monastic establishment to a saint named Ratannāth. As Bouillier tells us, 'Ratannāth's presence in the Caughera monastery today is not only in its narrative. The ritual makes him come to life in the person of the head of the monastery.' The ritual to which she refers is the annual pilgrimage that takes the *pīr*, as he is called, away from the monastery and to the Indian town of Devi Patan, to visit a goddess temple there. This is also the occasion of the annual installation of the new *pīr*. Much like Couture's Dvārakā, the holy man as locus of sanctity is a temporary entity. Every year a new *pīr* must be chosen and entrusted with the sacred duty of worshipping the main cult object in the monastery, the *amritapātra* or 'vessel of the nectar of immortality.' This centrifugal pull, as she describes it, has its parallel in the local legends told of Ratannāth. While Ratannāth is above all a son of the soil, deeply 'rooted in the landscape of Dang and even involved in the rise of the Dang kingdom as a poltical entity,' it is curious that the miracle stories that are told of him all take place outside of Dang. Indeed, Ratannāth receives his legitimation not from local leaders, but from the distant 'Badshah,' as he is called, the Muslim sovereign.

In the Nāth legends, Ratannāth is, paradoxically, a local saint, who is rarely mentioned outside the local tradition, at the same time as he earns his credentials to sainthood in his travels outside the area.

Bouillier describes how the pilgrimage to Devi Patan can also be understood as a confirmation from outside, this time by the goddess there, of the new *pīr*, the human embodiment of Ratannāth. The travels of the saint, in his legends and in his contemporary embodiment, raise now familiar questions about the dialectic between 'local and foreign' sacred space. Bouillier asks how precise historical circumstances, some of which remain obscure to us today, might have led religious groups to formulate notions of 'local' and 'foreign' that are more flexible than we might have otherwise suspected.

Kay Koppedrayer's essay, 'The Interweave of Place, Space, and Biographical Discourse at a South Indian Religious Centre,' unravels the complex skeins out of which a particular sacred site, in this case the distant Mt Kailāsa in the Himalayan mountains, is woven. Koppedrayer examines a south Indian religious institution, the monastery at Dharmapuram. Observation of contemporary ritual is also central to her investigation. Once a year, on the occasion of the new moon day of the month of Āṭi (July to August), the monastery holds a festival to celebrate Mt Kailāsa. This is curious in and of itself; Mt Kailāsa, regarded as the home of the god Śiva, is far from the world of Dharmapuram, if we are speaking in terms of terrestrial distance. However, there is no physical pilgrimage involved in this celebration for most of the celebrants, although the festival does commemorate the pilgrimage in 1959 to Mt Kailāsa by the twenty-fifth head of the centre. The distance to the holy site, a problem we have seen many times, is transversed during the festival by means of an icon, a painting of the mountain that is worshipped by the head of the monastery.

As a sacred site, Mt Kailāsa has multiple meanings for the members of the community, which Koppedrayer carefully unravels for us. It was at Mt Kailāsa that Śiva first taught the doctrine that eventually was transmitted to the group, and thus the group associates it with their legitimation. Members of the Dharmapuram monastery, in fact, call themselves the Kailāsaparamparai, 'the lineage of Kailāsa.' As Koppedrayer explains, 'For the members of the Dharmapuram Adhinam, the seat of their guru is Mt Kailāsa; the wisdom that animates their guru, embodied in the present Gurumahāsannidhānam, is descended from Śiva himself.' The icon of Mt Kailāsa that is displayed is also a special image, a painting that was made from the photograph taken at the time of the 1959 pilgrimage. It thus freezes and removes from the transitory realm of ordinary time both the act and the object of worship. Koppedrayer links the worship of Mt

Kailāsa by the Dharmapuram monastery today to earlier religious practices in Tamil Śaivism. As we follow her readings of this ritual and its multiple layers of significance, we see sacred space, historical process, biography, and ritual intersect to create a complex web of religious meanings.

The use of art to freeze a moment of worship and lift the sacred site and its rituals out of ordinary time into the timeless is also a theme in Jack Laughlin's essay, 'Portraiture and Jain Sacred Place: The Patronage of the Ministers Vastupāla and Tejaḥpāla.' Laughlin explores in detail the records of the donations made by the two brothers, Vastupāla and Tejaḥpāla, in thirteenth-century Gujarat. The brothers, who served as ministers under the local Vāghelā kings, were ardent Jains, although some of their donations were made to Hindu temples. Laughlin focuses on a particular kind of donation that these brothers seemed particularly eager to make: the donation of portraits of themselves, of members of their immediate family, and of the local rulers. He shows concretely something that other essays have suggested from a reading of the texts, namely, that the sacred site had intimate ties to the other world. He argues that the Jain temple was the *samavasaraṇa,* the heavenly assembly hall made by the gods for the Jina who had reached Enlightenment, and that the portraits of themselves and their relatives that the ministers erected, were meant to display them as gods, either as protectors of the quarters, or as the god Indra, the archetypical worshipper of the Jina in Jain mythology. Laughlin also suggests that by placing themselves in stone as perpetual worshippers, the brothers were able to perpetuate the merits of their worship long beyond the merits they might have gained from the simple physical act of worship accomplished by going to the temple, praying, and then departing.

The need somehow to lift the sacred site out of the mundane world of the transitory is here accomplished by fixing the worshipper in stone and by the arrangement of statues, which suggests that the worshipper himself is not mortal, but is one of the gods, if not in eternal submission, still engaged in devotion that far outlasts what the ordinary mortal can offer. The sacred site is transformed into heaven not by religious vision but by carefully articulated and, as Laughlin demonstrates, often politically motivated patronage. Laughlin's study clearly illustrates the role of politics and secular concerns in the patronage of holy sites, a theme we have seen in other essays.

Françoise Mallison, in 'Saints and Sacred Places in Saurashtra and Kutch: The Cases of the Naklaṃki Cult and the Jakhs,' provides us with a glimpse of these two poorly studied and poorly understood religious groups in late medieval India. She raises issues of the purely local versus outside concerns and of sectarian identity, issues that we have seen in other essays. The worship of Naklaṃki is associated with messianic beliefs in the coming of the tenth incarnation of Viṣṇu, whose more familiar name is Kalkin. The cult of Naklaṃki was confined to a few regions in India; Saurashtra may have been its centre, although messianic texts also exist from Orissa in the east. Mallison raises the issue of sectarian boundaries and local cults, and argues persuasively that the cult of Naklaṃki transcended sectarian boundaries. Indeed, she points out that the corpus of hymns known as the *Sant Vāṇī* was itself largely shared between different religious groups. Mallison discusses the founding of three Naklaṃki sanctuaries located in Pancal, in Saurashtra, all of which date from the nineteenth century. She suggests that the cult developed originally among the Isma'īlīs Khojas, perhaps even among Hindu converts. It used the language of *avatāras* or incarnations and borrowed some of its stories from the *purāṇas*. She proposes that the cult then became a Hindu cult.

The case of the Jakhs is equally complicated. The worship of the Jakhs seems, in fact, to have been confined to the area of Kutch. Sanctuaries of the Jakhs contain statues of seventy-two horseback riders who are said to have come from overseas to help the sick. Mallison discusses the competing theories about the origins of this cult and comments on how local religion in Saurashtra has had the ability to absorb and transform new cults with succeeding waves of immigration into the region.

As diverse as these essays are, it should be clear that they also have much in common. They examine how sacred place is created and understood by a religious group and the role that religious visions and imagination play in creating sacred space. Although the conference began with religious biography as an important component of its subject matter, as the conversation across traditions and disciplines progressed, it became clear that many of the issues raised centred on sacred place. These essays explore the role of sacred place in creating a specific local religious identity. Some of them examine the relationship between religious authority and secular authority and how that relationship crystallizes around a sacred place and sacred life; others explore issues of legitimation of religious authority and the role of biography and place in that process. Their topics reach across time and geographical boundaries and raise similar points for discussion. The diversity of the solutions and strategies that emerge suggests the complexity of the phenomena under study and points to the importance of engaging in ongoing discussions framed in a broad cross-cultural context, with scholars from different disciplines contributing their unique perspectives.

1

The Twenty-four Dioceses and Zhang Daoling: The Spatio-Liturgical Organization of Early Heavenly Master Taoism

FRANCISCUS VERELLEN

The Twenty-four Dioceses (*ershisi zhi*) provided the basic framework for ordering the spiritual space administered by the ancient Heavenly Master community (*Tianshi dao*) in the area of modern Sichuan in Southwestern China. Endowed with multiple cosmological correspondences, the dioceses were conceived as projections of the stellar lodges (*xiu*) on earth. They also constituted a hierarchically structured network of holy places, many of which commemorated deeds and events in the career of the community's founder Zhang Daoling. The sacred sites were marked by sanctuaries that served as the liturgical centres of the movement and as the seats of its ecclesial administration. Here the household registers of the parishioners were kept, their contributions collected, their confessions transcribed and submitted to the gods, and communal and individual rituals performed.

According to the founding myth of Heavenly Master Taoism, the investiture of Zhang Daoling in AD 142 as the first Heavenly Master made him Laozi's vicar on earth and conferred authority on him over both the community of the faithful and the pantheon of gods and demons now bound to the 'newly appeared Lord Lao' (*xinchu* Laojun) under the Orthodox One Covenant (*Zhengyi mengwei*). Almost all of the early sources on the Heavenly Master movement mention dioceses, and several refer explicitly to the Twenty-four Dioceses system.[1] Together with the institution of the Twenty-four Dioceses, a priestly hierarchy of Twenty-four Offices (*ershisi zhi*) was promulgated.[2] The latter was correlated with the hierarchical order of the dioceses, each priest being attached to a sanctuary and administrative district commensurate with his rank. The first of the Twenty-four Dioceses was Yangping zhi (A1) (see maps 1 and 2 on p. 21 for geographical location of the dioceses and the appendix at the end of the chapter for fuller descriptions). This was the see of the Heavenly Master himself, while 'libationers' (*jijiu*) administered the remaining dioceses, and lower ordination grades were in charge of lesser ecclesial units.[3]

Some of the earliest surviving sources devoted entirely to the system of the Twenty-four Dioceses reflect this liturgical and clerical order. The first, presented as a ritual protocol (*yi*), establishes precisely the connection between the cosmological order of the dioceses, ordination ritual, and the clerical hierarchy. This 'Liturgy of the Heavenly Master Dioceses,' *Tianshi zhi yi*, was written in Sichuan in ca. AD 552 by Zhang Bian, identified as the 'thirteenth generation Heavenly Master.'[4]

Another category of comparatively early sources is designated as 'diagrams' or 'charts' (*tu*). They appear to be derived from investiture documents of the ancient Heavenly Master liturgy, known generically as 'Charts of the Twenty-four Energies of the Orthodox One.'[5] These *tu* served as both charts and charters of the Heavenly Master realm, as constituted by the Twenty-four Dioceses, and were transmitted to the libationers upon ordination to a given diocese. Here we shall refer to two of the earlier specimens: the 'Chart of the Energy-Dioceses of the Orthodox One' (*Zhengyi qizhi tu*), reproduced in the Taoist encyclopedia *Wushang biyao* (ca. AD 574), and 'Heavenly Master Zhang's Chart of the Twenty-four Dioceses' (*Zhang tianshi ershisi zhi tu*). The latter survives in fragmentary quotations, the most complete of which is found in another Taoist encyclopedia, the *Sandong zhunang* by Wang Xuanhe (fl. AD 683). It appears from the textual parallels between them that the two specimens reproduced in these compendia derive from the same tradition of *tu*-charters. The period in which that tradition originated is difficult to determine.

Origins of the Twenty-four Dioceses System

The institution of the Twenty-four Dioceses is inseparable from that of Heavenly Master Taoism itself. It formed part of the founding event, Lord Lao's revelation of the Orthodox One Covenant (*zhengyi mengwei*) to Zhang Daoling, which is said to have taken place in AD 142 or 143. The terms of the New Alliance stipulated on that occasion and the acts of investiture conferred on Zhang Daoling included the 'transmission' of the Twenty-four Dioceses. Just as Zhang was appointed to preside over the new order designated as the Three Heavens (Santian), characterized by a distinct pantheon, theology, and priesthood, so was the sacred and ecclesial geography of the Heavenly Master realm entrusted to his administration. In time, Zhang Daoling and his successors were said to have added several categories of 'supplementary dioceses' to the system transmitted by the Heavenly Master tradition. The sources emphasize, however, that the original set of 'regular dioceses' (*zhengzhi*) were revealed by Laozi and had originated in heaven, at specific moments in mythical time.

As the 'Liturgy of the Heavenly Master Dioceses' (*Tianshi zhi yi*) explains, the Twenty-four Dioceses, grouped in three hierarchical sets of eight, were also known after their respective celestial founders as the Dioceses of the Supreme (Wushang zhi), of the Lao of Mystery (Xuanlao zhi), and of the Most High (Taishang zhi).[6] These founding deities were hypostases of Laozi, the Orthodox One (Zhengyi), who existed before creation and who was co-eternal with the universe itself.

The 'Chart of the Energy-Dioceses of the Orthodox One' (*Zhengyi qizhi tu*) specifies that the category of the eight superior dioceses (Shangpin zhi) had been established by Lord Lao of the Supreme Great Tao (Wushang dadao laojun) on the seventh day of the seventh month of the first year of the mythical Shanghuang era. On the fifth day of the tenth month in the first year of Wuji, the Most High of the Veritable Unlimited (Zhengzhen wuji taishang) established the eight middle dioceses (Zhongpin zhi). On the seventh day of the first month of the second year of Wuji Shanghuang, Lao of Mystery Lord Tao of Non-action (Wuwei daojun xuanlao) established the eight lesser dioceses (Xiapin zhi).[7]

The corresponding accounts in the *Zhang tianshi ershisi zhi tu* agree with this last version of the institution of the superior dioceses. The Veritable (*zhengzhen*) of the middle dioceses, however, is here called *zhenzheng*; as for the final group, there are small discrepancies with respect to the era's name and the divinity's title: 'On the seventh day of the first month of the second year of Wuji, the Perfected of Mystery Great Tao of Non-action (Wuwei dadao xuanzhen) established the eight lesser dioceses.'[8] Wuji (Limitless) is elsewhere identified as the celestial era corresponding to the reign of King You (Youwang,

781–771 BC) when Lord Lao transformed himself and left China for the western regions.[9]

The application of this geo-cosmological system created in heaven to the domain of Heavenly Master Taoism took the form of a promulgation: 'On the seventh day of the first month of Han'an 2 (AD 143), at noon, the Most High (Lord Lao) promulgated the Twenty-four Dioceses, [comprising the categories of the] superior eight, middle eight, and lesser eight ... He entrusted these to the Heavenly Master Zhang Daoling to reverently implement and proclaim at large.'[10] The additional dioceses were instituted by Zhang Daoling and his successors. They came in three separate categories:

1 Four complementary dioceses (*beizhi*),[11] also known as supplementary dioceses (*biezhi*).[12] A note at the end reads: 'On the seventh day of the first month of the first year of Jian'an (AD 196),[13] at sunrise, the Heavenly Master handed down these four dioceses. He entrusted them to the Successor (*sishi,* that is, Zhang Heng) who in turn entrusted them to the Second Successor (*xishi,* that is Zhang Lu).' These dioceses were said to have been created by Zhang Daoling in order to complete the match between the Twenty-four Dioceses and the Twenty-eight Stellar Lodges.

2 Eight adjunct dioceses (*peizhi*), established by the Heavenly Master, in affiliation with existing ones (B1, B2, B3, B4, B6, B7, B8, C1 – see map 1 and Appendix): 'At dawn, on the fifth day of the tenth month of Jian'an 1 (AD 196), the Heavenly Master instituted these eight adjunct dioceses. He entrusted them to the Successor who transmitted them to the Second Successor.'[14]

3 Eight movable dioceses (*youzhi*): 'Established by the Second Successor for promulgation on the fifth day of the tenth month, Jian'an 3 (AD 198).'[15] Zhang Lu appears to have instituted these following the displacement of his see Yangping zhi (A1) to Hanzhong. This was done in order to maintain the Heavenly Masters' religious authority over both the original and the supplementary dioceses after their removal from the movement's heartland.[16]

The above arrangements constitute what we might call the mythical or cosmological rationale for the Twenty-four Dioceses. As the last of the categories conceived by humans, the movable dioceses already suggests, however, the sites also played a very tangible role in the social and liturgical organization of the Heavenly Master movement.

It may indeed be justified to imagine their origin, prior to such increasingly elaborate cosmological rationalizations, in the social structure of religious communities at the end of the Han.

The term translated here as 'diocese' (*zhi*) had been used since the Warring States period (475–221 BC) in Chinese political philosophy and administrative nomenclature, including early Taoist writings. It stood for order, security, control, and the beneficent, civilizing effects of government. The latter included control of the forces of nature, especially water control, as well as those of the supernatural realm, that is, keeping demonic possessions and baleful influences at bay. The additional sense of 'healing' is clearly related to these activities. Finally, *zhi* had been a term used to describe the seat of a local administration since at least Former Han (206 BC–AD 8) times.[17]

In the present context, *zhi* were units of ecclesial administration – both the see of a ranking priest and the surrounding district under its jurisdiction. Modern Chinese writers use the word *jiaoqu*, corresponding closely to our 'diocese,' to circumscribe this meaning. Like the word 'see,' *zhi* was also used to refer simultaneously to the responsible priest's residence, the seat of his administration, and its liturgical centre or temple. Specifically, *zhi* were places in which control of the demon world was exercised and healing accomplished.

The *zhi*-dioceses constituted an important part of the military, administrative, and religious framework of Later Han Taoist movements,[18] and probably the first forms of truly large-scale communal organization in the history of Taoism. In Eastern China, a corresponding institution was called *fang*, a term referring at first to a military unit and title in the Yellow Turban movement:

> [Zhang Jue] established thirty-six *fang*. Fang was a title similar to that of imperial general (*jiangjun*). A major *fang* (*dafang*) had more than ten thousand men; a minor *fang* (*xiaofang*), six or seven thousand. Each [*fang* in his turn] appointed a chief (*qushuai*).[19]

The word *fang* had a range of meanings some of which overlapped with *zhi*. Henri Maspero understood the term as 'regional authority,'[20] Wang Chunwu more specifically as 'military and mutual aid unit.'[21] The word was interchangeable with *fang*, 'ward,' also meaning region, principality, or district, and could be used for *fang*, 'defence,' or refer to a room or building. The organizational principles evoked in the above passage, including the distinction between major and minor grades with corresponding levels of jurisdiction, are typical of the institutions of Han local administration as well as of Heavenly Master diocesan organization.[22]

Master Lu's Summary of Taoist Liturgy, the *Lu xiansheng daomen kelüe* by Lu Xiujing (AD 406–477), makes the connection explicit:

> The Heavenly Master set up the dioceses and instituted the offices (i.e., clerical hierarchy) on the model of the regional and local governments under the secular bureaucracy (*yangguan*), in order to administer (*zhili*) the population. The worshippers of the Tao all had their households registered and their records maintained; each had [his/her] place of affiliation.[23]

Lu mentions two specific offices performed by the diocesan priesthood, which remarkably resembled essential functions carried out by Han local governments. The first was the keeping of 'life registers (*mingji*),' necessary for obtaining divine protection, a substitution for the Han imperial system of household registration (*huji*). The second was the levy of 'pledge rice' (*xinmi*) in place of taxation by the government, which was especially controversial and largely responsible for the movement's reputation for sedition in official sources.[24] The pledges were ritually renewed and the census was updated, on the occasion of three annual Assemblies (*sanhui*) held at the seats of the dioceses. As places of registration, confession, healing, ritual, and imposition, *zhi*-dioceses served to structure the Heavenly Master community and to enforce its moral code. (I return to these institutions under the heading of liturgical organization below.)

The Mythical Geography of the Heavenly Master Realm

The geographical location of the Twenty-four Dioceses fell predominantly into a few clusters situated within the Sichuan basin, and especially in the Chengdu plain, delimited by the Dujiang yan irrigation system. (Map 1 uses a letter and number code to identify the location of the dioceses. This number-and-letter identifier corresponds to the description of the dioceses in the Appendix at the end of this chapter. Map 2 identifies the geographical location of the dioceses in the Chengdu plain.) The majority of the sites are located within a radius of less than one hundred kilometres around Chengdu, with the highest concentration in a small section of the plain to the northeast of Chengdu, in the modern counties of Jintang, 35 km from Chengdu (A8,

B1) ; Shifang, 48 km (C3, C4); Deyang, 55 km (A7, B2, B3); and Mianzhu, 75 km (A2, A6).

A smaller but important cluster was found in the area northwest of Chengdu, which had formed one of the centres of Shu civilization

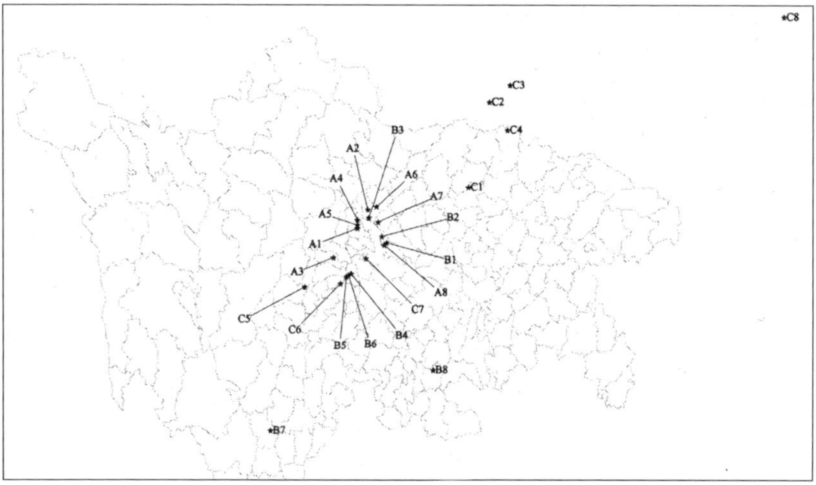

Map 1. Distribution of the Dioceses in Modern Sichuan Province [25]

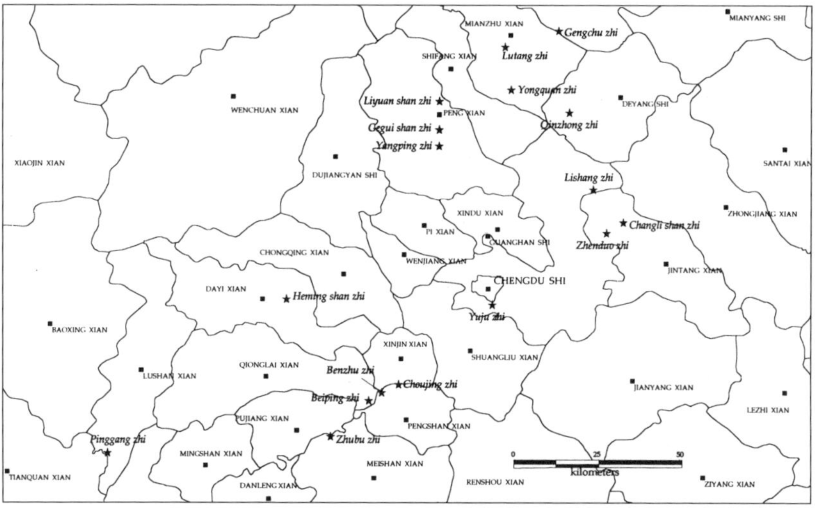

Map 2. Localization of the Dioceses in the Chengdu Plain.

prior to the rise of the ancient city of Chengdu, in Pengxian county, 35 km from Chengdu (A1, A4, A5). The more scattered sites in the area to the southwest of Chengdu were located in the districts of Xinjin, 45 km from Chengdu (B4, B6, post-Tang C5, B8?); Dayi, 65 km (A3); Pengshan, 70 km (B5); and Pujiang, 85 km (C6).

One diocese was located within the city of Chengdu itself (C7). A small number of the more distant dioceses were situated along the rim of the Sichuan basin. These included Langzhong, 200 km NE of Chengdu (C1); Yaan, 145 km SW (pre-Tang C5); and Luzhou, 235 km SE (B8?).

Only five of the original Twenty-four Dioceses were located outside the Sichuan basin region. One of these was in southern Sichuan at Xichang, 360 km SW of Chengdu (B7), and the remainder in southern Shaanxi or beyond – Mianxian, Hanzhong (C2, later A1); Nanzheng, Hanzhong (C3, C4); and Chang'an or Luoyang (C8).

As a rule, the main clusters of dioceses were situated in the heartland of the ancient civilization of Shu and not far from the areas of intensive rice cultivation in the irrigated lowlands of the Chengdu plain. By Later Han times, this cultivation had been practiced for five hundred years.[26] At the same time, the temples marking the seats of the dioceses tended to be in mountainous areas or at sites with some elevation above the plain (see map 3). As Wang Chunwu observed from the perspective of religious geography, the early Heavenly Master movement generally selected sites in the borderland where mountainous areas met the plain, preferably at the mouth of a river or on a communnicating road.[27]

The general location of the holy places can be determined with reasonable confidence from the historical sources. Many of the more important sites have in recent years been visited and explored on the ground by local, Japanese, and Western students of the Twenty-four Dioceses system, myself included.[28] Some are once again becoming major places of worship. Nevertheless, certain localizations remain problematic, either because their identification in the historical sources is ambiguous or because the texts propose conflicting localizations for one and the same site. Closer examination of these multiple and seemingly contradictory indications suggests, however, that some of the discrepancies are significantly due to changing historical circumstances. In reality, the system was never static, but was deliberately readjusted as it evolved.

The first diocese and see of the Heavenly Master, Yangping zhi (A1), as well as several others, were relocated to the Hanzhong area when

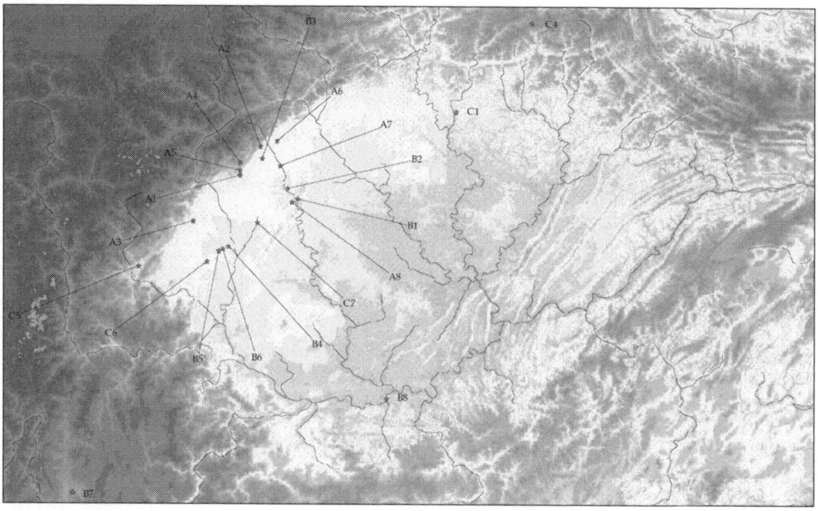

Map 3. Distribution of the Dioceses in the Sichuan Basin

the community settled there temporarily under the leadership of Zhang Lu at the end of the Han.[29] During the period of North–South division, a loose sense of spiritual lineage developed in several places outside the Sichuan area, prompting reinterpretations of the Twenty-four Dioceses cosmology and geography. A notable example is the effort of Kou Qianzhi (AD 365–448) at the Northern Wei court. In Kou's 'Hymnal Rules of Laojun,' Lord Lao explains the original institution of the *zhi* in Shu (Sichuan). Kou Qianzhi, however, advocated discontinuing the association of the dioceses with actual places in Shu. Libationers (the administrators or *jijiu*) were to be affiliated with the heavenly dioceses of the Twenty-eight Lodges (*ershiba xiu*), which replaced the former.[30] The projection of these holy places into idealized and increasingly abstract realms is discussed more fully below.

The reunification of the empire and the systematization of the Heavenly Master lineage under the Tang dynasty[31] also influenced the conceptualization of the Twenty-four Dioceses system. In addition to the work of Wang Xuanhe already mentioned, Sima Chengzhen's (AD 647–735) 'Plan of Celestial and Terrestrial Palaces and Residences' (*Tiandi gongfu tu*) and especially the anonymous 'Twenty-four Dioceses' (*Ershisi zhi*), compiled between the seventh and tenth centuries, attest to the revived interest. These different traditions are reworked into rubrics of the 'Twenty-four Divine Dioceses' (*Linghua ershisi*), a section of the comprehensive sacred geography titled 'Record of the Grotto-Heavens, Auspicious Sites, Holy Peaks, Marshes, and Famous Mountains' (*Dongtian fudi yuedu mingshan ji*) by the late Tang court Taoist Du Guangting (AD 850–933).[32]

The 'Twenty-four Divine Dioceses' was an evident attempt to systematize the disparate Tang and pre-Tang traditions. It also presents some striking departures from tradition, including several new localizations. The main innovations introduced by Du Guangting involve the abolition of the dioceses' hierarchical grouping and their integration into a global (that is imperial) system of sacred geography comprising the holy mountains, grotto-heavens, places of blessings, and so on. Furthermore, Du's scheme departs from some of the traditional cosmological correspondences associated with the dioceses.[33]

The cosmological rationale of the Twenty-four Dioceses[34] formed a central part of the founding myth of the Heavenly Master movement. As we have seen, they were thought to have originated in heaven. The principle of projecting terrestrial places onto heavenly counterparts was well established in Chinese tradition. As the 'Chart of the Energy-Dioceses of the Orthodox One' explains, the dioceses 'corresponded' with the Twenty-four Energies (*ershisi qi*) and 'accorded' with the Twenty-eight Stellar Lodges (*ershiba xiu*).[35] Cosmic time was structured into twenty-four 'energy nodes' (*jieqi*) or solar stations segmenting the solar year according to seasons arranged around the winter and summer solstices and the vernal and autumn equinoxes, with six subdivisions to each quarter. The Twenty-eight Stellar Lodges or mansions (*xiu*) constituted a circular zodiac of twenty-eight constellations near the ecliptic belt of the celestial sphere, each with a 'determinative star' (*juxing*). These asterisms were used for determining the positions of other celestial bodies, including the stations of the moon's sidereal orbit, and for a variety of astrological calculations.[36]

The Twenty-eight Stellar Lodges share certain features with the Indian set of twenty-eight lunar lodges.[37] A complete representation of the Chinese names of the twenty-eight lodges survives from the Warring States period. The characters for the names were found inscribed on the lid of a lacquer chest discovered in Hubei in 1978 in a tomb dated 433 BC. They are arranged in a rough circle surrounding the character *dou* for the Dipper and flanked by the Dragon of the East and the Tiger of the West.[38] A painting on the ceiling of a late Former Han tomb in Xi'an shows the Twenty-eight Stellar Lodges the way they were probably visualized by the Later Han followers of the

Heavenly Master movement (fig. 1): a belt of asterisms around the celestial equator, represented in the manner of traditional Chinese star maps as discs connected by straight lines. Beside the lodges, the incompletely preserved painting depicts Taoist and cosmological symbols including the sun and moon, the dragon, and cranes.

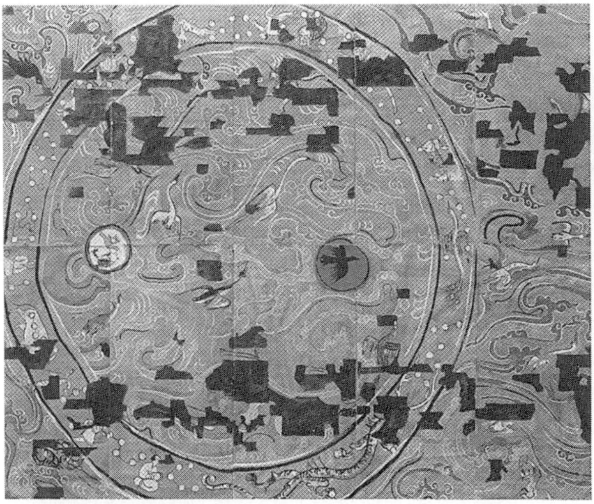

Fig. 1. The Twenty-eight Stellar Lodges (Late Former Han)
Reconstruction at Jiaotong University, from Chen Meidong, *Zhongguo gu xingtu*, pl. 3.

The idea of associating the Twenty-four Dioceses with sections of the sky such as the stellar lodges is grounded in the classical notion of *fenye*, the allocation of terrestrial 'fields' in correspondence with celestial domains. It was applied to a scheme that correlated the Nine Heavens with the Nine Provinces of ancient China, and later to match the twelve feudal states with the twelve stations of the planet Jupiter.[39] The notion of earth as a square with its geographical divisions circumscribed by a round heaven sectioned into the Twenty-eight Stellar Lodges survived into modern times.[40]

Since Chinese antiquity, the *fenye* system above all served astrological purposes: the presence of a baleful star or the auspicious motion of a heavenly body in a given sector of the sky would have repercussions in the corresponding geo-political region on earth. This concept applied, quite literally, to the system of cosmological correspondences for the Twenty-four Dioceses. One account speaks in connection with the creation of the dioceses and the institution of the Twenty-four Spiritual Offices (*yinguan*), of the 'descent of the Twenty-eight Stellar Lodges' true energies (*zhengqi*), penetrating the ground.'[41] A story by the Tang author Du Guangting about the Jade Throne diocese (Yuju zhi [C7]) in Chengdu relates that Zhang Daoling had sealed the grotto beneath this site with a large stone in order to prevent the energy of the inauspicious *fenye*-sector Gui, the corresponding stellar lodge, from penetrating there. Gui traditionally corresponded to ancient Yizhou, the region surrounding Chengdu.[42]

The Chinese penchant for 'correlative cosmology' is indeed a major factor in Heavenly Master mythology and the Taoist world-view in general. In Taoist cosmogony, the three cosmic energies (*sanqi*) at the origin of the universe[43] had their counterparts in the human body where the three 'spheres' were subdivided into sets of eight 'energies' each.[44] (See fig. 2.) Taoist sources, reflecting the ancient astro-calendrical system known as *liuren*, also posited cross-correspondences between the system of *xiu*-lodges and the divisions of the civil calendar.[45] The early cosmology, 'The Most High Lord Lao's Book of the Centre'

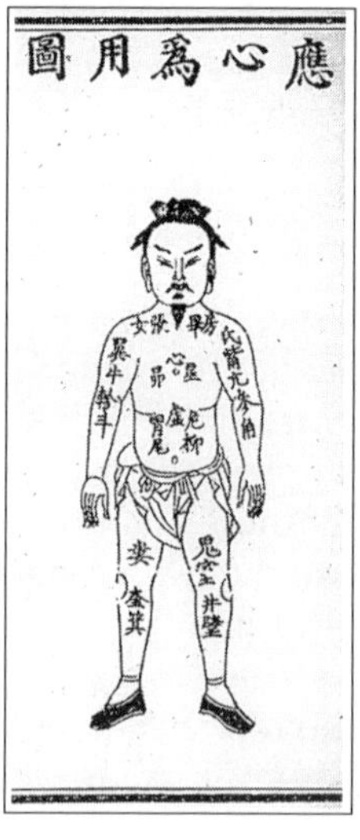

Fig. 2. Projection of the Twenty-eight Stellar Lodges onto the Human Body
Daode zhenjing jiyi dazhi 1.6a

correlates the gods of the universe with those projected onto the human body, and both sets in turn with calendrical units such as the phases of the moon, the cycle of sixty days, and the twelve periods of the day.[46] The Code of Nüqing lists the demons related to the different heavens, the sexagenary cycle, the twenty-eight *xiu*, and the stars of the Dipper constellation.[47] In the 'Diagrams of the Twenty-four Vital Energies,' finally, the messianic Latter-day Saint Lord Li (Housheng Lijun) visualizes the twenty-four cosmic *qi* as projections of the vital energies of his body. By means of twenty-four corresponding *fu*-talismans, the divinities associated with the twenty-four *qi* and located in the three centres of the human body could be invoked.[48]

As shown in table 1, correlations linked the main elements of space, time, and the destiny of individuals into a single system. Such comprehensive classification schemes are consistent with the highly organic view of cosmology in China as well as India.[49] Table 1 shows the system of correspondences between the Twenty-four Dioceses, the Twenty-four Solar Year Periods, and the Twenty-eight Lodges; beside these are found indications of the secondary associations with the spatio-calendrical cycles of sixty and twelve, which defined 'destiny' as determined by the hour of an individual's birth, and the Five Phases.[50]

Table 1: Schematization of Diocesan Correspondences

24 Dioceses 治	24 Solar Year Periods 節氣[51]	28 Lodges 宿[52]	Sexagenary Cycle 干支[53]	Duodenary Cycle 支[54]	Five Phases 五行[55]
A1 Yangping 陽平治	Cold Dew 寒露	El Jiao 角	1 甲子, 51 甲寅, 11 甲戌	5 辰	W-3 Metal 金
A2 Lutang 鹿堂治	Frost's descent 霜降	E2 kang 亢	55 戊午, 52 乙卯, 45 戊申	5 辰	E-4 Wood 木
A3 Heming 鶴鳴治	Beginning of Winter 立冬	E3 Di 氐[56]	17 庚辰, 29 壬辰	5 辰	W-3 Metal 金
A4 Liyuan 漓沅治	Slight Snow 小雪	E4 Fang 房	53 丙辰, 5 戊辰	4 卯	C-5 Earth 土
A5 Gegui 葛璝治	Heavy Snow 大雪	E5 Xin 心	16 己卯, 4 丁卯, 28 辛卯, 40 癸卯	4 卯	S-2 Fire 火
A6 Gengchu 更除治	Winter Solstice 冬至	E6 Wei 尾	3 丙寅, 37 庚子, 59 壬戌	3 寅	N-1 Water 水

Table 1 continued

24 Dioceses 治	24 Solar Year Periods 節氣	28 Lodges 宿	Sexagenary Cycle 干支	Duodenary Cycle 支	Five Phases 五行
A7 Qinzhong 秦中治	Slight cold 小寒	E7 Ji 箕	15 戊寅, 27 庚寅, 39 壬寅	3 寅	N-1 Water 水
A8 Zhenduo 眞多治	Severe cold 大寒	N1 Dou 斗	2 乙丑, 14 丁丑	2 丑	W-3 Metal 金
B1 Changli 昌利治	Beginning of spring 立春	N2 Niu 牛	46 己酉, 26 己丑	2 丑	C-5 Earth 土
B2 Lishang 隸上治	Rains 雨水	N3 Nü 女	38 辛丑, 50 癸丑	2 丑	N-1 Water 水
B3 Yongquan 涌泉治	Insects awaken 驚蟄	N4 Xu 虛	13 丙子, 60 癸亥	1 子 [57]	E-4 Wood 木
B4 Choujing 稠稉治	Vernal equinox 春分	N5 Wei 危	49 壬子, 19 壬午	12 亥	N-1 Water 水
B5 Beiping 北平治	Clear brightness 清明	N6 Shi 室	12 乙亥, 36 己亥	1 子	W-3 Metal 金
B6 Benzhu 本竹治	Grain rain 穀雨	N7 Pi 壁	42 乙巳, 18 辛巳, 48 辛亥	12 亥	E-4 Wood 木
B7 Mengqin 蒙秦治	Beginning of summer 立夏	W1 Kui 奎	11 甲戌, 23 丙戌	11 戌	S-2 Fire 火
B8 Pinggai 平蓋治	Small plenitude 小滿	W2 Lou 婁	54 丁巳, 6 己巳, 30 癸巳	11 戌	C-5 Earth 土
C1 Yuntai 雲臺治	Grain in ear 芒種	W3 Wei 胃	43 丙午, 7 庚午, 47 庚戌	11 戌	S-2 Fire 火
C2 Jinkou 濜口治	Summer solstice 夏至	W4 Mao 昴	22 乙酉, 34 丁酉	10 酉	E-4 Wood 木
C3 Houcheng 後城治	Slight heat 小暑	W5 Bi 畢	58 辛酉, 10 癸酉	10 酉	C-5 Earth 土
C4 Gongmu 公慕治	Great heat 大暑	W6 Zi 觜	21 甲申, 9 壬申, 57 庚申	9 申	W-3 Metal 金
C5 Pinggang 平剛治	Beginning of Autumn 立秋	W7 Shen 參	35 戊戌, 24 丁亥	9 申	N-1 Water 水
C6 Zhubu 主簿治	End of heat 處暑	S1 Jing 井	32 乙未, 56 己未, 20 癸未	8 未	W-3 Metal 金
C7 Yuju 玉局治	White dew 白露	S2 Gui 鬼	44 丁未, 8 辛未	8 未	N-1 Water 水
C8 Beimang 北邙治	Autumn equinox 秋分	S3 Liu 柳	25 戊子, 31 甲午	8 未 [58]	C-5 Earth 土

The Twenty-four Dioceses in the Legend of Zhang Daoling

Many of the episodes in Zhang Daoling's career are associated with the Twenty-four Dioceses, resting stations in his peripatetic ministry in Shu like the Stellar Lodges in the orbits of heavenly luminaries. Elements of Zhang Daoling's biography were already woven into the 'Heavenly Master Zhang's Chart of the Twenty-four Dioceses.' They include accounts of the saint's origins, studies, court appointments, the move to Yizhou (Chengdu), heavenly visitations, investiture with the *zhengyi mengwei* covenant, his role as instructor of princes, and finally his institution of the Twenty-four Dioceses and nineteen hermitages, *jinglu*.[59] The episodes located in specific dioceses can be grouped under two related themes: (1) events marking the progressive phases or different aspects of the founder's sanctification, and (2) acts of foundation, laying down a charter for the Heavenly Master movement and circumscribing the nature of its early community. The following analysis is based on the thirteenth-century Life of Zhang Daoling, in the 'Comprehensive Mirror of the Immortals Who Embodied the Tao Through the Ages' (*Lishi zhenxian tidao tongjian*, abbreviated below as LZTT), a composite hagiography drawing eclectically on all the sources available at that time. This text, which abounds with incongruities and anachronisms with respect to Zhang's assumed period of activity under the Later Han,[60] represents the fully established legend of the founder as elaborated after his official canonization under the Tang emperor Xuanzong (r. AD 712–756).

Sanctification of the Founder

Among the sites connected with Zhang Daoling's acquisition of the magical and spiritual powers that were the marks of an immortal,[61] the diocese Yangping zhi (A1) is mentioned first: thanks to spiritual exercises and the absorption of drugs, Zhang here attained the arts of flight, distant hearing, ubiquity, communion with spirits, and transformation; at Yangping he engaged in unflagging recitation of the *Daode jing*. At Mount Gegui (A5), Zhang made himself invisible and dwelled in a cave, fed on breath, and harmonized his spirits. At Yongquan zhi (B3), he acquired the ability to move through water and fire: thereupon he saved human beings and came to the rescue of creatures, performing concealed works of merit. At Zhenduo zhi (A8), he practised meditation and the visualization of gods, and became mindful of the Perfected. At Mount Beiping (B5), Zhang miraculously tamed wild beasts; at Choujing (B4) recited scriptures unperturbed by a specter. At Mengqin (B7) he received a divine visitation.[62]

Other dioceses provided Zhang with the natural resources or setting for medical and alchemical experimentation. The production of rare and curative substances is a traditional attribute of holy places in China.[63] Thus, at Changli shan zhi (B1), Zhang Daoling obtained drugs and fungi (see further examples listed in the Annex), while the beginning of his alchemical practice and eventual transformation is associated in the LZTT with Qinzhong zhi (A7), where he obtained the 'Secret Method of the Nine Perfected' (*jiuzhen bifa*), a term referring perhaps to the later Shangqing practice of evoking the spirits that resided in the vital organs of the body.[65] At Quting shan in the Heming diocese (A3),[66] Zhang Daoling refined the Divine Elixir of the Nine Crucibles (*Jiuding shendan*), completing it after three years. This refers to the Yellow Emperor Method for the Nine Crucibles Elixir, *Huangdi jiuding dan fa*, which had enabled the mythical sovereign to ascend as an immortal. Zhang is again said to have refined the Nine Crucibles Elixir at Lutang zhi (A2), before moving on to Pinggai zhi (B8) where he compounded a 'Great Drug of Nine-Fold Efflorescence' (*jiuhua dayao*).[67]

Zhang Daoling's ascension is also linked to diocesan sites, especially Yuntai zhi (C1), the Cloud Terrace Diocese. According to the 'Comprehensive Mirror of the Immortals,' Zhang had observed that the landscape there was exquisite and free from noxious influences. Thus he said to his chief disciple Wang Chang, 'This mountain is where I shall accomplish my merit and soar into Heaven.' Then he divined an auspicious place for alchemical experimentation and applied himself to meditation. At this juncture, Lord Lao manifested himself to reveal, among other things, a method for obtaining pardon for seven generations of ancestors and ascending together with them. Zhang practised acts of devotion and contrition to obtain the release of his ancestors, as well as rituals for his 'personal destiny' (*benming*) during a period of three years at Heming shan.[68]

The Cloud Terrace Diocese provides the setting for an episode in the legend of Zhang Daoling that is celebrated in Chinese art and letters, the 'seventh trial' in which the master tests his disciples' unconditional faith by requiring them to jump off a cliff in pursuit of peaches growing halfway down the chasm. The scene is featured in Zhang Daoling's early fourth-century *Shenxian zhuan* biography[69] and inspired the famous treatise on landscape depiction, 'An Essay on

How to Paint Mount Yuntai' by Ge Hong's near-contemporary Gu Kaizhi (AD 344–405).[70] Both the story and its depiction are rich in metaphors of transcendence: the peach, a symbol of immortality; the leap of faith, recalling the act of seekers of immortality on numerous 'suicide cliffs' in China; and the shape of the abyss, described by Gu Kaizhi as a *que* pillar gate.[71] This suggested a natural formation resembling the great monuments that marked the access to tombs in Han Sichuan,[72] and were frequently also depicted inside the tombs as symbols of the passage from this life to the next.[73] These metaphors stood for the promise of salvation extended to Zhang's tested and chosen disciples, Wang Chang and Zhao Sheng, and prefigured their eventual ascension with the master from Cloud Terrace.

Before accomplishing his definitive ascension, however, Zhang first returned to Quting shan to dwell in a cave until summoned to an audience in heaven with the Most High Celestial Worthy of Primordial Beginning (Taishang yuanshi tianzun). The Celestial Worthy bestows the 'method of the Orthodox One Covenant' (*Zhengyi mengwei zhi fa*) on Zhang and enjoins him to return with it to the world of mortals, to spread the Zhengyi method and toil for the salvation of the unenlightened. Apparently, the hagiographer here intended to invest the Taoist founder with the additional mantle of a compassionate bodhisattva. Zhang Daoling's protracted ascension eventually culminates with the apparition of two Jade Maidens who escort Zhang and his wife to the chariot in which they 'rose up from the Peak of Cloud Terrace in broad daylight, accompanied by attendants and the strains of Heavenly music.' According to the 'Comprehensive Mirror of the Immortals,' Zhang Daoling had been supernaturally conceived after his mother was visited in a dream by a celestial being descended from the Northern Dipper, and it appears that after his ascension, Zhang returned to that fateful constellation.[74] (See fig. 3.)

Acts of Foundation

Prior to his transformation into a deity, the Heavenly Master's investiture as vicar of Laozi and his prophetic announcement of the charter of the movement are associated with another key diocese, Mount Crane Call or Heming shan (A3). Situated in modern Dayi county, some sixty kilometres west of Chengdu, Mount Crane Call is considered the founding site of Heavenly Master Taoism.[75] The earliest texts agree that when Zhang Daoling set forth from his native

Fig. 3. Zhang Daoling in Communion with the Northern Dipper
From *Jiezi yuan huazhuan siji* (1818), supplement to the 'Mustard Seed Garden Manual of Painting' (1679–1701), after *Sancai tuhui* (1609).

principality of Pei (northern Anhui and Jiangsu) in quest of the holy mountains of Shu, he first settled at Heming shan.[76] The refining of the Nine Crucibles Elixir and the revelation of the Orthodox One Covenant are said to have taken place at nearby Quting shan.[77] Subsequently, Laojun appears in a dream to Zhang Daoling at Heming shan. The latter wakes to behold the descent of a heavenly cortège, including immortals bearing two exorcistic "divine swords" (*shenjian*), one male, one female, and a jade seal inscribed with the words 'Seal of the Inspector of Merit of Yangping diocese (*Yangping zhi dugong yin*).' A further apparition of Taishang Laojun, this time holding the *Wuming baoshan* fan, one of the insignia of high office in ancient China and a frequent attribute of Laozi, announces the establishment of the Twenty-four Dioceses and other institutions and confers numerous insignia of authority on Zhang. At Zhubu zhi (C6), the immortals honour him with a jade disk (*yubi*) finally, at Quting shan, Laojun's emissary bestows on Zhang a (funerary) jade tablet (*yuce*) and the posthumous *hao* Perfected Orthodox One, Zhengyi zhenren.

Later tradition attributed to the many revelations and visitations at diocesan sites the transmission of a variety of Taoist scripture in addition to the Heavenly Master founding charter: at Benzhu (B6), Perfected bestowed on Zhang the 'superior scriptures of Lingbao (*Lingbao shangjing*).[78] In AD 155, after the return of Zhang and his disciples to Mount Crane Call, Wang Chang and Zhao Sheng witness the descent of another celestial cortège. An immortal riding on a cloud confers on Zhang Daoling an 'arcane register' (*bilu*) of ordination. Next, Lord Lao descends from Mount Quting in a dragon chariot, accompanied by Perfected mounted on white cranes, to gather at the foot of the city wall of Chengdu. At the site of the future Yuju diocese (C7), a towering Jade Throne (*yuju*) surges from the ground. Laojun ascends it to predicate the essentials of the Tao, expand upon the significance of the *Zhengyi mengwei* covenant, and pronounce the 'Northern Dipper Scripture for Prolonging Life' (*Beidou yansheng jing*), the 'Southern Dipper Scripture' (*Nandou jing*),[79] and many others besides. After his departure, the throne disappears, the ground collapsing into a grotto.[80]

Clearly, in the hagiography of Zhang Daoling the Twenty-four Dioceses are foundation sites of the nascent community's institutions. It is at Heming shan that Lord Lao announces the promulgation of the system of the Twenty-four Dioceses themselves and their disposition in the mountains of Shu in correlation with the Twenty-eight Stellar Lodges. In the same place he stipulates the dispensations of the new covenant, transmits further registers, scriptures, alchemical recipes, exorcistic swords, and the 'One Thousand Two-hundred Officers Petitions' (*Yiqian erbai guan zhang*), referring to the 'Manual of the One Thousand Two Hundred Officers,' an early Heavenly Master pantheon, now lost, of celestial officials with their residences. A commentary to another passage indicates Gongmu zhi (C4) and Gengchu zhi (C6) as alternatives for the institution of the sacred geography. The other major elements of the subsequent system of Taoist mythical geography, the thirty-six hermitages (*jinglu*), seventy-two places of blessings (*fudi*), and 360 sacred mountains (*mingshan*), were said to have been instituted at Lutang zhi.[81]

Lutang zhi (A2), the Deer Hall Diocese in Mianzhu county in the Chengdu plain, is another key place in the founding myth of Heavenly Master Taoism:

> In the year Yongshou 1 (AD 155), the Most High Lord Lao led the Heavenly Master Zhang to this diocese to cleave asunder a rock in order to seal an oath with the generals who guard the four directions (*sizhen*) and the Great

> Year [star] (Taisui), as well as the hundred demons of the rivers and temples, that all would abide by the Way of the Orthodox One Covenant.[82]

Other sources describe a great assembly of the immortals of all the corners of the realm. At the heart of the Heavenly Master covenant was the definition of a new pantheon in which the benign Three Heavens of the new alliance replaced the pernicious Six Heavens of the demon-ridden past.[83] Spatial organization and the institution of a hierarchical sacred geography ultimately signified a comprehensive alliance, preceded by vigorous campaigns of exorcism and subjugation, with the deities controlling each holy place and natural feature of the land.[84]

On the level of the early community's social organization, the Twenty-four Dioceses are places of the transmission of the first Heavenly Master's instructions to his disciples, and of his insignia of authority to the successor. Thus at Lishang zhi (B2), he first instructed the disciples in the methods of 'nourishing vitality and lightening the body' (*yangxing qingshen*). At Quting, he expounds to Wang Chang, in the unlikely words of the late hagiographer, the importance for a gentleman desiring to rise to heaven to first serve the state[85] and found a family, and explains his exorcistic mission in Shu. At Cloud Terrace, Zhang harangues his disciples about the necessary qualifications for receiving his final instructions (a scene loosely based on *Shenxian zhuan*) before subjecting them to the Seven Trials. Once again, the group returns to Quting, where the Heavenly Master transmits the Arcane Three Heavens Orthodox One method (*Santian zhengyi bifa*) to Wang Chang and Zhao Sheng. The commentary adds that he also handed down 'final instructions' at Houcheng zhi (C3) and Yuju zhi (C7). At Liyuan shanzhi (A4) he further expounded his (*Santian zhengyi bifa*) method. At Yangping shan, he passed the 'levitation method of the flying immortals' (*feixian qingju*) on to the Successor.[86] The transmission of Zhang's alchemical methods took place at the site of his ascension, Yuntai. This is where Zhang Daoling finally passed on his swords, seal, jade tablet, and other insignia and laid down the rules of the Heavenly Master succession.[87]

Typology of the *Zhi* dioceses and Heavenly Master Sanctuaries

Sacred sites are marked, and in turn endowed with sanctity, by recognizable objects, structures, activities, and sensations. In Taoism, 'places of blessings' (*fudi*) are often locations for the procurement of rare and salvific substances, such as the metals and minerals used in alchemical preparations and medicinal drugs. Or they are sites of esoteric transmission and instruction in the form of recipes, methods, talismans or scriptures obtained through encounters with immortals or deities. The Twenty-four Dioceses were characterized by specific topographic features, such as the frequent proximity of mountains and rivers. The texts also regularly refer to natural and supernatural features like rocks, trees, vegetation, medicinal herbs, fungi, streams, sources, wells, holy water, and stones in the shape of various objects, especially of mirrors. Artificial markers include temples, halls, gates and pillars, sculptures, steles, and inscriptions.

Hagiographic accretion, the accumulated body of myths and legends defining a site, can also be considered a form of marker. The Twenty-four Dioceses are primarily places associated with the Heavenly Master foundation myths. Many were already holy places before the rise of Heavenly Master Taoism under the Later Han, typically as ascension sites or places where immortals practised their art; sites of manifestation and revelation; and sites connected with the cults of antiquity, including those of the mythical kings of Shu and immortals of the pre-Han and Han periods. Hagiographies, miracle tales, narrative fiction, as well as poetry from the Six Dynasties up to modern times describe encounters with immortals; miracles involving local products, plants, and water; rituals and temples; fairs and markets. They bear witness to the sanctity of the Twenty-four Dioceses as experienced in different periods and the place they continued to play in local Taoist communities.[88]

Besides representing a territory and the seat of a diocesan administration, a *zhi* was above all a sanctuary. There are a number of conflicting descriptions of *zhi* as buildings. A penal prescription in the *Taizhen ke* code evoking such structures runs as follows:

> Those who are condemned to Punishment Five, are fined provision of three thousand bundles of thatch for the roof of the Heavenly Master diocese; those who are condemned to Punishment Six, are fined provision of two thousand tiles for the building.[89]

Chen Guofu concluded from this passage that *zhi* were, unlike the elaborate and spacious Taoist temples of later times, simple thatched or tiled huts.[90] Another quotation from the same code cited by Chen, however, describes a rather substantial complex:

> Establishment of a Heavenly Master diocese: The ground should measure eighty-one paces, that is nine times the ritual number nine. There should only be the qi of rising yang. The centre of the diocese is called Chongxu tang. On an area for seven columns and six bays of 120 feet erect the main hall. On top of the two central bays a Chongxuan tai terrace is constructed on the upper story. In the middle of the terrace is placed a great incense burner, five feet in height. Incense is burnt constantly. Open three doors on the east, west, and south sides and install windows beside the doors. Provide two roads.
>
> The audience ritual is held on a platform beneath [the eaves of] the south door. The descendants of the Heavenly Master and *qingku jishi*-masters occupying the eight superior great dioceses as mountain retreats may ascend the platform to perform the audience ritual. The other officers and the great, minor, middle, and outer libationers all perform the audience ritual from a distance beneath the great hall.
>
> Fifty feet to the north of the Chongxuan tai terrace stands the Chongxian tang hall. It comprises seven bays of 140 feet and seven columns. To the east, construct the Room of Yang immortals, to the west the Room of Yin immortals. South of the [Chong] Xuantai, at a distance of 120 (feet), at the approach of the South Gate, erect a gatehouse of five bays and three columns. South of the east door of the gate house is the lodge (*she*) of the *xuanwei*-libationer.[91] West of the gate building is the lodge of the *jiqi*-libationer in charge. Other, smaller lodges are too numerous to list. The Twenty-four Dioceses should all be exactly like this.[92]

The Code of the Sublime Capital, *Xuandu lüwen*, details the dimensions for great, medium, and small dioceses.[93] It appears, then, that *zhi* is a generic term for a Heavenly Master sanctuary of various grades, as is evident from the system of placing libationers of corresponding rank in charge of them.

Some descriptions of major dioceses refer to upper and lower *zhi* within the same precincts, presumably referring to main halls and outbuildings of the main sanctuary. Yet in another context, the term 'upper diocese' (*shangzhi*) refers to the corresponding stellar lodge.[94] Similar ambiguities are encountered with respect to the terms 'oratory' (*jingshi*), 'hermitage' (*jinglu*),[96] and 'lodge' (*she*), which each have specific as well as generic meanings and can refer to sanctuaries at different levels of importance. Sometimes the term 'kitchen' (*chu*), name of a ritual banquet, is used to refer to a sanctuary or assimilated with the liturgical functions of a *zhi*.

Oratories are well documented in both historical and canonical sources and have been comparatively well studied.[97] The terminological range of the expression comprises (1) meditation room, private chapel, priestly residence, and bureau for writing and dispatching *zhang*-petitions; (2) temples in general, including those providing communal rituals; (3) penitentiary, especially a place for obtaining healing through reflection upon one's faults.[98] In functional terms, oratories served as places of healing both through confession and by intercession on behalf of others;[99] of communion and divination,[100] as refuges in times of danger,[101] and retreats used by literati for teaching and self-cultivation.[102]

The institution named *she* is more difficult to delimit. In the most general sense, the term designated not only the residences of minor clergy but also roadside lodges reserved for the people, especially the poor.[103] The intriguing term *yishe*, 'charity lodge,' discussed as 'auberges d'équité' by Rolf Stein,[104] does not to my knowledge occur in authentic Heavenly Master texts. The sources for the traditional association of the institution with the Heavenly Master community are descriptions by authors writing outside the movement, notably official historians. The biography of Zhang Lu, the Third Heavenly Master, in the *Wei shu* by Chen Shou (AD 233–297), states:

> The various libationers all established charity lodges (*yishe*), like today's relay stations (*tingchuan*),[105] and they provided charity rice and meat to be laid out in the charity lodges. Travelers could help themselves to as much as needed to fill their stomachs, but not more. If they exceeded that amount, the Way of the Demons (*guidao*) at once caused them to fall ill.[106]

The biography of Zhang Lu in the History of the Later Han, by Fan Ye (AD 398–445), repeats the above with minor variants.[107] And the *Dianlüe* (third century), quoted by the commentator Pei Songzhi (372-451) in the biographies of Zhang Lu in *Wei shu* and cited again in the corresponding passage in the History of the Later Han, states that:

> (Zhang) Lu in Hanzhong ... instructed [the faithful] to establish charity lodges (*yishe*) and place provisions of rice and meat in them for travelers to stop there. He further taught them self-restraint; violators had to repair a hundred paces of road to expiate their fault.[108]

The semi-official provision of 'charity grain' (*yigu*) by wealthy families, following the example of the governor of Wei commandery (in modern Hubei), is attested in the Later Han period. Similarly, court messengers were dispatched to deliver medicines and drugs in times of epidemics. Money provided for redeeming insolvent convicts (by converting their sentences) was called 'charity cash' (*yiqian*).[109]

Two types of antecedent may have inspired the *yishe*-institution, if it existed, or influenced the historians' interpretation of the function of the *she*-lodges that are in fact attested in Heavenly Master writings. The first is the Han institution of *ting*-communes or hostels mentioned in the above passages by Chen and by Fan, with commune chiefs or official hostel managers titled *tingzhang* whose task was to maintain law and order.[110] Ting were also watchtowers, a function relating them to the Taoist *guàn*, originally observation terraces from which encounters with immortals could be espied. The Taoist sanctuaries named *guǎn*, on the other hand, could no doubt be assimilated with the hostels and kitchens for travellers known as *ting chuan* and *chuchuan*. The hierarchy of Han local administration comprised territories (*yu*), districts (*xian*), communes (*ting*), and hamlets (*li*).[111] The same system, including the *ting*, was adopted as territorial units by the Taoist administration.[112]

A second possible model are the Buddhist charitable institutions designated *yi* that developed chronologically roughly in parallel with the institutions of Heavenly Master Taoism. Early fifth-century Buddhist associations were called *yiyi*,[113] and Buddhist public works for the benefit of communities had names like 'charity bridge' (*yiqiao*) or 'charity well' (*yijing*), sometimes with trees planted to provide shade for travelers.[114] The imposition of road repair work for penance attributed to the Heavenly Master in the passage cited above also resembles a perennial Buddhist charitable practice.[115] Travellers other than those who went about on official business and were entitled to use the government relay system were among the main beneficiaries of both Buddhist and Taoist charitable work, for they were by definition poor, homeless, or abroad in some form of religious pursuit.

The *Zhi* Dioceses in the Liturgical Organization of the Heavenly Master Community

Heavenly Master sanctuaries are also distinguished by their liturgical functions. We have already referred to the institution of the clerical hierarchy in parallel and in conjunction with that of the Twenty-four

Dioceses. Lay followers too were ranked, ordained, and affiliated with corresponding levels of the diocesan hierarchy. To cite 'Master Lu's Summary of Taoist Liturgy':

> The teaching of the dispensation says that when a member of the congregation (*min*) has performed three Services, that constitutes one Merit; if he has three Merits [to his credit], that makes one Virtue. A parishioner who has three Virtues is exceptional and becomes eligible for appointment with an [ordination] register. If he later proves worthy, he can be further promoted from a Ten Generals Register to one of One Hundred and Fifty Generals.[116]

The text continues to detail the necessary qualifications for several other offices and then discusses the conditions for transfer among the different levels of the dioceses, from supplementary dioceses (*biezhi*) through movable (*youzhi*) and lower (*xiazhi*) to adjunct dioceses (*peizhi*). Finally, the adept reaches the grade of Taoist master of a diocese of personal affiliation (*benzhi*).

The term *min* in the passage above indicates that Lu Xiujing was referring, at the initial stage, to ordinations among the lay community. The ritual codes *Taizhen ke* regulated the conferral of the registers mentioned by Lu on lay people (*suren*).[117] The 'Protocol for Exterior Registers According to the Zhengyi Canon' includes ritual memorials of thanksgiving for such occasions.[118] The registers gave an adept command over a graded number of spirit generals, beginning with a single one for a childhood consecration and culminating in one hundred and fifty upon marriage. From the age of twenty onwards, followers were admitted to the 'Rite of Passage According to the Yellow Book,'[119] a sexual rite conferring on couples the authority of their combined ordination registers.

Like the dioceses, the Twenty-four Offices were correlated with the Twenty-four Qi or vital energies, of which twelve were female and twelve male. The 'Liturgy of the Heavenly Master Dioceses' lists these Twenty-four Energies of Yin and of Yang (*yin yang ershisi qi*) in twelve pairs of left and right *qi*-energies in association with pairs of dioceses and the corresponding ranks and titles of 'official libationers' (*guan jijiu*). All of these elements are said to have been 'entrusted to Daoling' on the same day. A commentary explains that there were twelve *yang*-energies and twelve *yin*-energies, to the left and to the right, and that male and female clergy were ordained accordingly, attaining the

Twenty-four Energies in conjunction.[120] In addition to communal *zhi*, all male and female masters established their own personal dioceses.[121]

In addition to the annual assemblies and festivals, the liturgical functions of a communal *zhi* comprised kitchen banquets, communal rituals, in particular confession and repentance rites, the collection of pledge contributions, and household registrations. Priests appointed to a given sanctuary held graded 'kitchen feasts' (*chu*),[122] communal banquets that were commensurate in importance with their ordination rank and diocesan appointment. The level of the banquet was measured in terms of the number of participants: 'Those who are ordained [as head of a regular diocese] present a kitchen banquet to feed twenty-four sages ... Those who receive [complementary] dioceses feed eighteen sages ... Those who receive [adjunct] dioceses feed fourteen sages ... Those who receive [movable] dioceses feed twelve sages.'[123]

By all accounts, the Heavenly Master ritual was concerned with confession and repentance, and with healing as a function of absolution from sin. In this area, especially, the clergy occupied a key position as intermediaries between the divine and the human worlds. A quintessentially literate religion, in which the written word was held to be the most powerful instrument to move the gods, Heavenly Master Taoism looked upon its priests as official clerks and redactors capable of composing elaborate memorials and of conveying them to the appropriate addressee. The rites of healing involved, above all, the ritual redaction of confessions and the communication of formal *zhang*-petitions on behalf of the faithful. A large amount of primary liturgical material survives in the form of historical petitions and memorials, or of models preserved as aids for the correct composition of such documents.[124] Fragments of ancient ritual protocols, dating probably to the very beginning of the movement in the second and third centuries, have come down to us through the 'Rites for Entering the Diocesan Sanctuary and Going into Audience in the Oratory' and other documents assembled by Tao Hongjing (AD 456–536) in his 'Ascent to Perfection' (*Dengzhen yinjue*). These protocols describe the ritual entry into the sanctuary, the salutations addressed to the five directions of space, the offering of incense, the preparation of *zhang*-petitions, and the invocation of deities for the audience ritual.[125]

The controversial collection of taxes and other 'faith pledges' by the dioceses appears in a rather different light in the texts emanating from within the Heavenly Master community. Especially notorious was the imposition of 'five bushels of rice' (*wudou mi*) that earned the movement the name 'Way of the Five Bushels of Rice' (Wudou mi dao) and its clergy the epithet 'rice thieves' (*mizei*) among the detractors of the Heavenly Master church because of its apparent infringement on the imperial prerogative to raise taxes. These were normally levied in kind, particularly rice. The *Taizhen* code explains:

> The pledge rice of the faithful was five bushels. It served to establish good fortune and harmonize the vital energies (*qi*) of the Five Humors. The life register (*mingji*) of the members of the household depended upon this rice. In accordance with the annual assembly, they gathered on the first day of the tenth month at the Heavenly Master diocese to remit their payment to the Heavenly Granary (Tiancang).[126]

This tax, called 'pledge rice' (*xinmi*) or 'destiny rice' (*mingmi*), served two purposes when made as an offering by and to the community: on the one hand, it provided for the needs of the clergy and liturgy, supplied the roadside lodges for travellers, and maintained reserves against times of famine; on the other hand, it augmented one's store of life in the Heavenly Granary and contributed to the repayment of an individual's life debt to the Heavenly Treasury (Tianku).[127] In this religious perspective, the rice tax assumes the universal significance of a sacramental offering of which the ultimate benefit falls to the donor in the form of a transcendent grace.

The Heavenly Master system of maintaining life registers (*mingji*) of the diocesan populations constituted an ostensibly equally subversive activity because of its encroachment on another vital function of local civil administration, the registration of households. 'Master Lu's Summary of Taoist Liturgy' is once again instructive on this subject:

> [The Heavenly Master] commanded that on the seventh day of the first month, the seventh day of the seventh month, and the fifth day of the tenth month, Three Assemblies (*sanhui*) be held each year. All the faithful were to gather and present themselves at the diocese of their personal affiliation (*benzhi*). The master should then emend the record by deleting the deceased and adding the newborn, verifying the population numbers, and establishing exact name lists. Through proclamations and decrees they were to instruct the faithful to know the Rites (*fa*). On those same days, the officers of Heaven (*tianguan*) and the spirits of the Earth (*dishen*) all gathered at the master's diocese to collate the document.[128]

A passing reference to the system of registration in connection with the Twenty-four Dioceses is already found a century earlier in the 'Scripture of the Wuji Transformation of Lord Lao,' which in addition mentions the 'recording of household registers at the assembly of the Twenty-four Dioceses at Yangping' (A1).[129]

The relationship between the clergy and the diocesan congregations was circumscribed by the belief that the Twenty-four Dioceses were the seats of destiny gods.[130] The theological rationale of the system of household registration was that the registries were communicated to the destiny gods responsible for the family members concerned, thereby ensuring their protection. By correlating the cyclical characters for an individual's birth year with those associated with the spatial disposition of the Twenty-four Dioceses, the personal destiny (*benming*) of each member of the community was tied to a particular holy site and corresponding constellation.[131]

The second half of the preserved portion of the 'Protocol of the Dioceses of the Heavenly Master' is devoted to 'personal destiny talismans' (*benming fu*). Figure 4 shows an example of a talisman

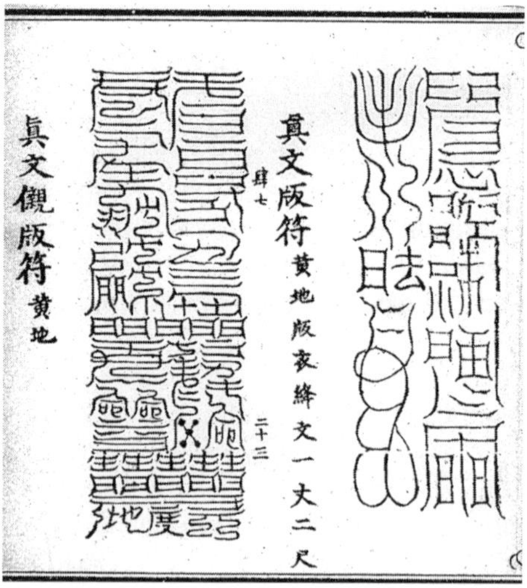

Fig. 4. Talismans Carved on Wooden Tablets for Presentation to the Gods upon an Adept's Initiation

From the 'Protocol of the Dioceses of the Heavenly Master' *Tianshi zhi yi* (Sixth century) ap. *Shoulu cidi faxin yi* 28b.

found in the Protocol. The text supplies samples of

> those symbolic writings which correspond to the individual energies. The master conferred these *fu* on each of the believers according to the latter's personality of 'fundamental destiny' (*benming*), determined at birth by the stars and planets. When the master gave this talisman to the adept, he caused him to 'pass' (*du*) into the system and become a member of the Orthodox One community, making him one of the 'Seed People' who would survive the end of this world in the Kingdom of Great Peace.'[132]

The 'Almanac for the Offering of the Petition to the Original Star,' a Six Dynasties calendar for determining an individual's horoscope complete with a liturgy for the cult devoted to his or her destiny star, contains a diagram for the arrangement of the central and fifteen surrounding altars laid out for this service (fig. 5). The outer twelve altars indicate positions for votive lamps for the Twenty-eight Stellar lodges, grouped counter-clockwise in four directional quadrants of seven asterisms each (beginning in the East). Four of these altars are

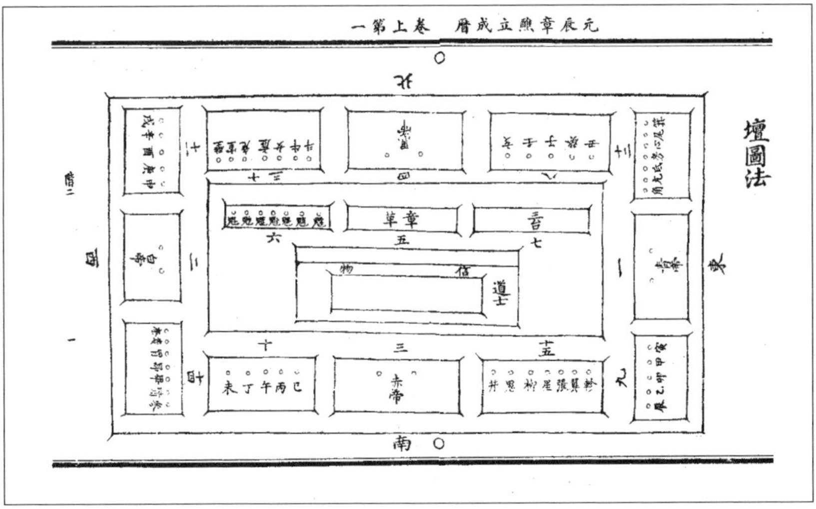

Fig. 5. Ritual Area for the Cult of the Star Presiding over an Individual's Destiny

From the 'Almanac for the Offering of the Petition to the Original Star' (Six Dynasties), *Yuanchen zhangjiao licheng li* A.1a–b.

devoted to the (gods of the) sexagenary cycle, each with alternating emplacements for three of the twelve Earthly Branches and two of the ten Heavenly Stems;[133] the middle altars on the four sides of the periphery are for the Green, White, Red, and Black Emperors of the four directions. On the side of the Taoist master's (*daoshi*) central altar are placed the pledge offerings. There are three tables in front of the central altar: a desk for drafting *zhang*-petitions (*zhangcao*) in the middle; an altar with emplacements for the seven stars of the Dipper to the left; and an altar for the Three Terraces (Santai) to the right (two constellations in Ursa Major that were predominantly involved with Fate).

The underlying objectives of the dioceses' liturgical agenda – payment of destiny rice into the Heavenly Treasury, inscription in the registers of Life, ordinations with personal destiny talismans, petitions addressed to destiny stars, and rituals performed on behalf of an individual's fate – was rooted in the eschatology of the age. The third-century apocalyptic harangue 'Family Precepts of the Great Tao' puts it this way:

> They shall behold Great Peace (Taiping) and be delivered (*dutuo*) from the cataclysm (*e'nan*), and they shall become the seed people (*zhongmin*) of the Latter Day generation (*houshi*). Even though there be calamities of war, disease, and inundation, they shall face adversity without coming to harm. Thus shall they be called the [congregation of the] Tao.[134]

Cataclysmic upheavals were widely believed to be imminent at the end of the Han and throughout the Six Dynasties period. To be consecrated as a member of the 'seed people,' who would survive the end of the world and form the germ of a renewed humanity of the 'Latter Day generation' was the main soteriological promise of the early Heavenly Master sect. The 'Orthodox One Heavenly Master's Oral Instructions to Zhao Sheng,' a fourth-century apocalypse purporting to contain Zhang Daoling's parting prophecies to one of his chief disciples, links the Heavenly Master promise of salvation expressly to the institution of the dioceses. There Zhang Daoling relates that after having been invested by Laojun as Lord of All Demons under the Orthodox One Covenant, he launched the Twenty-four Dioceses in correspondence with the Twenty-four Energies, and instituted the clerical and ordination hierarchies for the purpose of converting the followers of 'heretical and profane cults' (*xiesu*), that is, cults devoted to the gods and demons of the expired order of the Six Heavens. By adherence to the congregation of the Twenty-four Dioceses, this doomed humanity would be offered the prospect of salvation through the new dispensation of the Three Heavens. The names of the elect, including the clergy and ordained laity of the dioceses, would be inscribed in the heavenly registers of the seed people.[135]

In this way the Twenty-four Dioceses, grounded in the twenty-four-fold structure of the universe, the body, and time, formed a central part of the Heavenly Master charter for salvation. The 'Twenty-four Dioceses Charts' which provide a good deal of the information about the system available today, were themselves talismans of the elect. Heavenly Master Taoism as promulgated by the 'newly appeared Lord Lao' offered a response to the prevalent expectation of the end of the world with the end of the Han. Its vision of sacred space and sacred history, tending towards salvation across and in spite of the vicissitudes of the human condition, finds expression in the construction of the Twenty-four Dioceses system. The early Heavenly Master movement actively suggested it assimilate with the institutions of temporal administration by adopting a nomenclature for its diocesan organization that recalled the offices and functions, civil as well as military, of local government. As in the metaphor of Caesar's coin, however, the provocative analogy between temporal and spiritual authority ultimately throws the profound dissimalarity between the kingdoms of earth and heaven into sharper relief.

The Twenty-four Dioceses, for all their apparent emulation of the procedures of civil administration, had been created in heaven. They constituted an alternative space and source of authority within the territory of the declining Han empire. Beginning with the movement's refuge in Hanzhong, the system's geographical parameters had become increasingly fluid. They were eventually called into question altogether by Kou Qianzhi. The cosmological correspondences of the Twenty-four Dioceses with the Twenty-four Energies and the Twenty-eight Stellar Lodges provided a rationale for the spiritualization of their topography. As a result of the geographical and historical vicissitudes of the spread of Heavenly Master Taoism in China, the Twenty-four Dioceses were finally projected back into the heavens. Taoist priests today continue, on their ordination, to be attached to dioceses corresponding to their personal destiny, but the seats of these dioceses are entirely located in the stars.[136]

Like Augustine's (AD 354–430) redeployment of the Christian community to the City of God after the sack of Rome – the foundation stone of the early Church – the relocation of the Heavenly Master dioceses in heaven was situated against the background of a disintegrating world order. Under the Wei (AD 220–265) and the Northern Wei (AD 386–534) dynasties, Taoism began to form the symbiotic relationship with the empire that characterized much of its later history. Yet the messianic tide of the Heavenly Master movement during the centuries of disunion clearly envisaged salvation and renewal through a fundamental dissociation between *civitas terrena* and *civitas dei*, between the fallen Han empire and the 'seed people' of the Twenty-four Dioceses.

Appendix: Inventory of the Twenty-four Dioceses[137]

A. Superior Dioceses

A1 YANGPING ZHI

Localization: Xinxing, Pengxian, in the Chengdu plain. The diocese was moved to Hanzhong under Zhang Lu.[141] *Notable legends or features*: Important site in the mythology concerning the kings of prehistoric Shu. Yangping zhi was also known as the Successor Diocese, Sishi zhi, because the succession from Zhang Daoling to Zhang Heng was said to have taken place here. Chief diocese and seat of the Heavenly Master.

A2 LUTANG ZHI

Localization: Zundao, Mianzhu, in the Chengdu plain. *Notable legends or features*: Place of ascensions in antiquity. Zhang Daoling swore the oath of the Zhengyi mengwei covenant with the assembled gods and demons here in AD 155, before his own ascension at Yuntai zhi (C1). *Archaeology*: Discoveries in the 1970s of Warring States boat coffins and Ba bronze weapons.

A3 HEMING SHAN ZHI

Localization: Yuelai, Dayi, on the western edge of Chengdu plain. *Notable legends or features*: The founding site of Heavenly Master Taoism. All early sources agree that Zhang Daoling first settled here after moving to

Shu. Laozi's disciple Yin Xi presides over the site. *Archaeology*: Han period Taoist bronze seal with Ba-style inscription, discovered 1993.

A4 LIYUAN SHAN ZHI

Localization: Bailu, Pengxian, in the Chengdu plain. *Notable legends or features*: Adjacent to Lutang shan (A2). Drugs of immortality found here. The immortal Fan Li (fl. 496–465 BC) presides.

A5 GEGUI SHAN ZHI

Localization: Pengxian, Wannian xiang, Chengdu plain. *Notable legends or features*: Today also named Ge xian shan. Site of a major silkworm market under the Tang; temple fairs. Adjacent to Liyuan shan (A4).

A6 GENGCHU ZHI

Localization: Mianyuan, Mianzhu, Chengdu plain. *Notable legends or features*: The immortal Zhang Li attained the Way here.

A7 QINZHONG ZHI

Localization: Mengjia, Deyang, Chengdu plain. *Notable legends or features*: The fangshi Han Zhong received a celestial writ here and ascended into heaven.

A8 ZHENDUO ZHI

Localization: Huopen shan, Jintang, on the Tuojiang river in the Chengdu plain. *Notable legends or features*: Named after Li Zhenduo, sister of the immortal Li Babai. Site in the legend of Bieling, mythical king of ancient Shu. Fungi and divine drugs. *Archaeology*: Excavation in 1985 of Taoist objects (mirror, seal, and others) dating from the Han to the Song.

Middle Dioceses

B1 CHANGLI SHAN ZHI

Localization: Qixian, Jintang, in the Chengdu plain. Also known as Sanxue shan. *Notable legends or features*: Retreat of Li Babai. Large grotto, Three Dragon Gate with inscription. Drugs and fungi.

B2 LISHANG ZHI

Localization: Shoufeng, Deyang, Chengdu plain. *Notable legends or features*: Master Jizi, that is the Former Han diviner Sima Jizhu, presides and various immortals ascended here. Caverns, magic well.

B3 YONGQUAN ZHI

Localization: Bolong, Deyang, Chengdu plain. *Notable legends or features*: Later Han immortal and alchemist Ma Mingsheng ascended here in AD 180. Manifestation of Laojun. The spring, also called *lingquan*, produces holy water with healing power.

B4 CHOUJING ZHI

Localization: Five kilometres south of Xinjin city, Xinjin county, Chengdu plain. *Notable legends or features*: Residence of Xuanyuan, the Yellow Emperor; drugs for nourishing vitality and attaining immortality. Early site of Laozi worship, with an important Laozi temple. *Archaeology*: Site of Han cliff carvings and carved funerary bricks.

B5 BEIPING ZHI

Localization: Between the towns of Gongyi and Baosheng in Pengshan county. *Notable legends or features*: Pond, drugs of longevity. Pengzu practised longevity arts and the Han immortal Wangzi Qiao ascended here (among other places). According to one version (*Yizhou ji*), Zhang Daoling himself attained immortality here. *Archaeology*: Taoist bronze seal, discovered in the tenth century.

B6 BENZHU ZHI

Localization: Wenfeng shan, Dengshuang, Xinjin, between the dioceses Choujing and Beiping. *Notable legends or features*: Named after a bamboo grove planted there by the Yellow Emperor, providing 'bamboo for sweeping the sacred area.' The Han immortal Guo Zisheng ascended here.

B7 MENGQIN ZHI

Localization: Lushan, Xichang city, in what is now the Liangshan Yi Autonomous District in Southern Sichuan. *Notable legends or features*: Retreat of the Shang immortal Yi Yin; drugs of immortality; residence of Zhao Sheng. *Archaeology*: Site of continuous high civilization from the Shang to the Han periods.

B8 PINGGAI ZHI

Localization: Either Luzhou in Southern Sichuan or Xinjin in the Chengdu plain, depending on sources.[139] *Notable legends or features*: Jade statue, Han stone sculpture of Xi wang mu. Further sculpture of Cui Xiaotong who ascended here. Jade Maiden Spring.

C. Lesser Dioceses

C1 YUNTAI ZHI

Localization: Yuntai village, between Cangqi and Langzhong, on the northern rim of the Sichuan basin. *Notable legends or features*: Major site of ancient Ba culture. Early cult of immortals, alchemy. Site of the last of the seven trials to which Zhang subjected his disciples. Zhang Daoling is said to have ascended here in AD 156 with his wife and leading disciples, Zhao Sheng and Wang Chang. Master Gourd (Hu gong) and several later Taoists (Ge Hong, Chen Tuan) were associated with this place. *Archaeology*: Early Taoist seal, excavated in 1985.

C2 JINKOU ZHI

Localization: Mianxian in Hanzhong, Shaanxi. After the move to Hanzhong, Yangping zhi (A1) was transferred to this site. *Notable legends or features*: The immortal Chen Anshi ascended here.

C3 HOUCHENG ZHI

Localization: Originally seventy kilometres south of Nanzheng in Hanzhong, Shaanxi. Under the Jin, the diocese moved with Hanzhong refugees to Luoshui, Shifang, in the Chengdu plain. *Notable legends or features*: Immortal Nuan Ziran ascended here. Di Qiang peoples who adhered to the Heavenly Master movement from an early date inhabited the territory of Nanzheng. *Archaeology*: Shifang, major site of Warring States boat coffins, discovered between 1988 and 1995. Li Bing cult.

C4 GONGMU ZHI

Localization: Originally between Hanshan, Nanzheng, in Hanzhong (Shaanxi) and Nanjiang (Sichuan). Like C3, moved with Hanzhong refugees to Luoshui, Shifang, in the Chengdu plain under the Jin. *Notable legends or features*: Li Bing cult (tomb, ascension). Cult of Han immortal Tang Gongfang.

C5 PINGGANG ZHI

Localization: Original site at Lushan xian in Yaan district, in the territory of the Qingyi Qiang people to the Southwest of Chengdu. From the Tang onward, the diocese is localized at Xinjin in the Chengdu plain. Also known as Lingquan zhi. *Notable legends or features*: The Han immortal Li A ascended and mythical king Du Yu was active here. *Archaeology*: The Heavenly Master inscription *Jijiu Zhang Pu bei* (AD 173) was unearthed at nearby Hongya.

C6 ZHUBU ZHI

Localization: Changqiu shan at Tianhua, Pujiang. Notable legends or features: The Han archivist (*zhubu*) Wang Xing practised and ascended here, hence the name. The female immortal Yang Zhengjian also ascended at this place.

C7 YUJU ZHI

Localization: Near the old South Gate in the city of Chengdu. *Notable legends or features*: Lord Lao appeared to Zhang Daoling in AD 155 here, descending on a white deer or crane, while a throne surged from the ground for his predication. The throne's disappearance after Laojun's departure left a grotto.

C8 BEIMANG ZHI

Localization: Uncertain – Chang'an, Luoyang, or sites in Sichuan.

Notable legends or features: The immortal Wu Chengzi ascended here.

List of Chinese and Japanese References

Primary Sources

Chisong zi zhangli 赤松子章曆 (Six Dynasties). *D* 335-36, no. 615.

D: Zhengtong Daozang 正統道藏 (1445). Fascicule and work numbers according to Schipper and Verellen eds., *The Taoist Canon,* forthcoming, Chicago: The University of Chicago Press, 2003.

Dadao jialing jie 大道家令戒 (ca. A.D. 255). In *Zhengyi fawen tianshi jiaojie kejing* 正一法文天師教戒科經 12a-19b. *D* 563, no. 789.

Daode zhenjing jiyi dazhi 道德眞經集義大旨 (1299). By Liu Weiyong 劉惟永 and Ding Yidong 丁易東. *D* 431, no. 723.

Dengzhen yinjue 登眞隱訣 (c. 492-514). Compiled by Tao Hongjing 陶弘景. *D* 193, no. 421.

Dongxuan lingbao ershisi sheng tujing 洞玄靈寶二十四生圖經 (c. 400). *D* 1051, no. 1407.

Ershisi zhi 二十四治 (7th-10th c.). In *Yunji qiqian* 雲笈七籤 28. *D* 677-702, no. 1032.

Hanzhong ruzhi chaojing fa 漢中入治朝靜法 (2nd - 3rd c.). Cited and annotated in *Dengzhen yinjue* 3.

Hou Han Shu 後漢書 (398-445). By Fan Ye 范曄. Peking: Zhonghua shuju, 1963.

Huangdi longshou jing 黃帝龍首經 (Han). *D* 135, no. 283.

Huayang guo zhi 華陽國志. By Chang Qu 常璩 (fl. 350). In *Huayang guo zhi jiaobu tuzhu* 華陽國志校補圖注. Edited by Ren Naiqiang 任乃強. Shanghai: Guji, 1987.

Jin shu 晉書. By Fang Xuanling 房玄齡 (578-648). Peking: Zhonghua shuju, 1974.

Laojun bashiyi hua tushuo 老君八十一化圖說. Attributed to Shi Zhijing 史志經 (1202-1275). Ming ed. Reprinted in Florian Reiter, *Leben und Wirken Lao-tzu's in Schrift und Bild: Lao-chün pa-shih-i hua t'u-shuo*. Würzburg: Königshausen und Neumann, 1990.

Laojun bianhua wuji jing 老君變化無極經 (4th c.). *D* 875, no. 1195.

Laojun yinsong jiejing 老君音誦誡經. By Kou Qianzhi 寇謙之 (365-448). *D* 562, no. 785.

Linghua ershisi 靈化二十四. In *Dongtian fudi yuedu mingshan ji* 洞天福地嶽瀆名山記 (901), 11a-15a. By Du Guangting 杜光庭. *D* 331, no. 599.

Lishi zhenxian tidao tongjian 歷世眞仙體道通鑑 (pref. 1294). By Zhao Daoyi 趙道一. *D* 139-48, no. 296.
Lu xiansheng daomen kelüe 陸先生道門科略. By Lu Xiujing 陸修靜 (406-477). *D* 761, no. 1127.
Nüqing guilü 女青鬼律 (3rd c.?). *D* 563, no. 790.
Sanguo zhi 三國志 (297). By Chen Shou 陳壽. Peking: Zhonghua shuju, 1985.
Santian neijie jing 三天內解經 (5th c.). By Master Xu, 徐氏. *D* 876, no. 1205.
Shangqing huangshu guodu yi 上清黃書過度儀 (3rd c.?). *D* 1009, no. 1294.
Shangqing taishang dijun jiuzhen zhongjing 上清太上帝君九眞中經 (Six Dynasties). *D* 1042, no. 1376.
Shenxian ganyu zhuan 神仙感遇傳 (ca. 904). By Du Guangting 杜光庭. *D* 328, no. 592.
Taiping guangji 太平廣記 (987). Compiled by Li Fang 李昉 et al. Peking: Zhonghua shuju, 1961.
Taishang laojun jinglü 太上老君經律 (3rd c.?). *D* 562, no. 786.
Taishang laojun zhongjing 太上老君中經 (Later Han?). *D* 839, no. 1168.
Taishang miaoshi jing 太上妙始經 (5th c.?). *D* 344, no. 658.
Taizhen ke 太眞科 (4th c. and later). Reference to the evolving Shangqing code *Taizhen yudi siji mingke* 太眞玉帝四極明科, cited in numerous sources close to the Heavenly Master liturgical tradition. Cf. *Taizhen yudi siji mingke jing* 太眞玉帝四極明科經, *D* 77–78, no. 184.
Tiandi gongfu tu 天地宮府圖. By Sima Chengzhen 司馬承禎 (647-735). In *Yunji qiqian* 雲笈七籤 27. *D* 677-702, no. 1032.
Tianshi zhi yi 天師治儀 (ca. 552). By Zhang Bian 張辯. First part 上. In *Shoulu cidi faxin yi* 受籙次第法信儀 (Tang), 19b-30a. *D* 991, no. 1244. Cf. *Zhengyi xiuzhen lüeyi* 正一修眞略儀 (Tang). *D* 990, no. 1239.
Xuandu lüwen 玄都律文 (ca. 500). *D* 78, no. 188.
Yangping zhi 陽平治 (3rd c.). In *Zhengyi fawen tianshi jiaojie kejing* 正一法文天師教戒科經 20a-21b.
Yaoxiu keyi jielü chao 要修科儀戒律鈔 (ca. 715). By Zhu Faman 朱法滿. *D* 204-207, no. 463.
Yuanchen zhangjiao licheng li 元辰章醮立成曆 (Six Dynasties). *D* 1008, no. 1288.
Yunji qiqian 雲笈七籤 (ca. 1028). Compiled by Zhang Junfang 張君房. *D* 677-702, no. 1032.
Zhang tianshi ershisi zhi tu 張天師二十四治圖 ap. Sandong zhunang 三洞珠囊, 7.6a-15a. Compiled by Wang Xuanhe 王懸河 (fl. 683). *D* 780-82, no. 1139.
Zhen'gao 眞告 (499). Compiled by Tao Hongjing 陶弘景. *D* 637-40, no. 1016.
Zhengyi fawen jing zhangguan pin 正一法文經章官品 (Six Dynasties). *D* 880, no. 1218.

Zhengyi fawen taishang wailu yi 正一法文太上外籙儀 (Six Dynasties). *D* 991, no. 1243.
Zhengyi qizhi tu 正一氣治圖 ap. *Wushang biyao* 無上秘要 (ca. 574), 23.4a-9a. *D* 768-79, no. 1138.
Zhengyi tianshi gao Zhao Sheng koujue 正一天師告趙昇口訣 (Eastern Jin). *D* 1003, no. 1273.

Secondary Sources

Chen Guofu 陳國符. "Shezhi 設治" and "Shuzhi 署職". In *idem, Daozang yuanliu kao* 道藏源流考. Rev. ed. Peking: Zhonghua shuju, 1963.
Chen Meidong 陳美東, ed. *Zhongguo gu xingtu* 中國古星圖. Shenyang: Liaoning jiaoyu chuban she, 1996.
Gao Wen 高文, ed. *Sichuan Handai huaxiang zhuan* 四川漢代畫像磚. Shanghai: Shanghai renmin meishu chuban she, 1987.
Hachiya Kunio 蜂屋邦夫. *Chūgoku dōkyō no genjō* 中國道教の現狀. Tokyo: Kyūko shoin, 1990.
Li Houqiang 李后強, ed. *Wawu shan daojiao wenhua* 瓦屋山道教文化. Chengdu: Sichuan minzu chuban she, 2000.
Li Junming 李駿名. "Qingcheng shan yu Heming shan 青城山與鶴鳴山." *Zongjiao xue yanjiu* 宗教學研究 (1989.3-4): 15-16.
Luo Kaiyu 羅開玉. *Zhongguo kexue shenhua zongjiao di xiehe: yi Li Bing wei zhongxin* 中國科學神話宗教的協合—以李冰爲中心. Chengdu: Shu Ba shushe, 1990.
Pregadio, Fabrizio. "The Book of the Nine Elixirs and Its Tradition." *In Chūgoku kodai kagakushi ron* 中國古代科學論, vol. 2, 543–639. Edited by Yamada Keiji 山田慶兒 and Tanaka Tan 田中淡. Kyoto: Kyōto daigaku jimbun kagaku kenkyūjo, 1991.
Sawa Akitoshi 澤章敏. "Gotōbeidō seiken no shiki kōzō 五斗米道政權の組織構造." In *Dōkyō bunka e no tenbō* 道教文化への展望. Edited by Dōkyō bunka kenkyū kai 道教文化研究會. Tokyo: Hirakawa shuppan, 1994.
Wang Chunwu 王純五. *Tianshi dao ershisi zhi kao* 天師道二十四治考. Chengdu: Sichuan daxue chuban she, 1996.
Wang Chunwu 王純五. *Dongtian fudi yuedu mingshan ji quanyi* 洞天福地嶽瀆名山記全譯. Guiyang: Guizhou renmin chuban she, 1999.
Wang Jianmin 王健民, Liang Zhu 梁柱 and Wang Shengli 王勝利. "Zeng Houyi mu chutu ershiba xiu, bohu, qinglong tuxiang 曾侯乙墓出土的二十八宿青龍白虎圖象." *Wenwu* 文物 (1979.7): 40-45.
Wei Fuhua 衛复華. "Zhongguo daojiao Wudoumi dao fayuan di Heming

shan 中國道教五斗米道發源地鶴鳴山." *Zongjiao xue yanjiu* 宗教學研究 (1989.1-2): 6-11.

Xiao Dengfu 蕭登福. "*Taishang xuanling beidou benming yansheng zhenjing* tanshu (1-2) 太上玄靈北斗本命延生眞經探述." *Zongjiao xue yanjiu* 宗教學研究 (1997.3), 49-65; (1997.4), 30-39.

Xu Wenbin 徐文彬 et al., eds. *Sichuan Handai shique* 四川漢代石闕. Peking: Wenwu chuban she, 1992.

Yan Kaiming 顏開明. "Choujing zhi suozai di: Choujing shan Laozi miao 稠稉治所在地–稠稉山老子廟." *Zongjiao xue yanjiu* 宗教學研究 (1990.1–2): 15, 67.

Yan Kaiming 顏開明. "Daojiao Pinggai zhi yu Xinjin Guanyin si 道教平蓋治與新津觀音寺." *Zongjiao xue yanjiu* 宗教學研究 (1993.1–2): 21-23.

Yoshikawa Tadao 吉川忠夫. "Seishitsu kō「靜室」考." *Tōhō gakuhō* 東方學報 59 (1987): 125-62.

Zhang Zehong 張澤洪. "Wudou mi dao mingming de youlai 五斗米道命名的由來." *Zongjiao xue yanjiu* 宗教學研究 (1988.4): 12-17.

Zhao Zongcheng 趙宗誠. "Du Guangting *Linghua ershisi* de yixie tedian 杜光庭《靈化二十四化》一些特點." *Zongjiao xue yanjiu* 宗教學研究 (1990.1-2): 10-12.

End Notes

Research for this study was supported by the Research Grants Council of the Hong Kong Special Administrative Region (Project no. CUHK4019/99H).

1 For example, *Dadao jialing jie* 14b; *Laojun bianhua wuji jing* 2a, 6b; and *Zhengyi tianshi gao Zhao Sheng koujue* 1b. See the list of Chinese and Japanese sources in the Bibliography.

2 See Chen Guofu, 'Shezhi' and 'Shuzhi.'

3 Cf. *Sanguo zhi* 8.263: 'Those who had received their Tao and given a pledge were titled libationers. Each of them was in charge of a flock. If it was large, then he would be a superior libationer and head of a diocese. These [spiritual leaders] instructed [the people] to be sincere in their faith and truthful.'

4 Zhang, an aide in the household of prince Xiaoji of Wuling, the son of the Liang emperor Wudi (r. 502–550), probably composed this text when the prince served as prefect of Yizhou in Chengdu, Sichuan. Only the

first part survives within the Tang protocol 'Liturgy Concerning the Order of Ritual Pledges [due] on Ordination,' *Shoulu cidi faxin yi*.

5 See Kristofer Schipper, *The Taoist Body*, 62–66. Translated by Karen C. Duval (Berkeley: University of California Press, 1993).

6 *Tianshi zhi yi* 20b, 21b, and 22a, respectively.

7 *Zhengyi qizhi tu* 23.4a, 5a, and 6b, respectively.

8 *Zhang tianshi ershisi zhi tu* 7.7a, 9b, and 12a, respectively.

9 See *Laojun bianhua wuji jing* 1a; Adrianus Dudink, 'The poem *Laojun bianhua wuji jing*: Introduction, Summary, Text and Translation,' 66–67, in *Linked Faiths: Essays on Chinese Religions and Traditional Culture in Honour of Kristofer Schipper*, ed. by J.A.M. de Meyer and P.M. Engelfriet (Leiden: E.J. Brill, 1999).

10 See *Tianshi zhi yi* 22a–b and *Zhengyi qizhi tu* 23.4a.

11 *Tianshi zhi yi* 23b–24a. Cf. *Sandong zhunang* 7.5b–6a.

12 *Sandong zhunang* 7.2a.

13 The text has 'Jian'an 3' (AD 198). In view of the subsequent chronology, I adopt the reading from the *Taizhen ke* cited in the annotation. On the subject of chronology, it should be mentioned that most sources date Zhang Daoling's ascension into Heaven already in the year AD 155–156.

14 *Tianshi zhi yi* 24a–b. Cf. *Sandong zhunang* 7.2b-3a.

15 *Tianshi zhi yi* 24b–25a. Cf. *Sandong zhunang* 7.2b. The name, which is known from other sources, is only indicated here in the commentary.

16 According to the interpretation of Wang Chunwu, *Ershisi zhi*, 299. Additional hierarchical distinctions are indicated by the terms superior, inner, and great diocese (*shangzhi, neizhi, dazhi*). See *Sandong zhunang* 7.3b–5b.

17 The term was especially favoured under the Wang Mang interregnum (AD 8–23). See *Han Shu* 28A.1557 and *passim*, and Kristofer Schipper, 'The True Form: Reflections on the Liturgical Basis of Taoist Art' (forthcoming).

18 See Paul Demiéville, 'Philosophy and Religion from Han to Sui,' 818, in *The Cambridge History of China 1: The Ch'in and Han Empires, 221 BC–A.D. 220*, vol. 1., ed. D. Twitchett and M. Loewe (Cambridge: Cambridge University Press, 1986), 818.

19 *Hou Han Shu* 71.2299; Paul Michaud, 'The Yellow Turbans,' *Monumenta Serica* 17 (1958), 76, discusses this passages but erroneously refers it to *Hou Han Shu* 101.

20 Henri Maspero, *Taoism and Chinese Religion*, 287, trans. Frank Kierman (Amherst: University of Massachusetts Press, 1981); or (mistakenly, in this context) as 'magician,' ibid. 375–76.

21 Wang Chunwu, *Ershisi zhi*, 4-6.
22 Cf. *Hou Han shu* 28.3624, *Sanguo zhi* 8.263.
23 *Lu xiansheng daomen kelüe* 2a. For a translation of this work, see Peter Nickerson, 'Abridged Codes of Master Lu for the Daoist Community,' in *Religions of China in practice*, ed. D.S. Lopez (Princeton: Princeton University Press, 1996), 347–59.
24 *See Hou Han shu* 75.2435 and *Huayang guo zhi* 2.72.
25 The base map spatial data used in the maps in this essay were provided by Lawrence W. Crissman, Director of the Australian Centre of the Asian Spatial Information and Analysis Network (ACASIAN), Griffith University, in conjunction with the Electronic Cultural Atlas Initiative.
26 On the origins of this system under the Qin, see Luo Kaiyu, *Zhongguo kexue shenhua zongjiao di xiehe*: *yi Li Bing wei zhongxin*.
27 Wang Chunmu, *Ershisi zhi*, 200.
28 The most comprehensive account to date, combining observations based on field visits with source compilations, is Wang Chunwu, *Ershisi zhi*. See also Hachiya Kunio, *Chūgoku dōkyō no genjō*; Li Houqiang, ed. *Wawu shan daojiao wenhua*; Li Junming 'Qingcheng shan yu Heming shan;' Sawa Akitoshi, 'Gotōbeidō seiken no shiki kōzō;' Wei Fuhua, 'Zhongguo daojiao Wudoumi dao fayuan de Heming shan;' and Yan Kaiming 'Choujing zhi suozai di: Choujing shan laozi miao' *Zongjiao xue yanjiu* 1–2 (1990): 15, 67; 'Daojiao Pinggai zhi yu Xinjin Guanyin si.' See the list of Chinese and Japanese references below. As this volume goes to press I am informed that Volker Olles, a German scholar based in Chengdu, has begun publishing the results of a further field survey, but I have not been able to consult these.
29 See *Sanguo zhi* 8.263–4. According to *Dadao jialing jie* 14b, the community remained in Hanzhong for forty years.
30 *Laojun yinsong jiejing* 19a–20b.
31 See T. H. Barrett, 'The Emergence of the Taoist Papacy in the T'ang Dynasty,' *Asia Major* Third series, 7, no. 1 (1994), 89–106.
32 See Wang Chunwu, *Dongtian fudi yuedu mingshan ji quanyi*, and F. Verellen, 'The Beyond Within: Grotto-heavens (*Dongtian*) in Taoist Ritual and Cosmology,' *Cahiers d'Extrême-Asi*e 8 (1995), 265–90. The word '*hua*' in *Linghua ershisi* is a Tang substitute for *zhi* (diocese), observing a taboo in deference to the personal name of Emperor Gaozong (r. 649–683).
33 See Zhao Zongcheng, 'Du Guangting *Linghua ershisi* de yixie tedian' *Zongjiao xue yanjiu* (1990. 1–2), 10–12.
34 The author is indebted to Marc Kalinowski for providing valuable comments and materials on this subject.

35 *Zhengyi qizhi* tu 23.4a.

36 See Sun Xiaochun and Jacob Kistemaker, *The Chinese Sky Under the Han: Constellating Stars and Society*, (Leiden: E.J. Brill, 1997), 19–21, and Donald Harper, 'Warring States: Natural Philosophy and Occult Thought,' in *The Cambridge History of Ancient China: from the Origins of Civilization to 221 B.C.*, ed. M. Loewe and E. Shaughnessy, (Cambridge: Cambridge University Press, 1999), 833-43. See also the table and distribution of the lodges in Richard Stephenson, 'Chinese and Korean Star Maps and Catalogs,' in *History of Cartography*, Vol. 2, Book 2: *Cartography in the Traditional East and Southeast Asian Societies*, ed. J.B. Harley and D. Woodward, (Chicago: The University of Chicago Press, 1994), 517.

37 See Joseph Needham, 'Astronomy,' in *Science and Civilization in China* Vol. 3 (Cambridge: Cambridge University Press, 1959), 242–59.

38 Wang Jianmin, Liang Zhu, and Wang Shenglai, 'Zeng Houyi mu chutu ershiba xiu, bohu, qinglong tuxiang,' (1979.7): 40–45.

39 See Edward Schafer, *Pacing the Void: T'ang Approaches to the Stars*, (Berkeley: University of California Press, 1977), 75-79. On field allocation and various nonary arrangements in early geometrical cosmography, see also John Henderson, 'Chinese Cosmographical Thought: The High Intellectual Tradition.' In *History of Cartography*, ed. Harley and Woodward, 208–10.

40 See the eighteenth-century map reproduced in Henderson, 'Chinese Cosmographical Thought,' 209.

41 *Lishi zhenxian tidao tongjian* 18.13a. The dioceses are there called 'twenty-four blessed courts' (*futing*).

42 See F. Verellen, *Du Guangting* (850–933): *taoïste de cour à la fin de la Chine médiévale* (Paris: Collège de France, 1989), 117.

43 They corresponded to the categories obscure/black/heaven, initial/yellow/earth, and primordial/white/Tao, respectively. See *Dadao jialing jie* 12a–b. A translation of this work is included in Stephen Bokenkamp, *Early Daoist scriptures* (Berkeley: University of California Press, 1997).

44 Kristofer Schipper, *The Taoist Body*, 61–65. The subsequent creation of all beings was the result of the fusion of the *qi* of heaven and earth. See *Taishang miaoshi jing* 1b.

45 See *Huangdi longshou jing* 1.3a and Marc Kalinowski, 'The Use of the Twenty-eight Xiu as a day-count in early China,' *Chinese Science* 13 (1996), 55–81.

46 See *Taishang laojun zhongjing*, and Kristofer Schipper, 'The Inner World of

the *Lao-tzu chung-ching*,' in *Time and Space in Chinese Culture*, ed. Chun-chieh Huang and E. Zürcher. (Leiden: E.J. Brill, 1995).

47 *Nüqing guilü, passim.*

48 See *Dongxuan lingbao ershisi sheng tujing* 1b and *passim.*

49 Cf. Brian Smith, *Classifying the Universe: the ancient Indian* Varṇa *System and the Origins of Caste* (New York: Oxford University Press, 1994).

50 On these systems see Marc Kalinowski, *Cosmologie et divination dans la Chine ancienne: le Compendium des cinq agents (Wuxing dayi, VIe siècle)* (Paris: Ecole Française d'Extrême-Orient, 1991). The secondary associations here derive from different sources and are not always mutually consistent.

51 According to *Linghua ershisi.*

52 *Tianshi zhi yi, Zhengyi qizhi tu, Zhang tianshi ershisi zhi tu* et al.

53 Indicated only in *Linghua ershisi.* Cf. Zhao Zongcheng, 'Du Guangting *Linghua ershisi*,' 12.

54 According to *Yaoxiu keyi jielü chao* 10.3b–4a. This section is headed 'Diocese affiliations' (*zhi suo shu*). The dioceses listed there are said to preside over births corresponding to the respective cyclical characters, that is, to control the destiny of individuals born in corresponding years.

55 See *Tianshi zhi yi and Linghua ershisi.*

56 *Linghua ershisi*: 'Di, Fang, Xin.' The following are correspondingly displaced.

57 The series here is confused, and the text erroneously reads 'Beimang' for 'Beiping,' See category C8 of table below.

58 Number 6 does not feature in this list, and 7 is reserved for two supplementary dioceses.

59 *Zhang tianshi ershisi zhi tu* 7.6a–7a.

60 On Taoist attitudes to history, especially as conveyed by the *Lishi zhenxian tidao tongjian*, see the remarks by Schipper in 'The inner world of the *Lao-tzu chung-ching*,' 115.

61 For a discussion of the powers typically associated with immortals, see Isabelle Robinet, 'Metamorphosis and deliverance from the corpse in Taoism,' *History of Religions* 19 (1979), 37–70, and 'The Taoist Immortal: Jesters of Light and Shadow,' *Journal of Chinese Religions* 13/14 (1986). 87–105.

62 *LZTT* 18.4a, 18.4b–5a, 18.15b.

63 Beginning with the 'Book of Mountains and Seas' (*Shanhai jing),* compiled from the fourth century BC onwards. See the translation by Riccardo Fracasso, *Libro dei monti e dei mari (Shanhai jing): cosmografia e mitologia nella Cina Antica*, Venice: Marsilio, 1996.

64 Alchemy is an early but problematic feature of Zhang's legend. See F. Verellen, 'Zhang Ling and the Lingjing salt well,' in *En suivant la voie royale: mélanges en hommage à Léon Vandermeersch*, ed. by J. Gernet and M. Kalinowski (Paris: Ecole Française d'Extrême-Orient, 1997), 249–50.

65 *LZTT* 18.4b. See also '*Jiuzhen fa*' in *Shangqing taishang dijun jiuzhen zhongjing* 1.2b–11b.

66 In Linqiong (modern Qionglai). See *Dadao jialing jie* 14a. Qionglai county is adjacent to Dayi where the seat of the Heming diocese was located.

67 *LZTT* 18.5a, 18.21a. See Fabrizio Pregadio, 'The Book of the Nine Elixirs and its tradition,' in *Chūgoku kodai kagakushi ron*, vol. 2, 543–639. The Nine Crucibles elixir already features in the transmitted text of Zhang Daoling's biography from the *Shenxian zhuan* (ca. 320) by Ge Hong. See Verellen, 'Zhang Ling and the Lingjing well.'

68 *LZTT* 18.14a–15a, 18.15b. On Heavenly Master attitudes towards the dead and their redemption, see Ursula-Angelika Cedzich, 'Ghosts and Demons, Law and Order: Grave Quelling Texts and Early Taoist Liturgy,' *Taoist Resources* 4, no. 2 (1993), 23–35. Michel Strickmann considered the ancestor cult was accorded a minor place, or even rejected outright, by the early movement. See his 'Therapeutische Rituale und das Problem des Bösen im frühen Taoismus,' in *Religion und Philosophie in Ostasien. Festschrift für Hans Steininger*, ed. G. Naundorf et al. (Würzburg: Königshausen & Neumann, 1985), 189.

69 As quoted in *Taiping guangji* 8.55-58 and *Yunji qiqian* 109.19a-21a; *LZTT 18.66–17b.*

70 See Hubert Delahaye, *Les premières peintures de paysage en Chine: aspects religieux* (Paris: Ecole Française d'Extrême-Orient, 1981), 6–73.

71 Ibid., 31.

72 See Xu Wenbin et al., eds., *Sichuan Handai shique*.

73 See Gao Wen ed., *Sichuan Handai huaxiang zhuan*. Stephen Bokenkamp, in 'Into the clouds: the Mount Yuntai parish and early Celestial Master Daoism' (work in progress), relates the *que*-shape of Mount Yuntai to other gate metaphors in the mythical topography of early Sichuan.

74 *LZTT* 18.20a–b, 18.23b. See *Lishi zhenxian tidao tongjian* 18.1a-b; *Laojun bianhua wuji jing* 2a; Dudink, 'Poem *Laojun bianhua wuji jing*, 111-12.

75 See Wei Fuhua, 'Zhongguo daojiao Wudou mi dao fayuan di Heming shan.'

76 See *Sanguo zhi* 8.263, *Shenxian zhuan* ap. *Taiping guangji* 8.55–58 and *Yunji qiqian* 109.19a–21a, *Huayang guo zhi* 2.72–3, *Hou Han shu* 75.2435–6. The mountain is interchangeably called Heming shan or Huming shan (Mount Swan Cry). The call of the crane, mount of the immortals, signaled an ascension. See *LZTT* 18.5a.

77 *LZTT* 6b–8a, 18.5b–6a, 18.22b–23a. Scene no. 58 of the illustrated Laozi manifestations *Laojun bashiyi hua tushuo*, showing Lord Lao's descent in a dragon chariot, situates the 'Transmission of Zhengyi' at Mount Heming itself.

78 *LZTT* 18.15b. Another patent anachronism: the Lingbao scriptures, as known in history, were 'revealed' at the end of the fourth century.

79 See the versions of these popular Song scriptures in the Ming canon, titled *Taishang xuanling beidou benming changsheng miaojing* (D 341, no. 622–623) and *Taishang shuo nandou liusi yanshou duren miaojing* (D 341, no. 624), respectively. The former relates the legend of its revelation by Laozi in AD 155 at the Yuju diocese in Chengdu. The latter is attributed to Zhang's disciple Zhao Sheng. On these and related texts, see Xiao Dengfu, '*Taishang xuanling beidou benming yansheng zhenjing* tanshu (1–2),' and *Taishang shuo nandou liusi yanshou duren miaojing* tanshu.'

80 *LZTT* 18.21b–22a. The 'Dipper Predication' at the Yuju diocese is depicted as scene no. 59 of the illustrated Laozi manifestations in the Yuan polemic *Laojun bashiyi hua tushuo*.

81 *LZTT* 18.13a, 18.22b. Fragments of the ancient *Qian erbai guan yi* manual and petitions survive in *Zhengyi fawen jing zhangguan pin* and in *Dengzhen yinjue* 3.

82 *Zhengyi qizhi tu* 23.4a.

83 See *LZTT* 18.22a–b; *Santian neijie jing*, the 'Initiate's Explanation of the Doctrine of the Three Heavens' (trans. Bokenkamp, *Early Daoist Scriptures*).

84 SeeVerellen, 'Zhang Ling and the Lingjing well.'

85 *LZTT* 18.4b. This is in contradiction with many of the community's early rules of conduct; see Barbara Hendrischke and Benjamin Penny, '*The 180 Precepts Spoken by Lord Lao*: A Translation and Textual Study,' *Taoist Resources* 6, no. 2 (1996), 17–29, especially 22.

86 *LZTT* 18.5b–6a, 18.16a–17b, 18.20b, 18.20b–21a, 18.21a. Yangping zhi was also known as Successor Diocese, Sishi zhi.

87 *LZTT* 18.22b–23a. These and the resulting lineage were in fact constructed retrospectively under the Tang. See Barrett, 'Emergence of the Taoist Papacy.'

88 A sampling of this material can be found in Wang Chunwu, *Ershisi zhi*, under the headings of individual dioceses.

89 *Taizhen ke* ap. *Chisong zi zhangli* 2.19a, commentary.

90 Chen Guofu, 'Shezhi,' 335.

91 One of the sixteen ranks of libationers listed in the *Tianshi zhi yi*.

92 *Taizhen ke* ap. *Yaoxiu keyi jielü chao* 10.1a–b.

93 *Xuandu lü* [wen] ap. *Yaoxiu keyi jielü chao* 10.4a.

94 See *Tianshi zhi yi* 19b–22a.

95 *Zhen'gao* 18.6b–7a, for example.

96 These were instituted alongside the Twenty-four Dioceses. See *Zhang tianshi ershisi zhi tu* 7.7a.

97 See especially Yoshikawa Tadao, 'Seishitsu kō.' *Tōhō gakuhō* 59 (1987), 125–62.

98 See *Dianlüe* ap. *Sanguo zhi* 8.264: 'In addition, [Zhang Daoling] set up meditation chambers (*jingshi*) in which the sick had to dwell while reflecting upon their transgressions.'

99 See the story 'The Taoist Wang Zuan' in *Shenxian ganyu zhuan* ap. *Taiping guangji* 15.103–104: Wang Zuan helps victims of an epidemic during the war at the end of the Western Jin by dispatching a *zhang*-petition from his *jingshi* oratory. His prayers are answered by a resplendent apparition of Taishang Laojun and timely help.

100 See the story 'Linghu Xuan,' *Shenxian ganyu zhuan* 1.10a–11a, translated in F. Verellen, '"Evidential Miracles in Support of Taoism": The Inversion of a Buddhist Apologetic Tradition in late T'ang China,' *T'oung Pao* 78 (1992): 222–23.

101 See the example from *Zhen'gao* discussed in Michel Strickmann, *Le taoïsme du Mao Chan: chronique d'une révélation*, (Paris: Collège de France, 1981), 150–51. See also the story of Wang Ningzhi, son of the famous calligrapher Wang Xizhi (AD 303–361), who prays for supernatural protection during the Sun En rebellion, in *Jin shu* 80.2101–3.

102 See the example of Xie Lingyun discussed in Yoshikawa Tadao,'Seishitsu kō,' 128.

103 On the latter, see Rolf Stein, 'Remarques sur quelques mouvements du taoïsme politico-religieux au 2e siècle ap. J.-C.' *T'oung Pao* 50 (1963), 64.

104 Ibid., esp. 55–56.

105 The implication seems to be that they extended security, prosperity, and civilizing government to remote areas (cf. *Hou Han shu* 76.2459). *Tingchuan* were also meeting places for local administrators and scholars: 'Whenever [the statesman Liu Kuan (120–185)] went on a tour of inspection and stopped at a relay station (*tingchuan*), he would invite the academicians and libationers, as well as recluses and sundry scholars, to receive their instructions and explications' (*Hou Han shu* 25.887). *Guidao* is the term used here for the teaching of Zhang Lu.

106 *Sanguo zhi* 8.264.

107 *Hou Han shu* 75.2435-36.

108 *Sanguo zhi* 8.264 *Hou Han shu* 75.2436. Similarly, *Huayang guo zhi* 2.72.

109 See *Hou Han shu* 80A.2615; *Hou Han shu* 8.332 and 342; and *Hou Han shu* 58.1872. I am grateful to Donald Harper for having drawn my attention to these charitable practices under the Later Han.

110 See Stein, 'Remarques,' 59–76, and Hans Bielenstein, 'The institutions of Later Han,' in *The Cambridge History of China 1: The Ch'in and Han Empires, 221 B.C. -A.D. 220*, ed. D. Twitchett and M. Loewe (Cambridge: Cambridge University Press, 1986), 509.

111 See *Hou Han shu* 28.3624 n. 1.

112 See *Chisong zi zhangli* 5.1b and 6.22b–23a.

113 Stein, 'Remarques,' 56, maintains that Buddhist developments in this domain appear to have been later than their Taoist counterparts, but the historical evidence is uncertain. On *yiyi*, see Jacques Gernet, *Buddhism in Chinese Society: An Economic History from the Fifth to the Tenth Centuries*, translated by F. Verellen (New York: Columbia University Press, 1995), 259–77.

114 See Liu Shufen, 'Art, Ritual, and Society: Buddhist Practice in Rural China during the Northern Dynasties,' *Asia Major* Third series, 8, no. 1 (1995), 34–37.

115 See Barend ter Haar, *The White Lotus Teachings in Chinese Religious History*, 24–28 (Leiden: E.J. Brill, 1992), on lay Buddhist public works for acquiring religious merit under the Song and Yuan, including bridge and road building projects and the provision of tea and hot water to pilgrims and travellers.

116 *Lu xiansheng daomen kelüe* 5b–6a.

117 Quoted in *Yaoxiu keyi jielü chao* 10.4b–7b.

118 *Zhengyi fawen taishang wailu yi* 5a–9b.

119 See *Shangqing huangshu guodu yi* 1a.

120 *Tianshi zhi yi* 22b–23a.

121 *Zhengyi fawen wailu yi* 1a.

122 On the ritual background to this institution, see Rolf Stein, 'Spéculations mystiques et thèmes relatifs aux "cuisines" du taoïsme.' *Annuaire du Collège de France* 72e année (1972–73), 489–89.

123 On the kitchen banquet ritual, see *Yaoxiu keyi jielü chao* 12; *Tianshi zhi yi* 22b, 24a, 24b, 25a.

124 See especially the rich sampling contained in the 'Petition Almanac of Chisong zi,' *Chisong zi zhangli*, subject of a forthcoming study by the author.

125 See *Hanzhong ruzhi chaojing fa*, and Ursula-Angelika Cedzich, 'Das Ritual der Himmelsmeister im Spiegel früher Quellen: Übersetzung und Untersuchung des liturgischen Materials im 3. *chüan* des *Teng-chen yin-chüeh*.' (PhD Diss., Würzburg University, 1987).

126 *Taizhen ke* ap. *Yaoxiu keyi jielü chao* 10.2a. On the taxation system and its relation to the *cong*-tax levied on the Ba peoples by the Han, see Zhang Zehong, 'Wudou mi dao mingming de yulai,' *Zongjiao xue yanjiu*

(1988.4), 12–17.

127 See Hou Ching-lang, *Monnaies d'offrandes et la notion de trésorerie dans la religion chinoise* (Paris: Collège de France, 1975), 101–102, 108–109.

128 *Lu xiansheng daomen kelüe* 2a.

129 *Laojun bianhua wuji jing* 2a and 6b, respectively.

130 See *Sandong zhunang* 7.1a, quoting *Xuandu lü* (cf. *Xuandu lüwen* 11a–18a).

131 See the section headed 'Diocese affiliations' in *Yaoxiu keyi jielü chao* 10.3b–4a; in this chapter see table 1 'Schematization of Diocesan Correspondences,' under the Duodenary Cycle column.

132 Schipper, *Taoist body*, 63.

133 Here the sequence begins in the North and rotates clockwise. Numbers 5 and 6 are missing.

134 *Dadao jialing jie* 15a. The 'Scripture of the Wuji Transformation of Lord Lao' has a very similar passage, adding an exhortation about the prophylactic effects of *fu*-talismans and the method of reverently invoking one's protective deities with their help. See *Laojun bianhua wuji jing* 3a–b.

135 *Zhengyi tianshi gao Zhao Sheng koujue* 1a–2a.

136 Kristofer Schipper (personal communication). See also his 'Taoist Ordination Ranks in the Tunhuang manuscripts,' in *Religion und Philosophie in Ostasien*, ed. Naundorf et al., 133.

137 For detailed descriptions and sources, see Wang Chunmu, *Ershisi zhi*.

138 Ibid., 99–100.

139 Du Guangting has Xinjin. See Wang Chunwu, *Ershisi zhi*, 215–21.

Glossary

Bailu chang 白鹿場
Baosheng 保勝
Beidou 北斗
Beidou yansheng jing 北斗延生經
beizhi 備治
benming 本命
benming fu 本命符
benzhi 本治
biezhi 別治
bilu 秘籙
Bolong zhen 伯隆鎮
Cangqi 蒼溪
Chang'an 長安
Changqiu shan 長秋山
Chen Anshi 陳安世
Chengdu 成都
Chongxian tang 崇仙堂
Chongxu tang 崇虛堂
Chongxuan tai 崇玄臺
chu 廚 (kitchen banquet)
chuchuan 廚傳
Cui Xiaotong 崔孝通
dafang 大方
daoshi 道士
Dayi 大邑
dazhi 大治
Dengshuang 鄧雙
Deyang 德陽
Dianlüe 典略
dishen 地 神
dongtian 洞天
dou 斗
Du Guangting 杜光庭
Dujiang yan 都江堰
dutuo 度脫
e'nan 厄難
ershiba xiu 二十八宿
ershisi qi 二十四氣
ershisi zhi 二十四治 (Twenty-four Dioceses)
ershisi zhi 二十四職 (Twenty-four Offices)
fa 法 (ritual)
Fan Li 范蠡
fang 方 (military and mutual aid unit)
fang 坊 (ward)
fang 防 (defence)
fang 房 (room or building)
feixian qingju 飛仙輕舉
fenye 分野
fu 符 (talisman)
fudi 福地
futing 福庭
Ge Hong 葛洪
Ge xian shan 葛仙山
Gongyi 公義
Gu Kaizhi 顧愷之
guǎn 館 (sanctuary)
guàn 觀 (observation terrace)
guan jijiu 官祭酒
guidao 鬼道
Guo Zisheng 郭子聲
Han Zhong 韓衆
Hanshan qu 漢山區
Hanzhong 漢中
Heming shan 鶴鳴山
Hongya 洪雅
Housheng Lijun 后聖李君
houshi 後世
Hu gong 壺公

Huangdi jiuding dan fa 黃帝九鼎丹法
huji 戶藉
Huming shan 鵠鳴山
Huopen shan 火盆山
jiangjun 將軍
jiaoqu 教區
jieqi 節氣
Jiezi yuan huazhuan siji 芥子園畫傳四集
jijiu 祭酒
Jijiu Zhang Pu bei 祭酒張普碑
jinglu 靖廬
jingshi 靜室
Jintang 金堂
jiqi 祭氣
Jiuding shendan 九鼎神丹
jiuhua dayao 九華大藥
jiuzhen bifa 九眞秘法
Jizi 季子
juxing 距星
Kou Qianzhi 寇謙之
Kuixing 魁星
Langzhong 郎中
Li A 李阿
Li Babai 李八百
Li Bing 李冰
Li Zhenduo 李眞多
li 里 (hamlet)
Liangshan Yi 涼山彝族
Lingbao shangjing 靈寶上經
lingquan 靈泉
Lingquan zhi 靈泉治
Linqiong 臨邛
liuren 六壬
Lu Xiujing 陸修靜
Luoshui zhen 洛水鎮
Luoyang 洛陽
Lushan 廬山
Lushan xian 蘆山縣
Luzhou 瀘州
Ma Mingsheng 馬明生
Mengjia 孟家
Mianxian 勉縣
Mianyuan 綿遠
Mianzhu 綿竹
min 民 (congregation)
mingji 命藉
mingmi 命米
mingshan 名山
mizei 米賊
Nandou jing 南斗經
Nanjiang xian 南江縣
Nanzheng 南鄭
neizhi 內治
Nuan Ziran 暖自然
Pei principality 沛國
Pei Songzhi 裴松之
peizhi 配治
Pengshan 彭山
Pengxian 彭縣
Pengzu 彭祖
Pujiang 蒲江
qi 氣 (vital energy)
Qian erbai guan yi 千二百官儀
qingku jishi 清苦濟世
Qingyi Qiang 青衣羌
Qionglai 邛崍
Qixian 栖賢
que 闕 (pillar gate)
qushuai 渠帥
Quting shan 渠停山
Sancai tuhui 三才圖會
sanhui 三會

sanqi 三氣
Santai 三台
Santian 三天
Santian zhengyi bifa 三天正一秘法
Sanxue shan 三學山
Shanghuang 上皇
Shangpin zhi 上品治
shangzhi 上治
Shanhai jing 山海經
she 舍 (lodge)
shenjian 神劍
Shenxian zhuan 神仙傳
Shifang 什邡
Shoufeng 壽豐
Sima Chengzhen 司馬承禎
Sima Jizhu 司馬季主
sishi 嗣師
Sishi zhi 嗣師治
sizhen 四鎮
suren 俗人
Taiping 太平
Taishang yuanshi tianzun
太上元始天尊
Taishang zhi 太上治
Taisui 太歲
Tang Gongfang 唐公房
Tiancang 天倉
tianguan 天官
Tianhua xiang 天華鄉
Tianku 天庫
Tianshi dao 天師道
ting 亭 (commune)
tingchuan 亭傳
tingzhang 亭長
tu 圖 (diagram)
Tuojiang 沱江
Wang Chang 王長
Wang Mang 王莽
Wang Ningzhi 王凝之
Wang Xing 王興
Wang Xizhi 王羲之
Wang Xuanhe 王懸河
Wangzi Qiao 王子喬
Wannian xiang 萬年鄉
Wei shu 魏書
Wenfeng shan 文峰山
Wu Chengzi 務成子
wudou 五斗
Wudou mi dao 五斗米道
Wuji 無極
Wuming baoshan 五明寶扇
Wushang dadao laojun
無上大道老君
Wushang zhi 無上治
Wuwei dadao xuanzhen
無為大道玄眞
Wuwei daojun xuanlao
無為大道玄眞
Xi wang mu 西王母
xiang 鄉 (district)
xiaofang 小方
Xiapin zhi 下品治
xiazhi 下治
Xichang shi 西昌市
Xie Lingyun 謝靈運
xiesu 邪俗
xinchu Laojun 新出老君
Xinjin 新津
xinmi 信米
Xinxing 新興
xishi 系師
xiu 宿 (stellar lodge)
Xuanlao zhi 玄老治
xuanwei 宣威

Yaan diqu 雅安地區
Yang Zhengjian 楊正見
yangguan 陽官
Yangping zhi dugong yin 陽平治都功印
yangxing qingshen 養性輕身
Yi Yin 伊尹
yi 義 (charitable institution)
yi 儀 (ritual protocol)
yigu 義穀
yijing 義井
Yin Xi 尹喜
yin yang ershisi qi 陰陽二十四氣
yinguan 陰官
yiqian 義錢
Yiqian erbai guan zhang 一千二百官章
yiqiao 義橋
yishe 義舍
yiyi 義錢
Yizhou 益州
Yizhou ji 益州記
Youwang 幽王
youzhi 遊治
yu 域 (territory)
yubi 玉璧
yuce 玉册
Yuelai 悅來
Yuntai xiang 雲臺鄉
zhang 章 (petition)
Zhang Bian 張辯
Zhang Daoling 張道陵
Zhang Heng 張衡
Zhang Jue 張角
Zhang Li 張力
Zhang Lu 張魯
zhangcao 章草
Zhao Sheng 趙昇
zhengqi 正氣
Zhengyi mengwei 正一盟威
Zhengyi mengwei zhi fa 正一盟威之法
Zhengyi zhenren 正一眞人
Zhengzhen wuji taishang 正眞無極太上
zhengzhen 正眞
zhengzhi 正治
zhenzheng 眞正
zhi suo shu 治所屬
zhi 治 (diocese; seat of local government)
zhili 治理
zhongmin 種民
Zhongpin zhi 中品治
Zundao chang 遵道場

2

The Story of the Buddha's Begging Bowl: Imagining a Biography and Sacred Places

KOICHI SHINOHARA

Sacred biography and sacred places often intersect in Buddhism. The life of Śākyamuni Buddha is told through groups of stories centred around sacred places (for example, Foucher's eight pilgrimages). Conversely, Buddhist sacred places are often defined through references to incidents in the life of the Buddha.[1] In this essay I investigate some aspects of this complex relationship by examining how Buddhist sacred places were constructed, not so much as physical spaces filled with material objects, but rather as imagined spaces such as those described in recorded visions and scriptures, and how elements from sacred biographies are used in this effort.

I begin with a sermon on the Buddha's begging bowl; this sermon appears in the remarkable revelation that a prominent vinaya master Daoxuan (AD 596–667) is said to have received towards the end of his life. Although the record of this revelation is preserved in a rather chaotic state, in obscure fragments marked by numerous inconsistencies, I attempt to relate the sermon as an account with a coherent message. Unusual elements in the sermon become more intelligible when they are read against the background of a separate scripture, 'The Scripture of [a Non-Buddhist, called] Lotus-face' (*Lianhua mian jing*[2]), said to have been translated by Narendrayaśas though this attribution is questionable.[3] The second half of this scripture tells an elaborate story about the bowl.

In the sermon revealed to Daoxuan and in the Lotus-face Scripture the Buddha's begging bowl appears as an imaginary bowl. But a physical object known as the Buddha's begging bowl in fact existed as an important cultic object in Gandhāra, as carefully demonstrated by Kuwayama Shōshin. The story in the Lotus-face Scripture presupposes this cult of the Buddha's bowl in Gandhāra, and I believe that the sermon attributed to Daoxuan was, in turn, inspired directly by the account of this scripture. An element from the familiar life of the Buddha story was used as the centre of a cult, to construct a new Buddhist sacred place in a distant location, outside the area in which central events in the Life of the Buddha story occur. This cult was translated into a vision of cosmic dimensions, first through the Lotus-face Scripture and then through Daoxuan's record of the Buddha's sermon newly revealed in China, at even a greater distance from the Life of the Buddha sites.[4] I conclude by briefly reviewing how the remarkable cosmic vision that appears in the newly revealed sermons on the bowl and on other cultic objects used by the Buddha may have also affected Daoxuan's understanding of Buddhist sacred places in China. This remarkable story of Daoxuan's revelation was undoubtedly constructed from many pieces, and we need to trace its lineage in different directions to arrive at an adequate understanding. In this essay I trace one such connection, a particularly striking one since it enables us to see the source of this vision partly in a complex development that occurred in India.

The New Sermons of the Buddha Revealed to Daoxuan

Towards the end of his life in AD 667 Daoxuan is said to have had a remarkable experience. Gods appeared to him and instructed him on a variety of topics. The most detailed account of this incident appears in the encyclopedia *Fayuan zhulin* ('The Jade Forest in the Dharma Garden') compiled by Daoshi, Daoxuan's collaborator at the Ximingsi temple.[5] This account appears to have been written as an introduction to a record of the instruction Daoxuan received, entitled *Daoxuan lüshi zhuchi gangying ji* ('The Record of the Miraculous Communication to the Vinaya Master Daoxuan on the Preservation [of the Buddha's Teaching]').[6] Though the entire work does not exist today, and in fact may never have been completed, several passages from this and other related works are excerpted in subsequent sections in the *Fayuan zhulin*, all claiming to present the instruction Daoxuan received from the gods.[7] Some of these passages reproduce a record of the Buddha's sermon preserved in heaven; others take the form of exchanges between Daoxuan who asked the questions and the gods who answered them.[8]

The passages presenting the Buddha's sermons, particularly noteworthy as examples of Buddhist scriptures composed in China, begin by noting the circumstances under which the Buddha gave his sermons. He begins each sermon by recalling how at one time, either shortly after he had left his father's palace or shortly before he achieved enlightenment, some deity appeared and presented him with an object, such as a razor, a robe, or a bowl. The deity explains that the object had been passed from Buddha to Buddha during the present Cosmic Age of the Wise, and that he was entrusted with it by a previous Buddha so that he could give it to Śākyamuni. The message here is clearly that the object, used by previous Buddhas at a crucial point in their lives, was also used by Śākyamuni at the corresponding point, and this object is preserved further for the future Buddhas who will again use it in the same way. The focus of the sermon then shifts to that of the *stūpa* (a relic mound) in which each object is placed. Sometimes a *stūpa* is presented to the Buddha by a deity; sometimes the Buddha instructs deities and other Buddhas to construct one or more *stūpas*. The elaborate account of the *stūpa* is followed by the Buddha's instruction entrusting the *stūpa* to someone who is to guard it after the Buddha enters *nirvāṇa*. Various locations where the *stūpa* is to be kept are also mentioned, and in this context the Buddha frequently predicts that some time after his death evil monks and rulers will attack the True Teaching. Often bodhisattvas are instructed to take copies of the *stūpa* to all places, where they will serve to help preserve the True Teaching.

As this basic formula of the Buddha's sermons is repeated from passage to passage, each of which tells the story of different cultic objects, a picture of the preservation of the Buddha's teaching envisioned in the *Zhuchi ganying ji* emerges: the True Teaching that is revealed from time to time when a Buddha appears in the world is preserved at the present time in the many *stūpas* in which the various objects used by all the Buddhas of the present Cosmic Age are placed. After Śākyamuni enters *nirvāṇa*, there will be times when the existence of the True Teaching will be seriously threatened by hostile kings or evil monks who follow wrong teachings and violate monastic rules. Even at such times, the True Teaching is preserved securely in these *stūpas*, and the True Teaching can subsequently be re-established by building copies of these *stūpas* everywhere.

In the context of religious biographies and sacred spaces, I find it striking that many of these sermons focus on the cultic objects that Śākyamuni is said to have used in well-known episodes from the Life of the Buddha.[9] Daoxuan, or the author of these passages if it is not Daoxuan, used these objects, captured in the imagination, to establish a connection with Śākyamuni's life. In these sermons, specific yet imaginary sacred places, such as those where *stūpas* are built, are connected with the life of Śākyamuni Buddha, first by identifying the occasions on which these cultic objects were offered to him, and then noting that these objects were later kept in the *stūpas* in question. The sermons themselves are given by Śākyamuni at clearly specified points in his life. In addition, connections are established to previous Buddhas who are said to have used the same cultic objects on similar occasions.[10] Imaginary sacred places are constructed here with these elaborate references to the life of the Buddha.

The Sermon on the Buddha's Begging Bowl

The story of the Buddha's bowl[11] is told as follows: Daoxuan asked the god about the bowl. In answering the question the god said the following: In the thirty-eighth year after the Tathāgata attained enlightenment, in the two-storied lecture hall at the Jetavana temple, the Buddha told the bodhisattva Mañjuśrī, 'Go to the Ordination Platform and sound the bell, calling gods, dragons, monks, great bodhisattvas, and others from the ten directions to gather together at the Jetavana.' When they gathered, the Buddha transformed the Jetavana into a Pure Land, and with the ray of light from between his eyebrows the Buddha illumined everywhere. The earth shook in six ways. Billions of Śākyamunis gathered and millions of the Buddhas of Superior Light also came to the Jetavana. The World Honoured One sat cross-legged and entered the Diamond Samādhi. The earth again shook. Coming out of the *samādhi,* in a loud voice the Buddha told the following to all sentient beings in the three thousand realms:

> After leaving the city [of my father's palace], I came to Bimbisāra's kingdom and went into the mountain to practise the way. Māra led me astray, but the mountain god took me to the place where I was to practise, and said to me, 'In the past when Kāśyapa Buddha was about to enter *nirvāṇa,* he entrusted an old clay bowl to me, telling me to guard it and wait until a Tathāgata was born. He ordered me to pass it on to the World Honoured One. Before the World Honoured One attains enlightenment,

you must first accept this bowl from me, (and then the bowl of the Four Heavenly Kings).' I told the mountain god, 'I will attain enlightenment in the way you have described.' Later, when I had finished bathing in the river and was about to receive the milk gruel from two women, the mountain deity brought the bowl to me. I then took it and filled it with the milk gruel. The earth shook in six ways. I kept this bowl for thirty-eight years and did not damage it in any way.

The account of the bowl, passed from one Buddha to another and presented shortly before Śākyamuni Buddha achieves enlightenment, ends here and a new theme is introduced into the sermon. The setting is still that of the Buddha preaching to the assembly at the Jetavana thirty-eight years after his enlightenment:

[This morning] I went to Rājagṛha in response to the king's request. Having finished eating, I ordered Rāhula to take my bowl and wash it at the dragon's pond. As he washed the bowl, it broke into five pieces. I then repaired it with lead and zinc. This was not Rāhula's fault, but was a sign predicting that in the future evil monks and nuns will destroy the vessel containing the dharma. Five hundred years [after I enter *nirvāṇa*] my *vinaya* collection will be divided into five parts, my sūtra collection into eighteen parts. By the time the True Teaching is to be completely destroyed, my *tripiṭaka* will have been divided further into five hundred parts. Those ignorant monks, having no compassion and not having made the vow to save sentient beings everywhere, will be preoccupied only with doctrinal debates. Driven by their arrogance they will hasten the destruction of the True Teaching, and by one thousand years [after *nirvāṇa*] the True Teaching will be completely lost. Evil nuns, who are like prostitutes, failing to practise the eight kinds of respectful conduct, will take my bowl to drinking establishments or to houses of prostitution, filling it with wine and meat. How painful! The dharma will have been completely destroyed!

Then monks [in the assembly] simultaneously said to the Buddha, 'This morning we went into the city and begged for food. Having returned to our residence, each of us washed his bowl. The bowls broke at the same time, each into five pieces. We wanted to ask the Buddha about this. Having heard the World Honoured One predict the destruction of the dharma, we are filled with fear.' Then the Buddha said to the monks, 'I will leave behind bodhisattva monks (*pusaseng*), altogether eight billion people, who will not enter *nirvāṇa*, but protect the holy teaching in the

> later evil age. Each of them will be equipped with supernatural powers and teach evil monks to pay respect to the Buddha's bowl.'

The passage that follows this lament is particularly elaborate and confusing. Daoxuan believed Jetavana to be the place where the first Ordination Platforms were established.[12] In AD 667, when Daoxuan is said to have been receiving the god's instruction, he was also engaged in establishing the first Ordination Platform in Northern China at his temple Jingyesi, on Mt Zhongnan outside of the capital city Chang'an.[13] The miraculous event that is said to have occurred at the Jetavana temple in the course of this sermon by the Buddha thirty-eight years after his enlightenment needs to be read against this background.

> Then the World Honoured One rose from his seat and went to the Ordination Platform. He climbed it from the northern side. Monks offered their bowls and the World Honoured One accepted them. Then, he said to Rāhula, 'Bring my broken bowl here.' The Buddha took the bowl and threw it into the sky, and it reached to the highest point. In the same way the same-named *munis* [separate bodies of Śākyamuni that had appeared at the Jetavana?] all threw [the monks' bowls?] one after another. Linked together like the jewels of a necklace, the line of bowls reached to the highest point in the Realm of Form (that is, through the six heavens), and then gradually came down, straight to the Ordination Platform. Ten billion Buddhas who had gathered all ordered their attendants to take the bowls and offer them to Śākyamuni Buddha, so that they would together protect and preserve them, and make monks and nuns in the coming evil age repent [their sins]. When the World Honoured One accepted these bowls, he again threw them up into the higher realms, and they came down one after another, returning again to the Ordination Platform. At that time the World Honoured One transformed the broken bowl into something shaped like the golden umbrella in heaven, which emitted light that illumined realms in the ten directions.

The last part of the story of the Buddha's sermon on his bowl is devoted to another set of elaborate stories about the *stūpas* in which the bowl, or the now greatly multiplied bowls, were to be kept and worshipped. The following exchanges that begin with the phrase 'while the Buddha was still in the world,' appear to have taken place some time after the original sermon.[14]

> While he was in this world, the Buddha told the god Indra, 'You donate to me pearls and heavenly artisans.' He told Māra, 'You donate to me seven jewels.' He told the Dragon King Sāgara, 'You donate to me *maṇi* jewels.' Indra, the Dragon King, and others presented the jewels and within twenty-one days gathered at the Ordination Platform and constructed jewel *stūpas*. They were decorated with seven jewels and had a *maṇi* jewel on top. Due to the supernatural powers of the gods altogether eight hundred billion *stūpas* of pearls and seven jewels were completed in twenty-one days. The Tathāgata's clay bowls were placed in them.

Another story about one large *stūpa* for the Buddha's bowl follows. The story at this point appears to oscillate between multiple bowls, identified with the original bowl of the Buddha through the Buddha's miraculous feat at the Ordination Platform and housed in the multiple *stūpas* gods created for them, and the original single bowl for which Māra king produced a large *stūpa*:

> Then, Māra king said to the Buddha, 'I [would like to] build a jewel *stūpa* on my own and place the World Honoured One's bowl in it. Although I am Māra, I honour the Buddha's words. Therefore, I will in the future not let evil people damage the holy teaching. I will teach evil monks and make them repent their sins.' The Buddha then gave permission. And the Māra king built a large *stūpa*, forty *yojana* in height, using only *maṇi* jewels, and placed the Buddha's bowl in it.

The next passage that follows begins with the phrase, 'the time the World Honoured One enters/entered *nirvāṇa*.'[15] On one hand, this phrase may be read as a part of the ongoing instruction that the Buddha gave 'while He was still in the world';[16] he would then be speaking in the future tense, 'When I enter *nirvāṇa* [in the future] I will entrust ...' The phrase, on the other hand, could mark the beginning of a separate instruction. In this reading, the entry of the Buddha's bowl would be a separate sermon given as a part of the Buddha's last instruction. The subject, however, appears to be the singular *stūpa* created by Māra.

> At the time the World Honoured One entered *nirvāṇa*, he entrusted the *stūpa* built by Māra king to Indra, the Four Heavenly Kings, and the great king Māra. He said, 'You guard this. After my *nirvāṇa*, at the time the True Teaching has disappeared, take my bowl *stūpa* and place it safely to the South of the Ordination Platform, and keep it there for twelve years.

> You, the Four Heavenly Kings and others, must constantly make offerings to it day and night and protect it from any damage. After twelve years have passed, entrust it to the dragon king Sāgara and place it in the scripture hall in his palace where the *vinaya* is kept. Also, order the dragon king to make sixteen *stūpas* to surround the bowl *stūpa*. Another twelve years later entrust it to Indra and the Four Heavenly Kings, who will take it to the top of Mt Sumeru and keep it on the southern side of the Golden Sand Pond in Nandana garden.' The Buddha told the king of *gandharvas* and the eight divisions of deities, 'For forty years you must make heavenly music as an offering to the jewel *stūpa*, so that the disciples who uphold the precepts in the evil world will guard the bowl in the same way they guard [their own] eyes.'

The subject of the last part of this entry on the Buddha's bowl is again the multiple *stūpas*.

> The Buddha told Indra and the Four Heavenly Kings, 'Go to the Diamond Cave in Mt Sumeru and take the yellow sand there and build stone bowls. Place them inside the newly built *stūpas*. The size and shape of these bowls should be identical to those of my broken bowl. Make them as bowls made of five fragments and place them safely inside the *stūpas*. You must protect them from any harm. One hundred years later when King Aśoka has finished building his *stūpas*, you must take my *stūpas* everywhere, to thousands of kingdoms and billions of households. In large expanses of field, ten thousand miles in each direction, place two bowl *stūpas*. In those kingdoms, look for famous mountains and sites where ancient sages lived and place bowl *stūpas* there.' The Buddha told the King of the Northern Heavenly Realm, 'Go to Mt Laṅka and collect the Ox-head sandal-wood incense. Three times each day go to the sites of the *stūpas* and burn the incense as an offering. Do this without interruption. I will make the deity Maheśvara position the bowl *stūpas*. I will also send the Four Heavenly Kings and the king of *gandharvas* to offer incense and perform music, constantly making offerings. You, gods and dragon deities, do not yet understand my intention. I am doing this so that in the future monks and nuns deviating from the teaching can be made to reform their evil ways and turn to the good. For this purpose I keep the bowl *stūpas* in safety.'

The complex section describing how the *stūpas* are built for the Buddha's begging bowl and their multiple copies that concludes this quotation from Daoxuan's *Zhuchi ganying ji* in fact consists of possibly three different accounts of the construction of the *stūpas*. Perhaps several parallel accounts of this episode had existed, and the account reproduced in the quotation in the *Fayuan zhulin* is a clumsy synthesis of these separate accounts.[17]

The Buddha's bowl is also a topic of exchange between Daoxuan and a god in another passage, also preserved in the *Fayuan zhulin*.[18] Here Daoxuan poses a question: Why was the bowl placed on Mt Gṛdhrakūṭa for fifteen years after the Tathāgata's *parinirvāṇa*? The god answers with a story:

> Before the *parinirvāṇa*, when the Buddha was staying at the temple on Mt Gṛdhrakūṭa, he emitted thousands of clearly separated rays of light from between his eyebrows. One of these rays of light was to be given to his disciples in the Age of the Destruction of the Teaching. If those who uphold the precepts, or even those who have violated them, or gods, dragons, and other supernatural beings entertain one moment of good thought, they receive the gift of this light. At the time he attained enlightenment, the Four Heavenly Kings offered the bowl to the World Honoured One. The bowl is to be used only by him; others cannot use it. After the Tathāgata's *parinirvāṇa* the bowl was placed in Mt Gṛdhrakūṭa for fifteen years. This bowl and the white light, which first appeared at the temple on this mountain, together bring benefits to sentient beings. During the Age of the Destruction of the Teaching, people ought to follow the Buddha's bowl, and in kingdoms in other places they should offer food to monks. If gods, dragons, and others follow this instruction by the Buddha, even if they do something not in accordance with the Teaching, they will not be punished.[19]

The Story of the Buddha's Bowl in the *Lianhuamian jing* (Lotus-face Scripture)

In the *Fayuan zhulin*, fascicle ninety eight, the long passage on the Buddha's bowl from Daoxuan's *Zhuchi ganyingji* is preceded by a quotation about the Buddha's bowl taken from the Lotus-face Scripture.[20] Important themes in the sermon miraculously revealed to Daoxuan, such as the preoccupation with entrusting the bowl to supernatural beings and the breaking up of the bowl as a sign of the destruction of dharma, appear in this scripture and form integral parts of the continuing account of the Buddha's last days in this world.

This scripture, in two fascicles, describes how the Buddha announced to sentient beings in different realms his intention to enter *nirvāṇa* in the near future; he predicted the destruction of his teaching after this event. The story is summarized here in three sections: the Buddha's initial announcement in Vaiśālī that he will enter *nirvāṇa* in three months; his second announcement, at the site of the *bodhi* tree in Magadha, that he will enter *nirvāṇa* in fifteen days; and the announcement that he will enter *nirvāṇa* in seven days, made when the Buddha was still in Magadha but about to commence his last journey to Kusinagara.[21]

Three Months before Nirvāṇa

The story of the Buddha's first announcement and his entrusting (*fuzhu*) of the dharma to different categories of beings opens with a discussion of the Buddha's living body and his relics. Buddha was staying in a large two-storied building at the bank of the Markaṭa hrada pond in Vaiśālī; he was to give up his life shortly.[22] The Buddha told Ānanda that he would go with him to the city of Pāvā to convert an elder there. The Buddha bathed in the Aciravatī River, told Ānanda that the Buddha would enter *nirvāṇa* in three months, and instructed Ānanda to observe carefully the thirty-two marks of the Buddha. Tathāgatas appear very infrequently, billions of times less frequently than *udumbara* flowers that are themselves known to appear very infrequently; it is thus very difficult to get to see the Tathāgata's body. This body would disappear in three months. An elaborate description of the Buddha's body is followed by a statement that because Ānanda had attended to the Tathāgata's living body, he had accumulated an incalculable and inconceivable amount of merit.[23]

The Buddha then asked Ānanda whether he wished to hear how to worship in the future, after the Tathāgata had entered *nirvāṇa,* and only 'the broken body relics' (*suishen sheli*) of the Tathāgata remain. When Ānanda answers affirmatively, the Buddha said,

> At the time the Tathāgata enters *nirvāṇa,* he goes into the Diamond Samādhi, and his 'flesh body' (*roushen*) crumbles and breaks up into pieces as small as mustard seeds. One part of these relics goes up to heaven. Heavenly king Śakra and other gods see the Buddha's relics and realize that the Buddha has entered *nirvāṇa,* and rain down heavenly flowers to honour the relics. As if they are seeing the Buddha's [living] body, they circumambulate the relics clockwise and worship, some gods planting

seeds for achieving the ultimate enlightenment (*anuttara samyak-sambodhi*), others for Śrāvaka-hood and still others for Pratyekabuddha-hood.

One part of the relics goes to the dragon's world. Dragon king Sāgara and innumerable dragons, seeing the relics, perform a massive ceremony. Holding Indra jewels, Mahendra jewels, fire jewels, clear water jewels, and innumerable jewels of similar kinds, they circumambulate the broken relics clockwise and worship. At this time, dragons make vows, some to seek the ultimate enlightenment, some Śrāvaka-hood, Bodhisattva-hood, and some Pratyekabuddha-hood.

One part of the relics goes to the world of Yakṣas. King Vaiśravaṇa and other innumerable *yakṣa* generals, seeing the relics of the broken body, offer a variety of flowers, incense, lamps, and music to them; holding their palms together and circumambulating them clockwise, they worship the relics. Some make the vow to seek the ultimate enlightenment, some Śrāvaka-hood, and some Pratyekabuddha-hood.

The other parts of the relics remain in the Jambudvīpa. In the future a king called Aśoka will appear and bring all of Jambudvīpa under his rule. In order to honour these relics this king will build eighty-four thousand *stūpas*. Sixty-thousand other kings in the Jambudvīpa also will make offerings to the broken body relics. Presenting flower garlands, incense, lamps and music, they worship them by circumambulating clockwise, some planting the seed for ultimate enlightenment, others for Śrāvaka-hood, and still others for Pratyekabuddha-hood. Some immediately renounce the householder's life. Believing in the Buddha's teaching, they shave their head and beard, put on the dharma robe, cultivate the path diligently and all enter *nirvāṇa*.[24]

The Buddha is then said to have entertained the following thought: 'In order to ensure that the Buddha dharma, which I obtained after my efforts over the three *asaṇkhyeyas* of *kalpas*, continues to exist in the world for a long time, I should go to the places where gods, *asuras*, dragons, *garuḍas*, *mahoragas* (snakes) live and entrust the Buddha dharma to them.'[25] The idea appears to be that these beings, in their separate realms outside of Jambudvīpa, will be able to preserve the dharma when it is attacked and destroyed in the human world.

The Tathāgata disappeared from the Jambudvīpa and came to the Trāyastriṃśa heaven. Heavenly King Śakra saw the Buddha, prepared a high seat, and welcomed him, saying 'The World Honoured One, please accept this seat.' When the World Honoured One took the seat, Heavenly

King Śakra, along with numerous attendants, touched the Buddha's feet with their heads and sat on one side. The Buddha told Śakra and his followers, 'I will enter *nirvāṇa* shortly. I entrust this Buddha dharma to you. You must guard it.' When the Buddha said these words three times, Śakra shed tears, saying, 'Why must the Buddha enter *nirvāṇa* so soon? Why should the Tathāgata enter *nirvāṇa* so soon? The Dharma Eye of the World will disappear forever from here. The role that the Buddha assigned to me was to protect, to pay respect, and to make offerings. When the Tathāgata came from Tuṣita heaven into his mother's womb, with the gods of Trayastriṃśa heaven I guarded him. When he was born, with other gods I guarded him. When the Tathāgata sat under the *bodhi* tree and defeated Māra's huge army of eighty million *koṭi* and attained the ultimate enlightenment, I was on guard with other gods. When the Buddha turned the wheel of dharma at the Deer Park, in three stages and twelve steps, I protected him with other gods. [And yet,] now I am powerless to keep the Tathāgata from entering *nirvāṇa*. I am powerless to protect him.'[26]

The Buddha delivered various sermons, comforting and instructing gods in Śakra's heaven.

After he had told them to guard the Buddha dharma, the Buddha disappeared from heaven and came to the dragon king Sāgara's palace. The Buddha again instructed the dragon king that he was to enter *nirvāṇa* and that they should guard the Buddha dharma. In this way the Buddha appeared then in dragon king Takṣaka's palace, the black dragon's palace, yakṣa's world, and having entrusted the Buddha dharma to the Four Heavenly Kings, the Buddha finally returned to the Jambudvīpa. The Buddha entertained the following thought: 'All that I am to do has now been done. I have now subdued many evil sentient beings. I can enter the calm and quiet *nirvāṇa*.'[27]

The Buddha then told Ānanda that he was to enter *nirvāṇa* shortly. As if he had heard the news for the first time, Ānanda, behaving just like the god Śakra, the dragon king Sāgara, *yakṣa* generals and the Four Heavenly Kings, exclaimed in distress,

Why does the World Honoured One enter *nirvāṇa* so quickly? When the Eye of the World (the Buddha) has disappeared, for whom shall I hold the bowl, hold the fan and stand nearby? I will not hear the dharma, which is like the sweet drink of immortality (*amṛta*). Who will preach this dharma for me? Behind whom shall I now walk? I will no longer be able to see

> the face, superior and perfect like the sun and the moon. Venerable Śāriputra and other people of wisdom have already entered *nirvāṇa*. If the Buddha enters *nirvāṇa* now, the world will be in darkness, having lost the eye of wisdom. Mt Sumeru of wisdom is about to collapse and the Buddha tree is about to fall. The bridge of dharma is about to be cut off, and the boat of dharma is about to sink. The torch of dharma is about to disappear, and the sun and the moon of the True Dharma are about to fall on the ground. The gate of salvation is about to be closed. The gates leading to the inferior realms of rebirth are opened. The dharma gathered over the three *asaṅkhyeyas of kalpas* [by the Buddha] is about to disappear.[28]

The Buddha told Ānanda not to be distressed, explaining that life in the world is impermanent, and that the eternal dharma that cannot be destroyed does not exist. Having entrusted the dharma to him, the Buddha remained silent.

Seeing that Ānanda was deeply distressed, and thinking that he would now remove this distress, the Buddha asked Ānanda whether he wished to see events that would occur in the future. When Ānanda requested him to speak, the Buddha gave him the following prediction:

> In the future many monks, violating precepts, and yet wearing the *kāṣāya* robe, will wander around in cities and villages. These people are neither monks nor laymen. They will keep women, who will give birth to male and female children. There will also be monks who live in prostitutes' houses, monks who have sexual relations with nuns, monks who accumulate gold and silver, monks who engage in worldly employment to secure their livelihood, monks who serve as messengers to secure their livelihood, monks who specialize in medicine to secure their livelihood, monks who play dice games to secure their livelihood, monks who perform divination for others to secure their livelihood, monks who cast spells to make corpses revive and kill in revenge to secure their livelihood.[29]

The long list of evil activities continues. The Buddha concluded by stating that when they die these monks will go to hell. He compared them to the dead lion – wherever they die, other sentient beings will not dare to eat their flesh; only the worms born from the lion's body will eat the lion's flesh. The Buddha told Ānanda that his Buddha dharma will not be destroyed by others but by the evil monks who are inside his own dharma like poison in a wound. They will destroy the Buddha dharma he had accumulated over the three *asaṅkhyeyas* of *kalpas*.[30] The Buddha's

True Teaching is like a treasure boat, which has gathered many treasures from the treasure islands only to sink in the middle of the great ocean on its return journey.

After further exchanges on the evil monks who will appear in the future, Ānanda told the Buddha that the Buddha should quickly enter *nirvāṇa* so that he would not see these evil events. In the course of the exchanges that followed, the Buddha told Ānanda that in the future lay followers would be reborn in heaven while many of the monks would go to hell.

Following these exchanges between the Buddha and Ānanda, heavenly kings from many heavens appeared in front of the Buddha and greeted him. Kings of *asuras* and dragons followed the gods. Gods, *asuras*, dragons, *garuḍas, gandharvas, kiṃnaras,* and *mahoragas* filled the sky. They were there to see the Buddha for the last time. Then the Buddha told Ānanda the following:

> The site of enlightenment under the *bodhi* tree is most excellent and beautiful; the past Buddhas all achieved ultimate enlightenment (*anuttara samyak-saṃbodhi*) at this site. The future Buddhas will also achieve ultimate enlightenment at this site. In the present I too defeated Māra's army of eighteen *koṭi* at this site and achieved ultimate enlightenment. Thus, Ānanda, I am to enter *nirvāṇa* shortly. Furthermore, the Lumbinī garden is most excellent and beautiful. This is the place where the Buddha has had his last birth. Furthermore, Ānanda, Queen Māyā was endowed with a great deal of virtues and consequently gave birth to the jewel among men. Furthermore, Ānanda, King Śuddhodana was endowed with a great deal of virtues and became the most excellent 'jewel father' among all sentient beings. Vaiśālī is the most excellent city in its kingdom. Rājagṛha is the most excellent and beautiful city in the kingdom of Magadha.[31]

After remarking on a few other sites, the Buddha said that Jambudvīpa is a most excellent place; but sentient beings there indulge in lives of greed. Therefore, shortly after the Buddha enters *nirvāṇa* his teaching will be destroyed. In this way, the Buddha consoled Ānanda, bringing joy to his heart and removing the pains of his distress.

Fifteen Days before Nirvāṇa

Having entrusted the dharma to him, the Buddha told Ānanda that he will travel with him to different kingdoms.[32] The Buddha then went to the city of Pāvā, converting all those who requested to be conversion. They then visited many other places, converted numerous people, and finally came to the site of the *bodhi* tree in the kingdom of Magadha. The Buddha circled the tree six times and then sat under it. The Buddha said to Ānanda, 'The Tathāgata will enter *nirvāṇa* in fifteen days.' The gods and other supernatural beings thought that since the Tathāgata was going to enter *nirvāṇa*, they would come and worship him for the last time.

The second fascicle of the Lotus-face Scripture begins with the verses that gods and other supernatural beings, distressed by the news that the Buddha would enter *nirvāṇa* shortly, offered to the Buddha as the Buddha left the site of the *bodhi* tree. It is at this point that the Buddha tells the long story of the bowl in Gandhāra (Jibin). While he was at the palace of the dragon king Apāla, the Buddha predicted that after he has entered *nirvāṇa*, the kingdom of Gandhāra will prosper like the Northern Continent of Uttarakuru. The Buddha's teaching will prosper there; many *arhats* and disciples of the Tathāgata will go there. The place will be like Tuṣita heaven. The words of the Buddha will be collected into a variety of scriptures and treatises will be compiled. Five deities, including one called Kumbhīra, will be born in Gandhāra and hold a massive ceremony, of a scale unheard of in Jambudvīpa, for the followers of the Buddha's teaching. A remarkable story of the destruction of the Buddha's dharma and of his begging bowl follows:

> After the five deities die, a disciple of the non-Buddhist teacher Purāṇa [-Kāśyapa], called Lotus-face, will appear. An intelligent man learned in astronomy, Lotus-face will have a gold-coloured body. This great fool once made an offering to four *arhats*; on that occasion he also made a vow that in the future he would destroy the Buddha's dharma. Because of the merits acquired by making an offering to these *arhats* from one birth to another he obtained handsome bodies (in succeeding births), and in his last birth he will be born in a king's family. As king Mihiragula, he will destroy my dharma. This great fool will break my begging bowl. Having broken my bowl, he will be born in the *avīci* hell. After this great fool has died, seven deities will be reborn in the kingdom of Gandhāra one after another, and offer massive ceremonies for the Tathāgata's True Teaching. But, Ānanda, due to the breaking of the bowl, my disciples will gradually defile the pure precepts. At the time the bowl is first broken, though monks defile the pure precepts, their wisdom will still be like that of the king of oxen (the Buddha) and they can defeat the followers of non-Buddhist teachings. After a while, however, the monks in the Jambudvīpa,

having destroyed the pure precepts, will delight in committing immoral acts, stealing, ploughing fields and planting, accumulating beautiful robes and bowls, and not finding pleasure in reading the *sūtras*, *vinayas*, and *abhidharmas*. In this way people who find pleasure in reading and reciting the scriptures will disappear. Monks, insincere and jealous, will engage in evil deeds, and consequently rulers of many kingdoms will fail to follow the king's dharma. Because of this people in their kingdoms will commit the ten categories of evil deeds.[33]

The broken bowl of the Buddha then goes to the northern region, where seeing the bowl, sentient beings carry out a great ceremony, honouring the bowl with many kinds of flowers, incense, lamps, flower garlands, and music. Some will give rise to the thought of seeking ultimate enlightenment, some to the thought of seeking Śrāvaka-hood, and some to the thought of seeking Pratyekabuddha-hood. The bowl is then said to reach the kingdom of Parvata.[34] The people there honour it in the now familiar way, responding to the occasion by giving rise to the thought of seeking ultimate enlightenment, and so on. The bowl is then restored to its original [unbroken] state due to the power of the Buddha and in response to the good seeds planted by sentient beings.

Soon afterward, the bowl disappears from Jambudvīpa and appears in the palace of the dragon king Sāgara. When the bowl disappears from Jambudvīpa, darkness covers it for seven days and seven nights, the ground shakes, lightning fills the sky with frightful sounds of thunder. Terrifying winds arise. The Buddha tells Ānanda that when the bowl disappears, the Tathāgata's teaching also disappears. King Māra is delighted, and declares from the sky that Gautama's dharma is now destroyed and that he will now teach in his place. As a consequence of such misdeeds, Māra is eventually sent to the *avīci* hell.

The bowl is worshiped in the dragon's palace, with offerings of many jewels. Some dragons will give rise to the thought of seeking ultimate enlightenment, some to the thought of seeking Srāvaka-hood, and some to the thought of seeking Pratyekabuddha-hood. The dragon king Sāgara, while holding the bowl in his hand utters a verse: 'The bowl decorated with many remarkable characteristics, receives different kinds of food; filling the bowl with this food, I hold it [for the Buddha's] consumption.'[35]

The bowl disappears from the palace of the dragon king and appears in the palace of the Four Heavenly Kings. The Four Heavenly Kings carry out a massive ceremony that lasts for seven days and seven nights, offering many different kinds of flowers, flower garlands, perfumes and incense, lamps, and music. Some gods make the vow to seek ultimate enlightenment, some Śrāvaka-hood, and some Pratyekabuddha-hood. Then Virūḍhaka, the king of the Southern Heaven and the leader of *kumbhāṇḍa* ghosts, holds the bowl in his hand, and utters the verse: 'The Tathāgata took his last meal at the house of the blacksmith; in order to convert sentient beings, the bowl came to this place.'[36]

The Buddha tells Ānanda that after seven days the bowl will disappear from the palace of the Four Heavenly Kings and appear at the Trāyastriṃśa heaven. Seeing the bowl, the Buddha's mother Māyā is greatly distressed. In a manner that reminds one of the earlier formulaic accounts of the responses of different beings to the news of the Buddha's imminent entry into *nirvāṇa*, the mother says,

> 'Why is the Tathāgata's *nirvāṇa* occurring so soon? Why is *sugata* (the Buddha) disappearing so soon? The Eye of the World (the Buddha) disappears. The tree of the Buddha is falling. Mt Sumeru, the Buddha, is about to collapse. The torch of the Buddha is about to disappear. The Spring of dharma is about to dry out. The sun, the Māra of impermanence, is about to dry out the lotus flower, the Buddha.'
>
> Then Queen Māyā holds the bowl in her hands and speaks to gods, *asuras, gandharvas, kiṃnaras*, and *mahoragas*, 'Listen carefully, gods, this is the bowl that Śākyamuni, the Tathāgata used all the time. The shadow of the most brave one, whose face is even more perfect than the sun and the moon, appears on the bowl. Furthermore, gods, this is the bowl which in Rājagṛha received Śrīgupta's poisonous food.[37] Listen carefully, gods, with this bowl Śākyamuni, the ferocious hero, received the food in the house of Sumāgadhā (?). Listen carefully, gods, when the Tathāgata converted Uruvela-kāṣyapa and the dragons, he placed the dragons in this bowl ...[38] Listen carefully, gods, bcause of his great compassion Śākyamuni, the Tathāgata, received in this bowl the poorest people's food. Listen carefully, gods, Śākyamuni, the Tathāgata, also received a variety of food in dragon king Sāgara's palace. Listen carefully, gods, in the fourth month in the summer Śākyamuni, the Tathāgata, received our food again with this bowl. Listen carefully, gods, with this bowl Śākyamuni, the Tathāgata, covered the smallest child of Hāritī...'[39] Then Queen Māyā held the bowl in her hand and uttered a verse ...
>
> For seven days and seven nights heavenly king Śakra offered heavenly flowers, heavenly perfume, and incense of heavenly sandal wood, worshiping and circumambulating the bowl. When this offering was completed, some gods made the vow to seek ultimate enlightenment,

some Śrāvaka-hood, and some Pratyekabuddha-hood. Then the heavenly king held the bowl and uttered a verse ... [40]

The bowl then went to Yama heaven, to Tuṣita heaven, to Nirmāṇarataya heaven, receiving offerings for seven days. In each heaven, gods made the vows to seek ultimate enlightenment, Śrāvaka-hood, and Pratyekabuddha-hood.

The Buddha told Ānanda that after gods and other kinds of supernatural beings have made offerings to the bowl, they will send the bowl back to the palace of the dragon king Sāgara. The Buddha's bowls and relics from everywhere are gathered at the dragon king's palace. Some time in the future the Buddha's bowl and relics will be taken to Vajrakoṭi (*jingangji*, 'Diamond Limit'), eight hundred million *yojana* away. In the future, when the human life span is eighty-four thousand years, the Tathāgata Maitreya will appear.

'At that time my bowl and relics will leave Vajrakoṭi and come to Maitreya's place in Jambudvīpa. The bowl and relics will emit a five-coloured light of blue, yellow, red, white, and the various colours of crystal. The five-coloured light will reach all the heavens. When the light reaches a heaven, a voice uttering a verse will be heard in the light: "All phenomena are transient; all dharmas are selfless; and the quiet condition is *nirvāṇa;* these three are the marks of the dharma." The light then reaches all the hells, uttering the [same] verse ...' The Buddha told Ānanda, 'The light emitted by the Buddha's bowl and relics then reaches the worlds in the ten directions. In the light the [same] verse is uttered ...' The Buddha told Ānanda, 'Thus the light emitted by my bowl and relics, having finished the Buddha's work in the worlds in the ten directions, then returns to the place of the bowl and relics; a bright light illumines the clouds. At the sight of this great miracle eight thousand *koṭi* of sentient beings will obtain the fruit of arhat-hood, one thousand *koṭi* of sentient beings will shave their heads and renounce the householder's life, and ten thousand *koṭi* will conceive the thought of seeking ultimate enlightenment. All will attain the stage of non-retrogression.'

'Ānanda, after the bowl and the relics have widely instructed sentient beings, they will stand in mid-air in front of the Buddha Maitreya. Maitreya, holding the bowl and relics with his hand, will say to gods, *asuras, garuḍas, gandharvas, kiṃnaras,* and *mahoragas,* "You should know that this bowl and relics have been perfumed by Śākyamuni, the heroic and great being. Śākyamuni made one hundred *nayutas* of billions of sentient beings dwell in *nirvāṇa*. Because *udumbara* flowers have already appeared many billions of times,[41] the bowl and relics have come here [to be prepared for the appearance of another Tathāgata]." Then Maitreya builds a *stūpa* of four jewels and places the bowl and relics in it. Maitreya Buddha, gods, *asuras*, and other kinds of supernatural beings make offerings and worship the *stūpa* of bowl and relics.'

Seven Days before Nirvāṇa

The Buddha then tells Ānanda that he is to enter *nirvāṇa* in seven days.[42] The Buddha and Ānanda travelled through many cities, bringing salvation to numerous sentient beings. The *sūtra* concludes with an account of the Buddha's last days, mentioning the last meal at the house of Cunda-Karmāraputra, and describing how the Buddha taught his last disciple Subhadra while reclining between śāla trees outside of Kusinagara.

In this scripture, the emphasis shifts from the distress expressed by sentient beings at the news about the Buddha's imminent entry into *nirvāṇa* to the prediction of the disappearance of the Buddha's dharma, and finally to the restoration of the broken bowl, which is taken to the realms of different beings to be worshiped and then returns to Jambudvīpa at the time the future Buddha Maitreya appears. The bowl is the symbol of the Buddha's dharma, and its destruction and restoration stand for the destruction and restoration of the Buddha's dharma at the appearance of Maitreya.

In placing the quotation on the future destruction of the bowl in Gandhāra from this scripture immediately before the fragment from the record of the Buddha's sermon revealed to Daoxuan, the *Fayuan zhulin* indicates that the idea that the Buddha's begging bowl will break as a sign of the future destruction of his dharma, that appears in the sermon revealed to Daoxuan, is related to the story of the future destruction of the bowl in Gandhāra, predicted in the Lotus-face Scripture.[43] The setting of the Lotus-face Scripture, in which the Buddha, anticipating the future destruction of his dharma, entrusts the bowl to gods, dragons, and other beings, makes the story of the construction of the bowl *stūpas* in the sermon revealed to Daoxuan more intelligible; here again the god Śakra, the dragon king Sāgara, and Māra figure prominently. At one point in the Lotus-face Scripture, the Buddha speaks of the site of the *bodhi* tree as the place where all past and future Buddhas achieve ultimate enlightenment;[44] it is near this site[45] that deities pay their last respects to him, and the Buddha tells them the story of the broken bowl. The story culminates with the prediction that when the future Buddha Maitreya appears, the bowl, along with the relics, will appear in front of Maitreya, and that Maitreya will build a jewelled *stūpa*.[46] Though the idea that the same bowl will be used by succeeding Buddhas has not appeared here, the identification of the enlightenment of succeeding Buddhas is clearly made and Śākyamuni's bowl is passed on to Maitreya. Here, as in the sermon revealed to Daoxuan, the dharma entrusted to a variety of beings is preserved in *stūpas* as relics.

The Story of the Bowl Presented by the Four Heavenly Kings

Kuwayama Shōshin collected several passages in which the story of the begging bowl presented to the Buddha by the Four Heavenly Kings appears. Different versions of the story are found in the *Mahīśāsaka Vinaya*, the *Taizi ruiying benqijing*, the *Puyao jing*, and the *Fobenxing ji jing*.[47] Xuanzang's summary resembles the *Fobenxing ji jing* version.[48] In these versions the Buddha is said to have received food from two merchants shortly after enlightenment. When they offered the food, the Buddha is said to have thought that all ancient Buddhas received the gift of food in a bowl. Upon realizing this, the Four Heavenly Kings quickly produced four bowls and presented them to the Buddha, which the Buddha miraculously turned into one bowl.[49] The setting suggests that this story took place around the tree of enlightenment in the kingdom of Magadha.

According to the *Fufazang yinyuan zhuan*, or 'Circumstances of the Transmission of the Dharma'[50] and the biography of Aśvaghoṣa translated by Kumārajīva, the Buddha's bowl was taken by a foreign ruler (Yuezhi or Xiao Yuezhi) to some part of northwest India.[51] The record of Faxian's travels in the beginning of the fifth century locates the bowl in Puruṣapura and describes its appearance in some detail; the king of Yuezhi attempted to remove it from the city but failed.[52]

In Sri Lanka, Faxian heard an Indian monk recite an elaborate and remarkable story about the bowl from a scripture:[53] The Buddha's bowl was first in Vaiśālī, but it is now in Gandhāra. After a few hundred years (the exact number was given in the recitation) it will move to the kingdom of Yuezhi to the West, and after another few hundred years it will go to Khotan. Having stayed there for a hundred years the bowl will go to Kucha. After another few hundred years it will go to Sri Lanka. After still another few hundred years it will come to China. After yet another few hundred years it will return to Central India. Then it will go up to the Tuṣita heaven. Bodhisattva Maitreya will see it and say, 'Śākyamuni's bowl has arrived.' He will make offerings of heavenly flowers and fragrances for seven days. After seven days the bowl will return to Jambudvīpa, and the dragon king will take it to the dragon palace. When Maitreya is about to achieve enlightenment, the bowl will break up into four pieces and return to its place of origin on Mt Vinataka.[54]

When Maitreya is enlightened, the Four Heavenly Kings think that the (new) Buddha must follow the way of earlier Buddhas (and receive food in a bowl). The one thousand Buddhas of the Age of the Wise all use the same bowl. When the bowl disappears, the Buddha's dharma also disappears. After the Buddha's dharma disappears, the human lifespan becomes shorter and shorter to the point of being only five years. By this time rice and ghee[55] will have disappeared. People will have become wicked; turning grass and tree branches into swords and sticks, they will harm each other. Those who are lucky among them will flee into the mountains, and return only after the evil people have killed each other. They will then say to each other, 'In the past, the human lifespan was much longer. Only because of extreme evil deeds we have committed, our lifespan has become as short as five years. We will now together give rise to compassion and cultivate truthfulness.' As each of them cultivates truthfulness, their human lifespan will become longer, to the point of being eighty thousand years.

When Maitreya appears and turns the first wheel of dharma, he will first bring salvation to the followers of the dharma left by Śākyamuni Buddha, both those who have renounced the householder's life and those who have only accepted the Three Refuges, the five precepts, and the eight precepts of lay followers and honoured the Three Treasures. Then he will bring salvation to those whose conditions are ripe. On the occasion he heard this recited, Faxian wished to copy it, but the monk said he did not have a written copy of the scripture and that he recited it from memory.[56]

In this scripture as summarized by Faxian, the bowl that the Four Heavenly Kings offered to Śākyamuni is said to have been the same bowl used by all the one thousand Buddhas of the Age of the Wise, as in the sermon revealed to Daoxuan. The disappearance of the bowl marks the disappearance of the dharma. Though the disappearance of the dharma is described here rather differently, with reference to the changing human lifespan, the disappearance of the dharma (the Age of the Destruction of Dharma in other accounts) is again followed by the appearance of Maitreya. Faxians passage begins with an account of the places to which the bowl will be taken, but Kuwayama points out that references to Khotan, Kucha, and China in the scripture are rather unnatural and suggests that the account was reshaped by a later editor.[57] As Kuwayama has shown quite persuasively, and as will become clear below, the references to the movement of the bowl reveal an important fact about the nature of this cult of the bowl. Presumably the bowl was first moved from its original site near the site of the Buddha's enlightenment, in Magadha eventually to Gandhāra in northwest India, before being taken to other more remote sites.

The Bowl in Gandhāra

The physical object known as the Buddha's begging bowl actually existed at one time in Gandhāra. As Kuwayama discusses in detail, Chinese sources indicate that Zhimeng saw this bowl, with the four borders clearly marked, not much later than AD 404.[58] Tan Wujie (Dharmodgata?) saw it not much later than AD 420.[59] It must have been before AD 439 that Huilan saw it. Towards the end of the fourth century or early in the fifth century, Daopu had seen the Buddha's bowl.[60] The record of Faxian's travels in the beginning of the fifth century reports that the bowl existed in Puruṣapura.[61] The bowl is said to have had four borders, evidence of the fact that it was made from the four bowls presented by the Four Heavenly Kings. The attempt to move this bowl by a conquering Yuezhi ruler failed.

Tracing the earliest report on the bowl in Gandhāra to Fotudeng (AD 232–348), who had visited Gandhāra before AD 310 when he arrived in Luoyang, Kuwayama further speculates that the object known as the Buddha's begging bowl must have existed in Gandhāra by AD 310. Several reliefs from Gandhāra illustrate how this bowl was presented. The account in Zhimeng's biography suggests that worshippers often lifted the bowl, and the bowl changed its weight depending on the depth of the worshippers' faith.[62] By the time Xuanzang reached Puruṣapura in Gandhāra the bowl had been moved elsewhere ('to Persia'), and he only saw the jewelled base on which the bowl had formerly been placed.[63] As the Hephthalite Huns retreated from Gandhāra in the middle of the sixth century, Gandhāran society was thrown into confusion and Buddhism declined.[64] The story of the destruction of the Buddha's bowl may have developed against this background.

New Strategies for Constructing Buddhist Sacred Places

Kuwayama explains the significance of the cult of the Buddha's bowl in Gandhāra with a theory about constructing new Buddhist sites. The Buddhist sites in Gandhāra, where Buddhist images and *stūpas* were produced in great numbers in the second half of the first century, were constructed differently from those in the region around the Ganges River, the setting of Śākyamuni's life in the sixth to fifth century BC.[65] Whereas Buddhist sites in the Ganges region were constructed straightforwardly as places where familiar events in the life of the Śākyamuni Buddha took place, Buddhist sites in Gandhāra centred around more indirect relationships to the life of the historical Śākyamuni. Rather than making the transparently false claim that events in the life of historical Śākyamuni occurred in Gandhāra, Gandhāran Buddhists 'demonstrated the legitimacy of their own version of Buddhism' by creating sacred sites associated with Buddha's previous lives, relics, and other cultic objects such as the Buddha's begging bowl.[66]

Since the locations of the sites where familiar events in Śākyamuni's life are said to have occurred were widely known, new stories about his life had to be invented before new sites outside the circle of these familiar locations could be claimed as the places where other significant events occurred. Objects associated with his life could have been moved, or said to have been moved, and turned into focal points of Buddhist sacred places. New Buddhist sacred sites could also be constructed by claiming them as the places where widely known events in Śākyamuni's former lives took place. New sites could also develop based on stories about past Buddhas. In this way, references to the life of the Buddha carried spatial implications; some types of references were closely tied to specific locations, while others allowed greater flexibility. As Buddhism spread outside the boundaries of areas where Śākyamuni was originally believed to have lived, new Buddhist sacred sites were constructed, many of which still used references to the life of the Buddha but used them by means of different strategies. Numerous Buddhist sites in the Gandhāran region relied on these new strategies.

This analysis may be illustrated by reviewing Xuanzang's account of Buddhist sacred sites in the area around Gandhāra.[67] By the time Xuanzang travelled in this area in the seventh century, Gandhāra had declined as a Buddhist centre.[68] Nonetheless he mentions a number of sites that can be explained by Kuwayam's theory. The sites may be regrouped into three types.

(I) CONVERTED LOCAL DEITIES. Typically, Śākyamuni is said to have come to this area using supernatural powers. Thus, in Nagarahāra, Xuanzang mentions the place where the Buddha landed as he flew from central India using supernatural power. The Buddha also used supernatural power to arrive at the cave of the dragon Gopāla, where he left his famous shadow. In Gandhāra, a site is mentioned where Śākyamuni is said to have converted Hāritī.[69] In the story describing how Śākyamuni converted the dragon Apalāla in Uḍḍiyāna, it is again indicated that Śākyamuni arrived there miraculously, and the footprint Śākyamuni left on a rock near the spring is explicitly said to have been made after he converted the dragon.

(II) MOVABLE OBJECTS (RELICS AND OBJECTS) USED BY THE BUDDHA. There was a location in Nagarahāra where the Buddha's tooth was worshipped, and in nearby Hiḍḍa a building housed the Buddha's cranium, skull, and eyeball, as well as his *saṃgāti* robe and staff. In Gandhāra, Xuanzang saw the foundation of the building where the Buddha's begging bowl used to be kept. In Uḍḍiyāna was the *stūpa* where Uttarasena, the king of Uḍḍiyāna, is said to have placed the relics he received at the time the Buddha entered *parinirvāṇa*. The name of this king does not appear in standard accounts of the distribution of relics; this story was fabricated later on to bring this area into closer contact with the life of the Buddha.[70]

(III) PREVIOUS BUDDHAS AND PREVIOUS LIVES OF THE BUDDHA. In Nagarahāra, two sites refer to events that occurred as Śākyamuni encountered Dīpaṃkara Buddha in a previous life. In Gandhāra, two sites were associated with previous Buddhas, and four sites were based on stories of the Buddha's previous lives. In Uḍḍiyāna, Xuanzang mentions eight locations clearly associated with Śākyamuni's previous life. In Takṣaśilā, two sites are identified through references to the Buddha's previous lives. Two related sites refer to the past Buddha Kāśyapa and the future Buddha Maitreya respectively.

It was as a part of this general development, and perhaps as one of the more successful examples, that a certain physical object came to be identified as the Buddha's begging bowl. Stories about it were invented and inserted into the circle of familiar stories about the life of the Buddha. Since such a story would imply that the bowl, originally presented to the Buddha near the tree of enlightenment in Magadha, was moved at some point to Gandhāra, other stories about further movements of the bowl could easily be developed. Possibly in some connection with the decline of Gandhāra as a major Buddhist centre, stories may have developed about the relationship between the decline of the Buddha's teaching and the destruction of the bowl, like those we see in the scripture summarized by Faxian and the Lotus-face Scripture. The remarkable story told in the scripture revealed to Daoxuan in China drew many of its central ideas from this tradition.

Kuwayama argues that cults of physical objects used by the historical Buddha did not exist in central India or the area where Buddhism originated, but appeared in border regions.[71] The elaborate details in Daoxuan's stories about the Buddha's bowl and other cultic objects closely affiliated with the life of the Buddha suggest that as Buddhism moved further away from its homeland, through the border regions to China, these objects, imagined in increasingly fantastic terms, became the focal point around which the Buddhist teaching was situated in a larger Buddhist universe. The sacred places are increasingly detached from specific locations in India or elsewhere on earth and imagined as spaces in the Buddhist universe – Mt Sumeru, dragon king's palace, various heavenly realms, or even the Jetavana in its elaborate visionary existence. The chronological framework also expands, with explicit references to the past and future Buddhas, while the prediction about the future age of the Decline of the Buddha's Teaching is highlighted.

Cosmic Histories of Sacred Places in China Revealed to Daoxuan

We have reviewed above, following Kuwayama's analysis, how the cult of the Buddha's begging bowl appeared in Gandhāra and how stories about this bowl, possibly in connection with the decline of Gandhāra as a Buddhist centre, may have become combined with the story of the future decline of the Buddha's teaching. The theatre of the movement of the bowl expanded its horizon as the stories evolved. By the time the story of the bowl is told in the Buddha's sermon revealed to Daoxuan in China, the bowl is detached from Gandhāra, brought back to Jetavana, imagined by Daoxuan as the site of the original Ordination Platform and a central location in the Buddhist universe. This last stage of the evolution was also mediated by the logic of

Daoxuan's revelation. Daoxuan, or the author of the records attributed to him, transcended the geographical and historical distance between India of the Buddha's time and China in his time with the help of the story of a special revelation he received from gods. Records of the Buddha's teaching, presumably more extensive and reliable than the earthly scriptures, existed in heaven; the excerpts from the Buddha's sermon as well as the summary account of the Jetavana he left as the Jetavana Diagram Scripture[72] were taken from those heavenly records. Through the records preserved in heaven, Daoxuan, in China, was brought into direct contact with the Buddha's preaching and the original Jetavana, in the India of the Buddha's time.[73] Daoxuan's temple, where he established an Ordination Platform around the same time he received the revelation, became a site comparable to this cosmic Jetavana. Other locations in China could also acquire similar cosmic dimensions.

King Aśoka's *stūpas* are mentioned towards the end of the Buddha's sermons on the bowl and the robe, as revealed to Daoxuan. The *stūpas* containing the Buddha's bowl or those containing his robe were to be built everywhere; the sermon on the bowl specifically mentions famous mountains and places where ancient sages lived.[74] These comments suggest that Daoxuan related these cults of the Buddha's bowl and robe not only to abstract realms in Buddhist cosmology but also to more tangible sacred places similar to those where Aśoka *stūpas* and images were said to have been found in China. In fact, according to another version of the instruction Daoxuan is said to have received from the gods, an important part of this instruction centred around specific sacred places in China. These are Buddhist sites where miraculous events are said to have taken place in more recent times under Chinese dynasties. In response to Daoxuan's questions the deity presented cosmic histories of these sites, describing events that occurred in earlier stages in the evolution of the Buddhist teaching. A section of the *Daoxuan lüshi gantong lu*[75] is devoted to these cosmic stories, many of which supplement well-known Chinese Buddhist miracle stories. Through this rhetorical strategy, more familiar Buddhist sacred places in China were brought within Daoxuan's newly acquired cosmic vision.[76]

The 'Record of Daoxuan's Miraculous Communication,'[77] also known as the 'Record of Miraculous Communication on Monastic Rules,'[78] reproduces the content of the instruction in two parts: Daoxuan's questioning of the deity about 'matters that have to do with the Buddha,' and the discussion of monastic rules.[79] The first part consists of exchanges about a number of sites in China where ancient images and *stūpas* are kept. In these exchanges, gods instruct Daoxuan on the cosmic histories of these sites, images, and *stūpas* in China. Some of these histories concern sites about which famous miracle stories had been told and collected in Daoxuan's miracle story collection. Other exchanges tell both the stories of miracles that occurred under certain Chinese dynasties and the cosmic origins of the sites.

The first part begins with Daoxuan's question: When did the stone image of Prabhūtaratna Buddha in Chengdu in Yizhou spring out from the ground?[80] The answer to this question was very elaborate. Originally the capital city of this Shu region was situated at the peak of Mt Qingcheng, and the present-day Chengdu was in the middle of an ocean. In the past, at the time of the Kāśyapa Buddha, a man by the Xi'er river (in the Western region) produced the image, modelling it after the whole body of Prabhūtaratna Buddha. It was placed in the temple on the peak of the Eagle head Mountain (Grādhrakāūṭa?). Someone from (the original?) Chengdu went there as a trader and brought the image home. When he reached the temple where the image is kept today, the ocean god sank the boat. Earlier, this same man had seen the ocean god walking on the river bank, and mistaking him for a mountain demon, he had killed him. The god had become angry, and caused the man and the image to be drowned together. Prabhūtaratna Buddha was at the temple on the Eagle Mountain at an earlier time. The ancient site still remains, where there is a *stūpa* which constantly emits light.

The god, having told Daoxuan this story, identified the location of the Xi'er River, saying that the route of over three thousand *li* runs through Langzhou. The river is wide, and in the middle of the river is an island with a hill. There is an ancient temple where scriptures and images are kept but no monks live. Yet, occasionally bells are heard. People present offerings to the ancient *stūpa* twice a year. The *stūpa* is shaped like a three-level Ordination Platform and covered with numerous round tops. Locals call it a divine mound and offer vegetarian food every time it emits light. This part of the story concludes by noting that the location of this *stūpa* was not far from India, and then continues:

> At the time of the Jin dynasty (AD 265–419) a monk saw a dirt mound of a tomb appear from the ground [in Yizhou]. As he removed the dirt, the

mound came up again and he could not level the ground. Later he saw an opening, and mystified by it he excavated the place and discovered deep in the ground an image and human bones placed inside a boat. The skull, elbow, and shank bones were very large, several times as big as those of people today. This is because at the time of Kāśyapa Buddha, people in Jambudvīpa lived twenty thousand years. The lifespan of people today is shorter, and they are also smaller. When the image was first discovered, people could not pull it up. I (namely, the god instructing Daoxuan) appeared as an old man, and told them what to do and the image was then taken out. During the persecution of Buddhism under the [Northern] Zhou dynasty (that occurred in AD 574–578), the image was hidden temporarily, but as the support for Buddhism was restored, it was brought out again. People in Shu only know that the image came out of the ground, but have no idea about its ultimate origin. They noticed that the characters '*duobao*' (*prabhūta*) were written on its base, shaped like a [lotus] flower, and they named the image accordingly.

Daoxuan then noted that the standardized characters (*lishu*) for '*duo*' and '*bao*' appeared first under the Qin rule (221–207 BC), and wonders how there could have been writing in China at the time of the past Buddha Kāśyapa. The god answers by arguing that the *lishu* characters associated with the Qin minister Li Si (208 BC?) in fact had a long history, reaching back to the time of ancient Buddhas. At the present time, all countries in the southern parts of Jambudvīpa use the same phonetic scripts. Only in China, because of its isolation, is the ancient way of writing still used.

A variety of familiar strategies for constructing Buddhist sacred places appears in this story. The specific location in Chengdu is first of all the place where an ancient Prabhūtaratna Buddha image appeared from the ground. This image had been produced earlier, at the time of the past Buddha Kāśyapa, in a place called Xi'er River, not far from India, and was later transported from there to China. The site in China is thus connected to the Buddhas Prabhūtaratna and Kāśyapa through a story of a movable cultic object (a Buddha image). This specific location in China is, furthermore, identified as a part of the world in which Kāśyapa Buddha appeared and as a part of China under the rule of the Jin dynasty. The elaborate discussion about the inscription '*duobao*' in the *lishu* script serves to correlate Chinese history with Buddhist universal history. The invention of this style of writing, generally known to have occurred under the Qin dynasty, is now said to go a great deal further back in time to the time of Kāśyapa Buddha. Through this elaborate operation, a Buddhist site in China, generally known as the seat of an ancient image of unknown origin, is transformed into a part of the Buddhist world at one important point in the cosmic history of repeated appearances of the Buddhas. The distance between India, where Śākyamuni Buddha lived and taught, and China, with its own non-Buddhist history and civilization, represented here by a specific writing system, on the other, is first recognized as a real distance in the story of the moving of the image. But this difference evaporates in the end. The Chinese writing system was the writing system everywhere at one time in a very distant past. The spatial distance is overcome by temporal distance: if one goes back far enough in history, China was an integral part of a uniform Buddhist world that included China.

Variations of this same strategy appear repeatedly in the entries on other sites discussed by Daoxuan and the visiting gods. Some of the stories explain the origins and earlier histories of miraculous images whose more widely known stories are collected in Daoxuan's miracle story collection. Thus, answering Daoxuan's question about the origin of the rock image that appeared in Liangzhou, fulfilling the prediction given earlier by Liu Sahe who worshipped the mountain,[81] the god tells him how at the time of Kāśyapa Buddha, Bodhisattva Libin built a temple there and the great Brahma king produced an image which was no different from the Buddha himself. The image walked around and taught people. Later the temple and the Buddhist community around it were destroyed, but the mountain deity took the image out into a distant part of the sky, only later to bring it back and place it in a rock cave. Bodhisattva Libin is then said to have been Liu Sahe himself in an earlier life.

In this essay I attempted to examine an aspect of the complex relationship between religious biography and sacred places. Kuwayama's discussion of the Buddha's begging bowl in Gandhāra throws a great deal of light on the different ways in which Buddhist sacred places in different parts of India were constructed with references to the life of the Buddha. The cosmic fate of the bowl in Gandhāra is described in the Lotus-face Scripture, and the remarkable sermon on the bowl, attributed to the revelation Daoxuan is said to have received towards the end of his life, appears to be indebted to this scripture. As the distance from the original location of the Buddha's life expands, the horizons of the stories about the relationship between Buddhist sacred places and the life of the Buddha appears to expand. Many of the strategies used in constructing Buddhist sacred sites in Gandhāra reappear in Daoxuan's attempt to reconstitute Buddhist sites in China; Daoxuan's strategies are supplemented with a new theme of the instruction received from gods and heavenly scriptures.[82]

List of Chinese and Japanese References

Primary Sources

Banniyuan jing 般泥洹經 (T.6)
Dabanniepan jing 大般涅槃經 (T.7), translated by Faxian 法顯
Daoxuan lushi gantong lu 道宣律師感通錄 (T2107), attributed to Daoxuan 道宣
Daoxuan lushi zhuchi ganyying ji 道宣律師住持感應記
Fayuan zhulin 法苑珠林 (T.2122), compiled by Daoshi 道世
Fobenxing ji jing 佛本行集經 (T.190), translated by Jñānagupta
Fufazangyingyuan zhuan 付法藏因緣傳 (T.2058), attributed to Kiṃkārya and Tanyao as translators
Gaoseng Faxian zhuan 高僧 法顯傳 (T.2085), by Faxian 法顯
Ji shenzou sanbao gantong lu 集神州三寶感通錄 (T.2106), by Daoxuan
Guanzhong chuangli jietan tujing bingxu 關中創立戒壇圖經并序 (T.1892), compiled by Daoxuan 道宣
Lianhua mian jing 蓮華面經 (T.386), translated by Narendrayaśas
Luxiang gangton lu 律相感通錄 (T.1898), attributed to Daoxuan
Puyao jing 普曜經 (T.186), translated by Dharmarakṣa
Taizi ruiying benjijing 太子瑞應本起經 (T.185), translated by Zhi Qian 支謙
Tatang neidian lu 大唐內典錄 (T.2149), compiled by Daoxuan 道宣
Zhuanji boyuan jing 撰集百緣經 (T.200), compiled by Zhiqian 支謙

Secondary Sources

Kuwayama Shoshin 桑山正進, *Gandāra-kāpishi kenkyū.* ガンダーラ　カーピシー 研究 Kyoto: Kyo to daigaku jimbun kagaku kenkyūsho. 1990.

"*Keihin to buppatsu* 罽賓と佛鉢" *Tenbō Ajia no Kōkogaku: Higuchi Takayasu kyōju Taikan Kinen Ronshū.* 展望　アジアの考古学：樋口隆康教授退官記念論集. Tokyo: Shinchosa. 1990.
Nagasawa Kazutoshi 長沢和俊. *Hokkenden Sounkoki* 法顕伝宋雲後紀. Tokyo: Heibonsha. 1984.
Ogawa Kan'ichi 小川貫弌. *Bukkyo bunkashi kenkyū.* 仏教文化史研究 Kyoto: Nagata Bushodo. 1973.

End Notes

1 See A. Foucher, *La vie du Bouddha: d'après les textes et les monuments de l'Inde* (Paris: Payot, 1949), 18. Not all Buddhist sacred places are constructed with references to a Buddha, however. Xuanzang, for example, identifies Buddhist centres as places where famous masters lived and wrote treatises, in this way turning a particular temple into a sacred place. It is the legend about Bodhisattva Mañjuśrī that gives Mt Wutai its status as a Buddhist sacred mountain.

2 In *Taishō shinshū daizōkyō*, ed. Takakusu Junjirō and Watanabe Kaigyoku (Tokyo: Taishō Issaikyō Kankōkai, 1924–32), 386 (hereafter cited as *T.*).

3 Kuwayama Shōshin, 'Keihin to Buppatsu,' in *Tenbō Ajia no Kōkogaku: Higuchi Takayasu Kyōju Taikan Kinen Ronshū* (Tokyo: Shinchōsha, 1983), 604–606; *Gandāra-kāpishī shi kenkū* (Kyoto: Kyōtodaigaku Jimbunkagaku kenkyōsho, 1990), 151–54.

4 The cult of the Buddha's bowl in China is also discussed in some detail in Françoise Wang-Toutain, 'Le bol du Bouddha: propagation du bouddhisme et légitimité politique,' *Bulletin de L'école Française d'extrême-orient* 81 (1994), 59–82.

5 *Fayuan zhulin, T. 2122:53*. 353c–354b. I discuss this account in some detail in Koichi Shinohara, 'The *Kāṣāya* Robe of the Past Buddha Kāśyapa in the Miraculous Instruction Given to the Vinaya Master Daoxuan (596–667),' *Chung-Hwa Buddhist Journal* 13 (2000), 299–367.

6 *Fayuan zhulin*, 367c16.

7 Koichi Shinohara, 'Two Sources of Chinese Buddhist Biographies: *Stūpa* Inscriptions and Miracle Stories,' in *Monks and Magicians: Religious Biographies in Asia*, ed. P. Granoff and Koichi Shinohara (Oakville, ON: Mosaic Press, 1988), 166–67, 177–78, 214–19.

8 This irregularity of the format and style suggests that these passages were prepared on more than one occasion, possibly by more than one author. A series of attempts appears to have been made to present the content of

the instruction Daoxuan claimed to have received directly from gods.

The story of Daoxuan's encounter with gods who instructed him on a variety of topics appears in other works as well. *Daoxuan lüshi gantonglu*, or 'The Record of Miraculous Communication to the Vinaya Master Daoxuan' (*T.* 2107, ref. *T.* 1898) is devoted to this topic and reproduces the content of gods' instruction in considerable detail. References to this instruction appear in other places as well (for example, *T.* 1899: 45.890a-24b2). These different versions of the record do not agree with each other, again suggesting that multiple versions of the content of the instruction Daoxuan claimed to have received from gods existed at one time, and the effort to produced the definitive record, perhaps as it was attempted in the *Gantonglu* version, did not succeed entirely. Earlier versions, which may have existed only as draft paragraphs, may go back to Daoxuan himself; others may well have been prepared by his followers.

Daoshi was a close collaborator of Daoxuan. The *Fayuan zhulin*, in which the passages under examination here appear, was completed in the third month of AD 668, according to Li Yan's preface (269bl0). This was only several months after Daoxuan's death in the tenth month of AD 667 (50: 791a20). This suggests that the version of the instruction Daoxuan claimed to have received from gods that appears in fragmentary passages in the *Fayuan zhulin* may represent a relatively early stage in the evolution of this tradition. This version of the instruction focuses on the issue of the preservation and continued upholding of the Buddha's teaching (*zhuchi*), and tells elaborate stories about various cultic objects used by the Buddha.

Seven passages from the 'Miraculous Record on Preservation' appear in different parts of the *Fayuan zhulin*, and I designated them as Passages A to G, following the sequence in which they appear in this massive work: Passage A and B are found in fascicle 10 (353c–355b and 362b–363c respectively); Passage C in fascicle 11 (367c–368b); Passage D in fascicle 12 (376a–378a); Passage E in fascicle 35 (560a–563b); Passage F in fascicle 38 (589b–591a); and Passage G in fascicle 90 (1008a–1009a). Passage A begins with an introductory passage, mentioned above, describing the circumstances of the divine revelation (Passage A/1). The remaining passages are written in a highly formulaic manner, using two different formats. The remaining parts of Passage A, Passages B, C, E, and G are written as records of the Buddha's sermons given on different occasions. In contrast, Passages D and F are written as sets of Daoxuan's questions and god's answers to them. Sometimes the two formats are mixed. Thus, Passage F contains sections that use standard conventions that appear in the Buddha's sermons (590ab). The exchanges between Daoxuan and the god in Passage D are interrupted when the Buddha's speech is introduced abruptly (376c11–377b25).

9 Since these sermons are presented as those given by Śākyamuni himself in his life time, other references to familiar facts of his life also appear. Some of the sermons (in passages B, E, and G) are said to have been given in the Jetavana, for example, and familiar names of Śākyamuni's disciples appear. It is striking nevertheless that the content of the sermons focuses on these cultic objects.

10 The connection with Śākyamuni is also established on a different level, by specifying the times when the sermons were given very precisely as so many years after enlightenment, or as so much time before his *nirvāṇa*.

11 Passage G: 1008a–1009a.

12 *Guanzhong chuangli jietan tu bing xu, T.* 1892: 45.807c.

13 Ibid., 818b17.

14 *Fayuan zhulin,* 1008c5. The expression 'again' (*you*) that begins this new section may be a marker indicating a different source: 'again, according to another source that also tells a story about this subject.'

15 Ibid., 1008c15.

16 Ibid., 100c80.

17 This elaborate story about the Buddha's bowl, that has been passed on from Kāśyapa Buddha to Śākyamuni to be kept after Śākyamuni's *parinirvāṇa* in numerous *stūpas,* closely parallels another excerpt from Daoxuan's *Zhuchi gang-ying ji,* found in the *Fayuan zhulin* entry on dharma garment (Fragment E: fascicle 35, 560a–561; Shinohara, 'Kāṣāya Robe'). The subject of this passage is the robe of Śākyamuni, and the sermon reproduced here is said to have been given three months before *parinirvāṇa,* or fifty years after Śākyamuni's enlightenment, also at the Jetavana. After he had left his father's palace and gone into the forest, a tree deity, rather than the mountain deity in the bowl story, presented Śākyamuni with a robe, saying that the previous Buddha Kāśyapa entrusted it to him, to be passed onto Śākyamuni. Śākyamuni put the robe on at the time of enlightenment, and then placed it in a robe *stūpa;* since then he is said to have worn it every time he turned the wheel of the dharma. A scene at the ordination platform follows: Śākyamuni throws the robe *stūpa* high up into the sky, and the robe *stūpa* emits light, illumining millions of lands. All the Buddhas who had come to hear the sermon present their *saṃgahātī* robes, Māra king builds numerous *stūpas* for them. The story of the Buddha's instruction in

preparation for *parinirvāṇa* follows, more naturally here since the sermon is said to have been given only three months before *parinirvāṇa,* rather than only thirty-eight years after the enlightenment as in the begging bowl passage. Māra king tells the Buddha that he does not know to whom to entrust the *stūpa,* nor where to keep them safely. The Buddha tells Rāhula to get Ānanda, who in turn is told to get Mañjuśrī from the cave on Mt Qingliang in China, and Mañjuśrī is instructed to keep the *stūpa* of Kāśyapa Buddha's robe for twelve years, to the north of the ordination platform. Thus, for twelve years the robe *stūpa* was kept to the north of the ordination platform, while the bowl *stūpa* was kept to the south of it. There follows an elaborate prediction about the future persecution of the Buddha's teaching and the instruction that Mañjuśrī should take the robe *stūpa,* or *stūpas,* everywhere to collect the saṃghātī robes of monks who had been killed, and to take those still alive to the top of Mt Sumeru. The Buddha will then throw down a huge rocky mountain to destroy the evil kings. One thousand of his powerful sons will build temples in the Jambudvīpa and the other three continents. Mañjuśrī is then to take the robe *stūpas* everywhere in the universe and place them there safely. King Aśoka's *stūpas,* which will be built everywhere, are again mentioned. These close parallels between these stories, one about the Buddha's robe and the other about the Buddha's begging bowl, suggest that they were written in close connection with each other.

18 Passage F: 53.589c.

19 In the passage presenting the Buddha's sermon on the bowl, a brief reference to the Four Heavenly King's bowl appears out of context (given in parentheses in the summary translation). This appears to be a clumsy gesture by a later editor to harmonize the two stories about the Buddha's bowl, given to the Buddha just before he achieved enlightenment, by a mountain god according to the Buddha's sermon version, or by the Four Heavenly Kings according to the version claiming to record exchanges between Daoxuan and a god.

20 T. 386: 12.1070-1077; the quoted passage is in 1075c–1077b.

21 *Lianhuamian jing,* 1070b26; 1073c14; 1077b26. As noted above, in many cases the Buddha's sermons in the Fayuan zhulin passages reproducing the instruction Daoxuan is said to have received from gods begin with a note specifying at what points in the Buddha's life the sermons were given: shortly before his *parinirvāṇa* (Passages A, 354b20), in the thirteenth year after enlightenment (Passage B, 362b18), eleventh year after enlightenment (Passage C, 367cl8), three months before the parinirvāṇa (Passage E/1, 560a26), twenty-first year after enlightenment (Passage

E/2, 562a21), and thirty-ninth year after enlightenment (Passage G, 1008a17). At the same time, these sermons conclude with instructions describing how the objects about which the Buddha is speaking are to be preserved after his *parinirvāṇa*. Often, as in the case of the sermon on the bowl reviewed above, it is explicitly said that 'after the Buddha's *parinirvāṇa*' the objects in question are entrusted to specific deities: in Passage B the knife to Mañjuśrī and Samantabhadra (363b3) and the beard to the bodhisattva Speechless (363c2–3); in Passage D a jewelled *stūpa* to Śakra and the Four Heavenly Kings (376c19–20); in Passage E a comment on entrusting the robe appears (560b27, c6–8). The central theme of these sermons is the entrusting of these objects, housed in elaborate *stūpa*; their preservation beyond the life of the Buddha is emphasized. It seems therefore natural that references to the Buddha's *parinirvāṇa* occur frequently in these sermons. In fact, the explicit references to different points in the life of the Buddha as occasions of the sermon strikes the reader as somewhat artificial. As records of the entrusting of the Buddha's teaching after his *parinirvāṇa* the more natural occasion for these sermons appears to be the last moments of his life.

22 This is a familiar setting in the accounts of the Buddha's last days: *Banniyuan jing*,T. 6: 1.180b11; for Pāvā, *Dabanniepan jing*,T. 7: 197a1. The location also appears in a different context in *Zhuanji boyuan jing*, T. 200: 4. 203c2.

23 *Lianhuamian jing*, 12.1071a9–10.

24 Ibid., 1071a17–b14.

25 Ibid., 1071b17–20.

26 Ibid., 1071bc.

27 Ibid., 1072a26–27.

28 Ibid., 1072b1–10. This elaborate speech that Ānanda makes upon hearing the news of the Buddha's imminent entry into *nirvāṇa* suggests that this was the first occasion when the Buddha told Ānanda about this event. The reference to the Buddha's entry into *nirvāṇa* in three months that appeared at the beginning of the *sūtra* thus appears to have been added later.

29 Ibid., 1072b22–c2.

30 Ibid., 1072c26–28.

31 Ibid., 1073b19–29.

32 Ibid., 1073c8.

33 Ibid., 1075c5–24.

34 Ibid., Kuwayama, *Gandāra-kāpishī shi kenkyū*, 153.

35 *Lianhuamian jing*, 1076a26–27.

36 Ibid., 1076b7–8.

37 Ref., *T.* 2085: 51.921a.

38 Ref., *T*. 1428: 22.7930.

39 Ref., *T*. 1451: 24.36la4.

40 *Lianhuamian jing*, 1076b12–c12.

41 Ibid., 1077b1b. This indicates that the time between the appearance of two Tathāgatas has passed. Ref., Ibid., 1070b27–9.

42 Ibid., 1077b26.

43 Both Daoshi, who compiled the *Fayuan zhulin*, and Daoxuan were familiar with this scripture. *Daitang neidan lu*, ref., *T*. 2149: 55.275a28.

44 *Lianhuamian jing*, 1073b19–23.

45 Ibid., 1074a3.

46 Ibid., 1077bl0–19.

47 *T*. 1241: 22,339a; *T*. 185: 3.479ab; *T*. 186: 3.526bc, *T*. 190: 3.801b-802b.

48 *T*. 2087: 51.917c. Kuwayama, *Gandāra-kāpishī shi kenkyū*, 45–47. Also Kuwayama Shōshin, 'The Buddha's Bowl in Gandhāra and Relevant Problems,' *South Asian Archaeology* 9, pt. 2 (1987), 954.

49 The reference to ancient Buddhas is striking, though the point here is that ancient Buddhas all used different bowls and not that same bowl, as is said in the sermon revealed to Daoxuan.

50 *T*. 2058, 50: 315b.

51 Kuwayama, 'Keihin to Bappatsu,' 598; Kuwayama, *Gandāra-kāpishī shi kenkyū*, 47–8.

52 *T*. 2085: 51.858bc.

53 *Gaoseng faxian zhuan*, *T*. 2085: 51.865c. Kuwayama, *Gandāra-kāpishī shi kenkyū*, 48.

54 Ref., *T*. 186: 3.526c2.

55 Ref., *Lianhua mian jing*, 12.1975c25-27 'five flavours.'

56 The first half of this story is translated in Kuwayama, *Gandāra-kāpishī shi kenkyū*, 48. See also Nagasawa Kazutoshi, Hokkenden Sōunkōki (Tokyo: Heibonsha, 1984), 115–16; H.A. Giles, *The Travels of Fa-hsien* (AD 399–414), or Record of the Buddhistic Kingdoms (London: Routledge and Paul, 1959), 74–75; James Legge, *A Record of Buddhistic Kingdoms: Being an Account by the Chinese Monk Fa-Hsien of His Travels in India and Ceylong (A.D. 399–414) in Search of the Buddhist Books of Discipline* (New York: Pargon Book Reprint, 1965), 109–110.

57 Kuwayama, *Gandāra-kāpishī shi kenkyū*, 48.

58 Ibid., 50. *T*. 2145: 55.113b; *T*. 2059: 50.343b.

59 Kuwayama, *Gandāra-kāpishī shi kenkyū*, 51. *T*. 2145: 55.114a; *T*. 2059: 50.338c.

60 Kuwayama, *Gandāra-kāpishī shi kenkyū*, 52. *T*. 2059: 50.399a; *T*. 2059: 50.337a.

61 *Gaoseng faxian zhuan*, 51.858b. Kuwayama, 'Keihin to Bappatsu,' 599.

62 Kuwayama, *Gandāra-kāpishī shi kenkyū*, 55–58.

63 *Gaoseng faxian zhuan*, 51: 879c.
64 Ibid., 148.
65 Kuwayama, 'Buddha's Bowl in Gandhāra,' 298, 311.
66 Ibid. Similar issues are raised in David McMahan, 'Orality, Writing, and Authority in South Asian Buddhism: Visionary Literature and the Struggle for Legitimacy in the Mahayana,' *History of Religions* 37 (1998), 249–74.
67 Here I will follow Kuwayama and define Gandhāra as a large region including Nagarahāra to the west, Swat region to the north, and Taxila on the other side of the Indus River to the east (Kuwayama, 'Buddha's Bowl in Gandhāra,' 297).
68 Kuwayama, *Gandāra-kāpishī shi kenkyū*, 297.
69 Hāritī was a *yakṣī* associated with Gandhāra (ref., T.1451: 24.360–362c); Kuwayama,'Buddha's Bowl in Gandhāra,' 205n84; Ogawa Kan'ichi, *Bukkyō bunkashi kenkyū* (Kyoto: Nagata Bunshōdō, 1973), 35, 41.
70 Kuwayama, 'Buddha's Bowl in Gandhāra,' 223.
71 Kuwayama, 'Keihin to Bappatsu,' 598.
72 *T*. 1899.
73 See T.H. Barrett, 'Exploratory Observations on Some Weeping Pilgrims,' *The Buddhist Forum* 1 (1990); 99–110.
74 *Fayuan Zhulin*, 1009a2.
75 *T*. 2107.
76 Daoxuan's miracle story collection, *Ji shenzhou sanbao gantong lu* ('Collected Records of Buddhist Miracles in China,' T. 2106), is organized into three sections: miracle stories about *stūpas* (fascicle 1); images (fascicle 1); supernatural temples, scriptures, and supernatural monks (fascicle 3). Many of the stories, particularly those in the first two large sections, may be read as stories about the Buddha's presence in China. Since Daoxuan drew his material from existing sources, such as existing collections of monks' biographies, we may safely treat this material as a summation of views that existed among Chinese Buddhists leading up to Daoxuan's time. Thus, for example, along with *stūpas*, where Buddha's relics was kept, Buddha images were treated as embodiments of the Buddha's presence. To pay respect to a Buddha image is to pay respect to the Buddha. Stories about miraculous signs given by an image must have served to stress this identity.

Reading Daoxuan's miracle story collection in this way, I suggest that the stories about the well-known group of *stūpas* and images said to have been produced by King Aśoka, placed prominently at the beginning of the miraculous *stūpa* and image story sections in this collection, may be interpreted as further examples in which Buddhist sacred places were constructed by referring to the life of the Buddha. The locations of these *stūpas* and images are carefully noted. The stories of Aśoka *stūpas* imply that the relics were sent by king Aśoka to the places in China where these stūpas were built. Aśoka images were said to have arrived more recently in China, and were usually discovered in ways involving miracles.

In his miraculous image story collection (fascicle 2), Daoxuan collects stories that highlight the connection between miraculous images and the places where miracles occurred and the images were kept. These stories describe the often miraculous circumstances under which these images are said to have been discovered, reminding the reader over and over of the assumption that these images were brought to China from outside, ultimately from Aśoka's India. In this part of the collection, Daoxuan appears to have accepted the strategy of constructing Buddhist sacred places in China by telling stories that describe how relics and images were moved to China.

But certain new details begin to appear towards the end of this collection of image miracle stories, suggesting that Daoxuan may have begun to introduce new dimensions to his understanding of the nature of Buddhist sacred places in China. The second fascicle of Daoxuan's collection, devoted to miraculous images, contains fifty entries. These entries are organized chronologically around succeeding dynasties, with the last ten entries assigned to the Tang, mentioning dates from Wude (AD 619–26) (no. 40); Zhenguan (AD 627–649) (nos. 41, 42, 43, 44); Xianqing (AD 656–661) (no. 45); Yonghui (AD 650–656) (no. 46); and Longshuo (AD 661–663) (nos. 49, 50).

Story 40 speaks of a stone image that He Bian and He Ji dug out near the Ciwu River in Fangzhou. Daoxuan reports that, according to a local tradition, at the time of the past Buddha Kāśyapa forty images were hidden. Only two of them have been rediscovered so far, and others remain hidden in mountains. This image is said to have been just like the iron-ore image, discovered earlier under the Northern Zhou (AD 557–581) (story 34), that is kept in a garden to the east of the Yuhua shrine. Like the iron-ore image, the newly discovered stone image could not be carved. The note that appears in story 40 implies that this image, discovered during the Wude period (AD 619–26), was closely related to the iron image discovered under the Northern Zhou, and explains the relationship by referring to a group of images that were hidden at the time the past Buddha Kāśyapa lived. Story 34 does not speak of the image's origin at the time of the past Buddha Kāśyapa; the idea appears to have been introduced when story 40, about an image discovered during the Wude period, was added to the collection.

As I noted above, Daoxuan highlighted the well-known group of Aśoka images that appeared in China; he also told a long story about the image king Udayana produced during the time Śākyamuni lived in this world. But the comment appended to story 40 takes the origin of the image far beyond kings Aśoka and Udayana, to the time of the previous Buddha Kāśyapa. The horizon of the image miracle collection appears suddenly to have expanded as stories from the Tang period were added to the list of widely known stories of miraculous images in China.

Entries nos. 43 and 44 present stories of Buddha's footprints. In a rocky hill to the north of the Xiangxisi temple, 100 *li* to the West of Yuzhou (in Sichuan) were 12 pieces of the Buddha's foot print, 3 *chi* in length, 1 *chi* and 1 *cun* in width, and 9 *cun* in depth. Inside were patterns of fish (no. 43). On the rock to the north of the Lingkansi in the Xingning District to the northeast of Xunzhou (in Guangdong) were over 30 footprints of the Buddha, large ones as long as 5 chi. Visions of miraculous footprints seen under the Southern Song dynasty (AD 420–479) and later in the third year of the Zhenguan period (AD 629) under the Tang are also mentioned (no, 44). Other stories listed under the Tang in Daoxuan's collection are of a kind similar to those listed under earlier dynasties (nos. 45, 46, 47, 48). The large size of these footprints suggested great antiquity.

Since stories about Buddha's footprints are not reproduced with stories about Buddha images in the earlier part of the collection, these stories also appear to reflect the changing perspective Daoxuan introduced to his work at the time he completed this collection. While he was content to collect more conventional image miracle stories for the earlier periods, for his own times he broadened the category of the Buddha image to include other forms of the representations of the Buddha. Daoxuan may well have been affected by the prominent place given to Buddha's footprints in Xuanzang's account of Buddhist sacred places in India.

77 *Daoxuan lüshi gantong lu, T*. 2107.

78 *Lüxiang gantong lu, T*. 1898.

79 *Daoxuan lüshi gantong lu,* 52: 436a9/45: 875a29; 52:439c25-26/45: 879c5.

80 436a9/45: 875bl/53: 394a2.

81 Story no. 14.

82 It is also tempting to see in this a shadow of the medieval Daoist tradition of revealed scriptures. Future research is needed to explore this complex interaction.

Glossary

Chengdu 成都
chi 尺
Ciwu 慈烏
cun 寸
Daopu 道普
Daoshi 道世
Daoxuan 道宣
duobao 多寶
Fangzhou 坊州
Faxian 法顯
Fotudeng 佛圖澄
Guangdong 廣東
He Bian 郝辯
He Ji 郝積
Huilan 慧覽
Jin 晉
jingangji 金剛際
Jingyesi 淨業寺
Langzhou 郎州
Li 里
Li Si 李斯
Li yan 李儼
Liangzhou 涼州
Libin 利賓
Lingkansi 靈龕寺
lishu 隸書
Liu Sahe 劉薩何
Longshuo 龍朔
Luoyang 洛陽
pusaseng 菩薩僧
Qin 秦
Qingcheng 青城
roushen 肉身
Shu 蜀
Song 宋
suishen sheli 碎身舍利
Tan Wujie 曇無竭
Tang 唐
Wude 武德
Wutai 五臺
Xi'er 西耳
Xiangxisi 相思寺
Xianqing 顯慶
Xiao Yuezhi 小月氏
Ximingsi 西明寺
Xingning 興寧
Xuanzang 玄奘
Xunzhou 循州
Yizhou 益州
Yonghui 永徽
you 又
Yuazhi 月氏
Yuhua 玉華
Yuzhou 渝州
Zhenguan 貞觀
Zhi Qian 支謙
Zhimeng 智猛
Zhongnan 終南
Zhou 周
zhuchi 住持

3

Where Ascetics Get Comfort and Recluses Go Public: Museums for Buddhist Saints in Thailand

LOUIS GABAUDE

During the last fifty years, Thailand has faced tremendous distortions in its social fabric, growing from twenty million inhabitants in 1951 to more than sixty million in 1998. However, during this same period, the actual ratio of Buddhist monks to the population has decreased from 842 per 100,000 population to 450. The monks have lost most of their control over instruction and schooling, which means that they have lost their control over the construction of their world-view. Yet tourists have the impression that monks are ubiquitous: newspaper stands offer a broad range of Buddhist magazines, bookshops have sections of Buddhist books, and nearly every car and every person is adorned with a Buddhist medallion or amulet. On a drive in the country, one passes many billboards inviting one to make merit at a nearby Buddhist festival or pay respect to a saint living in the vicinity. There are also numerous new lavish temples, high *cetiyas* and huge Buddhas seated on hilltops. The temple, *cetiya* and Buddha images have been standard in Buddhist countries for centuries, but a new type of sacred monument has appeared in Thailand in the last ten years, the 'museum' of the saint.[1]

The Thai Context of Buddhist 'Sainthood'

The Connotations of Buddhist 'Sainthood' in English

The literature in English usually presents Buddhist Saints in Thailand through three descriptive categories: 'saints,' 'forest monks' and 'wandering monks.' As in other countries of Asia, designating Buddhist monks as 'saints' is convenient, but it may mask special connotations alien to the Western or Christian concept of saint. Nevertheless, many authors, such as S.J. Tambiah in the *The Buddhist Saints of the Forest and the Cult of Amulets: A Study in Charisma, Hagiography, Sectarianism, and Millennial Buddhism*, have used this term.[2]

The kind of spiritual achievement realized by a saint is also described by using more neutral, functional, and somehow more indigenous wording. Authors refer to the 'place' where most of these monks have lived, the 'forest.' I might cite as an example J.L. Taylor's *Forest Monks and the Nation – State: An Anthropological and Historical Study in Northeastern Thailand.* The reference to the forest not only corresponds to the place where these monks have actually spent the main part of their lives but also reminds us of the old and probably primitive tradition of 'forest monks,' the *araññāvāsin*, who distinguished themselves from monks living in 'villages,' the *gāmāvāsin*.[3]

Another indigenous word used by authors refers to the main activity practised by these monks: 'wandering', as in Kamala Tiyavanich's *Forest Recollections: Wandering Monks in Twentieth-century Thailand*.[4] The word wandering encapsulates several ascetic practises taken from a traditional set of thirteen 'austerities' (*dhutaṅga*) that Buddhist monks can practise at leisure, so to speak, to overcome their defilements.[5] Since the austerities involved in wandering are the most practised in Thai religious culture, their generic name, 'thudong,'[6] is actually used to describe specific austerities practised in wandering.[7] Usually, however, wandering does not necessarily connote sainthood, for example when it is practised by any young novice or monk during the March-to-May school holidays or outside the 'rain retreat' or 'watsa' (*vassa*), or when it is practised by monks who use their magical reputation to dupe the rural people. It is a fact, however, that most of the Buddhist monks considered to be saints have for some time practised wandering by being 'thudong' monks.

Beside the forest and wandering label, other terms may describe our saints in a spirit of devotion ('Masters'), or in a sociological context ('charismatic monks'). In some cases the cryptic one *Puang pho,*' a general honorific, is used.[8]

The Thai Wording of Buddhist Sainthood

If we turn to the Thai designations for our saints, the most classical one and closest to saint is certainly the term 'ariya' as in 'ariyasong,' the 'noble monk' (*ariya saṅgha*). This term is opposed to 'sommutti song,' the monk just by name or robe (*sammuti saṅgha*). According to the tradition, there are four main degrees of noble persons (*ariyapuggala*): the 'Stream Winner' (*sotāpanna*), the 'Once-Returner' (*sakadāgāmi*), the 'Non-Returner' (*anāgāmi*) and the 'Holy One' or our saint *par excellence,* the *arahant,* who has achieved enlightenment.[9] In popular Thai devotional literature, however, two of these degrees are used – the first one ('sodoban') and the last one ('orahan'). Nowadays, most of the Buddhist monks are considered as 'monks just by robe,' but there are a few dozen and sometimes a set of '101' or '108,' still living or dead, who are considered to be 'ariya.'

Other terms consider only one aspect of the life of the hero: 'Phra kammathan,' 'Phra vipatsana' or 'Phra thudong' connote either ability for concentration (*samādhi*), for insight (*vipassanā*), or for practise of austerities (*dhutāṅga*) related to wandering. Another word used to describe monks who are well known for their magical powers and their amulets is 'keji-ajan.' But Western scholars as well as their Thai saints, to say nothing of Western monks or Buddhists, would not readily call these magicians saints. As for the feeling of the Thai public, which would require a longer analysis that cannot be included here, let us just say that the frontier between the saint and the magician is not clear, simply because the public considers monks who have supernatural powers to be saints.

The Three Hierarchies: Vinaya, Administration, Popular

Calling somebody a saint or an 'ariya' creates a hierarchy of Buddhist spiritual achievement not only by 'grading' this attained perfection but by setting aside the majority who do not make it. The fact – and sometimes the problem – is that Thai Buddhism is structured by three separate hierarchies, which are supposed to measure Buddhist achievements: the first is the only hierarchy admitted by the Buddha, that which should come out of his *Vinaya* rules and which applies to small communities of monks. I refer to it as the *Vinaya* hierarchy. The second is the politically sanctioned hierarchy, recognized by the King, the government, and its administration, which I call the administrative hierarchy. The third emerges from popular reputation and is called the popular hierarchy.

I will not say anything here of the first hierarchy, that of the *Vinaya*, because if the criteria of imperfection are well described in the *vinaya*, the actual realization of perfection by such and such a monk is only well known in his community. This inner *Vinaya* hierarchy is in fact regulated if not superceded by the politically sanctioned one, the administrative hierarchy. This virtually government-appointed hierarchy is made up of monks who are responsible for the day-to-day routine of what is 'order,' not only in the eyes of the Buddha (or his *Vinaya*) but in the eyes of the political authorities. One knows that Theravāda kingdoms have generally taken for granted that monkish discipline was too serious a thing to be left to monks. So they devised rules and imposed sanctions to help the *śāsana* or the Buddha's teaching survive despite the flaws of monks and external political threats. This hierarchy is parallel to the civilian administration, from the patriarch who plays the role of a kind of religious king (*saṅgha-rāja*) down to the head of a temple who serves as a kind of village chief. The public is not generally concerned with this network of religio-political hierarchy except on formal occasions, or in the case of political mobilization by the government (against communism, for example), or in cases of criminal or sexual scandals involving a monk, when his spiritual as well as civilian superior must take sides or impose sanctions. In these cases, it appears that the theoretically parallel and mutually supporting rules of the *Vinaya* hierarchy and of the administrative hierarchy may in practise diverge and even collide.[10]

The popular hierarchy is made up of monks who are considered extraordinary in one way or another by the general public: they give winning lottery numbers through enigmas; they 'read' minds; they perform miracles; they prevent individuals from dying in car crashes; they live ascetic lives; they produce potent artefacts (medallions, Buddha images, phalluses) with special protective powers; or they preach well. There is no specific body to decide who will be a part of this hierarchy and who will be at the top. Often, it begins with local fame, which spreads throughout the country by word of mouth.

Now, however, word of mouth is more and more in the hands of newspapers, the weeklies, the TV talk shows, and the TV sermons. As a result, the popular hierarchy is more than before fabricated by professionals who visit, photograph, film, and interview monks, to feed their media outlet. It often happens that these professionals are urbanites, whose media cater to the tastes of the middle classes, composed of mostly Chinese men and women who own and operate small businesses.

These three hierarchies should or could correspond theoretically. The *Vinaya* rules in particular should constitute a unique spinal column for the three. When, for example, a popular monk becomes head of a temple, he becomes automatically positioned at the lowest end of the administrative hierarchy. However, the popular hierarchy which produces saints does not emerge from the administrative hierarchy, which the public frowns upon. Nor does it come from an official decision, or from a political authority's decision. It has to germinate from a genuine soil of its own, and once it emerges it needs to grow slowly, freely, and independently with the increasing support of the media and the middle class. The popular hierarchy may even generate an open conflict with the central power, as it did long ago, in the case of Khruba Siwichai in Chiang Mai.[11] Or it may explode into a national scandal, as it did more recently with Yantra Amaro.[12] Nonetheless, the popular hierarchy, over time, will be sanctioned by the government or by the educational institutions. The government may grant religious honorific titles, officially conferred by the King. The universities may grant *Honoris causa* titles, which the local hero of the popular hierarchy bears – or enjoys – with a smile. This comedy of honours and devotion contributes to the domestication of the hierarchy. We will see that the museum may be the highest peak, the apotheosis of this domestication, which signals the absorption of the popular hierarchy into the other more official hierarchies.

The Two Congregations: Mahanikai (Mahānikāya) and Thammayut (Dhammayutikanikāya)

These three hierarchies are affected by a split between two congregations (*nikāya*) which officially and legally form the Thai community of monks (*saṅgha*) – the Mahanikai (*mahānikāya*) and the Thammayut (*dhammayutikanikāya*).

The Mahanikai or the 'Large congregation' is a convenient name given to distinguish the majority of Thai monks from the Thammayut minority. This label has the disadvantage of reinforcing the false impression that the whole of what is now Thailand was once a uniform saṅgha. Very few studies have attempted to dig deeper than the surface into this rather hidden face of Thai Buddhism.[13]

The Thammayut came into existence in the first half of the nineteenth century as a result of the future King Monkut's wariness of 'wild' meditation and his desire to link orthodox practice (*paṭipatti*) to the Pāli texts (*pariyatti*). His ascension to the throne was a golden opportunity for the Thammayut as it gave them the protection of the royal family and the authorities. This 'central' protection allowed them to spread into the northeast region where they persuaded many Mahanikai monks to follow them, and to be ordained or reordained in the Thammayut lineage.

There is at least one notable exception, however. The saint who is the spiritual father of all the saints we will talk about, Man Bhuridatto, told one of his disciples, Cha Subhaddo, that it was not necessary for him to be re-ordained and that he should remain a Mahanikai. His order would have great consequences. Although the temples and communities which pretend to keep alive Man Bhuridatto's heritage are quite numerous in Thailand, those related to Cha Subhaddo are notorious for their influence on the West. Mahanikai monks insist that they are less pretentious than the Thammayut and do not frighten the *Farangs*, that is, the Westerners. This exception notwithstanding, the number of Mahanikai monks who slipped into the Thammayut has left sour memories in the hearts of those who stayed in the Mahanikai congregation. One Mahanikai monk told me that 'the Thammayut behaved like bandits' and 'preyed on the śāsana,' implying that true 'Buddhism' was represented only by the Mahanikai.

Those interested in a political analysis of this phenomenon remark that the Thammayut were an efficient tool in the integration of outer regions into the Bangkok polity, or, if one prefers, in the colonialization of the periphery by the centre. There is, however, a certain irony in the fact that a large number of the northeastern Thammayut monks became famous for putting meditation practice (*paṭipatti*) before proper study of doctrinal (*abhidhamma or vinaya*) manuals and before administrative responsibilities.[14] Their hagiographies mention not only conflicts with the Mahanikai, which were after all to be expected, but also with their own Thammayut hierarchy sent by the Bangkok government. This hierarchy appeared alien to them because the Thammayut from the northeast were not interested at all in Pāli studies, hierarchical promotion, or honorific titles, and even less in political activism. The fact that they successfully resisted the order to behave, to study more, and to be more sedentary, accounts now for their merit, their *pāramī* and what we finally call sainthood.

When we examine either the triple-layer hierarchy or the split in congregational affiliation, we find a recurrent phenomenon: the ability of the authorities or the centre to capitalize on what they had not necessarily had a part in inspiring, in creating, or in encouraging. While a saint is created from the forest by his own merits – his abiding by the *vinaya* – and out of the recognition by the public at large, the urban classes and authorities try and often manage to use the saint's magical powers for their own business and politicking; they manipulate his image for their own careers and achievements, or, to put it briefly, his otherworldliness for their worldliness. The contemporary success of the saints, including the building of the museums, bears witness to this tendency.

The Memorials for Saints

In 1998, I visited twenty-five sites in Northeast and North Thailand each of which has a building or buildings dedicated to a saint. By site, I mean either a temple with its well-defined limits and numerous buildings, or a simple monument sprouting right in the middle of nowhere. By building I mean something that is built, be it a *cetiya* ('jedi'), a *maṇḍapa* ('mondop'), an 'anusawari,' a *prāsāda* ('prasat'),[15] a pyre (*meru* or 'men')[16] or a museum.

I could not obtain in-depth knowledge of the history and functions of each site or building from my short visits; but I hope this essay provides a good overview of the growing phenomenon of the dedication of memorials to an ever-increasing number of saints. From my visits, I was able to identify the following characteristics of the sites:

- Eighteen of the twenty-five sites have one building (or monument) dedicated to a saint.
- Seven of the sites have two buildings dedicated to a saint. There are thirty-two buildings on the twenty-five sites dedicated to twenty-three saints – two of the saints are represented twice.
- Twenty-two sites are dedicated to dead saints, and three are dedicated to living saints. In one of the sites where the saint is still alive, there is no real building dedicated to him, except for a simple pyre built in advance on the cremation ground. The saint is afraid that devotees might build too costly and elaborate a pyre for him, which has happened for other saints.
- Of the thirty-two buildings dedicated to saints, thirteen are museums; nine are *cetiyas*; three are *cetiya*-museums; three are *merus*;

and there is one each of a *maṇḍapa, prāsāda* and an 'anusawari'; and one *maṇḍapa* – museum.

As we know, the building of *stūpas* for saints is as old as Buddhism, if not older. In Buddhist Southeast Asia, a polity could not survive without a *mahādhātu,* a great relic enshrined in a *cetiya.* These protective monuments contained not only one or several relics of the Buddha Gotama but also relics of former Buddhas and the first disciples of Gotama. The habit of building a small *stūpa* for a ruler or a famous monk or even for a commoner is not unknown.

In Southeast Asia, there are four traditional classifications for monuments which commemorate the Buddha or any other worshipful person[17] (1) the *dhātucetiya,* which contains one or several body relics; (2) the *paribhogacetiya,* which contains objects used by the worshipped; (3) the *dhammacetiya,* which contains a portion of the Dhamma, or the teaching of the Buddha; and (4) the *uddesikacetiya,* which contains objects such as images of the venerated person.

If we bear these classifications in mind, we can see that the new name of museum actualizes the traditional concern for the safe keeping of objects that belonged to a worshipped person in a *paribhogacetiya.* When visiting the monuments, one realizes that the names museum, *cetiya, cetiya*-museum, and *maṇḍapa*-museum refer to the same kind of building where relics (*dhātu*), belongings (*paribhogaka*), images and amulets (*uddesika*), and sometimes books (*dhamma*) are kept and displayed. These new buildings actually combine the four kinds of *cetiya* distinguished by the tradition.

The location of the sites and the buildings provide further information about the saints. Most of the buildings I took as *paribhogacetiya* are situated in temples, and in most cases, in forest temples ('Wat pa'). This indicates that most of the saints came from the forest tradition.

In ten cases, the buildings are situated near the entry of the temple so that visitors do not disturb the normal routine of the monks. However, in twelve cases, they are set on a more remote part of the temple grounds so that the visitor has to walk deep into the grounds. Four buildings are set on the top of a hill,[18] no doubt a reflection of a belief in the 'cosmic' symbolism of mountains. Five buildings are situated among other buildings of the temple, and one is outside the temple altogether.

Most of the *cetiya*-museums resembled *dhātucetiya* or *stūpa,* with a room having four doors in the four directions. In two of them, the hagiography of the saint is pictured in terra cotta bas-reliefs. The saint's real life is not only palpable through his belongings but through a visual rendering normally reserved for the Buddha's past lives or last life.

The standard contents of a *cetiya*-museum include bronze, wax, or resin image(s) of the saint; bone relics or 'crystallized relics'; personal objects the wandering monks carried with them on their journeys and belongings they used when they became sedentary; and, in certain cases, books written by the saint or amulets produced or consecrated by the saint.

Most of the museums have look-alike images of the saints that are made of synthetic resin. Their resemblance is so astounding that you really believe the actual saint is there before you. This has been the fashion in Thailand now for approximately twenty years. Near Bangkok, there is a museum dedicated to these images; it contains replicas of most of the great saints.

The bone relics or the 'crystallized relics' are the high point of the *cetiya*-museums. They are extremely significant because they offer a kind of scientific proof that the saint was an Arahant, a truly enlightened being, since his bones have become like crystal stones, either coloured or transparent. This transformation occurs sometime after cremation: quickly if the saint has been an Arahant for a long time; more slowly, if he had put an end to his desires recently. The story attached to crystallized relics is that after the cremation of a saint, a devotee carries away some remains of the bones and keeps them in a container. When he or she opens the container some months or years later, he or she discovers that the bones have crystallized, and out of respect, the devotee returns the relics to the temple.

The personal belongings of the saint are kept in display cases, with or without an inventory or description. In some cases however, the objects have not been organized at all and give the impression of the chaos of the village marketplace. Generally, the objects used in wandering are easy to display because they are very limited in number and variety. When it comes to the period when the saint became sedentary, old and paralyzed, the variety and the number of objects increase and the visitor is spared nothing – from enema syringes to commodes.

I have not been able to witness any important organized educational activity in these museums. There is the casual tourist visitor like myself – on one occasion a beggar took my companion's shoes away. There are ceremonies to commemorate the birth or death anniversary of the saint. In one museum, monks assemble and chant every last day of the month.

Conclusion

The transformation of the *cetiya* into museum should not come as a surprise – a *cetiya* was already a means for keeping sacred objects to remind people of their past. In the *cetiya*, the object – especially in the case of a relic – was not necessarily seen every day, or even seen at all. The museum, however, transforms the traditional *cetiya* into a showcase where nothing is to be kept aside or unseen. This phenomenon has occurred in conjunction with an increase in Thai tourism; an increase in fund-raising campaigns for the creation of provincial museums with the obvious purpose of keeping the past alive through the preservation of artefacts; and an increase in the number of saints, many of them confirmed Arahants. The Buddhist saints were thought to have been numerous at the beginning of Buddhism, but their numbers then decreased. For centuries, nearly everybody in Southeast Asia believed that there were no more Arahants. And what happens in this Kali Age? What grows in this world corrupted by Western culture? The saints!

Most of the saints' museums I visited belong to the Thammayut congregation. Even if I could have added Mahanikai examples, the statistics would still be in favour of the minority, the elite and, in some way, the royal sect. If our criteria had been magical powers, the gift for preaching, or social activism, the results would have been different. But if we consider such formal signs of approval as Arahantship certificates nobody can equal the *Thammayutinikāya.* The prestige of the Thammayut saints is enhanced by the high society figures who fund these expensive *cetiya*-museums. The alleged cost of one which is now under construction is anticipated to reach 2 billion bahts, somewhere in the region of U.S.$80 million. Such extravagant costs may not necessarily please the saints themselves. Bua Ñāṇasampanno's decision to build a simple pyre before his death may have been influenced by the cost of Cha Subhaddo's pyre (US$680,000) and by the fact that important names in Bangkok pride themselves on patronizing saints' funerals.

My visits suggest to me that this trend in glorifying the saints – in some cases even before they actually die – does contribute to their increasing care for their public persona, some could even say for their ego. While most of them have been shy and modest and have lived up to their reputations, some have posed for daring photographs on isolated mountains in grandiose and self-contradictory gestures of promoting their love of isolation! Of course they do this to please their followers and devotees. In such tactics and in the proliferation of saints' museums, we witness first-hand the process of hagioconstruction, beginning with the collection of articles from the saints' daily lives and culminating with the crystal-clear relics. Leaving crystallized relics is the ultimate certificate of Arahantship, the final proof that the saint has achieved complete extinction or *nibbāna*. While hagioconstruction no doubt occured throughout the history of Buddhism and all over Asia, in Thailand's museums for saints, the traditional concern for preserving the relics of special monks is given a contemporary gloss. The articles kept in the museum are taken as providing a kind of scientific proof of sainthood appropriate to this 'scientific age.'

Cetiya-Museum of Venerable Wan Uttamo at Wat Pa Aphai Damrong Tham, Song Dao District, Sakonnakhon Province, Thailand.

Museum of Venerable Chop Thanasamo at Wat Pa Khok Mon, Wang Saphung District, Loei Province, Thailand.

Window showing personal belongings of Venerable Chop Thanasamo at his museum, Wat Pa Khok Mon, Wang Saphung District, Loei Province, Thailand.

Museum of Venerable Chop Thanasamo at Wat Pa Khok Mon, Wang Saphung District, Loei Province, Thailand.

Resin image of Venerable Cha Subhaddo at his Museum, Wat Nong Pa Phong, Warinchamrap District, Ubon Ratchathani Province, Thailand.

Crystallized relics of Venerable Cha Subhaddo at his "Meru," Wat Nong Pa Phong, Warinchamrap District, Ubon Ratchathani Province, Thailand.

End Notes

1 I have based this essay on observations made from 26 April to 4 May 1998, when I drove 2000 kilometres from the north of Thailand to the northeast where most of these museums are located.

2 S.J. Tambiah, *The Buddhist Saints of the Forest and the Cult of Amulets: A Study in Charisma, Hagiography, Sectarianism, and Millennial Buddhism* (Cambridge: Cambridge University Press, 1984); Charles F. Keyes, 'Death of Two Buddhist Saints in Thailand,' in *Charisma and Sacred Biography*, ed. Michael Williams, *Journal of the American Academy of Religion, Thematic Studies* 98, pts. 3 & 4 (1982), 149-80.

3 J.L. Taylor, *Forest Monks and the Nation-State: An Anthropological Study in Northeastern Thailand* (Singapore: Institute of Southeast Asian Studies, 1993).

4 Kamala Tayavanich, *Forest Recollections: Wandering Monks in Twentieth-Century Thailand* (Chiang Mai: Silkworm Books, 1997).

5 These are: 1. wearing patched-up robes; 2. wearing only three robes; 3. going for alms; 4. not omitting any house whilst going for alms; 5. eating at one sitting; 6. eating only from the alms-bowl; 7. refusing all further food; 8. living in the forest; 9. living under a tree; 10. living in the open air; 11. living in a cemetery; 12. being satisfied with whatever dwelling; 13. sleeping in a sitting position (and never lying down). See Nyanatiloka, *Buddhist Dictionary: Manual of Buddhist Terms and Doctrines*, 4th rev. ed. (Kandy: Buddhist Publication Society, 1980), 59. For the practice of these austerities by Indian Buddhist Saints, see R.A. Ray, *Buddhist Saints in India: A Study in Buddhist Values and Orientations* (New York: Oxford University Press, 1994), at the index entry *dhutaguṇa*.

6 The Thai words are transcribed according to the rules of the Royal Institute in Bangkok and put in quotation marks. The Pāli words are in italics. Monks' names include normally their former first name followed by the religious name (*chāyā*) they took on their ordination. The first name is phonetically transcribed according to the rules of the Royal Institute while the religious name is transliterated according to the Pāli script.

7 Actually, all the first ten austerities and the twelfth listed in note 5 are practiced regularly by these wandering monks, while the eleventh and the thirteenth may be exercised only according to opportunities (proximity of a cemetery) and will (sleeping in a sitting position).

8 J. Kornfield, *Living Buddhist Masters* (Santa Cruz: Unity Press, 1997); Amara Bhumiratana, 'Four Charismatic Monks in Thailand' (master's thesis, University of Washington, 1969); and Anatole-Roger Peltier, *Introduction à la connaisance des hlvṅ ba1 de Thaïlande* (Paris: École

Française d'Extrême-Orient, 1977). *Hlvṅ bal* or 'luang pho' means something like 'Reverend Father' and, as such, does not imply at all the idea of holiness even if it may be used as a title for a large Buddha image. Depending on the relationship or the age, the same monk may be called 'Reverend Elder Brother' ('Luang Phi') or 'Reverend Grandfather' ('Luang Ta' or 'Luang Pu').

9 See Nyanatiloka, *Buddhist Dictionary*, op. cit.

10 For an example of this messy interplay of these roles and rules see L. Gabaude, 'La triple crise du bouddhisme en Thaïlande,' *Bulletin de l'École Française d'Extrême-Orient* 83 (1996), 241–57.

11 See Keyes, 'Death of Two Buddhist Saints' and Kamala Tiyavanich, *Forest Recollections: Wandering Monks in Twentieth-Century Thailand* (Chiang Mai: Silkworm Books, 1997), 43–45.

12 See Gabaude, 'La triple crise,' 250–53.

13 One exception I know of is François Bizot. See his *Le figuier à cinq branches* (Paris: École Française d'Extrême-Orient, 1976), *Le don de soi-même* (Paris: École Française d'Extrême-Orient, 1981), *Les traditions de la pabbajjā en Asie du Sud-Est* (Göttingen: Vandenhoeck & Ruprecht, 1988). See also François Bizot and François Lagirarde, *La pureté par les mots (Saddavimala)* (Paris: École Française d'Extrême-Orient, 1996). Kamala Tiyavanich, *Forest Recollections*, alludes frequently to this forgotten and plural past and is working on it.

14 On this, see J.L. Taylor, 'From Wandering to Monastic Domestication,' *Journal of the Siam Society* 76 (1988), 64–88; Kamala Tiyavanich, *Forest Recollections;* and L. Gabaude, 'Institution et réforme religieuse. Les cas de Man (1870–1949) et de Buddhadasa (1906),' in *Bicentenaire de Bangkok*, ed. Thida Boontharm, et al. (Bangkok: Ambassade de France, 1982).

15 In Thailand, a *maṇḍapa* or 'mondop' is a rather small and often square building, or a pavilion with a spired roof, having one room or hall inside, with elaborate decoration. An 'anusawari' is a monument, which can be anything from a statue to a building with a hall or a shrine. A *prāsāda* or 'prasat' is originally, in the Khmer world, a sanctuary-tower (Boisselier). In our case, it could also be a *cetiya*.

16 There are two types of pyres: one which is built before incineration and has the form of a *stūpa* – it could be turned into what would elsewhere be called a *cetiya* where the Saint's bones are kept and exposed; another which is also built in advance but is made of two small walls; the firewood is placed in between the coffin and the top wall.

17 For Thailand, see Damrong Rajanubhab, *Monuments of the Buddha in*

Siam, 2nd rev. ed., trans. Sulak Sivaraksa and A.B. Griswold (Bangkok: The Siam Society, 1973). For Burma, see Shway Yoe, *The Burman: His Life and Notions* (Arran, Scotland: Kiscadale, 1989), 154–55.

18 This 'hilltop' category is still obscured by the fact that I was not always able to decide whether the top of the hill was within the grounds of a temple or not. It was clear in two cases and not in two others.

4

Paradise Found, Paradise Lost: Harirām Vyās's Love For Vrindāban and What Hagiographers Made of It*

HEIDI PAUWELS

The Braj area in North India is an excellent place to study the intersection of sacred biography, sacred place, and community formation. This area saw a fervour of 'religious pioneering' activity in the late fifteenth and early sixteenth century, which laid the foundations for what is at the moment one of the most popular Hindu pilgrimage areas in North India. Demarcation of sacred space took place systematically and on a large scale. From the perspective of those engaged in such activities, it might be better to speak about reclamation of the lost sites of a glorious past. The places mentioned in the stories of Kṛṣṇa's life had of course been there all along; they were, so to speak, 'dormant sites' and merely needed to be identified. The pioneers who did so were not only engaged in a process of site-identification but also self-identification, not merely in the building of temples but also in the building of religious communities. The Braj area quickly asserted itself on the map as a new focal point of devotional activity.

On the one hand, such 'siting' of devotional fervour can be seen as a moment of integration, a major factor bringing together in Braj pioneers from such different areas as, say, Andhra Pradesh (Vallabhācārya) and Bengal (Caitanya Mahāprabhu). Yet at the same time, the process of 'settling' brought conflict and divergence. The charismatic figures of the first generation came soon to be regarded as 'founder-fathers' of sects, which increasingly chose to identify themselves in opposition to one another. This is also apparent on the map: different communities settled at different sites within the Braj area. Most prominent, perhaps, are the 'opposing camps' of Govardhannāth (Puṣṭimārga) and Vrindāban (Gauṛīya sampradāya). Even within Vrindāban itself, sectarian divergence came to be locally grounded around the temples erected for the images of the 'founder-fathers' of different sectarian groupings. For example, the followers of Hit Harivaṃś clustered around the Rādhāvallabh temple, and Gauṛīya activities focused upon the Govinddev temple. Within one *sampradāya* or sect, rivalling factions chose different headquarters: Haridāsī Gosvāmī-householders are nowadays associated with Bāṅke Bihārī temple, and the ascetics with the site of Taṭṭī Asthān.

Concerns of community demarcation are reflected in the sectarian literature, and perhaps nowhere as clearly as in the hagiographies. The hidden (and sometimes not so hidden) agenda of many hagiographers was the glorification of their own founder-father and hence their own community. This went hand in hand with an often obvious spatial demarcation vis-à-vis other communities. Some hagiographers 'cast their net widely,' seeing their community as broader than the particular sect in which they had been initiated. Others were more exclusionist in their approach. The hagiographies have a lot to tell us about community formation, but I will concentrate in this essay on where this intersects with sacred place.

The purpose of this essay is to investigate how perspectives on sacred place came to be interpreted over time. I do so by focusing on one non-sectarian representative of the early generation, Harirām Vyās (fl. mid-sixteenth century), his views, and what his hagiographers made of them. In the first section, I discuss the perspectives on sacred place as voiced by Harirām Vyās himself. In the second section, I outline some of the hagiograpical interpretations of Vyās's perspective.

Vyās's Perspective

Vyās's poetry provides us with a glimpse of how the 'first generation' of pioneers in Braj experienced their project of reclaiming sacred place. Vyās is particularly interesting because, in contrast to some of his contemporaries, he not only created poems on the Rādhā-Kṛṣṇa love play but also provided much social commentary on the period in which he lived. I will look at these so-called *sādhāraṇa* ('ordinary') or *siddhānta* ('instructional') *padas* because they reflect the personal experience of one representative of the pioneers of Vrindāban.

As always, there is the problem of authorship and authenticity.[1] Can we accept what has come down to us in modern editions as Vyās's authentic voice? We should be aware of the possibility that later concerns have crept into his *oeuvre,* as it was transmitted over the centuries. The three existing editions of Vyās's complete works or *Vyās Vāṇī*[2] differ in fine points of sectarian interest, but show a substantial agreement in poems attributed to Vyās as well as readings of individual lines. Since Vāsudev Gosvāmī's edition is the most readily available and indicates variants from the two other editions as well as from manuscript material, I will use it as the standard reference text and refer to it as V throughout. In any case, all three editions are based on manuscripts not older than the nineteenth century, which means that we have access to Vyās's poetry only in the form it took after a transmission of three centuries. I have tried to move closer to the time of Vyās by looking for older manuscripts and can claim some success. The picture of Vyās's work I will present here is the one that appears from the manuscript material I have collected.[3]

The oldest dated manuscript that contains the *siddhānta* poems was copied in 1737 (V.S. 1794). I refer to this manuscript as J, the Jhānsī Manuscript, because it has been preserved in that city by descendants of Vyās,[4] though it was actually written in Vrindāban. Not all the poems in the edited *Vyās Vāṇīs* are found in this manuscript, but even so, one suspects that this manuscript too must include a number of accretions. It is important because of its age; for all Vyās's *padas* I quote in this essay, it is the text of this manuscript that I present, even if it does not conform to modern orthographic standards.[5]

In addition, many of the poems quoted here are also found in some old manuscripts of anthologies or *padasaṃgrahas*. I refer to two in particular. The oldest one is referred to as M because it is preserved in Mathurā, in the Janmabhūmi library (number 360070, *padasaṃgraha* 4257).[6] It contains twenty-three padas by Vyās (fol. 145r.–50v.). It is dated 1701 (V.S. 1758) (fol. 46), but the date is written before the collection by Vyās, which may have been copied later.[7]

The other anthology is referred to as G because it is preserved in Jivaji University of Gwalior (number 113 in the catalogue).[8] It contains thirty padas by Vyās, which are given under the heading *atha śrī vyāsajī ke pada liṣyate* (fol. 81v.–105r.).[9] This manuscript is dated 1813 (V.S. 1870) and was copied in Kalyāṇpurī. Both anthologies have a total of ten poems in common, which gives us an idea about which of Vyās's poems were popular in the centuries following his death.

Thus, throughout the article, I refer to Vyās's poems mainly by two numbers, referring to the sequence of the poems in the best-known edition, V, and the oldest manuscript, J. Where appropriate I also refer to the sequence in the anthologies M and G. The quotations from Vyās's poems will be from the manuscript dated 1737, which is nearly a full century earlier than the manuscript material used in existing editions. However, it is still a bit more than a century and a half after the time that Vyās flourished. It is with such restrictions in mind that the use of 'Vyās' in the rest of the essay has to be understood as a reference to the oldest attested record of his poems, more than a century and a half after his period of activities.

On the basis of such textual evidence, it appears that Vyās's evaluation of sacred space is something like 'paradise found, paradise lost.' In many poems Vyās speaks of the idealistic discovery of the supramundane realm behind the mundane Braj. Vrindāban especially appealed to him. However in other poems, he also speaks of his disappointment in the very same mundane Braj once it became populated with people who were interested in exploiting such a vision for commercial purposes. I discuss first the poems in which Vyās speaks enthusiastically of this 'paradise found,' and then turn my attention to the poetry in which he voices his disappointment with 'paradise lost.' Finally I point out what Vyās does not say by identifying issues on which he is silent.

Paradise Found

In Praise of Holy Braj and Vrindāban

Let us first look at the 'paradise found' poetry. Vyās has straightforward songs of the *māhātmya* or 'praise' type, recommending different sites in the Braj area. The most ancient manuscript (J), like the modern editions, quotes a number of those poems under the rubrics *śrī vṛṃdāvana kī stuti* (J28–42), *śrī madhupurī kī stuti* (J43–4), *śrī jamunājū kī stuti* (J45). In the song *dhani dhani mathurā* (V58 = J43) 'Blessed, blessed Mathurā,' Vyās mentions Mathurā with its sights of 'Kesaurāy,' 'Catrabhuj,' Viśrānt ghāṭ. In *saṣī ho mathurā vṛṃdāvana vasīyai* (V59 = J44) 'O friend, settle in Mathurā and Vrindāban,'[10] he enumerates the major places in Braj: Mathurā, Vrindāban, Govardhan, and Gokul. Vyās promotes the *parikramā* or circumambulation of Mathurā-Govardhan in the song *duvidhā tava jaihai yā mana kī, nirbhaya hokau java sevahuge raja śrī vṛṃdāvana kī ... ini pāini parikaramā daihai mathurā govardhan kī* (V197 = J128) 'Only then this mind's confusion will end, when, fearless, I worship the dust of Vrindāban ... When these feet track the path around Mathurā and Govardhan.'

Of all the sights in the Braj area, Vyās found Vrindāban most appealing. He says simply, but movingly: *suṣada suhāvanau vṛṃdāvanu lāgatu hai ati nīkauṃ* (V45 = J34), 'Pleasant and pleasing Vrindāban is what I like best,' a poem reminiscent of the famous *alī mohai lāgai vṛṃdāvana nīkau* 'Friend, I like Vrindāban well,' attributed to Mīrābāī (including the rhyme in last line: *phīkau*). Poems on a similar theme are entitled *śrī vṛṃdāvana* (*kī sobhā*) *deṣata* (*mere*) *naiṃna sirāta* (V42 = J30 and V46 = J35) 'Seeing (the splendour of) holy Vrindāban my eyes turn moist.[11]

Vyās did not just make a pilgrimage tour to the Braj area. He decided to settle down in Vrindāban and spend the rest of his life there. Many of his poems express his desire to do so: *aisaihī kāla jāi jau vīti, nisi dina kuṃja nikuṃjani ḍolata kahata sunata rasa [r]īti ... nāṃcata g[ā]vata rāsa renu meṃ tanu chūṭai jau prīti* (V275 = J84 = G25 = M11), 'May time be such that it is passed, day and night roaming in the bowers, speaking and listening to the ways of delight (*rasa*) ... singing and dancing in the dust of the Rāsa dance, the love which transcends the body.'[12]

Vrindāban becomes nearly an obsession, the sole topic of conversation in the Vyās household, and the only possible place to reside: *śrī vṛṃdāvana merī ghara vāti, jāhi pīṭhi dai dīṭhi karau kita jita tita duṣita jīva vilalāta* (V89 = J229), 'The talk of my house is Śrī Vrindāban. Where should we look if we turn away from it? Everywhere [one sees] tormented souls lamenting.'

Occasionally, Vyās makes his point in language shocking in an orthodox Hindu context: *hohi mana vṛṃdāvana kau svāna! ... vrajavāsini kī jūṭhini jeṃvata ve[gi] milata bhagavāna* (V262 = J80) 'Become, o heart, a dog in Vrindāban ... Eating leftovers of the inhabitants of Braj, you will quickly find God.'

These are not mere theoretical statements. Vyās realizes his desire. He repeatedly stresses his commitment to staying there and speaks of his exclusive devotion: *hamāreṃ vṛṃdāvana vyauṃhāra ... sarvasu vyāsadāsa kauṃ vanahai vṛṃdāvanahi abhāra* (V91 = J230 = G1) 'My business is with Vrindāban only .... It has become Vyās's each and everything, Vrindāban is what he depends on.[13] The following poem is very telling:

V180 = J183
tṛṣṇā kṛṣṇa krapā vinu savakeṃ
jatī satī kau dhīraja na rahai māyā lobha vāgha ke vavakeṃ
jaga ghorāhi kāma dorāvata mārata āsā cābhuka ṭhavakeṃ
gahyau āsarau vṛṃdāvana kau kāṭara vyāsa bhayau hai avakeṃ

Without Kṛṣṇa all are thirsting.[13]
Yatīs and satīs can't stay calm,
  when the lions of illusion and greed are roaring.
Lust makes the world go round like a horse,
  cracking the whip of hope.[15]
Vyās got a hold of the saddle-knob, Vrindāban.
  From now on he is hanging on firmly.[16]

Vyās stuck to this commitment until the end of his life; he died and was buried there. His tomb or *samādhi* is still maintained by his descendants in the area called Kiśor Ban.

Vyās also made it a point to encourage others to come and settle in holy Braj, as in: *bhajahu suta sāṃce syāma pitāhi ... tere sakala manoratha pūjai jo mathurā lauṃ jāhi; ve gopāla dayāla dīna tū karihai kṛpā nivāhi; aura na ṭhaura anātha duṣita kauṃ, maiṃ deṣyau jagu cāhi* (V119 = J69) 'Sing, son, of your true father Śyām ... All your wishes will come true, if you go to Mathurā. He is Generous Gopāla, you are humble, he will protect you and bestow grace. There isn't any other refuge for the helpless and suffering, I've searched and seen the world.' And elsewhere: *vinatī sunīyai vaiṣṇava dāsī, ... tinikī pada raja sarana vyāsa koṃ gati vṛṃdāvana vāsī* (V282 = J148), 'Listen to my request, Vaiṣṇava girl, ... The dust of His feet is a refuge for Vyās, residents of Vrindāban [attain] deliverance.'[17]

The sacred place is often the site of re-enactment of social order[18] or construed as representing an ideal social order.[19] In a feudal society, it is not surprising to hear royal metaphors applied to sacred space. In his poems of praise of Vrindāban, Vyās styles Vrindāban as his capital, where Rādhā and Kṛṣṇa are queen and king: *asarana sarana syāma jū kau vānau ... rajadhānī vṛṃdāvana jākau, loka caturdasa thānau* (V70 = J66) 'Refuge for the refugee is the theology of Śyām .... Whose capital is Vrindāban, the fourteen worlds are [mere] sub-stations,' and *syāma dhana kau nāhī aṃta ... rajadhānī vana kuṃja mahala mahalī sarada vasaṃta* (V73 = J55) 'There is no end to the treasury of Śyām .... His capital is the forest, the bowers are the palace, the maidservants[20] are autumn and spring;' or *nava cakra cūḍā nṛpati mani sāṃvarau rādhikā taruni mani paṭṭarānī, seṃsagraha ādi vaikuṃṭha parajaṃta, sava loka thānemṃta vana rājadhānī* (V75 = J53), 'The young [prince] is crown-jewel of emperors,[21] a dark diamond, and tender Rādhikā is his treasured consort-queen. From the primeval abode of Śeṣa till Vaikuṇṭha (the highest heaven), all abodes are mere substations, the forest is the capital!' Vrindāban is considered to be the capital, not only of the world but of the entire universe, a topic to which we return below.

With all that said, of course, Vyās is quite aware that no matter in what metaphors he would cast them, his eulogies fall sadly short: Vrindāban's splendour is ineffable. Vyās concludes the above poem (V46 = J35) with: *trabhūvana ke kavi kahi na sakata kachū adbuta chavi kī vāta, vyāsa vāta nahiṃ muha kahiāvai, jyauṃ gūgahi guru ṣāta*, 'Poets from all three worlds can't begin to express anything at all of its (Vrindāban's and the Rāsa dance's) amazing splendour. Vyās, (human) tongue cannot put it in words: like a dumb man tasting sugar.' This theme of ineffability recurs in other poems about sacred space (for example V44 = J33).

RASA TRICKLING THROUGH: VRINDĀBAN AS *TĪRTHA* BETWEEN DIVINE AND MUNDANE

What is it about Vrindāban that attracted so many devotees? Like many sacred places in Hinduism, it functions as a 'crossing' (*tīrtha*) between different *lokas*, a place of strategic location in that sense. A place with, as Alan Morinis puts it, 'divinely infused ruptures in the continuous surface of the mundane, human, social world.'[22] In other words, a 'focusing lens' for the divine.[23]

In Vyās's case, it becomes clear from his poems that what attracts him first and foremost is Vrindāban's power to provide a glimpse of the divine; it is a place where the mundane and supra-mundane meet. Vyās is always on the lookout for a glimpse of the divine couple in Vrindāban's bowers: *vriṃdrāvana kavahi vasāihau, kara karavā haravā guṃjaṃni kau kaṭa kopīna kasāihau, ... vyāsadāsa kauṃ nīla pīta paṭa kuṃjani dura darasāihau* (V257 = J76 = G3),[24] 'When will I settle[25] in Vrindāban? Waterpot in hand, a garland[26] of guñja beads, [when] will I tie a loincloth[27] on my waist? ... [When will] Vyāsdās get a glimpse of the blue and yellow garments (of Rādhā and Kṛṣṇa) hidden in the bushes?'

So compelling is the overlay of the mundane with the divine for Vyās that when he talks about Vrindāban, he often shifts in and out from this world to the beyond. More often than not, it is difficult to determine which Vrindāban Vyās is describing, as in the poem already referred to above: *śrī vṛṃdāvana deṣata naiṃna sirāta ... saṃtata sarada vasaṃta veli druma jhūlata phūlata [g]āta,*[28] *naṃdanadana vṛṣabhānanaṃdinī mānahu mili musikyāta* (V46 = J35), 'Seeing holy Vrindāban, my eyes turn moist ... Eternally autumn and spring, its creepers swing on the trees, bristling bodies, as if Nanda's son and Vṛṣabhānu's daughter have met and smile together.'

Vyās came to Vrindāban because he aspires to such visions of the divine love play. In addition, he reports on the auditory possibilities. To Vyās's ears, mundane Vrindāban echoes with divine sounds: *vali jāuṃ vali jāuṃ rādhā mohi rahana dai vṛṃdāvana ke sarana, ... deṣauṃ keli veli maṃdira meṃ suni kiṃkiṃni rava śravana* (V264 = J82), 'I beg and beseech, O Rādhā, let me stay in the shelter of Vrindāban ... Let me see the play in the temple of creepers,[29] and hear the sound of your girdle bells with my own ears.'[30]

Vyās clearly had a propensity for erotic visions, facilitated by Vrindāban's fauna and flora: *vaiṭhe ali araviṃda viṃva para muṣa makaraṃda cucāta, mānahu syāma kaṃcu [kuca]*[31] *kara gahi, adhara sudhā pīvata vali jāta* (V46 = J35), 'A bee has settled on a lotus-heart, pollen dripping from its mouth. As if Śyām holds on with his hands to her bodice [and breast], drinking the nectar of her lips in total surrender.'[32]

Vyās is very explicit about liking best the nectar of the place: *śrī vṛṃdāvana rasa mohi bhāvai ho* (V121 = J222), 'I like the juice (*rasa*) of holy Vrindāban.' A few more lines from a poem already quoted above (V89 = J229) describe how all that divine nectar trickles through to the mundane level: *sahaja mādhurī kau rasa varaṣata haraṣata gore sāṃvala gāta, ... vivi araviṃda dravata makaraṃdahi piyahi jivāvahu dala patra cucāta,* 'Spontaneously, the *rasa* of sweetness rains down, a dark and fair body, filled with joy ... Two lotus-faces, trickle with pollen: she revives her beloved, the petals and leaves flutter down.'

Nectar (*sudhā, amṛta*) and sap (*rasa*) are of course central theological concepts in Rādhā-Kṛṣṇa *bhakti,* so it is not surprising that of Vrindāban's flora, fresh saplings, fruit-bearing trees, and juicy-leaved creepers attract Vyās's special attention: *virājai śrī vṛṃdāvana kī veli, ... kala phala pīna payodhara pīya ke hīya suṣa sāgara jheli* (V53 = J39), 'The creepers of Vrindāban are gorgeous ... Their beautiful fruit is like [Rādhā's] ripe breasts, her darling's chest swells with an ocean of joy.' And elsewhere the trees are personified as *rasikas* or aesthetic connoisseurs: *visada kadaṃvani kī kala vāṭī, vṛṃdāvana rasa vīthini rasamaya rasikani kī paripāṭī* (V233 = J114), 'Beautiful is the path with the lofty *kadamba* trees. Vrindāban has pathways of *rasa,* which are like an assembly of *rasikas* filled with *rasa.*'

Apart from the liquid 'juice,' the tactile dust, *raja* or *reṇu,* of Vrindāban is singled out for veneration (as in the lines quoted above from V197 = J128, V275 = J84 = G25 = M11, and V282 = J148).[33] The reason for Vyās's fondness for Vrindāban's dust is similar to that of his liking the *rasa*. Dust, too, functions as a conduit of bodily contact with the divine, as in: *pyārī śrī vṛṃdāvana kī raiṃnu, ... jahāṃ tahāṃ rādhā caranani keṃ aṃka virājata aina* (V49 = J36 = M19), 'Sweet is the dust of Vrindāban ... A treasurehouse,[34] everywhere adorned with the prints of Rādhā's feet.' For Vyās, one could say, Vrindāban is not only *rājdhānī* or abode of cosmic kings, but also *rajdhānī* or abode of dust.

However, whether through the audio-visual or tactile, Vyās is not content with merely witnessing the divine sport. He is interested in nothing less than actively participating in the action, in the form of a 'girlfriend' *sakhī* or *sahacarī*. As is well-known, many of the cults devoted to Rādhā and Kṛṣṇa encourage their followers to emulate the role of the female companions (*sakhī*) witnessing the rendezvous of the couple in the transcendent Vrindāban. The phenomenon is referred to as *sakhī-bhāva*.[35] Vyās says in the poem quoted above: *sahacari hvai terī sevā karauṃ pahirāūṃ ābharana* (V264 = J82), 'I'll become a companion of yours and serve you, I will help you adorn yourself.' Elsewhere Vyās refers to his providing the divine couple with a spittoon (as in J53 quoted above) *nava cakra cūḍā nṛpati mani sāṃvarau rādhikā taruni mani paṭṭarānī, ... palu na vichurata doū jātu nahi tahāṃ koū vyāsi mahalini līyai pīkadānī* (V75 = J53), 'The young [prince], is crown-jewel of emperors, a dark diamond, and tender Rādhikā is his treasured consort-queen ... Not for a second do they leave each other, and no one goes there. In [that] palace, Vyās has taken the spittoon.'

Vyās clearly thought of himself as a 'herself' participating in the divine goings-on. This is also apparent from many of the poems in his works specifically on Rādhā and Kṛṣṇa's love play. The best examples are the poems on the topic of Rādhā's pique or *Mān kī śṛṃkhalā*.[36] Vyās ensures a happy-ending for those poems with reconciliation of Rādhā and Kṛṣṇa, often by his own intervention. In the last line, he tends to use the *chāpa* or signature 'Vyāsi,' implying a feminine gender (at least such is the case in J), hence most lines can be read as an identification of Vyās with the female companion intervening to reconcile the couple. Some examples are: 'Upon hearing Vyāsi's words, the young lady showed mercy' (43.2.2); 'When Vyāsi presented the sweet envoy [to her]' (27.2.2); 'Upon hearing Vyāsi's plea, the silent one (*muni*) joins [Kṛṣṇa]' (63.4.2); 'Upon hearing this, she was pressed at [her] lover's chest, thanks to Vyāsi's grasping [her] feet' (56.2.2). Even more explicit is the identification of

Vyās with the *sakhī* in the following examples: 'Understanding the maid-servant Vyāsi's banter, she fetched the prince' (46.4.2; similarly 61.3.2); 'Heeding the advice of [her] friend (*sahacarī*) Vyās' (24.3.1). Sometimes Kṛṣṇa himself refers to Vyās, as for example: 'If you do not believe [me], take Vyāsi for a witness' (8.1.2); '[Your] friend Vyāsi has led me here by the arm' (12.2.2). Most unambiguous of all are the following references: 'Seeing [them] sport, [their] own maid-servant Vyāsi swells with joy' (44.3.2); 'Vyāsi [in] the body of a *sakhī*, smiled tenderly' (9.1.2); 'Know that Vyāsi is your own maid-servant' (20.1.2).

Tuning in to the Same Wavelength: Vrindāban and the Community of Devotees

A second major attraction for Vyās to settle 'on the spot' of the divine love play was the presence of a community of like-minded devotees. Vyās's devotion for devotees or *bhaktas* in general is apparent from his songs. In J, such poems even come first, immediately after the *maṅgalācaraṇa* 'auspicious invocation,' under the headings *sādhani kī astuti ke pada,* 'songs in praise of saints' (J6–22), and *sādhani kau viraha,* 'separation from saints' (J23–7 more or less corresponding to the edition V5–27). The theme has also been taken up by Vyās's hagiographers (cf. the refrain of the eulogy to Vyās, Chappāī 69, in Nābhādās's *Bhakt-māl* [see table 1 in the second section, 'The Hagiographies']: *bhakta iṣṭa ati vyāsa ke* 'Vyās's preferred [deity to worship] was the worshipper').

Frequently in Vyās's poetry there is an explicit connection of sacred space with holy men. Living in Vrindāban was all the more attractive because of the presence of people who were on the same wavelength, who thought and felt (and sang) like he did. For Vyas, sacred space and sacred men were linked automatically, as in the last line of this interesting poem:

V263 = J81
aisau manu kava karihau hari merau
kara karavā kāmari kādhe para kuṃjani mājha vaserau
vrajavāsini ke ṭūka bhūṣa meṃ ghara ghara chāchi maherau
chudhā lagai java māgi ṣāugauṃ ganahu na sājha saverau
rāsa vilāsa virti kari pāuṃ mere ṣūṭa na ṣerau
vyāsa videhī vṛṃdāvana meṃ hari bhaktani kau cerau

When will Hari give me such a mental attitude,

> That pitcher in hand, cover over shoulder, I'll take up living in the bowers?
> That, hungering for the crumbs of the inhabitants of Braj, in every house buttermilk and rich yogurt preparations;
> Whenever I'd get hungry, I'll beg and eat, and won't keep track of night or day?
> That I'll manage to follow the ways of the Rāsa sporting, in need of shelter nor house?
> That, says Vyās, carefree[37] in Vrindāban, of those devoted to God I'll be the servant?

For Vyās, those *bhaktas* are at the same time the way and the goal. Although his goal is to be with them and serve them, he also says he has to thank them for leading him to Vrindāban: *pahile bhaktani ke mana nirmala ... jinhai sei vṛṃdāvana pāyau vyāsa sukala janama phala* (V158 = J3 = G18), 'The hearts of the first *bhaktas* were stainless ... Worshipping them, Vyās found Vrindāban, the fruit of all[38] his births.'

Vyās talks also of how he shared delight with his companions in the holy dust of Vrindāban, in poem J 36, from which I have already quoted: *pyārī śrī vṛṃdāvana kī raiṃnu ... rasika ananyani kau muṣa maṃḍana duṣa ṣaṃḍana suṣa caiṃna* (V49 = J36 = M19), 'The sweet dust of Vrindāban ... An adornment of the face of exclusive devotees, extinguishing their sorrow, [sheer] bliss and peace.'

As in this last line, Vyās sometimes calls the group of devotees gathered in Vrindāban 'exclusionist connoisseurs' or *ananya rasika*. In several poems the connection with sacred space is made: *yaha taṃna vriṃdāvana jo pāvai, tau svāratha paramāratha merau rasika aninyani bhāvai* (V123 = J75[39]), 'When this body reaches Vrindāban, then my life's goal, the highest goal, pleases the *ananya rasikas*,' and *kara mana vriṃdāvana meṃ vāsa, ... syāmahiṃ gāvata gopī rasika aninya hota udās* (V260-78[40]), 'Settle down, my mind, in Vrindāban ... where the gopīs sing 'Śyām' and the *ananya rasikas* become ascetics.'

Among those *rasikas*, Vyās often singles out Hit Harivaṃś and Svāmī Haridās, with whom he shared the vision of divine 'dalliance in Vrindāban groves.' Many poems testify that Vyās saw his friends as actual participants in that vision in the form of *sakhīs*: *ava na aura kachu karanai rahanai hai vriṃdāvana, ... milahaiṃ hita lalitādika dāsī rāsa mai gāvata suṃna mana* (V258 = J92[41]), 'Now there is nothing left to do, just to stay in Vrindāban ... Hita and Lalitā (Haridās is regarded as the *sakhī* Lalitā) and the other girlfriends will join singing in the Rāsa, listen, my heart.' Or in this poem, which is worth quoting in full:

V256 = J7341
haṃma kava hoiṃge vrijavāsī
ṭhākura naṃdakisora hamāre ṭhakurāiṃna rādhā sī
saṣī sahelī kava milahaiṃ ve haravaṃsī haradāsī
vaṃsīkvaṭa kī sītala chāyā subhaga nadī jamunā sī
jā kī vaibhava karata lālasā kar mīḍata kamalā sī
itanī āsa vyāsa kī pujavo vriṃdāvipana vilāsī

When will I become a resident of Braj?
[When will] Nanda's young son (Nandakiśora) be my Lord, and the likes of Rādhā be my Lady?
When will I join those girlfriend companions, Harivaṃśī and Haridāsī,
In the cool shades of the Vaṃśīvaṭa-tree, [near] a beautiful river like Yamunā?
For such splendor, the likes of Kamalā (Lakṣmī) are longing, rubbing [their] hands (in regret),
Fulfill only so much of Vyās's desires, O
playboy of Vrindāban's groves.

Haridās and Harivaṃś are obviously comrades for Vyās, not only in Vrindāban-on-earth, but also in the supra-mundane world of Rādhā and Kṛṣṇa. He makes this clear by attaching the feminine suffix -ī to their name. In this particular poem, Vyās may in fact be referring to his deceased contemporaries. As in the modern expression, he may be using 'going to Braj' as a euphemism for death, or rather as a reference to a post-mortem state of bliss and realization of one's real form as *sakhī* in the supra-mundane Vrindāban.

Whatever the intended meaning of this poem, for Vyās, living in Vrindāban was one of the identifying characteristics of true *ananya rasikas*: *teī rasika ananya jānivai, ... tinakī jīvani-dhana vṛṃdāvana, jīvata marata vaṣānivai; vyāsa rādhikā ravana bhavana vinu teī kyoṃ pahicānivai* (V98 = J234), 'Count those among the *ananya rasikas*: ... For whom Vrindāban is the treasure of their life, alive or dead, they ought to proclaim such. Except by the abode of Rādhikā's lover, how could Vyās recognize them?' and *jāke mana vasai vṛṃdāvana, soī rasika anaṃnya dhani, jākeṃ hita rādhā mohana* (V100 = J221), 'Only the one in whose heart dwells Vrindāban, only that one is a blessed *ananya rasika,* who loves Rādhā and Mohan.'

Vyās does not merely wish to live in blessed company in Vrindāban, he also desires to die there. One poem refrains: *jīvata marata vriṃdāvana saranaiṃ* (V268 = J9142), 'Living and dying in the shelter of Vrindāban.' Elsewhere, he proclaims the desire to die in Vrindāban as a characteristic of true devotees: *rahi mana vṛṃdāvana kī sarana ... vyāsa anaṃnya bhakti kī jīvani vana meṃ maṃgala marana* (V261 = J79 also J87), 'Remain, O heart, in the shelter of Vrindāban ... Vyās says: exclusive devotees live by auspiciously dying in the forest.' Vyās even goes as far as to recommend 'Death in Vrindāban,' in a poem with the oxymoric line: *śrī vṛṃdāvana meṃ maṃju*[44] *marivo* (V122 = J89), 'It's fine dying in holy Vrindāban.' Vrindāban has become a substitute Kāśī for those tuned into Vyās's *ananya rasa*.

However, the 'in-group' for Vyās is not that 'exclusive.' It is not restricted to these *ananya rasikas* who dwell in Vrindāban and share his 'taste' for the Rādhā-Kṛṣṇa mythology, but also includes *nirguṇa bhaktas*, whom he praises lavishly in several poems.[45] He even mentions laudingly such stalwarts as Raidās and Kabīr in the same breath that he mentions the sacred space of Vrindāban. The following poem provides a good illustration:

V112 = J134

kahā kahā nahīṃ sahata sarīra
syāma sarana vinu karma sahāi na janama marana kī pīra
karunāvaṃta sādhu saṃgati vinu manahi dei koṃ dhīra
bhakti bhāgavata vinu ko meṃṭeṃ suṣa dai duṣa kī bhīra
vinu aparādha cahūṃ disi varaṣata pisuna vacana ati tīra
kṛṣṇa kṛpā kavacī [teṃ] uvarai (ura) poca vaṛhī u(pa)[ra] pīra[46]
nāmā saiṃna dhanā raidāsa dīnatā karī kavīra
tinakī vāta sunata śravanani suṣa varaṣata nainani nīra
cetahu bhīyā vegi kali vāṛhī kāla nadī gaṃbhīra
vyāsa vacana vala vṛṃdāvana vasi sevahu kuṃja kuṭīra

What all doesn't the body have to suffer?
Let go[47] of refuge in Śyām, and karma is of no avail against the anguish of birth and death!
Let go of the benevolent company of sādhus, and who would provide [you] peace of mind?
Let go of devotion and *Bhāgavatapurāṇa*, and who would comfort [you] and relieve the onslaught of sorrow?
Let go of provocation, yet from all four directions, sharp slings of slander keep showering down.

If [you] emerge from the harnass of Kṛṣṇa's grace, [you're] small game, anguish will pierce [your] chest.[48]
Nāmdev, Saina, Dhanā, Raidās, and Kabīr: [all of them] were humble.
Listening to their words is a joy to the ear, tears will trickle from the eyes.
Make up your mind quickly, brother, in Kaliyuga the river of death engulfs [you] till over your head.[49]
By the power of Vyās's words, settle in Vrindāban, devote yourself to the bower-huts.

Vyās may recommend especially the specifics of the Rādhā-Kṛṣṇa cult in Vrindāban, but he does not let that come in the way of his appreciation of others with different convictions, as long as their devotion is real.

More orthodox than thou: Vrindāban as focus for community-formation

In his more theoretical moments, Vyās has a theological justification for his devotion and ecstasy: he attributes to Vrindāban a cosmogonic significance. Such projections of 'sacred space' onto a cosmic timescale are quite common in general.[50] At the same time, the 'sacred space' may function as a microcosm, an 'icon for the world.'[51] In the following poem, Vyās paints his cosmological vision and shows how Vrindāban functions as a microcosm. The poem is worth quoting in full:

V39 = J2951

sadā vṛṃdāvana sava kī ādi
rasanidhi suṣanidhi jahāṃ virājata nitya anaṃta anādi
gaura syāma kauṃ sarana duṣa harana kaṃda mūla muṃjādi
suka pika ke[k]ī koka kuraṃga kapota mṛgaja sanakādi
kīṭa pataṃga vihaṃga siṃgha kapi tahāṃ sohata janakādi
taru trina gulma kalapataru kāmadhenu go vṛṣa dharmādi
mohana kī mansā teṃ pragaṭita aṃśa kalā kapilādi
gopini kauṃ nita neṃma prema pada paṃkaja jala kamalādi
rādhā dṛsṭi sṛṣṭi suṃdari kī varanata jaidevādi
mathurā maṃḍala ke jādava kula ati aṣaṃḍa devādi
dvādasa vana me tilu tilu [dharanī][53] *mukti tīratha gaṃgādi*
kṛṣṇa janma acalā na calai jauṃ hohi pralai manvādi
giri gahavara vīthī rati rana meṃ kālīṃdī salitādi
sahaja mādhurī moda vinoda sudhā sāgara lalitādi

savai saṃta sevata niravaira niraṣa[54] *māyā nāsādi*
seṣa aseṣa pāra nahī pāvata gavata suka vyāsādi

Vrindāban comes always at the beginning of everything![55]
Where the treasure of *rasa*, the treasure of joy, resides eternally, without beginning, without end.
[It is the place of] refuge with the fair and the dark one, [it is] a reliever of pain, its roots and tubers are primeval sacred grass.
[Its] parrots, cuckoos, peacocks, ruddy geese, deer, pigeons, and fawns, are (connoisseurs of music) Sanaka and his brothers,[56]
[Its] worms and moths, birds, lions, and monkeys are present there as primeval progenitors.[57]
[Its] trees, grassblades, and shrubs are wishing-trees, [its] cows are cows of plenty, [its] bulls are primeval dharma.[58]
Manifested from Mohana's mind are partial and minute [*āṃśa* and *kalā avatāras*], beginning with Kapila.[59]
For the Gopīs, the eternal rule is that of love, the water of [their] lotus-feet [drinks / gave rise to] Kamalā, et cetera.[60]
[From] the vision of Rādhā came the creation of beautiful women, Jayadeva was the first to describe [this].
The clan of the Yādavas in the area around Mathurā is utterly indestructible, they are foremost gods.[61]
Every grain of earth of the twelve woods is a cause of enlightenment (*mukti*), a crossing to spirituality (*tīrtha*), [like] the river Ganges.[62]
The earth of the birth place of Kṛṣṇa, does not move when Manu's subsequent universes will dissolve.[63]
[With its] mountains and overgrown paths in the arena of love, the Kālindī is the primeval river.
Natural sweetness, mirth and merriment, from the ocean of nectar [which taste] Lalitā and the other girlfriends.
Each and every holy man worships without enmity, realizing that *māyā* is the beginning of ruin.
The inexhaustible Śeṣa [with his thousand tongues][64] is unable to fathom about what Śuka and Vyāsa were the first to sing.

This is nearly a theological manifesto, proclaiming Vrindāban the first principle, the basis of everything. Part of it is clearly derived from traditional *tīrtha-māhātmya* formulae. As with such *māhātmyas*, what we see at work here is a process of identity formation. Vyās is engaged in a one-upmanship with more traditional orthodox Vaiṣṇava models.

Whatever the traditional Hindu cosmology might say is the first principle, Vrindāban came yet before that. Of course, he follows the Gauṛīya Gosvāmīs in stating that Vrindāban is a higher heaven than Viṣṇu's Vaikuṇṭha: *dhani dhani vṛṃdāvana kī dharani, adhika koṭi vaikuṃṭha loka teṃ śuka nārada muni varani* (V40 = J32), 'Blessed, blessed is the earth of Vrindāban, worth more than zillions of Vaikuṇṭhas, described by Śuka and Nārada the sage.'[65]

What is more important, Vyās states that all aspects of Vrindāban are more powerful than the traditional paraphernalia of brahminical ritualism: *rasika anaṃnya hamārī jāti, ... sevā vidhi niṣedha jaṛa saṃgati vṛtti sadā vṛṃdāvana vāsa, sumṛti bhāgavata kṛṣṇa nāma saṃdhyā tarpana gāyatrī jāpa, vaṃśī riṣi jajamāna kalapataru vyāsa na deta asīsa sarāpa* (V93 = J232 = G22 = M10), 'My caste is that of exclusive devotees ... Service is my moral dictum, the basis is good company, my method consists of uninterrupted residence in Vrindāban. My *smṛti* is the *Bhāgavata*, my *sandhyā*-libation formula is the name Kṛṣṇa, my *gāyatrī* is its rosary. (Kṛṣṇa's) flute functions as a seer, for sponsor I have the wishing tree. Vyās does not bless nor curse.' He is reacting against orthodox brahminical praxes, possibly of the type he had followed earlier in his life, given his caste. Such 'more orthodox than thou' poems seem to confirm at first glance brahminical practices, but in fact they undermine them by providing 'easy substitutes' and shifting the attention from ritual purity to loving devotion, a characteristic of *bhakti* in general.

This polemical attitude points to the fact that Vyās must have faced some opposition to his beliefs and praxes, in particular his settling in Vrindāban. This opposition probably came from caste or family members, or both. As we shall see, the hagiographers have worked out such incidents, but this also appears to be the case in Vyās's poetry: *garajatu hoṃ nāhina naikau ḍaru, aura sahāu karata haiṃ merau śrī gopāla dhuraṃdharu ... jāti pāṃti vallabha kula mereṃ vṛṃdāvana sācau gharu* (V238 = J104), 'I rave, but I am not afraid in the least. They are looking for another (means of) support, but I have the mighty Gopāl ... My caste and commensual group is the family of my beloved, my true house is Vrindāban.'

The green, green grass: Vrindāban as escape valve from moral corruption

In several of the poems already quoted, we find another reason for Vrindāban's importance: it provides, so to speak, an escape valve from the woes of existence. Vyās, like many of his contemporaries,[66] stresses that Vrindāban is transcendent, eternally fresh and green, above the grasp of time: *chavīlī vṛṃdāvana kī dharani, sadā harita suṣa bharita mohanī mohana parasata karani* (V41 = J33), 'The wonderful earth of Vrindāban. Always green, bursting with joy, touched by the hands of the Enchanter and the Enchantress'; *māyākāla rahita nita nautana sadā phūla phala pāta* (V42 = J30), 'Eternally devoid of illusion, always fresh flowers, fruit, leaves'; *rahi mana vṛṃdāvana kī sarana ... tarunī taruna pratāpa cāṃpa vala kāla [vy]āla kau ḍara na* (V261 = J79, also J87), 'Remain, o heart, in the shelter of Vrindāban. By the power of the powerful imprints of the tender young lady and man, there is no fear of the serpent of time'; *māyā kāla rahita vṛṃdāvana rasikani kī rajadhānī* (V43 = J41), 'Devoid of illusion and time is Vrindāban, the capital of the *rasikas*.'

As a consequence, in Vrindāban mundane concerns do not apply. Vyās says explicitly, in an apparently quite popular poem, *anaṃnyani kauṃna kī paravāhi ... śrī vṛṃdāvana ke deṣata bhāgeṃ nainani kī haravāhi* (V94 = J235 = G21 = M9), 'What would the exclusively devoted care about anything? ... [Merely] beholding Vrindāban has chased the lightness from their eyes.' In fact, living in Vrindāban will automatically bring about good side effects, such as the extinction of ignorance and duality: *śrī vṛṃdāvana sācau hai jākaiṃ, viṣaī viṣai bhiṣārī dātā nikaṭa na āvai tākaiṃ ... aisaiṃ hī rasasiṃdhu magana bhayeṃ rahai avidyā kākaiṃ* (V99 = J94), 'Those who hold holy Vrindāban true, are not touched by the sensual or senses, by beggar or patron ... Continually drenched in such an ocean of *rasa*, what room do they have for ignorance?' There simply is no need to look for anything elsewhere: *jau pai vṛṃdāvana dhana bhāvai, tau kata svāratha paramāratha lagi mūṃḍha manahi dairāvai* (V120 = J227), 'Once [you] like the wealth of Vrindāban, where, for the sake of immediate or higher goal, would [you] direct [your] mind, [like] a fool?' Vyās makes this clear also in a poem where he equates worldly concerns and goals with aspects of Vrindāban, that is, sacred space subsumes all secular goals: *hamāreṃ vṛṃdāvana vyauṃhāra, saṃpati gati vriṃdāvana mereṃ karama dharma karatāra*[66] *... sarvasu vyāsadāsa kauṃ vanahai vṛṃdāvanahi abhāra* (V91 = J230), 'I only have business with Vrindāban. Vrindāban is my my wealth and my goal, my karma and dharma, my maker ... It has become Vyās's each and everything, Vrindāban is what he depends on.'

In some poems, Vyās sets up an antagonism between the 'wealth' of Vrindāban and that of the world: *vṛṃdāvana sāṃcau dhana bhaiyā, kanaka kūṭa*[67] *koṭika lagi tajīyai bhajīyai kuvara kanhaiyā* (V176 = J88), 'Vrindāban is the true treasure, brother. Leave behind zillions of golden mountain tops and sing in praise of young Kanhaiyā,' and *ava maiṃ vṛṃdāvana dhana pāyau ... sūtoṃ hutoṃ viṣaiṃ maṃdira meṃ śrī guru ṭeri jagāyau* (V231 = J2), 'Now I have obtained the wealth of Vrindāban ... I was sleeping in the temple of the senses, but the venerable guru has called out and woken me up.'

Vrindāban is a haven for those fleeing from the corruption of the material world. Vyās speaks of Vrindāban's power to extinguish the burning questions of the human condition: *tahāṃ vyāsi vasi tāpa vujhāyau aṃtarahita kī jarani* (V40 = J32), 'By settling there, Vyāsi [note the feminine ending] doused the burning, the fire of his entrails / the secret fire.' In an autobiographical poem, which is not attested in J, Vyās actually gives this power of the sacred place as the reason he came to Vrindāban: *mosauṃ patita na anata samāi, yāhī teṃ maiṃ vṛṃdāvana kau sarana gahyau hai āi* (281), 'Nowhere else would a sinner like me fit. For that reason I have come here and held on to refuge in Vrindāban.' And elsewhere, he seems to encourage himself to stick with that plan: *mana tū vriṃdāvana ke māraga lāga, tereṃ na kou [na]*[69] *tūṃ kāhū kau māyā moha taja bhāga, yaha kalakāla vyāla viṣa bhoyau jagu soyau tū jāga ... vyāsa āsa kara rādhāvara*[70] *kī vrajavāsina ke kaurā māṃgu* (V254 = J74[71]), 'O my heart, stick to the path to Vrindāban. You don't have anyone of your own, nor do you belong with anyone: give up illusion and delusion and flee. Drenched with the poison of this snake of Kali times, everyone is asleep, you should wake up ... Vyās is aspiring to Rādhā's groom, begging crumbs from the residents of Braj.'

Paradise Lost

Notwithstanding all this praise, Vyās was not so idealistic that he would fail to notice how corruption had entered his pristine paradise. After the reassurances of Vrindāban's timeless status that I have just quoted, it may seem a contradiction when Vyās complains about what has happened to the mundane Vrindāban in the following poem:

V293 = J192

ava sāṃhī kalijuga āyau
pūta na kahyau pitā kau mānata karata āpanom[72] *bhāyau*
veṭī vecata saṃka na mānata dina dina molu vaṛhāyau
yā teṃ varaṣā maṃda hoti hai puṃnya teṃ pāpu savāyau[73]
mathurā ṣudati kaṭatu vṛṃdāvana munijana socu upāyau[74]
itanoṃ duṣu sahive ke kājeṃ kāhe kau vyāsu jivāyau

Now Kali has really arrived:
Sons don't obey their father's advice, they do as they please.
Selling their daughters, they have no scruples, prices rise daily!
For that reason the rains have been slow: sin has doubled compared to virtue!
Mathurā uprooted, Vrindāban destroyed, holy men inspire distress.
So much sorrow to endure! Why was Vyās allowed to remain alive?[75]

Gone is timeless Vrindāban! This poem is a realistic and pessimistic view of the times. It may refer to historical events, perhaps to the time of the political unrest marking the beginning of the Mughal dynasty and the Sher Shah interlude, which caused a substantial amount of anarchy and fighting in the Braj region.[76] There seems also to be an autobiographical element to this poem. Apparently, Vyās brought his family to live with him in Vrindāban, but his children, who did not heed their father's ways, disappointed him. Alternatively, one may read this more as a general statement about the climate of the times. Similarly, in yet another poem, Vyās complains that most people love their in-laws better than saints: *hari bhaktani teṃ samadhī pyāre* V295 = J194.[77]

PARADISE ABANDONED: TRAITORS CONDEMNED

Vyās decries openly the corruption invading his sacred space, without sparing the holy men there present. Here, Vyās makes it clear again who belongs to his 'in-group,' who are the true devotees, and who are 'out.' Clearly, those who leave Vrindāban are traitors in his eyes. Vyās says:

V54 = J220 = G2 = M21

śrī vṛṃdāvana ke rūṣa hamāre māta pitā suta vaṃdhu[78]
guru goviṃda sādhu gati mati suṣa phala phūlani kau gaṃdha
inahi pīṭhi dai anata dīṭhi karaiṃ so aṃdhani meṃ aṃdha
vāsa inahi chāṃḍai ru chuḍāvai tākau paraiṃ nikaṃdha[79]

The trees of Vrindāban are my mother, father, sons, kinsmen.
[My] mind and ways [are directed to] Guru Govinda and sādhus, [my] joy is in the smell of [Vrindāban's] fruit and flowers.
Those who turn away and set their goals elsewhere are the blindest among the blind.
Vyās says: those who leave or make others leave [Vrindāban] should be uprooted themselves![80]

Interestingly, one of the hagiographers, Nāgrīdās, has quoted this poem and read into it an existential crisis in Vyās's life, but it could also be read more generally as Vyās's anger with his less single-minded fellow *bhaktas* (I discuss this further below).

To some extent such utterances may be formulaic, part and parcel of the *māhātmya* tradition. Compare, for example, the above with the following verse shared by *Varāha* and *Skanda*: *Purāṇas: mathurāṃ tu parityajya yo'nyatra kurute ratim (matim), mūṛho bhramati saṃsāre mohito mama māyayā.*[81] 'The fool who abandons Mathurā and delights in other places wanders from birth to birth deluded by my power of illusion.' Yet Vyās sounds genuinely anguished. He does not spare his breath about those 'traitors': *[s]udhāryau hari merau paraloka, [śrī] vṛṃdāvana maiṃ kīnauṃ dīnauṃ hari apanoṃ nija oka ... carana dhūri mereṃ sira melī aura savani dai roka, te nara rākasa kūkara gadahāūṃṭa vṛṣabha gaja voka, vyāsa ju vṛṃdāvana taji bhaṭakata tā sira panhī ṭhoka* (V236 = J103), 'Hari has updated my heaven. In holy Vrindāban he has given me a dwelling place, he made me his own ... He has let me rub my face in the dust of His feet, but stopped all others. Those men are demons, dogs, donkeys, camels, bulls, elephants, goats, says Vyās, who leave Vrindāban and roam elsewhere. A kick with [my] shoe on their head!'

Similarly: *kara mana vriṃdāvana sauṃ heta, ... śrī vriṃdāvana taja je suṣa cāhata teī rākasa preta* (V259 = J7781), 'O my heart, love Vrindāban ... Those who leave Vrindāban in search for happiness are demons and ghosts.' And: *aisau vṛṃdāvana mohi saranai ... [ra]sika ananyani mohana vana teṃ [a]nata kahū nahi ṭaranai, vyāsa dharma taji bhakti gahī tāhū taji narkahi paranai* (V273 = J86), 'Such a Vrindāban is my refuge ... Exclusive devotees do not ever pass through the woods of Mohan to elsewhere. Vyās, those who left *dharma* for *bhakti*, and now give up *bhakti*, surely fall into hell.'

Apparently, this was a topic close to Vyās's heart, on which he must have sermonized on several occasions. Staying on in Vrindāban becomes a defining feature of the 'in-group':

V87 = J150

śrī vṛṃdāvanu na tajai adhikārī
jāke mana paratīti rīti nahi tāke vasa na vihārī
kaiseṃ jārahi bhajihai tajihai bhartārahi kula nārī
bhāgī bhakti lobha ke āgaiṃ maṃtrī ḍoṃma bhiṣārī
ko ko bhayau na para ghara haruvo tāta lajī mahatārī

mālahi pahiri gupalahi chāḍatu gurahi divāvata gārī
jyau gajakuṃbha vidārai siṃgha vālaka jhapaṭai jyau lyārī
aiseṃ vyāsa sūra kāyara kī saṃgati hari karī nyārī

Those who are qualified don't leave Vrindāban.
If there is no habit of faith in [your] mind, Bihārī does not come in [your] power.
How could a woman serve her lover and give up her true husband if she is noble?
Devotion flees when confronted with greed, in minister, low-caste, beggar.
So many left their own family, made their dad upset,[83] their mother ashamed.
With the mālā on their neck they give up Gopāla! So their guru becomes subject of slander.
Like when the elephant's lobe crushes the lion, the wolf pounces on the child,
So, says Vyās, Hari keeps aloof the hero from the company of cowards.

And yet elsewhere, Vyās makes a vehement plea to stay in Vrindāban, with definitions of the *ananya rasika* and the traitor (*vyabhicārī*):

V92 = J233

jāki upāsanā, tāhī kī vāsanā, tāhī kau nāma rūpa guna gāīyai
yahai ananya dharma paripāṭī vṛṃdāvana vasi ananta na jāīyai
soī vivicārī āna kahai āna karai tāko muṣu deṣai dāruna duṣu pāīyai
vyāsa hoi upahāsa trāsa kīyai āsa akṣata kita dāsa kahāīyai

The One you worship, is the One to desire, the One whose name, beauty and qualities you should sing.
This is the program of exclusive religion: stay in Vrindāban and don't go elsewhere.
This is a trespasser: who says one thing, but acts differently. If you as much as look at him, you're destined for sorrow.
Vyās says: 'You can mock and threaten, but with your lust intact,[84] how can you get approved as a servant [of God]?'

At this point one wonders if Vyās had in mind anyone in particular in the Vrindāban scene. A clue can be found in another poem, where he explicitly laments devotees occupied with promotion tours in Bengal and Gujarat: *bhaṭakata phirata gaura gujarāta* (V133 = J167), 'They ramble and roam in Bengal and Gujarat,'[85] and *sādhata vairāgī jaḍa vaṃga* (V138 = J191), 'Ascetics are worshipping, devoid of sense, in Bengal.'[86] One is tempted to read these as allusions to the trips to Gujarat to win disciples of Vallabha's successors Gopīnāth and in particular Viṭṭhalnāth,[87] and the efforts in Bengal of the Gauṛīyas, such as Jīva Gosvāmī's disciples, who became missionaries for the teachings of the six Gosvāmīs from the 1580s.[88] It seems highly likely, indeed, that Vyās lived to see such developments and disapproved of them. However, rather than trying to pinpoint the specifics of the people involved, suffice it to say that, in general, Vyās despised those who gave up true *bhakti* for commercial gain.

Paradise vended: hypocrites demasked

Nearly as bad as those 'leavers,' in Vyās's eyes, are the hypocrites who stay in Vrindāban and pretend to be *bhaktas* but are really after money. Vyās shows himself to be quite a realist and sceptic here. In such poems, Vyās sounds nearly 'Kabirian' in his strong reproach. In several poems, he lashes out against those who 'sell God in the market': *guru goviṃdahi vecata hāṭa* (V128 = J196), 'They hawk guru and Govinda in the market.'[89] The following poem is more clearly directed against the new settlers in Braj: *ava hama hūṃ se bhakta kahāvata, mālā tilaka svāgu dhari hari kau nāmu veṃci dhanu lyāvata ... kīyau akāju vyāsa kau āṃsā vana hī meṃ ghara chāvata* (V280 = J156 = M16), 'Now they would have me too call them a *bhakta*. They've donned the rosary and *tilaka* as disguise. Selling God's name they reap wealth ... They've ruined the hopes of Vyās, thatching their houses here in these woods.'[90] *Or, dharma duryau kali daiya diṣāī ... dāna laina koṃ vaḍe pātakī macalana koṃ vahmanāī ... upadesana kauṃ gurū gusāṃī ācaranaiṃ adhamāī* (V129 = J190), 'Obscuring *dharma* Kali shows its splendour[91] ... Great sinners, [to qualify] for receiving gifts. Brahminhood used for extortion ... For instruction [they play] 'Guru' and 'Gosvāmī,' but in their behaviour: plain meanness!'

As we saw before, even Vyās's own family let him down in this respect. He complains in self-reproach, to the point that he wonders by what grace he has deserved to live in Vrindāban: *hamāre ghara kī bhakti ghaṭī, upaje nātī pūta vahirmuṣa vigarī savai gaṭī, suta jo bhakta na bhayo tau va pitā kī garī kaṭī ... kihi kārana hari vyāsahi dīnī vṛṃdāvanahi taṭī* (V288 = J158 = G 27[92]), 'The devotion of my house has gone downhill. Infidel sons and grandsons were born, all ties are spoilt. If a son does not become a devotee, then he has as much as cut his father's neck ... For what reason has God granted Vyās a foot ashore in Vrindāban?'

In another poem, which deserves to be quoted in full, Vyās is even more belligerent:

V136 = J186

kahā bhayau vṛṃdāvanahi vaseṃ
jau lagi vyāpati māyā tau lagi kaha ghara teṃ nikaseṃ
dhana mevā kau maṃdira sevā karata koṭharī viṣai raseṃ
koṭi koṭi daṃḍavata kareṃ kaha bhūmi lalāṭa ghaseṃ
muṃha mīṭhe mana sīṭhe kapaṭī vacana (racana)[93] *neṃnani vihaseṃ*
maṃtra ṭhagorī kavahū na taṃtra gada mānata viṣaya ḍaseṃ
kaṃcana hātha na chūvata kamaṃḍala meṃ milāi vilaseṃ
vyāsa lobha rati hari haridāsani paramārathahi ṣaseṃ

So they settled in Vrindāban, so what?
As long as illusion has a hold on them, what did they accomplish by leaving their homes?
Serving in temples for money and delicacies,[94] enjoying themselves in brothels!
Let them do zillions of prostrations, what's gained by rubbing the ground with their forehead?
Their tongues are sweet, but their hearts are sour,[95] crafting treacherous words with a smirk in the eyes.
Their mantras for witchcraft, no way they'd regard Tantra as poison, [even] when stung by the senses!
They don't touch gold with their hands ... but merrily catch it in their begging bowl!
Vyās says: in their greed and lust, those 'Devotees of Hari,' let Hari, the highest good, slip away.

What seems to have bothered Vyās most is that in all the zeal of recruiting followers for the new creed, the original message got lost. Sectarian rivalry ate at the fundamentals of the message of love that *bhakti* was supposed to bring. Vyās frequently voices his protest to sectarian narrow-mindedness:

V142 = J176

jaisī bhakti bhāgavata varanī
taisī virale jānata mānata kaṭhina rahani taiṃ karanī
svāmī bhaṭṭa gusāṃī aginita mati kari gati ācaranī
prīti paraspara karata na kavahūṃ miṭai na hiya kī jaranī
dhana kārana sādhana kari hari para dhari sevā vana dharanī

viṣai vāsanā gaī na ajahū chāḍi vigūce gharanī
sahaja [pr]īti vinā paratīti na sisnodara kī bharanī
vyāsa āsa jauṃ lagi hai tau lagi hari vinu duṣu jīya bharanī

The devotion described in *Bhāgavata (Purāṇa)*,
Is known by few, and observed [by few]: it's tough to enact its way of life.
Countless Svāmīs, Bhaṭṭas, Gosvāmīs have philosophized on method and goal,
But never shall they love one another! The fire in their heart just doesn't get doused.
For wealth they foist devotion on Hari, and install worship on the earth of the bushes.
Even so their sensual desires haven't stopped, though they left their wife with trouble.[96]
Without spontaneous love, there is no belief, only stomach and penis get their full!
Vyās says, as long as there is desire, there is no Hari, and all you'll get your full of is suffering.

Devotion has become a sham for money, sectarian zeal has replaced the passionate love for God of the first generation of settlers in Vrindāban:

V144 = J181:

gāvata nācata ava tu lobha kaha
yāhī teṃ anurāga na upajatu rāga vairāga sova kaha
maṃtra jaṃtra paḍhi meli ṭhagaurī vasa kīno saṃsāru
svāmī vahuta gusāī aginita bhaṭṭani pe na uvāru
bhāva vinā sava vilavilāta arū kilikalā[ta] kari tehū
vyāsa rādhikā ravana kṛpā vinu kahū na sahaja sanehū

They arrive singing and dancing, but now out of greed!
No devotion can emerge from such (praxis), their passion and penance is all for show.
They read *mantra-yantra*, get involved with magic. It's the world that has them in its power![97]
Lots of Svāmīs, countless Gosvāmīs, even from Bhaṭṭas there is no release to be had.
Devoid of emotion, they're all just wailing, and cheering for selfish anger.[98]
Vyās says: without the grace of Rādhikā's enchanter, there never can be true love

In some poems, Vyās seems to put his finger on the cause of the 'decadence' of Vrindāban and especially this sectarian quibbling. It may well be that sectarian squabbles were caused by rivalry in seeking sponsorship from royals: *bhakta ṭhāḍhe bhūpani ke dvāra ... caṃdana mālā syāma vaṃdanī dai ulaṭe u[pa]hāra, vyāsa āsa lagi naṭa vādara jyoṃ nācata desa utāra* (V131 = J169), 'Devotees are knocking on the doors of kings ... Their sandalwood, initiation rosary, and black powder when provided are a poisonous gift. Vyās says out of greed they dance like acrobats and monkeys, to the ruin of the country.'

In some songs, it sounds like Vyās would prefer to put up a sign at the borders of Vrindāban, saying 'Kings not allowed,' and back it up with action: *anaṃnyani kauṃna kī paravāhi ... rījhata jāhi rājasī java tava mārata pāthara vāhi* (V94 = J235 = G 21 = M9), 'What cares do *ananyas* have? ... Whenever a pompous king[99] is attracted to anyone, he [chases him out by] throwing stones.' Vrindāban is of course in Vyās's eyes the capital of capitals, with its own king and queen: Kṛṣṇa and Rādhā.[100] This gives an interesting extra dimension to the sacred place being imagined in terms of worldly power. Vyās, it could be argued, uses the feudal metaphor to subvert the actual institution.

What Vyās Does Not Say

It is interesting here to point out what Vyās does not say and what he neglects to mention. First, there are places in Braj that hold no interest for Vyās. For instance, there is no reference of Rādhākuṇḍ anywhere in Vyās's poetry, which is quite surprising given the Gauṛīya activities there at the time. Vyās refers to 'Mānsarovar,' but it is not clear if he is referring to a site in Braj (for example, in *Rās-pañcādhyāyī* 26.3a, it is part of the *maṇḍala* of the Rāsa dance). Vyās does not often mention Barsānā, either. When he does, he seems to see it mainly as a mythical place, rather than as a spot on the map, since all occurrences are in connection with poems praising Rādhā: *dhani terī mātā jini tū jāī, vraja naresa vrasabhāṃna dhaṃni jihi nāgari kuvari ṣilāī, ... dhani varasānau haripura hū teṃ tākī vahuta vaḍāī* (V79 = J62), 'Blessed your mother who gave birth to you. Blessed the king of Braj, Vriśabhānu, who raised the clever young lady ... Blessed Barsānā, which is even greater than Haripur,'[101] and *kula devī rādhā varasānau ṣerau vrajavāsini so pāṃti* (V93 = J232 = G22 = M10), 'My family deity is Rādhā, my village is Barsānā, my commensual group are the residents of Braj.' (A few other occurrences in V are not attested in J.)

In his interpretation of Vrindāban as sacred space, there are again elements that might be expected but that are left out. Vyās never connects the sacred place with the physiology of the human body in Tantric fashion. Although he speaks of the Rāsa dance of Rādhā and Kṛṣṇa as a *maṇḍala* (in his *Rās-pañcādhyāyī* 26,[102] and also in several poems, V624 = J544, V635 = J556, V639 = J560, V640 = J561, V675 = J594), he does not explicitly apply this to the geographical site of Vrindāban.

Vyās does make use of the term *alaukika* only once, but not as a theoretical statement: *phūlata doū jhūlata ḍola, racyau alaukika kautika nirașita rati pati dījatu vola* (V661 = J580), 'Bristling with joy the couple is swinging on the swing, observing the transcendental joy they created, Rati's husband (Kāmadeva) looks for shelter.'[103] Similarly, Vyās does not seem interested in the theological concepts of *prakaṭa* and *aprakaṭa līlā*, although he uses the terms, mostly in a non-technical sense: *śrī vṛṃdāvana pragaṭa sadā suṣa ceṃna* (V46 = J35), 'Holy Vrindāban is manifest eternal abode of bliss'; *volāi laiṃu hoṃ vṛṃdāvana kī ... viṭapa veli prati keli pragaṭa* (V47 = J40), 'I surrender to Vrindāban ... Their play manifest in each creeper wound around a tree.' The term is also used for the birth of Rādhā and Kṛṣṇa: 'they became manifest.' The only other instances where the term is used are: *tahāṃ pragaṭī naṭanāgari ṣelati rati sauṃ rati pachitāi ...* (V360 = J309), 'There the dancer and his clever lady make their play manifest, the goddess of Passion (Rati) herself envies such passion'; and *rati rasa subhaga suṣada jamunāṃ taṭa, nava nava prema pragaṭa vraṃdāvana viharata kuvara nāgari nāgara naṭa* (V667 = J586), 'The flavour of passion, beautiful and charming, on the banks of the Yamunā. Ever-new love, manifest in Vrindāban, the clever young lady is sporting with the expert dancer.'

Surprisingly, witnessing the corruption taking hold of his environment does not make Vyās turn to seek 'Vrindāban in the heart.' Maybe he was too involved with the pioneering movement to be engaged in the reversal, the 'negation of localization.'[104] Though there are certain affinities between Vyās and Kabīr, here is one of the points where they part company. Kabīr lived in Benares, a place established for centuries. Naturally his major task is radical opposition to all the abuses that come with routinized sacred space. Vyās is still enthusiastically involved with the discovery of sacred space, and though he recognizes the abuses, he cannot quite shake off the original enthusiastic message.

To summarize Vyās's ideas on sacred space: his poems speak of his dedication to life in Vrindāban and disgust for those who would leave the place or abuse it for commercial purposes. Notwithstanding his reservations about sectarian demarcation, Vyās himself was actively involved in setting up boundaries between the 'in-group' and the 'others.' The 'in-group' consisted of a whole raft of *bhaktas* of times past and present, in particular, the connoisseurs or *ananya rasikas*, especially Haridās and Hit Harivaṃś. The 'others' as I have shown elsewhere, are called *śākta*.[104] In connection with sacred space, the outsiders are those who defile it by their commercial transactions or do not appreciate its value fully and leave it for other places. For Vyās, the 'other' was everyone who was not *ananya* or 'exclusive,' literally, 'without other.' Had Vyās been into designing slogans for bumper stickers, he might have quipped: If you have an 'other,' you are the 'other' (*hoi tumharo anya, na bhayau ananya*).

The Hagiographies

Having outlined Vyās's ideas on sacred space, in this section I outline how Vyās's hagiographers dealt with his interpretation of sacred space. For convenience's sake, I provide a chronologically organized overview of the hagiographical literature about Vyās in table 1. Obviously, I cannot deal with all hagiographies, so will focus on those that comment in an interesting way on Vyās's perspective on sacred space. I discuss cases of sectarian appropriation and instances where hagiographers have linked up the issue with two favourite hagiographical *topoi*, namely that of the debate between pandit and *bhakta* and between saint and king.

Table 1. Hagiographies on Vyās

DATE	AUTHOR	WORK and REFERENCE
late 16th C?	Bihāriṇīdās	(*Aṣṭācāryoṃ kī Vāṇī*), 305–6[106]
end 16th C?	Nābhādās	*Bhakt-māl* 92(87)[107]
fl. 1593–1641	Dhruvdās	*Bhakti-nāmāvalī* 41–43[108]
ca. 1650	Bhagvatmudit?	*Rasik-ananya-māl, paracaī* 2[109]
ca. 1680	Uttamdās	*Rasik-māl, prasaṃga* 4[110]
1712	Priyādās	*Bhakti-ras-bodhinī* 368–73[111]
1718	Priyādās	*Bhakti-sumariṇī* 106[112]
?	Priyādās	*Ananya-modinī* 50–3[113]
1720	Rāghavdās	*Bhakt-māl* 288–9 (256 – 257)[114]
1676 – 1766?	Lalitkiśorīdev	(*Aṣṭācāryoṃ kī Vāṇī*), 353–61[115]
ca. 1750	Lāldās or Bābā Kṛṣṇadās	*Baṃglā bhakt-māl, caritra* 100[116]

fl. 1723-64	Nāgrīdās	*Pad-prasaṃg-mālā, prasaṃga* 27–35[117]
ca. 1750	Kiśordās	*Nij-mat-siddhānta, madhya khaṇḍa* 235–48, 358–59[118]
1770-90?	Bhagvatrasik	*ananya-niścayātmak-granth* 8, 36, 38[119]
1800?	Caturdās	*Ṭīkā on RbhM* 393–98 (389 – 94)[120]
fl. 1821-37	Sahacarīśaraṇ	*Lalit-prakaś (pūrvārddha)* 185–241[121]
pre-1843	Gopālkavi	*Vṛndāvan-dhām-anurāgāvalī, adhyayana* 16–17[122]
1846	Raghurājsiṃh	*Rām-rasikāvalī, adhyāya* 56[123]
1892	Pratītrāy Lakṣmaṇa Siṃh	*Lokendra-brajotsav* 157–93[124]

Visions of Vrindāban: Sectarian Appropriation by Rādhāvallabhans

As we have seen, inter-sectarian rivalry had already started in Vyās's time, and he himself spoke out virulently against this. Ironically, by the middle of the seventeenth century, Vyās himself had become the focus of such squabbles. Unlike Hit Harivaṃś and Svāmī Haridās, no sectarian movement grew up around Vyās, yet he was later claimed by several sects. Vyās was famous enough to attract the attention of hagiographers eager to 'beef up' the prestige of their own sect by counting Vyās among the disciples of their founder-guru. The first to stake their claim on Vyās were the followers of Hit Harivaṃś, the Rādhāvallabhans. Their claim is the best-known, but other sects were to follow suit, notably the Mādhva-Gauṛīyas[125] (whom I do not discuss here, since there is not much of interest about sacred space in their writings) and to some extent the Haridāsīs (see 'Visions of Vrindāban' and 'Sectarian Perspective...' below).

The first work expressing the Rādhāvallabhī claim is *RAM*. A whole chapter (*paracaī*) is devoted to building up carefully the story of Vyās's initiation by Hit Harivaṃś. This work is usually ascribed to Bhagvatmudit,[126] who was apparently initiated into the Gauṛīya-sampradāya.[127] Bhagvatmudit's affiliation with a different sect is cited by the Rādhāvallabhans as proof of the neutrality of the work. They argue that the initiation by Harivaṃś must be true if someone from the rival sect affirms it. Yet *RAM* obviously has the intention of establishing the Harivaṃś's priority, either directly or indirectly. It describes only followers of Harivaṃś. The latter is praised in an introductory Dohā at the beginning of every chapter (*paracaī*), and only the dedication (*mañgalācaraṇa*) and, significantly, the introduction to the chapter about Vyās, mention Caitanya.[128]

For our purposes, it is interesting to see how sacred place is interpreted in a sectarian sense. First, *RAM* ascribes the reason for Vyās's traveling to Vrindāban to the influence of Hit Harivaṃś. Vyās is described as residing in Orcchā, and in order to bring about the contact between Vyās and his future guru, the author brings on stage a liaison, a follower of Harivaṃś, Navaldās (whose own life story is described in a later chapter of *RAM*). Navaldās visits Vyās and entertains him with a song by Harivaṃś, which has the desired impact on Vyās (RAM 12–17 and Dohā). The hagiographer makes it clear that it is upon hearing the song describing the beauty of Rādhā and Kṛṣṇa by Harivaṃś and on Navaldās's explicit command (*cali vṛndāvana darśana kīje, RAM* 19) that Vyās goes to Vrindāban. Right from the beginning of the chapter, sectarian identity formation is at work: the distinction is set up between *nirguṇa bhaktas*, such as Kabīr, Raidās, and Nāmdev, who command Vyās's respect (see 'Tuning in to the same Wavelength' above) on the one hand, and Hit Harivaṃś, who is associated with Vrindāban, on the other.[129]

Next, Vyās's decision to stay in Vrindāban is attributed to the influence of Harivaṃś. What follows is the heart of the sectarian argument: a conversion episode. This is portrayed as a debate between a learned pandit (Vyās) and a simple but powerful devotee (Harivaṃś). The outcome is, of course, in favour of the latter and this is dramatically underlined by Vyās's immersing his books he had brought for debate in the Yamunā (*RAM* 34), a symbolic farewell to his old life of erudition.

Next, the hagiographer turns to how Vyās organized his new life, once he decided to settle in Vrindāban. The hagiographer models this new lifestyle on that of Harivaṃś, implying that Vyās copied Harivaṃś's adoration of the divine couple (*jugala upāsanā*) and his way of relishing (*rasa rīti*) (*RAM* 35), as well as the celebrating of the Rāsa Līlā (round dance of Kṛṣṇa and the Gopīs or the staging of the miracle plays of that name) (*RAM* 36). The hagiographer is more explicit while describing Vyās's worship (*sevā*), which he says was according to the tradition of Hit (*hita paddhati*) (*RAM* 39). Furthermore, he says that in Vyās's shrine Rādhā was symbolically represented by a cushion or throne (*gādī*) (*RAM* 38), as is the case in the Rādhāvallabha temple founded by Harivaṃś. The discovery of Vyās's image (*mūrti*) is also ascribed to the grace of Harivaṃś (*RAM* 40).[130] The phrasing in this part of *RAM* is often reminiscent of Nābhādās's *Bhakt-māl*.[131] Since the latter work must have been familiar to the hagiographer's public, it lends the story a more authoritative ring.

Throughout his story, the hagiographer supports his claims either by directly quoting from Vyās's songs or by making indirect reference to them. It is important that only after the initiation by Hit Harivaṃś is Vyās's voice heard. Not surprisingly, nearly all the poems quoted are in some way connected with Hit Harivaṃś. Interesting for our purposes is that of the five poems quoted, two explicitly link the sacred space of Vrindāban with Hit Harivaṃś. This is most evident in the first, a simple poem in praise of Hit Harivaṃś: *namo namo jai śrī harivaṃsa ... namo jayati vṛṃdāvana sahaja mādhurī rāsa vilāsa prasaṃsa* (V10 = J11), 'Hail, hail to and glory to Śrī Harivaṃś. Hail and glory to Vrindāban's natural sweetness, praise to the Rāsa play'; and, *hutau suṣa rasikani kau ādhāra, vinu harivaṃsahiṃ sarasa rīti kau kā pai calihai bhāra ... śrī vṛṃdāvana kī sahaja mādhurī kahihai kauna udāra* (V24 = J24 = G4), 'He was the basis of bliss for the *rasikas*. Without Harivaṃś, who will take the responsibility of promoting the sensuous ways ... Who will be so generous as to reveal holy Vrindāban's natural beauty?' Here Vyās ascribes to Harivaṃś a power to reveal the secrets of the supra-mundane Vrindāban behind the phenomenal one. Singled out on their own, they are used by the hagiographer to support his initiation claim. This is a conscious move, because the author himself points out the importance of 'internal evidence' in the concluding Dohās of *RAM*, where he argues that the words of the disciple (*śiṣya*) must provide final proof in deciding who his guru is (*RAM* second of final Dohās).

What has the hagiographer been up to? Most obviously, he has been concerned to attribute Vyās's love for Vrindāban to Hit Harivaṃś's influence. It is by the grace of Harivaṃś that Vyās first came to Vrindāban and then decided to settle there. We have a clear instance in which sacred space has been submitted to sectarian boundary-formation. In fact, our author has been very successful. As we shall see, several later hagiographers, even those without any sectarian interest, take over the story wholesale, including such authors as the Dādūpanthī Rāghavdās in the eighteenth century (see table 1 for details).

Our hagiographer has been up to more. He has linked the concept of sacred space with the *topos* of the conflict between learning and devotion. Vyās, the pandit, has been transformed into a devotee in the sacred precincts of Braj, and the river Yamunā has washed away his books. I will return in more detail to the link of sacred space with the topos of the conflict of *bhakti* and learning. For the time being, let us look at another example of sectarian appropriation of Vyās's vision of sacred space.

Visions of Vrindāban: Sectarian Appropriation by Haridāsīs

Vyās's *oeuvre* contains several songs in praise of Haridās. Understandably, these songs have always been popular with the Haridāsīs, which some authors saw as an endorsement of the philosophy of their founder-father (Bihārinidās and Lalitkiśorīdev, see table 1). So it should not be a cause of wonder that we find Vyās portrayed as a respectful associate of Haridās in *Nij-mat-siddhānta*, a lengthy prose work from the mid-eighteenth century. This work was authored by Kiśordās, who belonged to the ascetic (*sādhu*) branch of the Haridāsīs and was strongly concerned with apologetics defending his branch against the householder Gosvāmīs.[132]

The context is that of a gathering of devotees around Haridās, where a *kṣatriya* from Lahore approaches him for initiation. Haridās sends the man on to the Gauṛīyas (!) on the grounds that he initiates only ascetics, not householders. But the story goes on to stress Haridās's capacity to provide his devotees with a glimpse of the divine behind the mundane world, which he does in response to a request by Vyās. This passage evokes the *Bhagavadgītā,* where Kṛṣṇa provides Arjuna with a divine eye to behold the magnificent manifestation of his cosmic form.

v. 240

...

vyāsadāsa bole kara jorī, śrīharidāsa lakhau hama orī
yah kṣatrī ātura cali āyo, tākoṃ kahā naina darśāyo
ina adbhuta kīnī astūtī, varṇana kīnī sakala vibhūtī
sabake sunata tattva mukha gāyo, tāke hṛdaya kauna vidhi āyo
so samujhāya kahau saba svāmī, rasika ananya nṛpati nita nāmī
Dohā
srī haridāsa prasanna hvai, haṃsi bole mṛdu vaina
jo una nija dṛga taiṃ lakho, so nirakhau tuma naina

v. 241

jaisaiṃ paradā deta uṭhāī, tyoṃ saba keli dṛgana darśāī
camakata taṛita bhaī tyo jhāṃkī, ghana madhi chipata tāsu vidhi ḍhāṃkī

saba adbhuta nirakhyau sukha sārā, astuti karana lage uccārā
tina tina tāsu samaya mili bhākhī, tākī sunoṃ yathā ratha sākhī
ananya nṛpati śrī svāmī haridās ...
śrī vṛṃdāvana reṇu tana mana bhaja taji loka veda kī trāsa ...

...

v. 242
...

Dohā
sakala rasika nainani lakhyo, śrīharidāsa svarūpa
vyāsa kahata kara jori yaha, aho rasikamaṇi bhūpa

v. 243
maiṃ pratāpa tumharo aba jānyo, mo mana alipada kamala lubhānyo
mo mana maiṃ yaha bhāva pakāsā, tuma sataguru maiṃ tumharo dāsā

v. 240
Vyāsdās said with folded hands, 'Śrī Haridās look [gracefully] in my direction.
This *kṣatriya* has come eagerly, what [have you] shown [before] his eyes?
[You] have sung a wonderful hymn, described the splendour completely.
While all heard it [your] mouth has sung the essence, how can [your technique] find root in his heart?
In order to make us see, tell all that, Svāmī, who in eternity are named the king of the *ananya rasikas.*'
Srī Haridās was satisfied, smilingly, he said: 'What he has seen with his own eyes, look at that with yours.'

v. 241
As if he had lifted a curtain , he showed the whole play [before] their eyes.
A glimpse like lightening, flashing, [then] hiding in the clouds, veiled, in such a way.
All saw the wonderful essence of bliss, and (started to) raise their voices in praise.
All those who were gathered at that moment put it in words.
Listen to the objective evidence of this: [quotation of Vyās's poem V12 = J12]
'Śrī Svāmī Haridās, king of the exclusive devotees ...
Worshiping the holy dust of Vrindāban with body and soul, he left behind

fear of conventional morality ...'
[also quotes from Govindsvāmī]
v. 242 [quotes from Agradās, Nābhādās's *Bhakt-māl]*

...

All *rasikas* had seen Haridās's true manifestation with their own eyes.
Vyās said with joined hands: 'O king of the jewels among the *rasikas,*

v. 243
Now I have come to know your glory, my heart is like a bee, eager for your lotusfeet.
In my heart this feeling is shining forth, that you are the true guru, and I am your servant.'

Like Bhagvatmudit, Kiśordās is eager to portray Vyās in a subservient role vis à vis the founder-father of his own sect. In both cases, sacred space functions prominently in the story. Haridās's ability to reveal the divine behind the ordinary is the cause of Vyas's admiration. Both authors also feel the need to back up their claim with 'proof from the mouth of Vyās': like the Rādhāvallabhan hagiographer, the Haridāsī quotes a song by Vyās which connects Vrindāban with the spiritual authority of the founder-father.

Sacred space: Locus of Debate Between Pandit and Bhakta (Radhavallabhans)

Let us return to the *topos* of the conflict between the *bhakta* and the pandit. This is a favourite one in *bhakti* hagiographies and fits, of course, with the tenets of the *bhakti* movement that logic and philosophy are futile in the light of devotion. Grand debates, so prominent in the hagiographies of great philosophers like Śaṅkara,[133] are irrelevant from the *bhakti* point of view.

So it should not surprise us that the theme does occur in *RAM*, quoted above, and is eagerly picked up by later hagiographies, such as a slightly later Rādhāvallabhan work, Uttamdās's Rasik-māl.[134] This work is inspired by *RAM* in content and in wording, but is much less directly polemical. One reason for this may be that the basic sectarian claim had already been established by *RAM*. The *Rasik-māl prasaṃga*[135] elaborates a bit on the incident:

23. *tina saumṃ caracā kaisai kījai, aba tau carana sarana gahi lījai*
24. *vyāsa bheṭa pada eka caṛhāyau, astuti kara tika maṃtra ju pāyau*
pada vyāsa jū kṛta
namo namo jai śrī harivaṃśa
Caupāī
25. *pothī thokṣī jāni bahāi, kuṃja keli rasa līlā gāī*
26. *īna uni kau arau saṃvāda, liṣau kahā lagi aṃtu na ādi*
27. *śrī rādhā carana muṣya kari jānaiṃ, karma dharma vrata asada visānai*

23. 'How could I have dispute with him? I would better take refuge at his feet.'
24. Vyās composed a pada, and offered this as a gift. Praising him, he also received the mantra.[136] A song composed by Vyās:
'Hail, hail and glory to Śrī Harivaṃṣ' (V10 = J11).
25. Considering his books useless, he set them aflow [in the river]. [All he did was] sing about *līlā* and *rasa* of the bower-sport.
26. The discussion of the former and the latter got stuck,[137] to which extent can I describe it, it has no beginning nor end.
27. Now he recognized Rādhā's feet as the main thing, and action, duty and vows as under the tyranny[138] of untruth.

The incident of immersion of the books in the sacred river, which we have already encountered in *RAM*, provides a powerful dramatization of the basic message that the pandit's approach and the *bhakta's* don't rhyme. The author of *Rasik-māl prasaṃga* also links this antagonism with sacred place. In line 25, the books are contrasted with the bowers (*kuñja*). We could say that, for our author, the library and the bower are spaces at odds. And he does not leave us in doubt about which one he (with Vyās) prefers.

Sacred space: Where the Digvijaya Comes to a Stop

Yet all this contempt for scholarship and debate has not impeded *bhaktas* from going on 'conversion tours,' known as 'world victory tours' or *digvijayas*. And the hagiographers have been only too happy to take up the set piece of *digvijaya* description. A famous example constitutes the tours of Vallabha according to the *Caurāsī-baiṭhak-caritra*.

This theme is also picked up by Vyās's hagiographers, who tend to combine it with the story of Vyās's conversion by Harivaṃś. This is the case in a mid-eighteenth-century prose hagiography, *Pad-prasaṃg-mālā* (*PPM*). The author's pen-name is Nāgrīdās, alias Sāvant Siṃh, the retired king (1699–1764/5) of the small Rājasthānī principality of Kishangarh. His work was not written out of sectarian concerns for orthodoxy. In fact, the sectarian allegiance of Nāgrīdās himself has been debated between the Vallabha- and Nimbārka-Sampradāyas.[139] The ex-king seems to have been especially inspired by Vyās: he relates no fewer than nine episodes (*PPM* 27–35) from Vyās's life[140] and quotes liberally from Vyās's poetry, even in chapters on other *bhaktas*.

In the chapters on Vyās proper, Nāgrīdās quotes some of the songs by Vyās that we have discussed above and provides contexts for them. The song instructing women (V282 = J148), for instance, is connected with a quarrel between Vyās and his wife (*PPM* 33), and the 'more orthodox than thou' song (V93 = J232 = G22 = M10) is placed within the well-known story of Vyās's breaking his sacred thread to substitute for Rādhā's anklet in the Rāsa Līlā, alluded to already in *Bhakt-māl* 92.[141]

Let us now turn to the way Nāgrīdās tells the conversion story and links it with the *digvijaya* theme (*PPM* 28):

buṃdelkhaṃḍ ke ek prohit vyās jī mahā paṃḍit digbijai kauṃ phirat he. so śrī bṛṃdāban hū āi nikase. pūchyo ihāṃ koū paṃdit bhī haiṃ? tab kā hū naiṃ kahyo harivaṃsjī haiṃ.

tab bād karibe kauṃ haribaṃs jī pās āe. kahyo mosauṃ vidyā kī carcā karo. tā samaiṃ haribaṃs jī ṭhākur kai rasoī karata hē tab vīās jī bole bhalai vidyā kī carcā rasoī kari cukaiṃ pīchaiṃ kariyaiṃgā. itne kachū sulap saṃbhāṣan to kie jāie.

tab śrī haribaṃs jū ṭokanī utāri cūlā jal taiṃ bujhāi dayo. tab vyās jī bole itnauṃ kyauṃ kiyo doū bāt karat jāte. tab śrī haribaṃs jū tāhī samai nayo pad banāi sunāyo. so pad sunat hī vyās jū sarva pustak sagrah ūṃṭana taiṃ lade utāri śrī jamunā maiṃ ḍāri die. bibād udbeg choḍi vṛṃdāban vās kiyo. yā bhāṃti vyās jākaiṃ upades lagyo.

A *purohit* from Bundelkhaṇḍ, the great pandit Vyās, was travelling with the aim of [establishing] national superiority (*digvijay*). He showed up in Vrindāban too, and asked: 'Is there also a paṇḍit here?'

Someone said: 'There is Haribaṃsjī.'

Then, for the sake of discussion,[142] he approached Haribaṃs. He said: 'Engage in a philosophical debate with me.' At that time, Haribasjī was preparing the food for Ṭhākur. Vyāsjī said: 'Fine, the philosophical debate should be postponed till after you have finished the cooking. Meanwhile, just a short conversation can work.'

Then Śrī Haribaṃsjī lifted the utensils [from the fire] and extinguished [the fire of] the oven with water. Then Vyāsjī said: 'Why did you take so much

> [trouble]? You could do both jobs [at the same time].' Then Haribaṃs instantly composed a new song and recited it.
>
> As soon as he finished listening to the song, Vyāsjī started unpacking his whole book collection, which was loaded on his camels, and threw them in the Śrī Jamunā. He gave up the excitement of debating, and settled in Vṛṃdāban. In this way, Vyās's instruction (initiation) had lasting effect.[143]

Nāgrīdās has changed the conversion incident, doing away with the function of the 'intermediary' Navaldās, who figured so prominently in the Rādhāvallabhan versions. Instead, he chooses to portray Vyās as a pandit with a mission: establishing his own prominence. There is arrogance in his question whether there might be someone who could carry out a decent debate in Vrindāban. Underlying this, we sense an agenda of defending Vrindāban, a relatively unknown religious centre, and making the point that it may not be famous for its pandits and brilliant debates, but has something much more important to offer, namely, devotion. There is an undercurrent of tension between the urban centre of sophistication and learning and the rural countryside where simple devotion can blossom. This contrast fits well with the Kṛṣṇa *bhakti* movement's preference for Kṛṣṇa, the simple cowherd in Braj, rather than for the cosmic king of Vaikuṇṭha, instructor of the *Bhagavadgītā*. For *bhaktas*, the institution of the *digvijaya*, with both its royal and instructional overtones, becomes meaningless. Vrindāban is the last stop on the pilgrim's progress, so to speak.

A more elaborate story on the same theme is found in the *Lokendra Brajotsava*. This work is in fact the account of a pilgrimage to Braj and Citrakūṭ, by the king of Datiyā, Bhavānī Siṃh. It was written in 1890–1 (V.S. 1947–8) by Pratītrāy Lakṣmaṇ Siṃh.[144] Vyās's lifestory was probably included because the minister of the king, at whose behest the work was written, was a descendant of Vyās. In this version, Vyās is portrayed as a successful pandit touring the country and scoring victories in debates. This time we see him reach Benares, which is, of course, the most prestigious of all urban religious centres. Upon Vyās's approach, the local pandits are nervous and ask Śiva to intervene on their behalf. The God agrees and approaches Vyās in the form of a child and impresses him by speaking Sanskrit. He then reveals that Vyās is in fact an incarnation of the *sakhī* Viśākhā and exhorts him to leave Benares and go to Vrindāban. To the general relief of the local pandits, Vyās follows his advice (Lokendra-brajotsav 160–73). Although the pandits get what they want, the real message is of course again that, in the light of *bhakti*, all philosophical wisdom becomes irrelevant. The hagiographer concludes the section by quoting a Dohā by Vyās (V *sākhī* 112) that expresses his disregard for worldly praise.

The way the story is told in *Lokendra-brajotsav* is reminiscent of similar stories told about Vallabha in the *Caurāsī Baiṭhak Caritra*.[145] However, there is no need to go far afield to find sources of inspiration for the story. Vyās's poetry itself offers many illustrations of the conflict between *bhakti* and scholastic learning. One might also suspect that the hagiographers felt that the title 'Vyās,' virtually synonymous with 'pandit,' was in conflict with his primary inclination to *bhakti*. One hagiographic strategy for dealing with unwanted characteristics of a saint is to relegate them to a period before the saint's conversion. So, Vyās's role as a pandit, implicit in his name, was stressed for the 'pre-conversion' phase, in order to highlight the contrast with his 'post-conversion,' real identity as a *bhakta*.

Whatever the sources of the story, it is interesting that a new element has been introduced in Vyās's hagiology in the form of the *digvijaya* motive. Vrindāban is portrayed as the stopping place of all worldly aspirations and scholarly pride. Implicitly, an antagonism has been set up between the 'viper nest' of urban Benares and the rustic paradise of sweet Braj.

Sacred Space as Locus for Meeting between King and Saint

Another favourite hagiographic topic is the conflict between worldly and spiritual power. Most hagiographies indulge in stories where a saint has an audience with a king, often turned around as the king approaching the saint for an audience. By the end of such meetings, of course, the saint always comes out ahead. Often he demonstrates that the king's worldly power has no hold over him. Secular power structure fails to oppress, or even impress, the divinely inspired. This topic becomes closely linked with the theme of sacred place in the hagiology of Vyās. The story goes that Vyās used to be in the service of a king, before he dropped everything and moved to Vrindāban. The king did not appreciate Vyās's desertion and followed Vyās all the way to Vrindāban with the purpose of bringing him back in his service. But Vyās refused to leave the sacred space. Priyādās, is the first to tell this story (*BhMṬ* 368):

āye gṛha tyāgi vṛndāvana anurāga kari
gayau hiyau pāgi hoya nyāro tāsauṃ khījhiyai
rājā laina āyau aipai jāyabau na bhāyau
śrīkiśora urajhāyo mana sevā mati bhījiyai.[146]

He left his home and came [here],[147] he got attached to Vrindāban, his heart steeped [in love]. If someone had to leave, he would get upset with him.[148]

The king came to take him [with him], but he did not like to go. Kiśorajī had entangled his heart, his mind was absorbed in devotion (*sevā*).

Whereas older hagiographies (for example, *RAM* 2) merely describe Vyās's father as a respected court pandit, the character of the king has come to play a more prominent role in this source. Priyādās says the king personally tried to get Vyās to leave Vrindāban and return to his court. Priyā also mentions that Vyās was upset with people trying to leave Braj. No doubt, he had in mind Vyās's many songs to that effect, which we examined earlier (see 'Paradise Abandoned' above). We had not found a reference before, though, to a king trying to convince Vyās to leave.

Later hagiographers followed suit. The story came to be associated with one song by Vyās, quoted above, in which he praises the trees of Vrindāban and expresses his feeling that dwelling there is superior to all other activities (V54 = J220 = G2 = M21). Nāgrīdās is the first to include a grandiose scene contextualizing this song with the story of the king coming to fetch Vyās. In Nāgrīdās's version of the story, the king (who is by this time identified as the Buṇḍelī ruler Madhukar Śāh of Orcchā) repeatedly pleads with Vyas to go back with him. However, Vyās is simply unable to leave Vrindāban. So, he begins to weep and embrace all the trees of Vrindāban as a farewell. The hagiographer somewhat dryly remarks: 'There are indeed many trees in Vrindāban, and he had much emotion in his heart, and the wilderness extended endlessly' (*PPM* 30). It is at this point that Vyās composes the famous song. I will quote the story here in full:

PPM 30

Śrī vyāsa jū bṛdāban āya bāsa kiyo. tinkau le jāybe ke vās taiṃ buṃdelā rājā śrī bṛṃdāban āyo. bohot haṭh kīno. rājā kahyo tum na caloge to maiṃ hūṃ yahāṃ taiṃ na jāūṃgo. tab vyās jū kūṃ ye bātai suni suni bohot dukh bhayo. vṛṃdāvan choḍyo na bhāyo.
tā samay ek nayo pad kanāy gāvata rovata phirana lage. jā vṛccha sauṃ jāy milaiṃ

> *tā vṛccha kūṃ choḍaiṃ nahīṃ vṛṃdāvan maiṃ to vṛccha bahot inke citt maiṃ anurāg bahot aru ye akele kahāṃ lag milaiṃ. dvai tīn din binā prasād jal aiseṃ bitīt kīneṃ. so jā pad kauṃ gāy gāy roy roy vṛcchan sauṃ mile so vah yah pad ...*

> Śrī Vyāsjū came to Bṛṃdāban, and settled there. With the wish[149] to take him away [from there], the Bundelā king came to Śrī Bṛṃdāban. He was obstinate (about staying).[150] The king said: 'If you won't go, than I will not go from here either.' Then, on hearing such pleas again and again, Vyās became very sad. He did not like to leave Vrindāban.
>
> In those days he started roaming around, crying and singing the new song he had composed.[151] Each tree he went and embraced, he could not leave. There are indeed many trees in Vrindāban, and he had much emotion in his heart, and the wilderness extended endlessly. A few days he spent like this, without *prasād* or water. So the song he kept singing, when he embraced the trees, crying without a pause, was the following: ... (quotes V54 = J222 = G2 = M21)

There are two interesting features in this story. First, Nāgrīdās (like Priyādās) concentrates on the moment of conflict itself, rather than resolving it by the king's softening and giving in to the saint's wish. The reason for Nāgrīdās may well be that the song is central to the story. Second, Nāgrīdās interprets the song with reference to a specific moment of existential crisis for Vyās. Obviously, that is not the only way it could be read; it could also be seen to express Vyās's anger with his less single-minded fellow *bhaktas* more generally. However, Nāgrīdās's is part of a distinguishable trend, which we also notice in other hagiographers, interpreting Vyās's angry poems with reference to particular incidents in his life, rather than as having general relevance.

Sectarian Perspective on Locus for Debate between King and Saint (Haridāsīs)

The sectarian concerns of Sahacarīśaraṇ, a Haridāsī, led him to retell the same story in a different way. Like the hagiographer Kiśordās (see 'Visions of Vrindāban'), he also belonged to the ascetic (sādhū) branch of the Haridāsīs and was the leader of the Taṭṭī Asthān *āśrama*. He is the first to elaborate on the 'king meets saint' incident from a Haridāsī point of view (LP 201–219). In this version, when the obstinate king, Madhukar Śāh, insists that Vyās should leave Vrindāban and come with him, Vyās responds by falling in the dust and pleading with his own feet not to leave, saying that true heroism is to stay in Vrindāban.

Vyās then invokes the trees, asking them to let him stay in their shadow, and invokes the Yamunā river. He calls the whole of Braj his family, and goes as far as to call Rādhā and Kṛṣṇa the treasury of royalty, in front of the king. This has the desired effect: the king becomes ashamed (*LP* 204). The author comes up with several metaphors of how the most impossible things would happen before Vyās would leave Braj (*LP* 205).

Finally, the author proffers his sectarian interpretation. Apparently, even with all this pathos and drama, the king has not budged. To break the stalemate, Vyās proposes to bring the matter before Svāmī Haridās (*LP* 208). The implication is, of course, that the verdict of the saint eclipses secular jurisdiction. This is dramatically underlined by the king's donning a simple loincloth (*dhotī*), rather than his royal garb, as a sign of humility, for his meeting with Haridās (*LP* 209). In most other sources, the king, Madhukar Śāh, is said to be Vyās's disciple,[152] but here Vyās is depicted as a mere matchmaker between the king and his guru Haridās. To return to the story, Haridās ordains that Vyās should stay in Vrindāban and that the king should go back to his royal duties. He deigns to instruct the king in his wisdom and grants him by way of consolation the spiritual power to recognize Vrindāban in his own kingdom (*LP* 210).

The Haridāsī hagiographer does not differ much from his Rādhāvallabhan counterparts we studied earlier. He has the same intent, namely to talk up the founder-father of his own sect. Also, his rhetoric is similar: he ascribes to Haridās the power to reveal the spiritual Vrindāban to his disciples. To some extent in parallel with Harivaṃś, Haridās can also determine who gets to stay in the worldly Vrindāban or leave. There are two elements introduced here – the stress on how spiritual power eclipses secular authority and the consolation prize given to Madhukar Śāh: apparently, a vision of the divine Vrindāban can be had outside of Vrindāban's boundaries.

Sahacarīśaraṇ also retells the story of Vyās's arrival in Vrindāban. Again, his version is very similar to that of the Rādhāvallabhans, except for the fact that it features Haridās in the main role. For instance, Haridās is said to foretell to Vyās the discovery of the image, Yugalakiśora (*LP* 197–200). The Haridāsī hagiographer even uses the same techniques as the Rādhāvallabhans to substantiate his claims, frequently referring to songs by Vyās. Sometimes Sahacarīśaraṇ refers to the content of these songs, for example, when Vyās refuses to leave Vrindāban (*LP* 202, 204–205). Sometimes, he uses vocabulary highly reminiscent of Vyās's songs (*LP* 397). Elsewhere, songs in the hagiography are presented as if by Vyās, Madhukar Śāh, or Kiśordās, but they cannot be traced in the available manuscript material.

The Emperor Akbar and His Visit to Sacred Hindu Space

Many hagiographers of the *bhakti* movement, in their eagerness to demonstrate how spiritual power inevitably prevails over even the highest mundane authority, tell stories about the Mughal emperor Akbar's humiliation in front of all kinds of *bhaktas* (from Haridās and Sūrdās to Mīrābāī). Surprisingly, such stories rarely have a communal feel, but rather follow within the general 'king meets saint' genre. In the hagiology about Vyās, kings appear early on, yet Akbar himself does not appear until quite late.

A meeting between the emperor and the saint is described for the first time in the first half of the nineteenth century[153] in the work *Vṛndāvan-dhām-anurāgāvalī* by Gopālkavi.[154] This author does not appear to foster any particular sectarian goals, although he had links with the Haridāsīs.

Gopālkavi relates how Akbar became interested in a song by Vyās (V75 = J53, quoted above in 'Rasa Trickling Through') with the closure formula (*chāpa*) 'Vyās with the spittoon' (*vyāsa pīkadaṃnī liyai*). The emperor visited the saint and kept him talking all night. Vyās was thus impeded in his duty of providing the spittoon in the divine *līlā*. The next morning, he showed Kṛṣṇa's and Rādhā's spittle as proof to the emperor, who repented and offered Vyās his services.[155] Vyās asked for a place for his family to stay in Vrindāban so that he could provide the deity with better service.

At the end of the episode, Gopālkavi provides the background information that Akbar, despite being a Muslim, was really an incarnation of a certain Mukad Brahmācāri. Gopālkavi may have used as his source *Caurāsī vaiṣṇavan kī vārtā*, where a similar story is told about Sūrdās and Akbar alias Bālmukund Brahmācārya.[156] In contrast to the story about Sūrdās, the conflict between mundane and spiritual power loses some of its edge in the story about Vyās. Whereas Sūrdās is described as refusing any imperial gifts and asking instead to be left alone, Vyās is shown to accept land from the emperor, albeit with the stipulation that his ultimate purpose is better service to God.[157]

This episode is also interesting in that it introduces a miracle to illustrate how the phenomenal Vrindāban is inextricably linked with the divine one. The *rasas*, in the form of juices of betel, have quite literally trickled through to the mundane level. The king is merely a foil to witness such testimony and serves to confirm officially the role Vyās claims to play in the divine world. Although we find the claim of access to the divine world in Vyās's poetry itself, the need for 'proof' seems to arise late in the hagiology.

What the Hagiographies Do Not Say

Now that I have explored how some of Vyās's songs were contextualized by his hagiographers, we should also pause for a moment and reflect on what they did not say, which contexts they did not provide, and which songs they did not pick up on.

Surprisingly, the ability to cure, a universal trait of saints and sacred places, does not figure in the hagiology of Vyās. Hypothetically, Vyās's songs on the dust of holy Vrindāban might have been contextualized with references to healing miracles, but none of the hagiographies I have seen does so. Such power comes to be ascribed to Vyās only in one late source.[158] Here Vyās is said to have cured a leper by applying the dust of Vrindāban.[159] Specifics are given, such as the name of the leper (Umed) and the circumstances of the cure: Vyās allegedly was on his way to Jagannāthpurī.

More important, the hagiographers are unanimous in portraying Vyās's story as a success story of 'Paradise found' only. Rarely do they elaborate on the 'Paradise lost' side of his poems. The dismay Vyās felt at the end of his life and his disenchantment with his neighbours in Vrindāban is, if not actually downplayed, at least not stressed.

Here we should look in some more detail at Priyādās, who gives Vyās some space for his more pessimistic poems in his *Ananya-modinī*.[160] First, he introduces Vyās, promisingly, as demasking 'those turned away from religion' or *vimukhas*:

baṛe kulīna mahanta vara, paṇḍita parama pravīna
rasika ananya pramāna ati śrīmat vyāsa raṃgīn
kiye bahuta pada ati sukhada, vimukhani ke mukha tora
tāmeṃ kachuka sunāiyai, bhakti ananya nicora

Of very high caste, a choice *mahant*, a very clever pandit,
He was the foremost of the exclusively devoted, colourful Mr. Vyās.
He created many charming songs, tore the mask of sinners,

Let me quote a few, the gist of exclusive *bhakti*.

Priyādās continues to quote some of Vyās's songs related to sacred space that were discussed in the first section of this essay.[161] However, significantly, the songs of social critique that Priyādās quotes have no explicit reference to Vrindāban and sacred space. Moreover, when he is done quoting Vyās, Priyādās resumes his work by discussing the greatness of Vrindāban: (*jetika hari ke dhāma haiṃ sarvopari vana dhāma, mahā mahā aiśvarya hū koṭi madhura viśrāma* [55], 'Among the many abodes of Hari, the highest is the holy forest space. Even the most elevated majesty zillion-fold [finds here] sweet rest'). This is not an oversight. Priyādās is aware of the 'paradise lost' poems. In his trendsetting work, *BhMṬ*, he briefly indicates this awareness when he mentions that Vyās would get upset with those who would leave Vrindāban (quoted above, in 'Sacred Space as Locus...'), yet, he does not elaborate.

A possible reason for such peculiar silence may be that Priyādās himself resided in Vrindāban and was Gauṛīya.[162] Given that part of Vyās's criticism likely concerned the Gauṛīya promotion tours in Bengal, it may be not so surprising that he chose not to elaborate on this type of poetry.

Since Priyādās is so influential, some later hagiographers repeat the piece of information about Vyās's disgust for 'leavers.' However, no one has worked out any story connected with it. This is all the more surprising because Priyādās hints at an incident that could have easily been made to fit the bill: (*saṃta saṃpuṭa meṃ ciraiyā dai hita soṃ basāye haiṃ* [*BhMṬ* 370], 'He put a bird in a holy man's basket and made him stay with love'). Only late commentators have worked out the full story, which is about Vyās's trying to convince a visiting saint to stay in Vrindāban. It involves a practical joke. When the saint insists on leaving, Vyās secretly substitutes the image (*mūrti*) in the saint's basket with a bird. When the man stops a short distance outside Vrindāban, in order to do his ritual worship or *pūjā*, he sees his '*mūrti*' fly off, back in the direction from which he has come. He has no alternative but to return.[163]

The story would have fit well with Vyās's condemnation of those who decide to leave the sacred place. It is only surprising that none of the earlier hagiographers chose to discuss the issue at greater length. One would especially expect such from the *nirguṇī* hagiographers, but they seem content to repeat Priyādās's information (*ṭīkā* on

Rāghavdās's *Bhakt-māl*[164] 391): *ciriyāṃ dhari saṃpaṭa sādha basāye*, 'By putting a bird in his basket he made a saint stay.' Even in the late source (RR), no poetry by Vyās is quoted to support the incident. From what we have learned about Vyās's poems on Vrindāban, we would have imagined that some creative hagiographer would have come up with a piece of evidence.

Conclusion

In this essay, I first explored Vyās's ideas on sacred space. In addition to his enthusiasm for having found 'paradise,' he voices his disgust for those who transformed it into a 'paradise lost.' Vyās is at the same time opposed to sectarian formation and yet is himself involved in demarcating a religious community, setting up boundaries between the 'in-group' of the connoiseurs or *ananya rasikas* and the 'others,' who had concerns other than *bhakti*. Ironically, the 'others' are not *ananya* or 'exclusive' (literally, 'without other'). The link with sacred space is that the former are able to have and share their vision of the supra-mundane level of sacred space, while the latter defile sacred place by their commercial transactions, or do not appreciate its value fully and leave it for other places.

I then examined how the hagiographers evaluate Vyās's perspective. Several hagiographers rework Vyās's decision to go and settle in Vrindāban from sectarian points of view. To strengthen their case, they also use the 'pandit debates with *bhakta*' and *digvijaya* motifs. Several hagiographers combine the theme of Vyās's vow not to leave Vrindāban with the *topos* of 'saint meets king.' All these incidents serve the glorification of sacred space. The hagiographers tend to leave Vyās's social critique poems out, as if they were felt to be discordant with the tenor of their own works.

If they refer to Vyās's negative poems, the hagiographers tend to provide a specific context for them, which narrows the interpretative possibilities. The poems are cast in the light of conflict within Vyās's family, in line with the *topos* of 'the householder versus the ascetic,' or conflict with representatives of secular power, the topos of 'the king versus the saint.' Hagiographers do not quote the songs criticizing other *bhaktas*, which, one might imagine, they could have filled out with specifics about Vyās's contemporaries. The hagiographies concentrate on songs about other *bhaktas* only if these are positive and fit the hagiographer's sectarian allegiance.

This sectarian agenda of the hagiographers is something of which Vyās would not have approved. Vyās saw himself mainly as a devotee participating in the happenings of supra-mundane Vrindāban. For him, what happened in the mundane Vrindāban became an unpleasant distraction. Vyās's main agenda was not the demarcation of sacred space on earth, nor the organization of a group of followers for whom he would create a script for future acting out of his devotional ideas. Those issues arise later in the hagiographies. The Rādhāvallabhan hagiographers cast Hit Harivaṃś in the role of 'pioneer of sacred space' or 'pathfinder.' They are eager to portray their founder as the one who laid 'networks of paths through unmarked territories, led by culturally derived maps.'[165] For the Haridāsīs, it is Svāmī Haridās who led the way. In both cases, Vyās is cast in the role of one of the first to be guided by the founders.

What we see in process is sectarian formation on a much narrower level, along lines of specific sectarian allegiance rather than 'good *bhakta*' versus 'bad *bhakta*.' Paradoxically, we see a growing irenic concern at the same time as we see the inter-sectarian rivalry growing. As sectarian boundaries get fixed, spiritual visions are watered down. What we see at work in the hagiographer's evaluations of Vyās's perspective on Vrindāban may be part of a larger process of 'routinization,' or 'transformation from highly spiritual act to one of ritualistic formulism.'[166] In the process, Vyās, who on the basis of his own poetry came across as an 'angry not-so-young man,' is transformed into a harmless model for the hagiographer's brand of '*bhakti* without sharp edges.' Sarcasm has apparently no place when hagiography takes over. Hagiographers are, after all, engaged in eulogy and under the onslaught of beautification, realism and scepticism are felled. Meanwhile, on the map, urbanization invades the sylvan countryside. In contemporary Vrindāban, there are fewer and fewer trees to hug as temples mushroom in a once idyllic paradise, lost over and over again.

End Notes

*This essay is based on the manuscript material I collected during field research in India from 1987 to 1988, which was made possible by a scholarship from the Indo-Belgian Cultural Exchange Program. I gratefully acknowledge the generous help I have received with the translation and interpretation of several of the poems quoted here from Śrī Baldev Lāl Gosvāmī and Buddhi Prakāś of Vrindāban, India. I am also grateful to the late Professor Alan Entwistle of the University of Washington, Seattle, who supervised my Ph.D. research (1990–94), Professor Monika Boehm-Tettelbach, now at Heidelberg University, with whom I had the chance to study in Cologne (1989–90) thanks to a stipend from the DAAD, and Dr. Winand Callewaert of K. University Leuven, Belgium, who taught me the value of text criticism.

1 See John Stratton Hawley, 'Author and Authority in the Bhakti Poetry of North India,' *Journal of Asian Studies* 47, no. 2 (1988), 269–90.

2 *Śrī Vyās-vāṇī*, 2 vols., ed. Akhila Bhāratavarṣīya Śrī Hita Rādhāvallabhīya Vaiṣṇava Mahāsabhā (Vrindāban: Śrī Vrajendra MachinePress, V.S. 1991 [1934]). *Śrī Vyās Vāṇī: Siddhānt aur Ras sahit*, ed. Rādhākiśor Gosvāmī (Mathurā: Agravāl Press, V.S. 1994 [1937]). Vāsudev Gosvāmī, *Bhakt kavi Vyāsjī* (Mathurā: Agravāl Press, V.S. 2009 [1952]).

3 For full textual details of my manuscript study, see Heidi Rika Maria Pauwels, 'Harirām Vyās's *Rās-pañcādhyāyī* and *Mān kī śṛṅkhalā*: A Critical Interpretation' (PhD diss., University of Washington, 1994), 135–148, and *Kṛṣṇa's Round Dance Reconsidered: Harirām Vyās's Hindī Rās-pañcādhyāyī*, London Studies on South Asia, 12 (London: Curzon Press, 1996), 13–72.

4 I thank the brothers Ghanśyām and Lalit Prasād Gosvāmī, Mohanlāljī kā mandir, Manik Cauk, Jhānsī for kindly allowing me to photograph the manuscript.

5 I have made minor emendations, mostly for *akṣaras* that are illegible in the original. Otherwise, I cite my reasons for emendation in each. All emendations are indicated by square brackets for proposed additions and round brackets for proposed omissions.

6 This manuscript is clearly Rādhāvallabhī in inspiration in that it starts nearly each new section with *śrīrādhāvallabho jayati*, and contains also praise of Hit Harivaṃś (fol. 46). It contains Nanddās's *Rās-pañcādhyāī* (fol. 25–46); *Ras-siddhānt-cintāmaṇi-granth* (fol. 46–53); *Śṛṅgār-cūṛāmaṇi* (fol. 53–67); *Ās-tyāg* (fol. 67–72); *Ras-muktāvalī* by Dhruvdās (fol. 72–81); *Nem-battīsī* (fol. 81–83); *Śṛṅgār-sat* (fol. 83–108); *Bhakti-pratāp* (fol. 108–16); *Sant-pratāp* (fol. 116–27); *Vimukh-bhajan* (fol. 127–33); poems by Bihāridās (fol. 133–44); by Vyās (fol. 145–50); miscellaneous poems (fol. 151–60); a story called *Gītā-līlā* (fol. 160–63), and some poems by Tulsīdās (fol. 163).

7 On fol. 83r., a different date seems to be given in riddle form: *saṃvat*

sāgara siddha rasa śaśi, which might be taken to be 1764 or even as late as 1830 (V.S. 1821 or 1887).

8 This manuscript contains also a *Guvāl-paherī* (fol. 1–8r.); a *Rādhākṛṣṇa-vilās* (fol. 45v.–86r.); and Rādhāvallabhī Kavittas (fol. 86v.–91v.). It seems to have some Rādhāvallabhī sectarian inclination, judging by the latter sections and references to Harivaṃś (for example, fol. 45v.). I am grateful to the personnel of the Jivaji University Library for allowing me to photocopy parts of the manuscript.

9 The numbering of the *padas* in the manuscript is very confusing: the scribe numbers poem 7 as 8 and from 8 onwards (fol. 85r.ff); the scribe misnumbers as 11 onwards; from poem 11 onwards, he numbers as 15 onwards; from 16 onwards as 21 onwards; from 24 onwards as 33 onwards; from 26 onwards, as 36; from 29 onwards as 40; and 31 as 44. I am not sure why he does so; he might have mistakenly skipped a few *padas* from his *exemplar*. To avoid confusion, I have referred here to the assigned number of the logical sequence.

10 This song's refrain seems to echo a half-verse from *Skanda Purāṇa*, namely *kuru bho· kuru bho vāsaṃ mathurākhyāṃ purīṃ prati*. See *Śrīskanda Mahāpurāṇam*, vol. 2 (Delhi: Nag Publishers, 1986), 5.17.31.

11 In fact, literally, 'turn cold,' which does not make much sense in English. The idea is that the eyes cannot shut anymore once they have beheld such beauty; hence my free translation.

12 G has a variant for this line: *nācata gāvata suṣa upajāvata vāṛhata prema pratīti*, 'singing and dancing, making others happy, causing love and faith to grow.'

13 I read *abhāra* as *ābhāra*, though I did not find attestation of such a variant. G has the variant reading: *vyāsadāsa kī saravasa vṛṃdāvana jahāṃ nitya vihāra*, 'Vrindāban is the each and everything of Vyās, where the love-play is eternal.'

14 Note the wordplay with internal rhyme of Kṛṣṇa and *tṛṣṇa*.

15 Literally: 'restraining by beating with the whip of hope' (taking *ṭhabak-* as synonymous with *ṭhamak-*).

16 Literally, 'he has become strict' ('unyielding,' 'fanatic').

17 This poem is also quoted by Priyādās in *Ananaya Mohinī* (see table 1 and 'Sacred Space' in the second section of the essay).

18 Alan Morinis, *Pilgrimage in the Hindu Tradition: A Case Study of West Bengal* (Delhi: Oxford University Press, 1984), 246–49.

19 *Encyclopedia of Religion*, s.v. 'Sacred Space,' by Joel E. Brereton (New York: Macmillan, 1986–87).

20 I am not sure how to interpret *mahalī*; it could be related to *mahal*, 'palace.'

So maybe 'palace maid servants' is intended. Alternatively, it might be a variant for *maharī*, 'woman of water-carrier caste.' Since the two seasons mentioned are masculine, the feminine form seems a bit out of place.

21 The word order is unusual here. One would have expected the more formulaic *cakra nṛpati* and *cūṛā maṇi*, which is how I have translated it. Possibly the reason has to do with the fact that this way *maṇi* can also be applied to *sāṃvarau*: 'black jewel.'

22 Morinis, *Pilgrimage in the Hindu Tradition*, 280.

23 *Encyclopedia of Religion*, s.v. 'Sacred Space,' by Joel E. Brereton, quoting Jonathan Z. Smith.

24 This poem is written in J in a different, more ornamental and curly handwriting.

25 Literally, this seems to be a transitive form: 'to cause to dwell' or 'to settle (land).'

26 The word *haravā* is apparently a derivative of *hāra*. See Vidyānivās Miśra, *Sāhityik Brajbhāṣā koś*, vol. 3 (Lucknow: Uttar Pradeś Hindī Saṃsthān, 1990), 328.

27 The word *kopīna* is synonymous with *laṃgoṭī*, see Ambāprasād 'Suman,' *Kṛṣak-jīvan-sambandhī Brajbhāṣā-Śabdāvalī*, 2 vols. (Allahabad: Hindustānī Academy, 1960–61), vol. 1, 352.

28 J has *ghāta*, but that seems inferior in meaning: 'tricks blossoming.'

29 Note the wordplay with internal rhyme: *keli veli*.

30 The last half-line could also be interpreted as 'having listened to the sound of your girdle bells for "service of the word"' (*śravaṇa* in its sense of one of the nine praxes leading to devotion).

31 This word is not there in J, but it may be a case of haplology because the meter clearly requires an additional two *mātrās*.

32 The line is hypometrical, so one wonders whether an irenical correction has taken place, adding *adhara*.

33 Editions of Vyās's work also have a poem with refrain *mohiṃ bṛṃdāvana raja soṃ kāja* (V84 = J228), 'I only have business with the dust of Vrindāban.' However, in J, the reading is *vṛṃdāvana rājā*, 'the king of Vrindāban,' which seems a better reading and a better internal rhyme of which Vyās is so fond. Nevertheless, the poem still refers to the water of Yamunā and also to the food of Braj. In connection with the latter topic, there is also a poem on the 'spinach' or *sāg* of Vrindāban: *rucata mohiṃ bṛṃdāvana kau sāga* (V 81), 'I am fond of Vrindāban's vegetables,' but this is not attested in J.

34 Or, 'its paths' (*aina* can be either 'path,' 'abode,' or 'storeroom,' 'treasure-house').

35 See Alan W. Entwistle, *Braj: Centre of Krishna Pilgrimage* (Groningen: Egbert Forsten, 1987), 91–92.

36 I have edited and translated them in Pauwels, 'Harirām Vyās's *Rās-pañcādhyāyī and Mān kī śṛṅkhalā*,' 340–537, to which all the following numbers refer.

37 Literally, 'free of body,' 'unconscious,' 'free of care for the body.'

38 I have interpreted *sukala* as *sakala*. Alternatively, it can be seen as *śukla*, which seems to be the name of Vyās's father, who also was his guru. The edition by V has the variant reading *suphala* 'successful,' which is confirmed by the reading in G.

39 This poem is written in an ornamental hand, which is different from the main scribe's handwriting. It seems that someone rewrote several pages of the manuscript at a later date, likely to repair some damage. There is no evidence of significant alteration of the readings during the repair.

40 This poem is also written in the same ornamental hand.

41 Ibid.

42 Ibid.

43 Ibid.

44 Ibid.

45 See also Heidi Rika Maria Pauwels, 'Harirām Vyās and the Early Bhakti-Milieu,' in *Studies in South Asian Devotional Literature: Research Essays 1988–1991, Presented at the Fifth Conference on Devotional Literature in New Indo-Aryan Languages, Held at Paris-École Française d'Extrême-Orient, 9–12 July 1991* eds. Françoise Mallison and Alan W. Entwistle (New Delhi: Manohar; Paris: École Française d'Extrême-Orient, 1994).

46 Emendations of this line are carried out on metrical grounds and because a corrector of J has already added in the margin the missing *teṃ*. Clearly there is a case that ura belongs somewhere in the line, most naturally before *pīra*, it seems. The editions of Akhila Bhāratavarṣīya Śrī Hita Rādhāvallabhīya Vaiṣṇava Mahāsabhā, vol. 2, 219, and Gosvāmī, vol.1, 218 read both *kṛṣṇa kṛpā kavacī taiṃ ubarai soca vaṛhī upa pīra, soca* probably being a *lectio facilior*, 'If you emerge from the harness of Kṛṣṇa's grace, sorrow swells, close to pain.'

47 In this and the following three lines, I have translated the parallel constructions with *binu*, literally, 'without,' somewhat freely to render the rhetoric effect of the poem.

48 Literally, 'In the breast of the insignificant anguish has risen.' The reading of J (*upapīra*) does not make much sense, hence the emendation. Other readings substitute the first *ura* in J by shoving in a postposition *teṃ*, which is, in my opinion, preferable.

49 Literally, 'The river of death has swollen deeply.'
50 *Encyclopedia of Religion*, s.v. 'Sacred Space,' by Brereton.
51 Ibid.
52 For the interpretation of this poem, I am grateful to Phyllis Granoff for many valuable suggestions. All mistakes remain my own.
53 Not in J, supplied for meter on the basis of V and Gosvāmī, vol. 1, 42. The edition by Akhila Bāratavarṣīya Śrī Hita Rādhāvallabhīya Vaiṣava Mahāsabhā, vol. 1, 4 gives: *dvādaśavanameṃ tiḷu tilu mukti aru tīratha gaṃgādi.*
54 In J one *akṣara*, recognizably the letter *t* has been eradicated by a later hand. V has *rivairina lakhi.*
55 Every line ends on the rhyme word *ādi*, which can mean 'beginning' or 'foremost,' and is hence ambiguous. In this poem, it is often written together with another word, thus indicating it forms a compound. In Sanskrit compounds of the form X-*ādi* usually mean 'having X for its beginning,' or simply 'et cetera.' Braj compounds do not consistently take this form, so we can simply translate them as 'beginning of X,' that is, 'primeval X.' In most lines both interpretations are possible, but the second is often the most meaningful in context. The theme of the *pada,* as indicated in the *ṭeka* line, is the cosmic importance of Vrindāban, as primeval source of everything, and most lines equate Vrindāban's flora and fauna with primeval cosmic characters and events.
56 In this line the final compound *sanakādi* is a formulaic one, usually meaning 'Sanaka et cetera,' that is: 'Sanaka and his brothers.' This conventional meaning is conflated with the meaning in context on the parallel of the other lines of the poem: 'primeval Sanaka.'
57 This line is reminiscent of *Skanda Purāṇa's* verses: *mathurāyāṃ ca yat puṇyaṃ tat puṇyasya phalaṃ śṛṇu, mathurāyāṃ samāsādya mathurāyāṃ mṛtā hi ye; api kīṭapataṃgādyā jāyaṃte te caturbhujāḥ, kūlātpataṃti ye vṛkṣāste ' pi yāṃti parāṃ gatiṃ. Śrīskanda Mahāpurāṇam* 2:5.17.47–48.
58 The god of dharma, Yamarāja, is often associated with a buffalo. This line may also be construed to refer to the 'cow of *dharma*.'
59 The sage and Sāmkhya teacher Kapila is in *Bhāgavatapurāṇa* described as an *avatāra* of Viṣṇu. See *Śrīmad Bhāgavata Mahāpurāṇa: With Sanskrit Text and English Translation*, 2 vols., 2nd ed., ed. and trans. Chinman Lal Goswami and M.A. Śāstrī (Gorakhpur: Gita Press, 1981), 3:24–33.
60 Likely intended to subjugate Lakṣmī, Viṣṇu's consort, to the Gopīs. This line could also be interpreted as '[their] lotus feet are the primeval water lotuses.'
61 Compare to *Varāha Purāṇa's* half-verse: *mathurāvāsinaḥ sarve te devā*

naravigrahāḥ, in Varāha Purāṇa: Text with English translation, ed. Anand Swarup Gupta, ed. and trans. Ahibhushan Bhattacharya (Varanasi: All-India Kashiraj Trust, 1981), 164:53.

62 Compare to *Skanda Purāṇa's* half-verse: *pade pade tīrthaphalaṃ mathurāyāṃ caturmukha. Śrīskanda Mahāpurāṇam*, 2:5.17.3.

63 One might be tempted to read *acala* 'mountain' and see a reference, not to Kṛṣṇa's birth, but rather to the incident of Kṛṣṇa lifting the mountain Govardhana against the flood caused by Indra, which would make a nicer parallel with the flood and Manu.

64 Literally: 'With not even a remainder left,' a pun on the name of the cosmic serpent Śeṣa, which means 'remainder.'

65 Another poem, not attested in J, has *vara mathurā baikuṃṭha loka teṃ sukhada nikuṃjani aina*, 'Mathurā is peferable to the heaven Vaikuṇṭha, the abode of the bowers is charming' (V 50).

66 Entwistle, *Braj*, 74.

67 This line is added in the margin in J.

68 In J something is added after *kūṭa* and before *ṭika*. It looks like *kosarā* or *dosarā*, neither of which makes sense.

69 Not in J, but clearly a case of haplography, and emended on the basis of other manuscripts.

70 V reads *rādhādhava*.

71 This poem is also written in the ornamental hand referred to in note 39, and this passage is particularly difficult to decipher.

72 G has the variant *āpa mana*.

73 The second half of this line in G is: *adharma desa maiṃ chāyaṃ*, 'lawlessness has spread in the country.'

74 This line is not found in G.

75 Or, 'Why has Vyās given birth?'

76 Entwistle, *Braj*, 145.

77 This poem seems more explicitly autobiographical. Vyās apparently was chided by his sons for feeding holy men: *phorata kāna hamāre*.

78 This poem appears in G with a minor variant in the *ṭeka* or refrain: *vṛṃdāvana ke phūla hamāre māta pitā suta vaṃdhu*.

79 A variant in G: *tini kau pariyau kaṃdhu*.

80 The last word, *nikandha*, may be a rhyming variant for *nikanda* 'uprooting,' or it may be related to idioms such as *kandhā denā*, 'to take a corpse on its bier,' an understanding confirmed by the reading in G. In both cases the implications are the same.

81 *Varāha Purāṇa*, 150.17; *Śrīskanda Mahāpurāṇam*, 5.17.36.

82 In J, this poem is written in the same ornamental hand mentioned

above.

83 Literally, 'Who all didn't become [loyal to] another family.' I have interpreted *haruvo* as a verbal form from *huruā-* (v.i.). See Dīndayāl Gupta and Premnarāyaṇ Ṭaṇḍan, *Brajbhāṣā Sūrkoś* (Lucknow: Viśvavidyālay Hindī Prakāśan, V.S. 2031 [1974]) (hereafter cited as *BBSK*). It is possible to translate as 'debased their dad.'

84 The word *akṣata* can be interpreted as an adjective, meaning 'undivided,' 'intact,' or as a verb form, as compared to its variant in V *achata* meaning 'remaining.' The intended meaning is the same.

85 For the full translation, see Pauwels, 'Harirām Vyās and the Early Bhakti-Milieu,' 36.

86 Ibid., 37–38.

87 Entwistle, *Braj*, 151, 154, 160–65.

88 Ibid., 167.

89 Translated in Pauwels, 'Harirām Vyās and the Early Bhakti Milieu,' 35.

90 Most likely a reference to the awkwardness of the pioneering movement, which in search for pristine pastoral environs, ruins them with settlements.

91 Probably ironic use of the verb *diṣāī de-*, 'to come out,' 'to appear.'

92 G has some minor variants: in the first line *pūta kapūta* (for *nātī pūta*) 'sons and bad sons' and at the end of the second line *gudī vaṭī* (for *garī kaṭī*), likely to be translated as 'twisted my neck' (taking *vaṭī* as from the verb *baṭ-*). G also a different sequence in the last line: *kahi kārana hari dīnī vyāsahi* ... with no change of meaning.

93 J's line is hypermetric. Probably the word *racana* should be left out as it is in V.

94 Note the ingenious wordplay on *sevā-mevā*.

95 Note the ingenious wordplay on *mīṭhe-sīṭhe*, the latter literally meaning 'bland,' 'devoid of *rasa*.'

96 Probably *bigūce* is to be taken as a ppp. of the verb *bigūc-*, 'to be in a tough situation,' 'to get caught' (*BBSK*). One could also read this line as 'They got caught leaving their wife.'

97 The second half-line is probably purposely vague. Vyās seems to make the point that though magic is intended to influence worldly phenomena and thus establish one's power over the world, in fact, in doing so, one is taken in by worldly concerns oneself.

98 I have interpreted *tehū* as a rhyme word variation for *teha* (m.) in the sense of 'anger.'

99 The word *rājasī* is attested in this meaning (*BBSK*), although one might also translate as 'one in whom the *guṇa* of *rajas* is predominant' or 'passionate people,' as supported by the variant indicated in V (but not

confirmed in J nor G): *tāmasī.*

100 On same theme: *aisaihiṃ basiyai braja bīthini,* not in J, but also in *Sūrasāgara,* vol. 1, 4th ed., Nāgarīpracāriṇī Granthmālā 35, ed. Nanddulāre Vājpeyī et al. (Benares: Nāgarīpracāriṇī Sabhā, V.S. 2021 [1964]), 427–28, *pada* 1108/490.

101 Haripur is apparently another name for Dvārkā. See Nirmalā Saksenā, *Sūrsāgar Śabdāvalī: Ek sāṃskritik adhyayan* (Allahabad: Hindustānī Academy, 1962), 172.

102 See Pauwels, *Kṛṣṇa's Round Dance Reconsidered.*

103 The intended meaning seems to be that they shame the god of love himself. Translation on the assumption that *vola* is synonymous with the variant reading from V *ola.* Otherwise, it would also be possible to translate as 'Kāmadeva marks with sound,' that is, 'applauds.'

104 *Encyclopedia of Religion,* s.v. 'Sacred Space,' by Brereton.

105 Pauwels, 'Harirām Vyās and the Early Bhakti-Milieu,' 33–38.

106 See Hargūlāl, *Sarvopari nityavihāriṇī ras-sār* (*Aṣṭācāryoṃ kī Vāṇī*) (Vrindāban: Śrī Prem Hari Press, V.S. 2028 [1971]). Text and translation are provided in Pauwels, 'Harirām Vyās's *Rās-pañcādhyāyī* and *Mān kī śṛṅkhalā,*' appendix 1.

107 The first reference is to the standard editions such as: *Śrīmad Gosvāmī Śrī Nābhājī kṛt Śrī Bhaktmāl, Śrī Priyādāsjī kṛt kavittamayī Bhakti Ras Bodhinī ṭīkā sahit,* vol. 3, 3rd ed., ed. Bhaktmālī Gaṇeśdās and Rāmāyaṇī Rāmeśvardās (Vrindāban: Rāmānand Pustakālay, V.S. 2039 [1982]); *Nābhājī kṛt Śrī Bhakt Māl, Bhakti Ras Bodhinī ṭīkā evaṃ Bhakti Rasāyanī vyākhyā sahit,* ed. Rāmkṛṣṇadās Garge (Vrindāban: Viyogī Viśveśvar Nimbārkācārya Pīṭh, 1960); *Nābhādās Bhaktmāl,* ed. Sītārām Śaran. and Bhagavānprasād Rūpkalā (1910; reprinted Lucknow: Tejkumār Book Depot, 1969), 609–10. The second reference is to the critical edition, *Bhaktmāl: Pāṭhānuśīlan evaṃ vivecanā,* vol. 2, ed. Narendra Jhā (Patna: Anūpam Prakāśan, 1978), 32.

108 See *[Śabdārth evaṃ pramukh viṣayoṃ ke śīrṣak yukt] Śrī Bayālīs Līlā tathā padyā-valī: Racayitā: Śrī Hit Dhruvdāsjī Mahārāj,* ed. Lalitācaraṇ Gosvāmī (Vrindāban: Bābā Tulsīdās, V.S. 2028 [1971]), 30.

109 See Lalit Prasād Purohit, *Rasik Ananya Māl: Mūl evaṃ gadya rūpāntaraṇ,* vol. 2 (1960; reprint, Vrindāban: Veṇu Prakāśan, 1986), 4–6 (hereafter cited as *RAM* with references to the line-number of the *Vyās Parcaī,* the chapter on Vyās, of this edition).

110 This important hagiography has not been edited, but a manuscript dated 1778 (V.S. 1835) is preserved in the Vrindāban Research Institute (acc. no. 4398, fols. 17r–20v.). Text and translation of the chapter on Vyās are

given in Pauwels, 'Harirām Vyās's *Rās-pañcādhyāyī and Mān kī śṛṅkhalā,'* appendix 2. An older manuscript (V.S. 1799) is preserved in the Caitanya Pustakālay in Patna (reference from N.C. Bansal, personal communication, January 1988), but was not available to me.

111 See *Śrīmad Gosvāmī Śrī Nābhājī kṛt Śrī Bhaktmāl, Śrī Priyādāsjī kṛt kavittamayī Bhakti Ras Bodhinī ṭīkā sahit,* vol. 3, 126–145; *Nābhājī kṛt Śrī Bhakt Māl, Bhakti Ras Bodhinī ṭīkā evaṃ Bhakti Rasāyanī vyākhyā sahit,* 577–583; *Nābhādās Bhaktmāl,* 610–16.

112 The reference is to a manuscript preserved in the Vrindāban Research Institute (acc. no. 4512F). This manuscript is dated 1718 (V.S. 1775) according to the catalogue, but this is based on the date when Priyādās finished his work as given at the end. In the editions this corresponds to v. 107. See *Śrīmad Gosvāmī Śrī Nābhājī kṛt Śrī Bhaktmāl, Śrī Priyādāsjī kṛt kavittamayī Bhakti Ras Bodhinī ṭīkā sahit,* vol. 3, 39; *Priyādāsjī kī granthāvalī,* ed. Bābā Kṛṣṇadās (Kusum Sarovar: Bābā Kṛṣṇdās, 1950), 35.

113 See *Śrīmad Gosvāmī Śrī Nābhājī kṛt Śrī Bhaktmāl, Śrī Priyādāsjī kṛt kavittamayī Bhakti Ras Bodhinī ṭīkā sahit,* vol. 3, 21–25; *Priyādāsjī kī granthāvalī,* 17–21; *Ananya Modinī tathā Cāhvelī* (*Priyādās viracit*), ed. Śyāmsundar Śarmā (Bhelsā [Gwalior], n.p., V.S. 1991 [1934]), 7–22.

114 The first reference is to Svāmī Nārāyaṇdās, *Śrī Svāmī Rāghavdāsjā viracit Bhaktmāl: Svāmī Caturdāsjī kṛt padya ṭīkā tathā bhakti-caritra prakāśikā gadya ṭīkā sahit* (Pushkar: Dādūdayālū Mahāsabhā, 1969), 411–17; the second to Agarchand Nāhaṭā, *Rāghavdās kṛt Bhaktmāl: Caturdās kṛt ṭīkā sahit,* Rājasthān Purātan Granthmālā 78 (Jodhpur: Rājasthān Prācya-vidyā Pratiṣṭhān, 1965), 129–30.

115 See Hargūlāl, *Sarvopari nityavihāriṇī ras-sār* (*Aṣṭācāryoṃ kī Vāṇī*), 713. Text and translation are provided in Pauwels, 'Harirām Vyās's *Rās-pañcādhyāyī Mān kī śṛṇkhalā,'* appendix 1.

116 See *Bhakt Māl Granth,* ed. Durgadās Lahilī (Calcutta: Bangladāśī Electric Machine Press, B.E. 1312 [1905]), 364–66. The *caritra* consists of 63 unnumbered couplets, which I will refer to by logical sequential number. It also contains one *pada* by Vyās.

117 See Kiśorīlāl Gupta, *Nāgrīdās granthāvalī*, vol. 2, Ākār Granthmālā, 9 (Benares: Nāgarīpracāriṇī Sabhā, 1965), 377–82 (hereafter cited as *PPM*).

118 See *Nijmat Siddhānt: Śrī Mahant Kiśordāsjī kṛt,* vol. 2 (Madhya Khaṇḍ), ed. Caraṇsevak Lālā [Vaiśya] Kedarnāth (Lucknow: Anglo-Oriental Press, V.S. 1971 [1915]), 107–14, 166.

119 See *Śrī Bhagavat Rasik Devjī kī Vāṇī,* ed. Vrajvallabh Śaraṇ (Vrindāban: Śrījī Mandir, V.S. 2044 [1987]), 60, 68–69.

120 The first reference is to *Śrī Svāmī Rāghavdāsjī viracit Bhaktmāl: Svāmī*

Caturdāsjī kṛt padya ṭīkā tathā bhakticaritra prakāśikā gadya ṭīkā sahit, 411–17; the second to Nāhaṭā, *Rāghavdās kṛt Bhaktmāl*, 129–30.

121 See *Lalit Prakāṣ*, ed. Caturvedī, Banmālīlāl (Lucknow: Tālukdār Press, 1931), 46–54 (hereafter cited as *LP*).

122 An edition of this work is in preparation by Dr. N.C. Bansal to whom I am grateful for providing me with copies of the manuscript dated 1843 (*vadi* 10 Pūs V.S. 1900) from the library of Advaitācaraṇ Gosvāmī (microfilm, Vrindāban Research Institute), reel 666, acc. no. H5(3). The chapters on Vyās are on fols. 118–33.

123 Raghurājsiṃh, *Bhakt Māl arthāt Rām Rasikāvalī*, ed. Khemrāj Kṛṣṇadās (Bombay: Lakṣmī Veṇkateśvar Steam Press, V.S. 1971 [1915]), 769–72.

124 Pratītrāy Lakṣmaṇ Siṃha, *Lokendra Brajotsava* (Lucknow: Naval Kiśor Press, 1892), 14–17.

125 The Rādhāvallabhan initiation of Vyās was first disputed by the Mādhva-Gauṛīya-sampradāya. This sect regards Caitanya as its founder, and claims that he himself was spiritually affiliated with the Mādhva-sampradāya. The claim that Vyās belonged to this sect is made in the middle of the eighteenth century in the so-called *Baṃglā bhakt-māl*. This work by Kṛṣṇadās Bābā, alias Lāldās, purports to be a translation of Nābhādās's *Bhakt-māl* into Bengālī. However, in the process Lāldās adapted it for Mādhva-Gauṛīya sectarian purposes. He not only claimed that Vyās belonged to the Mādhva sect, but also that Harivaṃś himself was initiated by a follower of Caitanya. See Rupert Snell, *The Eighty-Four Hymns of Hita Harivaṃśa: An Edition of the Caurāsī Pada* (Delhi: Motilal Banarsidass, 1991), 25–27.

126 Ibid., 15–16.

127 Bhagvatmudit is mentioned in Chappāī 198 of Nābhādās's *Bhakt-māl*. According to Garge, however, this is an interpolation (*Nābhājī kṛt Śrī Bhakt Māl*, 898). Priyādās in his commentary (Kavitta 626–629) says that he was a disciple of a *pūjārī* of the Govindadeva temple, and as such a follower of Caitanya.

128 The oldest manuscript available was clearly written in a Rādhāvallabhan milieu, because the opening verses are *śrī rādhāvallabho jayati. śrī vyāsa-nandano jayati*. For speculations about the authorship, see Pauwels, 'Harirām Vyās's *Rās-pañcādhyāyī* and *Mān kī śṛṅkhalā*,' 4.3.1.

129 As I have described elsewhere (ibid., 38–40), a contrast is set up in *RAM* 5-11, between Hit Harivaṃś, the true guru, and other possible candidates for guruhood mentioned in Vyās's poetry, such as Kabīr, Raidās, Nāmdev, and so on. To be sure, *RAM* 10 mentions that Vyās was aware of the Vrindāban scene, but his actually going there is the

result of this 'conversion-prep' by Navaldās.

130 This reference occurs in the edited text of *RAM* only; it is not confirmed by the reading in the manuscript.

131 For instance, the terms *tilaka* and *dāma* in *RAM* 37.

132 Entwistle, Braj, 156, 194. The section on Vyās is found in the middle part (*madhya khaṇḍa*) of the work.

133 P. Granoff, 'Scholars and Wonder-Workers: Some Remarks on the Role of the Supernatural in Philosophical Contests in Vedānta Hagiographies,' *Journal of the American Oriental Society* 105. no. 3 (1985), 464–65.

134 Snell, *Eighty-Four Hymns of Hita Harivaṃśa*, 17–21.

135 Pauwels, 'Harirām Vyās's *Rās-pañcādhyāyī* and *Mān kī śṛṅkhalā*,' appendix 2.

136 Or, 'the *ṭīkā* and the mantra,' but this is likely a faulty reading.

137 I have interpreted *ar-* as synonym of *aḍ-*: 'to take a stand,' 'get stuck.'

138 I have interpreted *visā-* in the sense of *vaś cal-* (*BBSK*).

139 Entwistle, *Braj*, 210.

140 Though some of the episodes are quite short, they are relatively numerous, compared with only five on Nāmdev and Mīrā each, four on Sūrdās Madan Mohan, three on Tulsīdās and Sūrdās, to mention only the longest. In addition, there is also one episode about Vyās's patron, Madhukar Śāh (*PPM* 52) and Vyās's son Kiśorīdās (*PPM* 56).

141 In addition, there is a song in which Vyās enumerates several *bhaktas* as forming his family (V21 = J21), which Nāgrī sees as an answer by Vyās to criticism by those who do not understand his associating and interdining with *bhaktas* outside his caste. Another song (V201 = J105) is interpreted as his testament, and yet another one (V26 = J26 = G11) is contextualized by the death of Vyās's fellow-*rasikas*.

142 According to *BBSK*, *bāda* is synonymous with the Skt. *vāda* and has the meaning of *tark, bahas; vivād*.

143 One of the meanings of *lagnā* can be *baratan ke tal meṃ rah jānā*. Hence the translation for *upadeś lag-*: 'instruction to be ascertained,' with the implication that he became a worthy '*pātra*' for instruction.

144 See table 1.

145 This is especially true in the chapters on Ujjain, or Avantikā Purī, and on Benares. *Caurāsī baiṭhak caritra*, ed. N. Śarmā (Mathurā: Śrī Govarddhan Granthmālā, V.S. 2024 [1967]), 171–77.

146 *Śrīmad Gosvāmī Śrī Nābhājī kṛt Śrī Bhaktmāl, Śrī Priyādāsjī kṛt kavittamayī Bhakti Ras Bodhinī ṭīkā sahit*, vol. 3, 126.

147 The opening of this line seems to be formulaic; cf. Priyādās's account (Kavitta 365) of Harivaṃś's life. See Snell, *Eighty-Four Hymns of Hita Harivaṃśa*, 14.

148 Another possible translation is: 'If somebody else would leave, he would be angry with that person.' This could be taken to refer to incidents where Vyās is annoyed with people who leave Vrindāban (cf. the last line of Kavitta 370). Most commentaries interpret it this way, and some quote a relevant *pada* from *Vyās-vāṇī.* See *Śrīmad Gosvāmī Śrī Nābhājī kṛt Śrī Bhaktmāl, Śrī Priyādāsjī kṛt kavittamayī Bhakti Ras Bodhinī ṭīkā sahit,* vol. 3, 129–30.

149 The repetition of the word *vāsa* is a bit confusing. For the meaning of the second occurrence, cf. *BBSK* which equals *bāsa* with *vāsanā.*

150 Or, if referring to the king, 'He insisted a lot.'

151 This is clearly the meaning of *kanāy*, although the only possibly relevant meaning that is attested in dictionaries is as a synonym of *kanāī* (f.): *vṛkṣa athavā paudhe kī patlī śākhā.* Cf. Miśra, *Sāhityik Brajbhāṣā koś,* vol. 1, 295.

152 See Pauwels, 'Harirām Vyās's *Rās-pañcādhyāyī* and *Mān kī śṛṅkhalā,*' 4.2.

153 This work must have been written by 1843. See Entwistle, *Braj,* 272.

154 *Vṛndāvan-dhām-anurāgāvalī, adhyayana,* fols. 127–28, ch. 16, *vyāsajī kau gherau.*

155 A similar story about a meeting of an anonymous king (*pātasā*) with Vyās and two of his companions is also told in *Baṃglā bhakt-māl caritra* 100:46–63 (see table 1). Lāldās stressed that the saints refused to go to the king's court, but were forced to. When they wanted to return after a few days, the king permitted at first only Vyās to return, because he considered as indispensable Vyās's role in the divine play as spittoon-provider.

156 *Bhāv-prakāś* at the end of *Sūrdās kī vārtā.* See Richard K. Barz, *The Bhakti Sect of Vallabhācārya* (Faidabad: Thomson Press, 1976), 122.

157 This story is also told in one of the genealogies, where Vyās's wish (much like Sūrdās's) is to be left alone, but the emperor is said to have granted him land anyway. Gosvāmī, *Bhakt kavi Vyāsjī,* 118.

158 The *Guru-śiṣya-vaṃśāvalī,* preserved in a manuscript dated V.S.1936. See ibid., 33–35, to which I did not have access.

159 Ibid., 114.

160 See table 1.

161 See V93 = J232 = G22 = M10, V282 = J148 = G14, as well as V234, not in J (*tana avahī kau kāmai āyau ... dhanya carana mere śrī vṛṃdāvana gahi anata na dhāyau,* 'Finally my body is of use ... Hail to my feet which have reached Vrindāban and refuse to go elsewhere').

162 He was connected with Rādhāramaṇ temple via his guru Manoharrāy. See Entwistle, *Braj,* 186.

163 The earliest source I have been able to detect for this story is a work dated 1846, Raghurājsiṃh, *Bhakt Māl arthāt Rām Rasikāvalī,* 56:4.

164 Nāhaṭā, *Rāghavdās kṛt Bhaktmāl,* 129–30.

165 Morinis, *Pilgrimage in the Hindu Tradition,* 279.

166 Ibid., 252, with regard to the Christian medieval pilgrimage.

5

Pilgrimage as Revelation: Śaṅkaradeva's Journey to Jagannātha Purī

PHYLLIS GRANOFF

Introduction: The Paradox of the Divine Pilgrim

Pilgrimage is often a central event in the biography of a holy man in medieval India. During the course of his journeys the saint may meet his guru and receive the transmission of the teaching, often in the form of books that are considered most authoritative and important to his teachings; he may also defeat opponents in debate and begin to gather around himself his own followers, thus initiating the religious community that will survive him and recount his deeds in the wide range of biographical texts that have come down to us. The saint may also act as an ordinary pilgrim, visiting holy sites and praying at famous temples. He may in addition create his own holy sites, by the miracles that he performs as he moves from village to village, temple to temple.

Despite this centrality of pilgrimage in religious biographies, the saint as pilgrim often seems to be problematic in biographical texts. In the *Śaṅkaradigvijaya*, when Padmapāda, Śaṅkara's famous disciple, wants to set off on a pilgrimage, his guru tells him that pilgrimage is not particularly productive of spiritual ends.[1] In the words of the text (chapter 14),

sa kṣetravāso nikaṭe guror yo vāsas tadīyāṅghrijalaṃ ca tīrtham /
gurūpadeśena yadātmadṛṣṭiḥ saiva praśastākhiladevadṛṣṭiḥ // 2

śuśrūṣamāṇena guroḥ samīpe stheyaṃ na neyaṃ ca tato 'nyadeśe /
viśiṣya mārgaśramakarśitasya nidrābhūtyā kim u cintanīyam // 3

saṃbhāvyate kva ca jalaṃ ca nāsti pāthaḥ śayyāsthalaṃ kvacidihāsti na ca kva cāsti /
śayyāsthalījalanirīkṣaṇasaktacetāḥ pāntho na śarma labhate kaluṣīkṛtātmā // 5

jvarātisārādi ca rogajālaṃ bādheta cet tarhi na ko 'pyupāyah. /
sthātuṃ ca gantuṃ ca na pārayeta tadā sahāyo 'pi vimuñcatīmam // 6

Dwelling near to one's guru is called dwelling in a holy place; the water used to bathe the guru's feet is holy water. And seeing the self through the instructions of a guru is the highest vision of God.

One who wishes to serve his guru should stay near him and not journey abroad. How can a person practice contemplation when he is overcome by sleep, exhausted and weary from his travels?

For the traveller is beset with worries. Where will he find water to drink, and where not? Sometimes there will be a place to stay and sometimes not. His mind absorbed in looking for water or a place to stop, the traveller is in turmoil and finds no peace.

Fever and dysentery, all manner of ills may beset the traveller; what can he then do, unable either to go on or to stay. And at such a moment his companion deserts him.

Padmapāda is not deterred, however. He agrees that his teacher's words contain a germ of truth, but he nonetheless repeats that he is eager to see new places: *anekān deśān avīkṣya hṛdayaṃ na nirākulam me,* 'Unless I see many places my heart will know no peace' (v. 8). Padmapāda readily agrees that the journey is difficult. But he adds, it is never easy to acquire merit: *mārgo hi vidyeta na suvyavasthaḥ sukhena puṇyaṃ kva nu labhyate adhunā,* 'It may well be that the path is not lined with comforts, but these days how is merit to be acquired without hardship?' (v. 9). Even the threat of illness does not make him turn back; after all, disease is a result of previous karma, and that will come to fruition whether one stays at home or sets out on the road: *sādhāraṇād iha ca vā paradeśake vā karma hyabhuktam anuvartata eva jantum*, 'Whether here or in a foreign land, karma that has not been exhausted by living it out, will surely follow a person' (v. 10). Padmapāda then seeks to counter a common prejudice against travelling in foreign lands:

iha sthitaṃ vā parataḥ sthitaṃ vā kālo na muñcet samayāgataścet /
taddeśagatyā amṛta devadatta ityādikaṃ mohakṛtam janānām // 11

Death comes to a man, whether he stays at home or goes abroad, if his time has come. It is just superstition that makes people say, 'It was going to that place that killed Devadatta.'

Padmapāda further argues that some men go abroad on pilgrimages and return in good health, while others stay at home and die in the meantime (v. 14). He then goes on to extol the virtues of pilgrimage:

sattīrthasevā manasaḥ prasādinī deśasya vīkṣā manasaḥ kutūhalam /
kṣiṇotyanarthān sujanena saṃgamas tasmān na kasmai bhramaṇam virocate // 16

Visiting an excellent holy place gladdens the heart, while seeing a new place stimulates the mind. Meeting fine men puts an end to misfortunes. Who would not delight in travel?

And so Padmapāda undertakes his longed-for pilgrimage.[2] The text suggests, however, that there are still incongruities in a holy man journeying to a holy site. In the course of his travels, Padmapāda stops to visit his maternal uncle. His relatives welcome him and then say,

caranti tīrthānyapi saṃgrahītuṃ lokaṃ mahānto nanu śuddhabhāvāḥ /
śuddhātmavidyākṣapitorupāpās tajjuṣṭam ambho nigadanti tīrtham // 89

True it is that the great, pure in heart, make pilgrimages out of a desire to help others. For they have already destroyed their own sins through their pure knowledge of the true soul; indeed they say that the water such men use is the real holy water.

This is actually a very significant verse; it introduces us to an important theme in the treatment of pilgrimage in religious biographies, namely, that there is something incongruous in a sage being a pilgrim. The sage is already pure and does not need to make a pilgrimage, the purpose of which is to remove sin, often by bathing in holy water. Indeed such a person's own bath water purifies others of sin. What need would he have, then, of making a pilgrimage? The answer given here is simple: The sage makes a pilgrimage to help others. He does so by setting an example, and by providing them with the chance to be in his presence.[3]

The problem of the sage as pilgrim is even more acute when the sage is regarded as a God or incarnation of a God. This is the case of all the figures in medieval Hinduism who were the main subjects of religious biographies. The question then arises, why would God ever need to travel to see God? The *Madhya Līlā* section of the *Caitanya-caritāmṛta* by Kṛṣṇadāsa describes in great detail Caitanya's pilgrimage to Purī and other sacred sites.[4] At one point on the journey the text tells us,

tīrthe pavitra karite kare tīrthabhraman /
sei chale nistāraye sāṃsārika janān // 10.11

Great men make pilgrimages to purify the holy sites. That is how they save people caught in transmigratory existence.

Kṛṣṇadāsa then quotes the *Bhāgavata Purāṇa*, as he often does, as textual support for his view on holy men and pilgrimages.

bhavadvidhā bhāgavatas tīrthībhūtāḥ svayaṃ vibho /
tīrthīkurvanti tīrthāni svāntasthena gadābhṛtā // 1.13.10

Great devotees like you, O Lord, are themselves holy. They sanctify supposed holy places by the presence of Viṣṇu, who resides in their hearts.

The verse from the *Bhāgavata Purāṇa* is spoken by Yudhiṣṭhira to Vidura, who has returned to Hastināpura after making a pilgrimage. It lends support to at least part of Kṛṣṇadāsa's statement, that holy men do not need to make pilgrimages for their own sake; indeed the verse seems to say that the presence of such men is what makes a place holy. They bring with them God, who is said to reside in their hearts, that is, who is the constant focus of their thoughts. We then must go back to Kṛṣṇadāsa's own verse to understand why in fact someone who carries the divine within him would seek God in a pilgrimage place. The answer is simply that somehow this is part of the holy man's efforts to rescue people from the cycle of rebirths.[5]

Religious biographies treat the holy pilgrim in a number of ways and adopt a variety of strategies to show that the saint is not an ordinary pilgrim. Although in much of the *Madhya Līlā* Caitanya seems just that, as he visits well-known temples and prays to the famous images, there are indications that he has an unusual relationship with the God to whom he prays: in many cases he is that God. Thus when Caitanya goes to Remuṇā to pay homage to the image of Gopīnātha there, an unusual event transpires. The garland that was on the head of the God suddenly finds itself on Caitanya's head instead.[6]

Despite the fact that the biographical tradition of Caitanya in stories such as this one recognizes the inherent incongruity of the divine Caitanya bowing to God as an ordinary pilgrim might, the accounts of Caitanya's pilgrimage overwhelmingly suggest an extraordinary but nonetheless human quest. Caitanya does at times exhibit unusually strong emotions in his overwhelming love of the God he sees; thus in the temple of Jagannātha at Purī, he rushes to embrace the image and falls into a swoon (2.5.144; 2.6). Caitanya bows down, dances, and sings before certain images (2.6.235), but more often he just worships in various temples without any mention of anything unusual. He also simply meets various people who will become his disciples. Most important, perhaps, he meets his teachers and receives the holy books that will form the basis of his ecstatic religion. Caitanya, on one pilgrimage, receives a copy of the important *Brahmasaṃhitā* (2.9.23-7) and of the *Kṛṣṇakarṇāmṛta* (2.9.306). In each case, he has copies of the manuscripts made. It was on an earlier pilgrimage to Gayā that he had met Īśvara Purī, who had initiated him. The *Caitanya Bhāgavata* of Vṛndāvanadāsa describes this as Caitanya's *mantra dīkṣā*, his initiation through the transmission of a mantra (1.7.105).[7]

In this text, when Vṛdāvanadāsa describes Caitanya's visit to the temple of Jagannātha, mentioned above, he does remark on the unusual situation of Caitanya's fainting and swooning in joy at the sight of God, given the fact that Caitanya is himself God. He says simply,

kṣeṇeke paḍilā hai ānande mūrchita /
ke bujhe e īśvarer agādha carita // 3.2.430

For an instant he fell down, swooning in joy. Who can comprehend the unfathomable deeds of God?

Thus the paradox remains. We are left with the anomaly of God in a swoon over Himself as proof of the fact that God's ways are beyond human comprehension. Vṛndāvanadāsa does not stop here, however; he seems to be intensely concerned by the strangeness of the Divine Pilgrim and offers an alternative explanation for Caitanya's pilgrimages. On his trip to Purī he has Caitanya say that he really came not to see the deity, Jagannātha, but to see the human Sarvabhauma, who will become one of his most faithful devotees (3.3.11–12). Caitanya repeats this assertion later (3.3.143). Here the seemingly ordinary events of the pilgrimage are put into service as an explanation for the enigma of God travelling to worship Himself. God has another design, which is to meet a human devotee and bring him into His worship. We might compare this with Kṛṣṇadāsa's assertion that the Divine Pilgrim acts to save mortal beings caught in the cycle of rebirth.

Sometimes bringing God to mortals requires an extraordinary revelation and thus there are moments during the pilgrimages when Caitanya's divinity becomes immediately apparent to his devotees. We have seen one such moment in the story of the garland of Gopīnātha of Remuṇā being miraculously transferred onto Caitanya's head. On the banks of the Kṛṣṇaveṇā River, Caitanya is recognized as an incarnation of Rāma when he embraces a certain tree in the Daṇḍaka Forest and the tree vanishes to heaven (2.9.314).[8] Pilgrimage in this biographical tradition is thus a complex phenomenon, offering the occasion for the divine saint to reveal his divinity, and theoretically serving in some way to save the mass of humanity. Nonetheless, most often Caitanya's travels seem to be part of a very human quest of an emotionally sensitive devotee, who along the way finds his teachers and his books, and worships fervently at various holy sites, as we might imagine other human pilgrims do. At the same time, behind the account of all of these activities, as we have seen, there lurks a suspicion of their very appropriateness. In varying ways the biographers all question the point of a holy man making a pilgrimage. In the end Vṛndāvanadāsa offers as an explanation the inscrutability of God's ways, while Kṛṣṇadāsa suggests that holy men make pilgrimages to save others. Both tell stories that highlight the anomalous nature of Caitanya's pilgrimage, of God praying to God. Pilgrimage is thus both a major event in the biographies of Caitanya and a major problem.

When we look at the biographical tradition surrounding another Northeastern Indian Vaiṣṇava saint, Śaṅkaradeva of Assam, the problem of pilgrimage seems even more acute. Like Caitanya, Śaṅkaradeva was regarded as divine by his followers. There is thus the incongruity of the God going to worship Himself. But there was another problem with pilgrimage for the Assamese Vaiṣṇava community, which advocated the sole reliance on the worship of Kṛṣṇa, particularly on reciting the name of Kṛṣṇa in these degenerate times. Thus, in the biography of Śaṅkaradeva by Rāmacaraṇa, we are told,

kalita śaṅkare śunā nirantare bhaktar sādhibe gati /
tānta vine ān saṃsār tāraṇ kalita nāhi samprati //
bhailanta udita śaṅkara vidita prakāśilā nijadharma /
deva tīrtha vrata yāg yoga yata dūr kailā āna karma // 3444

Listen now, in this time of Kali Yuga, Śaṅkara will save his devotees. There is no other means now in this Kali Age to cross the ocean of transmigratory existence, but Śaṅkara. Śaṅkara, like the sun, has now risen, spreading the light of his religion. He has cast far away other religious practices, worship of the Gods, pilgrimage to holy places, fasts, sacrifices, meditation and all.[9]

Despite this bold assertion, that Śaṅkara's new religion rejects all ritual, including pilgrimage, pilgrimage remains a central event in the biographies told of Śaṅkaradeva. Like Caitanya, Śaṅkaradeva goes to Purī and to Gayā. In the rest of this essay, I explore how his pilgrimage is treated by one biographer, Rāmacaraṇa.[10] I argue that the suspicion of pilgrimage in the Assamese Vaiṣṇava community led the biographer to treat the holy pilgrim very differently from the way in which other holy pilgrims had been treated by their biographers. I try to show that unlike Caitanya, Śaṅkaradeva was not described as either an ordinary or a particularly fervent human devotee, but more consistently as God. Śaṅkaradeva is not an ordinary pilgrim; he does not find a guru on his journey, and he does not collect books. His pilgrimage is more a series of divine revelations, in which, in dreams and visions, he shows the faithful his true nature as God. Pilgrimage has become so problematic that it has ceased to be a pilgrimage at all for the pilgrim, and became a spiritual journey for the onlookers.

Śaṅkaradeva's Journey

Despite Śaṅkaradeva's unambiguous rejection of pilgrimage in Rāmacaraṇa's biography of him, people do make pilgrimages throughout the text. The biography begins with a detailed account of Śaṅkaradeva's ancestors. All of Śaṅkaradeva's ancestors were born in somewhat unusual circumstances, to parents who were childless until they obtained a boon from a god or goddess. As the biography opens, we hear of a woman Indunī, whose husband rejects her. In the years since the celebration of her *puṣpotsava*, the festivities celebrating her reaching puberty, her husband has not once come to her bed. One day he finally relents and comes to her (1.29). She prays fervently for a child, and reflecting on the fact that if a son is born a husband's ill-fame as sterile is removed, while if a daughter is born, a wife is no longer rebuked for having been the cause of infertility, she prays to Śiva for a daughter (1.31). She gives birth to a daughter Kṛṣṇakānti, who is the Śakti of Kṛṣṇa. This Kṛṣṇakānti is later miraculously made pregnant by Śiva, who makes Viṣṇu's seed fall from the heavens into her mouth (1.40). We learn of this child's, Laṇḍādeva's, descendants, who include Sūryavara, born after his parents worshipped the sun God, Sūrya, and Śaṅkaradeva's father, Kusumavara, born from a boon obtained when his father, Sūryavara, worshipped the Lords of the Quarters, the Dikpālas. Kusumavara is childless and he and his father together make a pilgrimage to a famous Śiva *liṅga* situated in a cave at Sṛgarikā. Kusumavara tells the priest that he has come seeking a child. The priests give him some *prasāda* and offer an oblation into the sacred fire (1.319–320). A garland on the Śiva *liṅga* falls onto Kusumavara, in this case, confirming that he has received a boon from the God.

The child born to Kusumavara is Śaṅkaradeva, who thus ironically seems to owe his very birth to the ritual of pilgrimage that he later rejects. The birth of Śaṅkaradeva's first wife is also the result of a pilgrimage. We are told of one Satānanda Bhuā, who went to Purī to worship. He prayed to Subhadrā for a daughter. That night Subhadrā appeared to one of the temple priests in a dream. She predicts the birth of a son, Harikhā, who will father a daughter, Sūryavatī. It is this Sūryavatī who will wed Śaṅkaradeva (2.1659ff.).

After a long account of the unusual circumstances of Śaṅkaradeva's conception and birth, the biography goes into great detail about Śaṅkaradeva's early history; indeed we are given a day-by-day account of his exploits for much of his infancy. The biography tells us again and again that Śaṅkaradeva is Kṛṣṇa; his childhood is filled with pranks that resemble those of Kṛṣṇa. Like Kṛṣṇa, he is naughty and torments his mother; like Kṛṣṇa, he kills various threatening creatures.

But the author of the biography does not simply stop at drawing these obvious parallels; he actually makes his text an extension of the authoritative texts that tell the life of Kṛṣṇa, for example the *Bhāgavata Purāṇa*. Thus when Śaṅkaradeva kills a snake, we are not just told that this was like Kṛṣṇa, who had once killed a snake. We are told that in a former life the snake was Satrājit, the father of Kṛṣṇa's wife, Satyabhāmā. Satrājit had verbally abused Kṛṣṇa, who had turned him into a *vidyādhara*, predicting that he would be reborn as a snake when Kṛṣṇa himself was reborn as Śaṅkaradeva and that Śaṅkaradeva would bring about his final release from *saṃsāra* (2.1226ff.). The life of Śaṅkaradeva is here seen as a continuation of the life of Kṛṣṇa, its very events foretold during Kṛṣṇa's own lifetime.[11] I might add that this also makes Rāmacaraṇa's text something of a new *Bhāgavata Purāṇa*, continuing the account of Kṛṣṇa into the present.

In this way, Rāmacaraṇa frequently takes events in the life of Śaṅkaradeva back into the world of the *Bhāgavata Purāṇa* as he attempts to establish without question the identity of Śaṅkaradeva with Kṛṣṇa. Thus when Śaṅkaradeva's father dies an early death we are told why: He was Nanda, Kṛṣṇa's father in an earlier birth, and he had not believed the children when they had told him of Kṛṣṇa's marvelous exploits. And so it was that he had to pay for his lack of faith with a gripping fever that carried him off early in life. Śaṅkaradeva's mother also dies young; we are told that this is because as Kṛṣṇa's mother, Yaśodā, she had tied Kṛṣṇa up after he had made a mess of the house (2.1139ff.). Rāmacaraṇa frequently cites some *purāṇa* as an authoritative source as he explains how events in Śaṅkaradeva's life are prefigured and foretold in the accounts of Kṛṣṇa. Thus at one point he cites the *Nārada Purāṇa* (2.1258); at another, the *Viṣṇu Purāṇa* (2.1303).

We are thus amply instructed in the biography that Śaṅkaradeva is Kṛṣṇa. It seems natural, then, when we do come to the point in the biography where Śaṅkaradeva is ready to make his first pilgrimage, that the question is raised openly about the suitability of someone we know to be God going on a journey, the ostensible purpose of which is to see the visible God in His temple. Śaṅkaradeva has gone to take leave of his guru, Mahendra Kandalī. Here is the exchange between them in our text:

śaṇkare śuniyā hariṣa kariyā bolanta śuniyo vāṇī /
jagannātha kṣetre yāive icchā bhilā vidāya diyo āpuni // 1753
guruve bolanta tumi ye īṣvara kṣetrata kaman kāma /

> *brahmāṇda loka sabe nistariba tomāther gāyā nāma // 1754*

> Hearing his words, Śaṅkara was delighted and said, 'Hear my words! I wish to go to the holy place of Jagannātha. Give me leave to go.' The teacher said, 'But you are God! What could you possibly want with a holy place! All the beings in the universe will be released just by chanting your name!'

Śaṅkaradeva's reply is not terribly helpful:

> *Śaṅkare bolanta nubulibā guru sisaba vākya amāka /*
> *diyo anumati yāiboho samprati tīrtha kṣetra dekhibāka // 1755*

> Śaṅkara said, 'Please don't say such things to me, O teacher! Give me your permission. I must go now, to see the holy place, the holy site!'

The guru next proposes to consult the almanacs to determine the propitious day on which Śaṅkaradeva should set out; Śaṅkaradeva dismisses all of that with contempt and gets permission to make the journey (1755-1756).

Śaṅkaradeva has obviously not answered Mahendra Kandalī's very fundamental question: Why would God need to go on a pilgrimage to find or see Himself? The text does give us its answer, although somewhat later on. At this point, Śaṅkaradeva is still on his pilgrimage. Along the way he has picked up Rūpa and Sanātana Gosvāmī, the famous followers of Caitanya. Śaṅkaradeva has bathed in a sacred spot and offered memorial oblations to his ancestors.[12] Some pilgrims are gathered under a large tree that has miraculous fruit; eating the fruit of this tree instantly stills both hunger and thirst. But no one is able to reach the fruit. As Śaṅkaradeva approaches, the fruit falls down to him, all by itself. Rūpa and Sanātana are both amazed. The pilgrims under the tree include four priests, who were sleeping at the time. They see a dream in which Śaṅkaradeva assumes the appearance of Rāma. Sītā is worshiping him with songs of praise. The priests ask Rāma from where he has come; Rāma replies that he has been born in Kāmarūpa as Śaṅkara, in a family of *śūdras*. He proclaims the doctrine of exclusive refuge in Kṛṣṇa and he has come on a pilgrimage to prove this (*tīrthaka lāgiyā āilo dekhāite pramāṇa,* 2049). With these words Rāma vanishes and the priests see Śaṅkara right before their eyes, shining like the full moon (3.2042-2050). This phrase, *dekhāite pramāṇa,* 'to show proof,' occurs again, when

Śaṅkaradeva is in Vṛndāvana. One of his followers asks him, *dharibek nijarūpa dekhiyo pramāṇa*, 'take on your real form and show us proof' (3.2101). They then all fall asleep and in a dream they see Śaṅkaradeva, who has taken on his real form as Kṛṣṇa, surrounded by the *gopas* and *gopīs* (3.2102). The purpose of Śaṅkaradeva's pilgrimage is thus to show proof of his divinity by revealing his true, that is, his divine nature. As we go back now and look at some of the other events that take place during Śaṅkaradeva's pilgrimage, we shall see that this is exactly how Rāmacaraṇa depicts the pilgrimage. It is a visionary experience, not so much for Śaṅkaradeva himself, as for the select devotees to whom he reveals his divine nature.

Once he obtains permission from Mahendra Kandalī to make the pilgrimage to Jagannātha, Śaṅkaradeva first settles some important matters at home. He arranges for his daughter's marriage and he performs more *śrāddha* rituals with appropriate gifts to Brahmins. He is then ready to set out. As if to remind us of that other Śaṅkara's words to his disciple, Padmapāda, with which I began this essay, the first major incidents in the pilgrimage have to do with the efforts of the pilgrims to obtain food and drink along the way. In one incident the party has not been able to find any inhabited place to stop; they are forced to camp out in the wilderness. They are worried that they will not find anything to eat and they lie down to sleep. Suddenly a shining and handsome man, his body aglow like the sun or moon, appears. He is accompanied by others and they have together brought all that the pilgrims require. The two disciples, Sarbajaya and Balarāma, are awake and see the shining person; they pinch a third person, Rāmarāma, so that he wakes up.[13] Śaṅkaradeva tells them to wake up all the other pilgrims so that they can eat. When the pilgrims awaken and see the food, they ask who has brought it all. Śaṅkaradeva tells them that he had gone and brought the food. Rāmarāma then speaks up; he says that it is unlikely that anyone could have found a market and a store in that wilderness; Śaṅkaradeva has brought the food from heaven. He describes the glowing apparition and the fourteen others who accompanied the shining person. Balarāma, Sarbajaya, and Rāmarāma then all tell the others what they had seen (3.1901ff.). Mahendra Kandalī is among the pilgrims and he declares that Śaṅkaradeva is himself Jagannātha; what need have they of going to Purī, when Jagannātha is among them? (3.1908).

This incident, early in the pilgrimage, sets the tone for what will follow. During the pilgrimage Śaṅkaradeva will repeatedly reveal his divinity to select devotees, either in visions or in dreams. Others who are present often do not see the dreams or visions, although they may later be told about them. Soon after the vision in the wilderness, the party reaches the Ganges and Mahendra Kandalī has a dream in which he sees nine beautiful women. They are all richly bejewelled, though the one at their lead is particularly richly appointed. This woman places a gold garland on Śaṅkaradeva's head calling him Nārāyaṇa, and proclaims herself his servant. She says that he will purify her. She tells Śaṅkaradeva that once before she had gained release from touching his foot. With this, all the women bow to Śaṅkaradeva and Mahendra Kandalī wakes up (3.1913). Kandalī is overwhelmed and cries. He rushes to where Śaṅkaradeva and the other devotees are and he tells them of his dream; he tells them how the women praised Śaṅkaradeva and proclaimed him to be Kṛṣṇa. The pilgrims are all astounded and they rush to the Ganges River. Śaṅkaradeva also goes to bathe in the river and to deposit the bones of his father and grandfather there. A beautiful woman comes out of the river. She praises Śaṅkaradeva. This vision is both the fulfillment of Mahendra Kandalī's dream and a somewhat private revelation; the pilgrims do not recognize the woman as the Goddess Gaṅgā, although they do see her rise out of the water and hear her words glorifying Śaṅkaradeva (3.1926ff.).

The pilgrims continue along their way to Jagannātha, stopping at Gayā to perform *śrāddha* rituals. When Śaṅkaradeva is about to reach Jagannātha, there is yet another revelation of his divinity. This time Jagannātha speaks to his priests in a dream, telling them that Śaṅkaradeva is coming and that he is Jagannātha's Lord (Prāṇanātha, 'Lord of My Life,' 3.1934). He describes Śaṅkaradeva to them so that they will know him and instructs them to offer him food from the temple along with Jagannātha's greetings. The priests do as they are told, and even explain to Śaṅkaradeva that this was what Jagannātha had instructed them to do in a dream. In this scene, the God sends food from the temple to the pilgrim, instead of the normal course of events, in which a pilgrim would be expected to go to the temple himself or herself and receive food. Śaṅkaradeva, though a pilgrim, is thus not really a pilgrim at all.

In another negation of his status as a pilgrim, the three Gods of the temple at Purī then come to Śaṅkaradeva at night. Jagannātha himself, Balarāma and Subhadrā come disguised as cats (3.1957). This, too, is a reversal of the normal order of things, since pilgrims come to see gods and not the other way around. The text further makes clear that it is the Gods who are the real pilgrims, for when they visit Śaṅkaradeva in this surreptitious night visit they eat what Śaṅkaradeva has left uneaten; in other words they take *prasāda*, food eaten by the God, from Śaṅkaradeva, which is what pilgrims do, taking *prasāda* from a temple that they visit. The ever watchful Sarbajaya sees the cats and tries to shoo them away, but Śaṅkaradeva stops him. The cats vanish. Now the three pilgrims, Sarbajaya, Rāmarāma, and Kandalī, have a dream in which Jagannātha comes to them and says that he has eaten the *prasāda*. He tells them that it was he who came in the form of a cat. With that he vanishes and they wake up. Once more we have an incident in which the divinity of Śaṅkaradeva is revealed to select disciples, for this is what it means for Jagannātha to take *prasāda*, which is the word that designates the food given to the God and then distributed to the worshippers. The incident tells us that Jagannātha is the worshipper and Śaṅkaradeva is the God.

The same relationship between Jagannātha and Śaṅkaradeva is confirmed by what happens when Śaṅkaradeva finally enters the temple. In an incident that closely recalls what we saw happen to Caitanya at Remuṇā, when Śaṅkaradeva approaches the image, Jagannātha gives his garland to him. While no one actually sees him transfer the garland from his own head onto Śaṅkaradeva's head, they all see the garland on Śaṅkaradeva. The pilgrims all praise Śaṅkaradeva as the highest lord (3.1973–4).

Perhaps the most striking of all of the divine revelations during the pilgrimage occurs to the pilgrims at Dvārakā. The visit to Jagannātha is over and the pilgrims are making a tour of various holy places. They go to Prayāga and Puṣkariṇī, for example. We are told that at each place they visit, the pilgrims see dreams and know that there is no higher God than Śaṅkara (3.2963). The group then comes to Mathurā. The pilgrims ask Śaṅkaradeva to show them Dvārakā; they want to see the palace of Rukmiṇī (3.2064ff.). Sarbajaya explains that at the time of the equinox Rukmiṇī's palace rises from the ocean (3.2065). He and Balarāma and Paramānanda beg Śaṅkaradeva to take them and he agrees. They make their plans to go to the sea at the time of the equinox. As the four of them, Śaṅkaradeva, Sarbajaya, Balarāma, and Paramānanda, all sit by the shore in the lotus position, facing West, they hear a rumble from the depths of the ocean. Śaṅkaradeva tells them to close their eyes and he moves away from them. When they open their eyes and do not see him they are afraid, but then they see someone in the midst of the ocean. They cannot tell if they are in heaven or in the underworld, but they realize the divine person that they are seeing is their own Śaṅkaradeva (3. 2075). They also see a divine city with palaces like golden suns. It has groves, lakes, and ponds, and Śaṅkara is in the middle of all this. There are sixteen thousand palaces that all glow like the sun, but among them is one palace even more glorious than the others. There is a woman in this palace, seated on a jewelled throne. They see Śaṅkaradeva by her side on the jewelled throne. A heavenly retinue from Viṣṇu's heaven, Vaikuṇṭha, waits on the couple. The three pilgrims are astonished. They know that Śaṅkaradeva is God and that he has left their side and is in the divine palace on a jewelled throne (3.2086). And then the vision vanishes. They look around and Śaṅkaradeva is with them again. They praise him and are ready to move on. They have seen Dvārakā, which is as wonderful as heaven itself.[14]

This vision, although more detailed and splendid than the other visions on the pilgrimage, is perfectly consistent in character with the other divine revelations that have taken place during Śaṅkaradeva's travels. It is an esoteric vision, given only to select disciples and Śaṅkaradeva is the object of the vision and not its recipient. There was a tradition in medieval Indian writing on pilgrimage that emphasized the visionary quality of the goal of pilgrimage and its exclusivity; this text is not unique in associating pilgrimage with private visions. At the same time, I would stress that it is distinctive in that here it is not the prime pilgrim who has the visions; Śaṅkaradeva does not receive visions but somehow causes others to see him in a vision. He is thus not really a pilgrim here, as he was not a pilgrim in Jagannātha's temple; he is the God, the goal of someone else's pilgrimage.[15] However pilgrimage is defined, whether as visionary experience or as an ordinary journey to a temple, it is difficult to characterize Śaṅkaradeva as a pilgrim in either sense.

It is also as instructive to note what does not happen to Śaṅkaradeva on the pilgrimage as it is to study what does happen. Śaṅkaradeva does not find a guru, nor does he receive any teaching in the form of books, both important events for Caitanya on his pilgrimage as we saw above. Śaṅkaradeva is regarded as an innovator by his biographer; although Mahendra Kandalī is referred to as his guru, he does not teach Śaṅkaradeva anything that one might consider to be the basis of Śaṅkaradeva's religious doctrine. Mahendra Kandalī had been Śaṅkaradeva's childhood teacher and had taught him the rudiments of Sanskrit and had been responsible for his early education. The biography at one point tells a curious story of Nārada and Uddhava, both famous from the *Bhāgavata Purāṇa*. In the story, Uddhava makes fun of Nārada, saying that he has no guru. Nārada vows to take the first person who comes along as his guru. God comes disguised as an outcaste, reeking of liquor and carrying a pig. The outcaste has no wisdom to impart to Nārada, so Nārada must teach him something that the outcaste can then teach back to him! (5.2694). This story seems to me to mock the need for linear transmission that was the concern of so many medieval Indian religious sects. It is thus perhaps not surprising that Śaṅkaradeva does not use his pilgrimage to seek or find his teachers.[16]

Śaṅkaradeva also does not collect books on his travels. The books come to Śaṅkaradeva, while he stays at home. Thus we are told how a Brahmin from Tirati goes to Purī to recite the *Bhāgavata Purāṇa* in front of Jagannātha. Jagannātha appears to him in a dream and tells him to go and recite the text to Śaṅkaradeva, for Jagannātha and Śaṅkaradeva are one (4.2161ff.). Thus the *Bhāgavata* comes to Śaṅkara. If one function of the pilgrimage in religious biographies is to bring the holy man in contact with his teacher and teachings, then in this sense, too, Śaṅkaradeva is not a pilgrim.

Finally, Śaṅkara does not make most of his converts on his pilgrimage; they, too, come to him. In fact, one particular disciple, Nārāyaṇa, seems to collect many of the others around Śaṅkaradeva. We are left with the impression that in this text, Śaṅkaradeva's pilgrimage seems to be the very antithesis of a pilgrimage, however conceived.

Conclusion

I began this essay by trying to show that despite the importance of pilgrimage in religious biographies, these texts are often ambivalent about the spiritual benefits to be gained from pilgrimage. The *Śaṅkaradigvijaya* both doubts the usefulness of pilgrimage in a search for religious knowledge and suggests that there is some fundamental incongruity in the very idea that the holy man, who makes holy places wherever he goes, should have something to gain from visiting a place that popular opinion holds to be sacred. I briefly noted how, in the biographical tradition concerning Caitanya, the ambiguities surrounding pilgrimage are often explicitly discussed. We have seen that stories are told that clearly problematize the notion that God would go to worship Himself, while reasons other than worshipping God are offered for going on pilgrimages. At the same time, however, it seems undeniable that Caitanya can and does often act as an ordinary pilgrim, going from temple to temple, meeting his teachers, and collecting texts that he carefully has copied.

By contrast, in the biography of Śaṅkaradeva ascribed to Rāmacaraṇa, pilgrimage has been radically transformed. In keeping with the strong emphasis throughout the biography on Śaṅkaradeva's identity with Kṛṣṇa, Śaṅkaradeva is portrayed as a highly unusual pilgrim. He does not go to worship, but to be worshipped. Pilgrimage becomes the occasion for him to reveal his divinity. That he does so at famous pilgrimage sites, for example Jagannātha at Purī, and Dvārakā, surely attests to the importance of these places at the time when the biographies were written. Nonetheless, attention is deflected from the holy sites onto Śaṅkaradeva himself. Thus, at Purī, it is Śaṅkara's lodgings that become the temple when Jagannātha, Subhadrā, and Balarāma go there and eat Śaṅkara's leftover food. And without the presence of Śaṅkaradeva, the pilgrims would not have seen Rukmiṇī's palace in Dvārakā at all; they certainly could not have seen the God in Dvārakā, since that was Śaṅkaradeva himself.

Regional religious movements with their emphasis on vernacular writing are obviously more locally rooted than religious movements writing in a language that transcends local boundaries. It may not be irrelevant that this biography, while allowing pilgrimage to pan-Indian holy sites a place in Śaṅkaradeva's story, at the same time denies many of its defining characteristics. It is perhaps not surprising that even after Śaṅkaradeva's pilgrimage is over, Jagannātha travels again to see Śaṅkaradeva, coming as far as Assam, to the place where Śaṅkaradeva holds his prayer sessions (4.2330). The devotees know that he has come by the divine fragrance that suffuses the assembly. Śaṅkaradeva even has an image of Jagannātha made and consecrated (4.2298ff.). Jagannātha in this text retains his authority, but not his position as the God in a particular temple which was the goal of pilgrims from all across India.[17] Now Jagannātha is the pilgrim, and the religious centre remains in Assam, wherever Śaṅkaradeva and his followers gather. God as pilgrim in this text is thus both a problem and a solution to another problem, that of creating and maintaining regional religious identity.

If there is a concern in Rāmacaraṇa's biography to transcend the strictly local through pilgrimage, it would seem to emerge not in any search for legitimacy outside Assam at an established centre or fixed place. Rather, it takes the form of creating links between Śaṅkaradeva and the other Vaiṣṇava saints of medieval India that seem to defy the natural boundaries of time and space. Pilgrimage helps to accomplish this goal either by bringing Śaṅkaradeva into contact with major Vaiṣṇava leaders from other sects or by giving the author of the biography the opportunity to state explicitly the essential unity behind their doctrines. We have seen how Śaṅkaradeva on his first pilgrimage met and impressed Sanātana and Rāpa Gosvāmī, the famous followers of Caitanya. It is instructive to reflect on how their encounter is described; there is no question of rivalry or hostility. We are told that when Śaṅkaradeva reaches the place in which Rāpa and Sanātana are residing, the two brothers rush to meet him. Seeing him, they are beside themselves with joy; they lose all sense of reason and fall to the ground at his feet (3.2021). Śaṅkaradeva lifts them up and embraces them. He asks them what religion they follow and they reply with a brief summary of Śaṅkaradeva 's own doctrine on the sole reliance on reciting the name of Kṛṣṇa. They also praise Śaṅkaradeva as the supreme God (3.2023–4). There is no question of conversion or conquest, familiar to readers of medieval Indian religious biographies such as the *Śaṅkaradigvijaya,* with which I began this essay. The supremacy of Śaṅkaradeva 's position is amply demonstrated by showing that it is in accord with what other great Vaiṣṇava leaders teach.

In addition to this encounter with these two men who were known as Caitanya's followers, the biographies tell us that Śaṅkaradeva made a second pilgrimage which was to bring him into contact with other leading Vaiṣṇava saints. One of his stops is at the home of Kabīr's daughter. She relates to Śaṅkaradeva some incidents from Kabīr's life and concludes with an account of how Hindus and Muslims alike refused to cremate Kabīr and the corpse was left unattended until Caitanya took care of it (5.3327–54). Caitanya is given an opportunity to explain the fundamentals of his religious beliefs, which of course accord completely with the doctrines that Śaṅkaradeva preaches! When Kabīr's daughter finishes her account, Śaṅkaradeva praises Kabīr. In this single episode we are encouraged to see in Kabīr, Caitanya, and Śaṅkaradeva three exemplars of the one correct religious belief and life. If pilgrimage in religious biographies is in part a quest for legitimacy, here that legitimacy comes not from a single conquest or moment of divine approbation in an established religious centre, but from creating a sense of community that goes beyond time and place: Kabīr is dead and

Caitanya is placed back in the closing moments of Kabīr's life story; we may see in Śaṅkaradeva their living spiritual descendant. Here pilgrimage has little to do with a fixed point in time and space and everything to do with timeless truth. As the text itself explains, Śaṅkaradeva's purpose was to make known the true doctrine of non-duality and save people; pilgrimage was simply the convenient excuse to do so (5.3367).

Finally, I would like to suggest that there were political reasons as well as religious reasons for maintaining the centrality of pilgrimage in Śaṅkaradeva's biographies. The biographies are open about the hostility that the orthodox Brahmins displayed to the new religion promulgated by the low caste *śūdra* Śaṅkaradeva. One of the accusations they made against Śaṅkaradeva in the court of King Naranārāyaṇa was that Śaṅkaradeva rejected Vedic rituals and therefore threatened the security of the kingdom. Both Śaṅkaradeva and his disciples use the fact that Śaṅkaradeva went to Purī twice as evidence of his eagerness to maintain orthodox rites.[18] Pilgrimage to an established religious centre takes on a very different significance here; it is a necessary compromise with established religious authority. Nonetheless, we have seen how our texts at the same time undermine the existing religious authority and seek to create new religious authority in their descriptions of what transpired on the pilgrimages that Śaṅkaradeva undertook.

End Notes

1 [Vidyāraṇya], *Śaṅkaradigvijaya,* Ānandāśrama Saṃskṛta Granthāvali 22, ed. Vināyak Gaṇeśa Āpaṭe (Puṇe: Ānanda Āśrama 1932). In the discussion several participants reminded me that the notion of a God worshipping himself is not confined to these texts; indeed, the daily ritual of worship in the *Āgamas* involves the worshipper first becoming a God and then worshipping. On this, see Richard Davis, *Ritual in an Oscillating Universe: Worshipping Śiva in Medieval India* (Princeton: Princeton University Press, 1991). The Vedic gods also perform sacrifices. I would argue that what makes the question of the saint/god going on pilgrimage different is that the texts themselves self-consciously highlight the incongruity and seek to find a suitable explanation for what they regard as an anomaly. Text citations in this essay are to chapter and verse.

2 Véronique Bouillier pointed out the similarity between this exchange between the guru and his disciple, and the ritualized exchange between the young student and his family during the *upanayana* ceremony. Information on this may be found in her article 'Preliminary Remarks on Bālajogīs or Ascetic Children,' in *Recent Research on Nepal*, Schriftenreihe Internationales Asien Forum, Band 3, ed. Klaus Seeland (München: Weltforum Verlag, 1985), 12–15.

3 Indeed one definition of a holy place is a place where sages and saints dwell: *gosiddhamuninivāsāśca deśāḥ puṇyāḥ prakīrtitāḥ*, Ballalasena, *Dānasāgara*, Bibliotheca Indica 274, ed. Bhabatosh Bhattacharya (Calcutta: Asiatic Society, 1953), 326, quoting Vyāsa.

4 The text is edited by Śrīmadbhaktikevala Auḍulomi Mahārāj (Calcutta: Gauḍīya Mission, 1957). Bimanbihari Majumdar has an extensive discussion of the pilgrimage routes and a comparison with other biographies of Caitanya in his *Śrīcaitanya-cariter Upādān* (Calcutta: Calcutta University, 1959).

5 It is interesting to note the way in which the text problematizes pilgrimage here; pilgrimage is problematic for any holy man and not just for one who is regarded as an incarnation of God. This statement of the problem does not allow the text to solve the dilemma simply by playing upon the very notion of a divine incarnation, who can act at times as an ordinary human being although he or she is divine. We shall see that even when the problem is the incongruity of God journeying to meet Himself, the concept of *līlā* is not necessarily offered as the solution, although such a device would have readily been available to the biographer. Instead other explanations may be sought to explain the divine journey or, as we shall see, the pilgrimage will serve as proof of the divinity. In these cases, the fact that God is also human does not seem to be part of the discussion.

6 This incident is told in Karṇapūra's *Caitanyacandrodaya Nāṭaka* (Calcutta: Sarasvati Press, 1885), 6.9, and the *Caitanyacaritāmṛta* of Kṛṣṇadāsa 2.4.12–13. Majumdar dates the first text to 1572 (*Śrīcaitanyacariter Upādān*, 102), while S.K. De dates the second to around 1615. See his *Early History of the Vaiṣṇava Faith and Movement in Bengal* (Calcutta: Firma K.L. Mukhopadhyay, 1961), 56.

7 The text is edited by Śrīmadbhaktikevala Auḍulomi Mahārāj (Calcutta: Gauḍīya Mission, 1961). S.K. De dates the text roughly to sometime just before AD1550. He cites Majumdar (*Śrīcaitanyacariter Upādān*, 183) in his speculation about the date (De, *Early History*, 47–48 n.).

8 The complexity of conceptions about the divinity of Caitanya has been

amply explored by Tony K. Stewart in his 'Biographical Images of Kṛṣṇa-Caitanya: A Study in the Perception of Divinity' (PhD diss., University of Chicago, 1985). I thank Tony Stewart for a copy of this thesis.

9 Rāmacaraṇa, *Śaṅkaracarita*, ed. Harinārāyan Dattabarua (Nalbārī: Dattabarua Publishing Company, 1996). I thank Dr Dilip Kalita of the ABORILAC Institute, Guahati, for providing me with a copy of the text.

10 On Rāmacaraṇa see Maheshvar Neog, *Early History of the Vaiṣṇava Faith and Movement in Assam Śaṅkaradeva and His Times* (Delhi: Motilal Banarsidass, 1965), 5–7. The extant biography ascribed to Rāmacaraṇa is now thought to be a late text, written around 1688. To avoid being tedious, I refer to the author by the name 'Rāmacaraṇa,' with the understanding that this is nothing more than a traditional ascription.

11 It is difficult for me to assess at this stage of my research the extent to which Rāmacaraṇa is an innovator in extending purāṇic stories this way into the life of Śaṅkaradeva. The corresponding sections in an early biography of Śaṅkaradeva by Daityāri do not do this. See Daityāri, *Śaṅkaradeva-Mādhvadevar Jīvan Carita*, ed. Haribilas Gupta (Tezpur: n.p., 1990). On Daityāri, see Neog, *Early History*, 5. Daityāri is the son of Rāmacaraṇa. In general Daityāri gives only a very brief account of Śaṅkaradeva's early life.

12 This is probably the most frequently performed Brahmanical ritual in the biography. The author devotes considerable space to details of the funerals that are carried out and the later offerings to the ancestors. It is one of the more striking inconsistencies of the biography that, despite this meticulous observance of rituals connected with the ancestors (*śrāddha*), this is supposedly one of the rituals that Śaṅkaradeva is said to have rejected (see page 486 of Rāmacaraṇa's text).

13 These three individuals, and sometimes Mahendra Kandalī as well, play a special role on the pilgrimage. They seem to be the most frequent recipients of the visions and dreams that attest to Śaṅkaradeva's divine status. They also act as mediators between Śaṅkaradeva and the other members of the pilgrimage party by explaining to them what they have experienced and that Śaṅkaradeva is actually God. Rāmarāma and Balarāma are both mentioned by Neog, *Early History*.

14 It is worth noting that both pilgrimages to Purī and Dvārakā are very differently treated in a later biography. In Puvārāma Mahanta's *Bardowā-gurucarita*, ed. Maheśvara Neog (Guwahati: Guwahati Book Stall, 1977), the pilgrimage to Purī is very briefly described; the only unusual event is that the local priests are told in a dream not to make

the offering in the temple but to bring the offering to Śaṅkaradeva; there is also no visionary experience at Dvārakā, although Śaṅkaradeva does carry two devotees into the ocean to see the temple of Rukmiṇī. The vision of Śaṅkaradeva in the ocean is reminiscent of the vision of Kṛṣṇa and Balarāma in the Yamunā that Akrūra witnesses in *Bhāgavata Purāṇa* 10.39.

15 I have written about the visionary and esoteric nature of medieval pilgrimage in my articles, 'Rāma's Bridge: Some Notes on Journeys Real and Envisioned,' *East and West* 48, nos. 1–2 (1998), 93–117; 'Medieval Jain Accounts of Mt. Girnar and Śatruñjaya: Visible and Invisible Sacred Realms,' *Journal of the Oriental Institute Baroda* (forthcoming); and 'Defining Sacred Place: Contest, Compromise and Priestly Control in Some Māhātmya Texts,' *Annals of the Bhandarkar Oriental Institute* 79 (1998), 1–28.

16 Given the importance of transmission in medieval Indian religions, Winand Callewaert suggested that this feature might offer some internal evidence for a late date of the text. Neog suggests as a context for the biography ascribed to Rāmacaraṇa the efforts by Kanakalatā Āi and Śaṅkaradeva's descendants to set up *sattras* of their own under the leadership of Kanakalatā Āi at the newly rediscovered birthplace of Śaṅkaradeva, Bardowā. Perhaps the denial of the necessity of belonging to a direct line of transmission reflects an atmosphere of sectarian division.

17 In the late biography, the *Bardowā-gurucarita*, the importance of Jagannātha is both acknowledged and subtly compromised. A wonderful story is told of the devotee Dhvajāi, who takes his leave of Śaṅkaradeva and goes to Purī. He sustains himself for a few days by begging, but eventually gets nothing to eat. He climbs up on the image of Jagannātha, placing his foot on the image, and steals the God's crown. He sells it in the bazaar and buys something to eat with the money. The priests of the temple find out from the shopkeeper that it was Dhvajāi who stole the crown and they seize him and are about to beat him. He runs to the image and throws his arms around it, begging Jagannātha to save him. He disappears into the image. The priests see the traces of Dhvajāi's death on the image and are amazed. His feet are hanging out! The text tells us that Śaṅkaradeva told this story to his devotees (chapter 24). This is not an easy story to analyze; surely there can be no greater insult to an image and to the God it represents than to place one's feet on the image, or for that matter, steal what belongs to the God. Śaṅkaradeva's devotee does both of these things and is still saved by

the God. The meaning of the story must be at least in part that as a ritual object under the control of the priests Jagannātha is not important; what saved the devotee is his devotion to the God according to the practices that Śaṅkaradeva has taught.

18 In the biography by Puvārāma Mahanta, *Bardowā-gurucarita,* chaps. 29 and 30.

6

The 'Early Hindi' Hagiographies by Anantadās

WINAND M. CALLEWAERT

Introduction

Some time before or around 1600, Anantadās, an ascetic of the Rāmānandī order in Rajasthan, felt inspired to bring together in a poetic composition the different legends he had heard about the great Bhaktas of his times. He most probably did not use ink or paper, but sang and composed as he recited, convinced that he earned great merit by doing so. It is not unlikely that the story he himself sang a couple of years later was slightly different, because of a particular need or bias in an audience or because he had learned something more in the meantime. But the purpose was always the same: To sing the praises of the saint and proclaim the supremacy of devotion (*bhakti*) to God (called Hari or Rām).

He sang about Nāmdev, Kabīr, Raidās, Dhanā, Angad, and Trilochan and Pīpā. More famous *bhaktas* he could not have chosen. Four of them (Kabīr, Dhanā, Pīpā, and Raidās), he says, were initiated by Rāmānand. Nāmdev, Angad, and Trilochan were too faraway in the past, even for his sense of history, to call them disciples of Rāmānand. The association with Rāmānand was repeated by Nābhā and Rāghavadās in their *Bhaktamāls*, and by later tradition, but it has been called into question recently by Parśu Rām Chaturvedi and modern scholarship.[1] Many legends about the saints must have been at the disposal of Anantadās. Already in his day dozens of legends about the famed Kabīr and Raidās of Benares circulated in Rajasthan. For the other Bhaktas, he had to be satisfied with just a couple of legends.

The Parcaīs of the Saints

These *parcaīs* composed by Anantadās became very popular matter for travelling singers and Bhaktas who drew great inspiration from the miracles, the encounters of the saints with Brahmins and Qazis, their unfaltering trust in God never deserting them. The travelling singers who memorized the *parcaīs* of Anantadās were themselves also poets, capable of adding or changing a line or two. The result of their genius and creativity is a headache and a challenge for the text critic who looks at manuscripts and tries to restore what Anantadās must have originally recited.

A study of the *parcaīs* of Anantadās gives us an insight into a very creative period of oral transmission, as well as late-sixteenth-century social and religious thinking. I briefly summarize below some of the *parcaīs*, before discussing in greater detail the *parcaīs* of Pīpā.

The Pīpā Parcaī

By far the longest and most interesting *parcaī of Anantadās* is the one about Pīpā. With its 756 double verses in 35 chapters, it is longer than the *Bhagavadgītā*.[2] It is easy to see the basic purpose of Anantadās when looking at the *parcaīs*: through the stories he brings home the basic ideas of the Bhakti movement. What the devotional singers tried to achieve with their *pad*-singing, and commentaries (*pravacan*) on these *pads*, Anantadās tries to achieve through the stories. His *parcaīs* are a great patchwork of stories, with a few colourful threads running through them in the form of lessons or morals. The purpose of a hagiography is not historical, and with Anantadās one has the impression that the saint is less important than the sermon the author wants to give with each story told. These hagiographies must have aroused sincere faith in devotees, but they might also be called texts of subtle indoctrination. Even for a devotee of Rām,[3] the appearance of Mother Goddess Bhavānī before Pīpā must have been awe-inspiring. If Anantadās used her authority to say that 'only the worship of Rām brings salvation,' one can imagine that the villagers listening to

Anantadās's account must have been very impressed indeed.

There are several miracles mentioned in the *Pīpā parcaī*, but they are less prominent than those in the Nāmdev *parcaī*, for example, who is much more remote in history than Pīpā. In the *Pīpa parcaī* – and in that of Trilochan – a woman plays an important role. I cannot shake the feeling that this woman, the youngest queen of Pīpā called Sītā, is perhaps the more important personality in the story. Although she performs a striptease in public, with the consent of her husband, in the beginning of the story, she emerges at the end, at least in the words of Anantadās, as a very impressive personality. Again – and this is no doubt part of the role model of an ideal woman in Indian tradition – her final fulfillment lies in the service of Rām and her husband.

The Nāmdev Parcaī

The saint Nāmdev lived around AD1300, or about three hundred years before Anantadās wrote or sang about his life. In *The Hindī Songs of Nāmdev*,[4] Mukund Lath and I devote a complete chapter to a discussion of the hagiographies of Nāmdev, from the very earliest (the *parcaī* by Anantadās) to the end of the twentieth century. From that survey it appears, as one would expect, that specific details about Nāmdev start to grow in number as time goes on, and the miraculous nature of the events increases. Of the ninety different 'data' about Nāmdev in all these 'biographies,' as few as twelve are referred to in the *parcaī*. These are mainly miracles performed by Nāmdev. The story of the *ekādasī* fast and the reviving of the Brahmin takes 17 verses of the total of 49, while the weighing of gold against half the name of Rām takes 22 verses (together 39 out of 49).

The Trilochan Parcaī

The delightful *Trilochan parcaī* gives only one simple story (in 31 double verses) with a clearly drawn meaning. It is the story of Trilochan and his faithful wife, who are so busy serving God that they have no time for their material needs. God visits them one day in the person of a servant, who says:

> I come from nowhere, I am going nowhere.
> I stay with the person who puts me up.
> I have no father and no mother,

no family and no brothers.
I have become a servant when people employ me,
I serve them as they order me. (vs. 5–7)

That is no problem for Trilochan, but the servant (God!) has only one condition:

I am always hungry, never satisfied.
Grinding wheat and preparing bread for me,
where I live the housewife despairs.
I do not ask wages, I only want to live:
where people show me love, there I stay forever. (vs. 8–9)

He even tells them his name, 'Indweller,' or one who stays in the family. *Antaryāmī* or 'Indweller' is of course a very common name for God as well. The servant also promises that he will always be faithful to them, but 'if your love diminishes I shall have to go,' he warns (v. 17). Anantadās cannot help 'explaining' the meaning of the story, as he does in other *parcaīs*: 'Neither gods nor men know His essence, but He is always dependent on His devotees' (v. 27).

Very soon, the servant appears to be an expert in all trades, and every wish of Trilochan is immediately fulfilled, but his wife grows thin because she has to go on and on preparing food for the servant! He 'is never satisified.' And at the very moment the wife goes to complain about this to a neighbour, the servant (God) vanishes. Trilochan is very sad (Anantadās says nothing about the feelings of the wife), until God appears to him in a dream and says: 'If you insist I shall come back, I shall stay all your life and never go again.' Trilochan explains to his wife Haridāsī and to the audience:

Like a servant He wanders from door to door.
We have sinned, not knowing His true nature.
Why, Hari, if You were prepared to appear before me,
did You not come in your four-armed form? (vs. 27–28).

Dhanā

Dhanā, too, was a popular saint in medieval hagiographies; he often figures in a list of saints ending with '... and Dhanā.' Four hymns are ascribed to him in the *Gurū Granth*. Macauliffe, most probably relying on Punjabi informants at the end of the nineteenth century, mentions that Dhanā was born near Tonk (Rajasthan) in AD1415. Interestingly, the two main events in Dhanā's life are associated with agriculture: God eats the offered food, while Dhanā grazes his father's cows; seeds for sowing are all given to an ascetic (= God) and yet an abundant harvest is reaped; gourds are found to be full of wheat. The moral of the stories is clear: 'Whatever comes in your hands, first consider it not your own. This attitude is dear to Hari' (5.9).

Raidās

Around 1600, when a Rajasthani writes or sings about Benares, what stereotypes does he have about the city and what does he emphasize? I cannot help thinking that in the *parcaī* of Raidās (and of Kabīr) the focus seems to be on the interaction with the Brahmins. Most incidents are in fact confrontations between *bhaktas* of Hari and the ritualist Brahmins. Of course, other saints, too, were not spared such confrontations:

– Nāmdev: 'Hari comes in the form of a Brahmin,' who tries to convince him of the supremacy of *bhakti*. The portrait of this Brahmin may be called 'neutral'. After the miracle of weighing of 'half the Name of Rām,' the Brahmins are furious. They are used to enjoying extensive sponsorship by the merchant community, which now chooses Nāmdev instead.
– Dhanā: The Brahmin (God Himself?) in this account appears as a friendly helper, who gives the young Dhanā the chance of finding God by worshiping a stone (*śāligrām*).
– Trilochan: God appears as a servant who claims that 'he knows all the obligations of a Brahmin' (verse 7).
– Pīpā: The Brahmins appear here mainly as the proponents of the traditional, ritual worship (1.7) to whom food and donations have to be given (1.10; 9.4; 26.14ff.; 31.20ff.); they are in charge of the horoscopes (3.11); they are greedy and stubborn (9.6ff.; 32.11ff.) and proud (28.1ff.).
– Angad: The Brahmins are hardly mentioned in this *parcaī*.

In the *parcaī* of Raidās the Brahmins in Benares are harshly treated, and in each encounter they are defeated. Their behaviour in defeat can hardly be called an example of religious surrender. Punished to be born as a Śudra because in a previous birth he was a Brahmin who ate meat (1.3) or 'did not know Hari' (12.6), Raidās will all his life confront the Brahmins as a Śudra. Because of his excellent preaching and singing, the Brahmins are angry (4.11) and advise him that he 'should remain content by remembering Hari's name, but never must you worship the *śāligrām*' (4.15).

The Brahmins even ignored the king's decree (4.17). All of chapter 5 is devoted to this confrontation. As in traditional debate, the Brahmins produce arguments quoted from the scriptures to prove that the low-caste people should stay away from rituals (5.14ff.), but Raidās gives equally compelling examples to prove his point. This reaches a climax when eventually the *śāligrām* comes to Raidās not the Brahmins (6.16).

Five years later comes the episode with the queen of Chittaur. There again the Brahmins propose themselves as sole initiators (7.8), eager to get a free ride to Benares. The queen eventually has to play hide-and-seek with them. The Brahmins are especially furious because she received initiation from a low-caste person (8.2). Verses 8.3ff. are a pathetic litany of hysterical Brahminical behaviour. Another low-caste man, Kabīr, is called upon to settle the dispute. After this tumultuous confrontation, the *parcaī* continues smoothly, until the queen arrives back home and there has to confront her Brahmins 'who died of jealousy' (11.8). The queen does not hesitate to tell them, and everyone in Rajasthan:

> One is mean if one's actions are mean,
> one is excellent if one performs meritorious deeds.
> Excellence and meanness are in one's actions,
> in the human body alone there is no excellence at all.
> Desire, anger, greed and the nine gates,
> through these all are Chamārs.
> One who conquers these becomes excellent –
> who speaks there of Brahmins or of famous Vālmīkīs?
> Caste and family have no importance
> one who sings of Rām is dear to Rām (11.9–11).

However, Raidās advises her 'to make them happy ... and grudgingly she decides to feed the Brahmins' (11.14), who eventually are converted and admit that Raidās is a saint and 'we are sinners' (11.22). Does one often hear such a statement from the mouth of a Brahmin? At the end of the *parcaī*, they throw away their sacred threads and become the disciples of Raidās (12.9).

Angad

In six chapters, Anantadās tells us the story of Angad who was converted to *bhakti* by his wife and who experienced only one major event in his life: He found a precious crown while looting a castle and donated it to Hari, even when his nephew Salahdī wanted it very badly and threatened to kill him. Angad's sister (aunt?) is persuaded to poison him, but Angad is saved by God, 'because the food had already been offered as *prasād*':

> If Hari protects you, tons of poison will disappear.
> How can a devotee be harmed by poison?
> It is stated in the Vedas and in the Bhāgvat Purān
> that meditation on Hari protects everyone.
> Even if the whole world intends to harm them,
> the Sants of Hari cannot be killed. (4.23–24)

Eventually Angad leaves the country, but is chased by Salahdī. Under pressure he throws the diamond in a river, and a short while later the diamond surfaces 'on the chest of Jagannāth' (5.13).

The Historical and 'Biographical' Data of the *Pīpā Parcaī*

In the *Pīpā parcaī*, Anantadās reports that Pīpā was a king of the Khici clan, in the city of Gagraunī (1.1ff.):

> No one could harm the people in his land.
> His actions were based on correct policy;
> he was brave in war, virtuous and wise.
> People of all castes lived in his city.
> Deeds of merit graced every home.
> Pīpā was a worshipper of the Great Mother, Bhavānī,
> she was considered the real queen of the city and its fortress.
> He worshipped the Goddess in every prescribed way,
> for him there was no other deity. (1.3-5)

Pīpā carries on this way for twelve years, until one day he has a frightening experience (see 'The Goddess Bhavānī, below) and taking the advice of the Goddess he travels to Benares (4.10) to meet Rāmānand. There he is tested by Rāmānand, jumping into a well until the guru saves him (4.10), and after initiation Pīpā returns home (5.16), where he starts to serve people (6). After an invitation, Rāmānand decides to travel to Dvārkā and, en route to stay with Pīpā. Kabīr and Raidās join him (6.9). Great festivities mark the arrival of Rāmānand, and Pīpā decides to leave his kingdom and his queens. Sītā's sincerity is tested (8.7). And then the journey starts, with many adventures. Severe famine is described in 33.2ff., the date of which is given as AD1463 in the *Bhaktmāl* (163). A precise reference is given to Angad, when Anantadās says that he lived in the fort of Rāisen, where Salahdī ruled (1.3).

The Main Stories and Their Lessons

In the 35 chapters of the *Pīpā parcaī,* we can discern more than a dozen stories, some of which are spicy, considering the times and the religious environment in which they were sung. Only a few are discussed here.

The Goddess Bhavānī

In the *Pīpā parcaī,* Anantadās reports that Pīpā was a worshipper of Bhavānī, and that he worshipped the Goddess in every prescribed way (1.4–5). He did this for twelve years, until one day

> He woke up in the middle of the night
> and started to cry intensely.
> That very moment the Goddess came to him, and said:
> 'Ask from me whatever you want' (1.13). (Pīpā replied:)
> ...
> 'as your servant, please grant me liberation.' (1.19)

The story of the dialogue with the Goddess continues in the next chapter, but Anantadās concludes chapter 1 with a *dohā,* which, one can imagine, the audience repeated as a refrain after the singer:

> True wisdom arose in Pīpā
> because of the deeds of his past life,
> but without the words of the satguru,
> he was unable to meditate on Hari. (1.20)

The *parcaī* may have had the function of a *līlā*, which is a performance of the adventures of Kṛṣṇa or of Rām. When the curtain opens for chapter 2, we see that

> The Mother could say nothing in reply and stood still,
> not knowing what to do.
> Pīpā said to her: 'Listen to me, O Giver of Joy,
> please release me from my bondage.' (2.1)

With the authority of a Goddess who had been worshiped in India for more than two millennia, Bhavānī startles the audience when she says:

> If you have no devotion for Hari in your heart
> and are without divine knowledge, you cannot find liberation.
> When have you ever seen anybody find liberation through me? (2.4).
> ...
> I can give you every other joy,
> if that satisfies you then serve me.
> But if you hope to find liberation,
> then worship only Hari, without hesitation.
> Give all you have to the devotees of Hari,
> there is no other path for you.
> Then Hari will be pleased with you, and
> without delay give liberation to you and your family. (2.5–6)

The reaction of Pīpā (and of the listeners?) is dramatic: He is so 'frightened, that he falls on the floor in a swoon, his whole body begins to sweat profusely, as if he had been struck with a high fever' (2.7). These are signs of a very intense experience. The Mother takes care of Pīpā until he regains consciousness, but as he jumps up on the stage, he shouts:

> I worshipped you thinking that you grant liberation.
> You cheat, why did you not tell me earlier,
> why did you not tell me right at the beginning
> that your worship is not to my benefit?
> What is the point in having faith in someone
> who cannot lead to release from rebirth? (2.11–12)

An equally high authority, the Vedas, is quoted by the Goddess

Herself, when she replies:

You never asked me.
You never told me that you are looking for liberation.
Do not blame me falsely.
Why should I stop you from worshipping me.
Fool, I have no access to liberation,
The Vedas and Purāṇas proclaim this clearly.
...
All the gods are servants of Hari:
they are many only in name.
Hari knows everything from beginning to end.
Such is Hari and he is pleased by bhakti.
Hari creates the world and destroys it.
Other gods have fear; Hari alone is beyond fear. (2.13–15)

The Goddess continues praising Hari and concludes chapter 2 with a *dohā*: 'He who worships Hari with a meek heart will never be born again.'

In this story some may see the event of Pīpā's conversion. It is aptly used, with the authority of the Goddess Herself, to bring home the point that one should worship Hari and no one else. It is also the Goddess who eventually advises Pīpā to go to Benares and there seek initiation from Rāmānand (3.3) and amazingly, 'she touched Pīpā's feet as she left'!

Sītā, the Wife of Pīpā

The remarkable story of the test of Pīpā's youngest queen, Sītā, also has the dramatic power of a performance. In the courtyard of the castle, where the whole town seems to have been present (7.11), Pīpā takes leave of his twelve queens. They put up quite a show, but eventually withdraw to their apartments when Pīpā depicts the dangers and hardships of the travel of a life with dedicated ascetics. Echoes of dramatic situations in medieval India resound when Anantadās makes the queens say:

It is not proper that we should leave you and go back alone.
The thread always follows the needle.
Without you, O husband, where can we go? (7.13)

In the words of Rāmānand, Anantadās takes this opportunity to describe what is expected of a fully committed devotee of Hari:

He will wander in strange lands, living on alms,
with a shaven head and garb of an ascetic.
He has given up all attachment to caste, status and family honour –
a king and a beggar are equal in his eyes.
He has no thought of sleep or hunger or pain or pleasure.
Sometimes he might wear clothes, at other times he will go naked.
This is my path, consider whether you can walk on it. (7.15–17)
...
If you can do the same, then you can come with us, ladies.
If not, remain at home. (7.18)

Seeing all individuals as equals and giving up honour and status are favourite themes of Anantadās.

The youngest queen, Sītā, 'beautiful as the heavenly Rambhā' (8.10), volunteers to suffer the hardships and to stay with Pīpā. Very daring, indeed, in the composition of Anantadās is the request he puts in the mouth of Rāmānand, who 'asked her to dance in the nude.' Sītā does not hesitate:

She put down all her jewellery,
while the other eleven queens looked on from afar.
She discarded her clothes until she was naked –
she dropped all shame and thus left the world behind.
The whole town witnessed this spectacle,
but Sītā just ignored them as if they were grass. (8.8–9)

Rāmānand advises Pīpā to take her with him, as the sacrifice of giving up his kingdom is sufficient. Celibacy may be too much for him. Equally provocative is Pīpā's reaction:

What will I do with her?
She is of no use to me, give her to someone else. (8.12)
...
By force or deceit women beguile men,
and loving them can only be an obstacle for knowledge.
In the house of a king she becomes a queen,
in the house of a yogī she becomes a yoginī.

Not only men, even gods are infatuated with women,
forgetting bhakti, they plunge into the dark well of a household.
I know, Svāmī, the mind and deeds of women. (8.12, 14-16)

This statement is harsh and shocking, but it is a subtle trick in the composition of Anantadās. Like Sītā of the *Rāmāyaṇ* epic, who enjoys the final victory when she disappears into the earth after the ordeal by fire, this Sītā of Anantadās, too, will emerge victorious at the end of the performance.

The Attack of the Pathan

It is in this story of the attack of the Pathan (12.14-13.23) that Sītā, for the first time, seems to play an important role. Pīpā takes the non-violent stance and simply gives his wife up:

I am an ascetic and this is my woman.
I spend my days worshipping the Creator.
If you want to use violence, do what you desire. (12.17)

He only regrets having taken her with him in the first place (12.19)! After the lecherous talk of the Pathan and his earnest attempts to touch Sītā, she trembles with fear and 'fixes her mind on Govinda' (13.8), and 'suddenly there appeared a fearless man,' who hit the Pathan. When he regains consciousness, he begs 'the faithful Sītā as though she was his mother' for forgiveness. The story has a standard message:

Such is the protection of Gopāl,
that no one can harm you.
Whoever remains true to Hari,
can never be lost. (13.23)

At the same time, however, Anantadās subtly inserts a gentle moral remark, when the defeated Pathan admits: 'I will never behave in this shameful manner again, dreading even to look at another's wife.' (13.16) After this frightening incident, Pīpā again suggests that Sītā should return home, but she appears to be the ideal believer, reminding her husband of real faith:

'But Keshav is with us,' replied Sītā,

'Where then is the cause for fear, my lord?
Rām is constantly looking after us,
sing His name without fear.' (14.2)

Subduing Tigers

In 'Strategies of Prestige in Sufi Legend,'[6] Simon Digby describes how the motif of riding a tiger or a lion (or a wall) is used in Sufi hagiography. In the *Pīpā parcaī*, this is reduced to the mere control and conversion of tigers, suggesting that even animals enjoy the full protection of Rām (14.17). In this case, there is one condition: the tigers should give up eating humans and cows (14.15) and become vegetarians! And 'without fear' (14.20) Pīpā and Sītā continue their travels, in the same way that the Goddess Bhavānī had suggested, for 'Hari alone is beyond fear' (2.15).

Sītā as a Prostitute [1-4]

The *karmaṇy evādhikāraste*, or 'action should be your main concern,' of the *Bhagavadgītā* (2.47) has been open to criticism for its possible justification of all means, if the purpose is right. We may find an echo of this undercurrent of Indian thinking when Anantadās tells his audience:

Without hesitation Pīpā and Sītā spent everything,
firm in their service for the benefit of others.
You cannot sin if you help a worthy person,
if you organize devotion to Hari by crooked means,
or if you pawn another woman's jewellery,
if by any means you serve devotees,
even if you do not honour any god:
you will be rewarded in heaven
and you will not have to come back in another body. (33.15–16)

The four incidents in which Sītā serves as a prostitute for the good cause seem to exemplify this principle. Seeing the extreme poverty of their hosts, it is Sītā who volunteers 'to walk the streets.' 'Indeed, Pīpā sent her to go and sit in the fields' (15.14). Being very beautiful she does not fail to attract many men and to receive many presents, although nobody manages to touch her. All the presents are given to the devotees, for, Anantadās concludes:

If for the benefit of others,
you give all that you have,
so will God also give to you. (15.23)

The second episode of Sītā as a prostitute (20) illustrates again that for a good cause – here 'feeding devotees' – much leeway is allowed. A lecherous merchant becomes an important patron, provided Sītā is ready to spend the night with him. As it was a rainy night, Pīpā even volunteers to carry her on his shoulders, for, as he explains to Sītā, 'Your feet will get dirty in the mud, the merchant will not like it. He is a sophisticate and will send you back' (20.8). The merchant is so impressed with her husband's spirit of tolerance, that he becomes Pīpā's disciple. The moral of the story: 'Truth cannot turn into falsehood, for those who take shelter with Hari' (21.1).

When for a third time Sītā is expected to serve as a prostitute (21.19ff.), one wonders whether it is meant to drive home the religious principle emphasized in chapter 21: there is no devotion as long as there is 'mine' and 'thine.' Only he knows who has forgotten 'mine' (21.16). Pīpā welcomes the men heartily (21.20), saying:

'You say you are devotees of Hari,
because of him take whatever you want.'
...
'Now take this maidservant,' said Pīpā,
'do not feel embarrassed in front of me.
She was with me only for a few days,
she was with You forever.
Nothing in my house is mine.' (22.1, 5-6)

This time, however, the story develops into a miracle, with a tigress sitting in the place of Sītā (22.7). In the fourth case of 'prostitution,' Sītā is again made available, but somehow the lecherous person cannot touch her. At the end he becomes a devotee, and realizes, 'If one is totally committed to God, nobody can touch what belongs to him.' (24.2)

For the first time in the *Pīpā parcaī,* we see after this episode a change in the tone of Pīpā (and of Anantadās) with regard to Sītā. All of chapter 24 is a tribute to Sītā and to the 'faithful wife' in general. Here Pīpā even sings her high praises. But the submissive tone remains, even in Sītā's reply to his praise:

If a woman has only joy and no suffering,
if her husband shows her too much love
and all the time fulfills all her desires,
how can she be called an ideal wife?
If a wife helps her husband in distress,
then she is really a faithful wife. (24.16-17)

It is as if Anantadās reminds all women of rural Rajasthan in the seventeenth century of their role – even if your husband is cripple or a thief, even if he goes to prostitutes, and 'you have no clothes or food *and do not complain*,' only then are you a truly faithful wife (24.18-25): 'If she does not mind the mistakes of her husband, this faithful woman will find liberation'(24.25).

The Miracles

The first miracle in the *Pīpā parcaī* is introduced by Anantadās in order to establish the superior status of Rāmānand, at a point in the drama when Pīpā has decided to leave everything behind and follow his guru. An obnoxious Brahmin sees his income disappearing with the departure of Pīpā and blackmails him by committing suicide. Pīpā feels responsible for this and agrees to die with him on the funeral pyre. But Rāmānand insists that one cannot 'be responsible, if a man dies because of his stupidity' (9.15) and brings 'the Brahmin back to life and gives him the water his feet have been washed in.' The lesson of this episode is to be seen in the light of the Rāmānandī background of Anantadās: 'When the Brahmin was gone, Pīpā's doubts disappeared: he knew that Rāmānand was a part of Govind himself' (9.18).

A similar incident – with a different didactic purpose – is related in the *Nāmdev parcaī*, but there it is the saint himself who revives the Brahmin. Nāmdev is a strict observer of the *ekādasī* fast, and he refuses to give cereals (prohibited by the fast) to a begging Brahmin (= God). The Brahmin pretends he is dead and Nāmdev is accused of the heinous sin of Brahminicide (1.18). Nāmdev decides to join him in the fire, and 'as he started to burn along with the Brahmin, Hari jumped down from the pyre and ran away laughing.' This incident gives Anantadās the opportunity to lash out at ritual observances:

Praised be Nāmdev the true bhakta:
he gave up his ekādasī fast and became truly liberated (2.2).

> Ritual observances are fetters shackling the world.
> Can anyone cross samsār without Rām?

This theme is frequently emphasized in the *parcaīs*. In the *Pīpā parcaī* ritual observances are called futile by Bhavānī Herself (1.6ff.). A strong statement of Anantadās is found in 21.17:

> As long as you are interested in the praise of the world,
> and you do not give up your desire for worldly enjoyments,
> you cannot find Rām, with all your dancing and singing.

Even stronger is his statement in 21.4:

> If one ignores the restrictions of traditions and scriptures,
> then one is in the company of Rām.
> If you remember God all the time,
> He will appear in your heart.

Of a miraculous nature in the *Pīpā parcaī* is the visit of Pīpā and Sītā to the underwater city of Kṛṣṇa at Dvārkā (10.13–12.13). It consists of two parts. First there is the visit proper and the description of the city as the visitors see it, when

> Hari instructed Pīpā again and again,
> making him see the presence of Brahman in every living thing.
> 'I dwell in your heart, I am never far from you,
> consider what your guru has taught you.' (11.10, 14)

It is Kṛṣṇa Himself who eventually tells them that they cannot stay there. They have a mission to fulfill: 'Go back to Kaliyug and devote yourself to *bhakti*, remove the suffering of others' (12.11).

This is followed by the account of Pīpā entering the town, much to the astonishment of the people who had thought he and Sītā had drowned. The outcome of the account is somewhat expected and, in fact, reflects a common reaction to saints that one can hear even today: 'They finally decided that Pīpā was a partial *avatār*' (12.12). Minor miracles are recorded, too – for example, Pīpā makes a bamboo put down roots (15.6) and robbers find a snake instead of treasure (16.8).

The incident in which Pīpā wants to have Sen, the wife of Sūraj, is another occasion for Anantadās to expound a basic tenet of *bhakti* theology: unconditional respect for the guru. The request of Pīpā is strange, to say the least, and even Sūraj is slightly concerned (25.17). However, the trickery of Pīpā is disconcerting. When Sūraj enters his house he sees a lion, while outside he sees Pīpā, and then again inside he finds a baby 'lying close to his wife and sucking her breast' (25.3). But the message is clear: 'Even if the guru is mad or strange, a wise disciple will never leave him' (25.9).

Several more miraculous events are mentioned in chapters 26–33 of the *Pīpā parcaī*. Each event has its moral. After the incident with the thieves, Pīpā states: 'the Indweller lives in you' (28.24); when Shrīrang thinks of his cobbler, we hear: 'caste and family make no difference' (29.10); when death comes to fetch a person, we are reminded: 'without devotion to Hari, you are in great trouble' (30.15); and 'to those who serve the devotees of Hari, Yam's assistants say nothing: they are afraid' (30.18). With such statements no devotee will ever hesitate to rely on the generosity and hospitality of the benefactors! In the dire need caused by famine, it is Sītā who 'is always truthful, and says: Our Creator is not far from us now' (33.9).

The bilocation (or multilocation) of Pīpā deserves our attention because it seems to be a routine event in the lives of saints, reminding one of the omnipresence of Kṛṣṇa in the *Rās Līlā*. It is described also in that very important hagiography of the seventeenth century in Rajasthan, the Life of Dādū,

> Whenever devotees came to take him somewhere,
> Swamiji's form appeared there.
> Everyone tells this story
> of Dādū's appearance in seven different places.[7]

Also in the *Raidās parcaī*:

> As in many mirrors you see the same body,
> the transcending body was seen everywhere.[8]
> He sat down to eat with everyone and
> on all sides he could be seen.
> Seeing this marvel, everyone was astonished,
> there were as many Raidāses as there were Brahmins.
> Then someone ran to the place where Raidās was camped,
> and found the devotee of Raidās there as well.
> Everyone said, 'He is great, He is great,'

and the Brahmins hid their faces. (11.18ff.)

A similar description is found in the *Pīpā parcaī*:

After that five letters came with an invitation,
to be present at five celebrations.
Five replies were given at the same moment,
that Pīpā was coming to the five villages.
If on one day he did not go to all,
they would be very unhappy.
When Pīpā was leaving for the celebrations,
just at that moment some guests arrived.
They would not let him go away,
and Pīpā began to feel sorry.
Wherever Pīpā was supposed to go,
there God went, taking his form. (34.16-19)

Attitudes Promoted in the Parcaīs

Anantadās and Women

The *Pīpā parcaī* leaves us in no doubt about its attitude towards women (as revealed in the treatment of Sītā above). In the *Angad parcaī*, as well, Anantadās does not have very good words for women:

Women have confused minds,
they cannot discern evil from good.
What is the point in their being instructed by a svāmī?
They are impure and always full of lust. (1.10)

In fact, Anantadās does not hesitate to load all the sins of the world onto them:

A woman is called a source of disagreement and pain.
Gods, men and demons – she brings them all to naught.
She draws everyone with her beauty and dance,
leaving no place to escape even in hell.
A woman leaves no one,
she turns around both householders and ascetics. (2.6b.1–2)
....

Ascetics may live in caves and hills, eating only fruits
and controlling their bodies in yogic exercises,
controlling their māyā and conquering their senses –
their vows are all broken by a woman!
Wise and virtuous men, warriors, poets, and scholars –
their vows are all broken by a woman.
A man may be well versed in philosophy,
but a woman takes different form and destroys it all.
Even a powerful king
who has authority everywhere
and conquers impregnable forts
is powerless in front of a woman.
A woman makes everyone dance.
Who can save you if you do not concentrate on Hari?
Everyone listens to the instructions of a woman
and accepts her opinion, whether good or bad.
Some women take you straight to hell,
while others take you on the path of bhakti. (2.7–11)

But he makes exceptions:

The wife of Angad was a fine lady,
she took good care of her beloved.
He was on the way to hell
but she directed him towards Vaikuṇṭha,
avoiding rebirth in many bodies.
Blessed is the woman who is good for her husband
and stops his downward fall. (2.11–12)

Without a Guru a Person Is Totally Helpless

The need for a guru is stressed again and again by Anantadās. Pīpā was at a loss because he had no guru. Although,

True wisdom arose in Pīpā
because of the deeds of his past life,
without the words of the satguru,
he was unable to meditate on Hari. (1.20)

In 7.7, Rāmānand suggests that in the service of his guru, Pīpā will 'have a double result, never to return again in the body.' In the context of queen Jhālī, searching for a guru in the *Raidās parcaī*, we hear Anantadās tell his audience and all generations after them, 'If your guru never comes to your house, your human birth remains useless' (10.4). The frustrated wife of Angad has taken refuge with a 'guru,' and that gives Anantadās the opportunity again to bring home his point:

> A guru is like a father and mother.
> What he says has to be acted upon.
> Nobody can equal a guru,
> I have looked everywhere. (1.13)

At the height of the story of Angad, when his aunt/sister is being persuaded to poison him, Anantadās subtly remarks that in fact the woman should be excused: 'How could she now be better?' For,

> How can a person have right insight, friends?
> Only by the grace of the guru!
> Otherwise one does not stop hurting,
> brothers and dear friends. (4.14)

Hari and the Devotees Are One

Anantadās stresses the importance of the community of devotees in verses such as this:

> Do not think that Hari and his devotee are different,
> as gold and a golden jewel are not different.
> Hari, guru, devotee: we say 'three,' they are one.
> Understand this like the shore, the traveller and the boat. (Angad 2.9–10)

Therefore, serve the devotees!

Conclusion

The *bhakti* poets in North India (sixteenth and seventeenth centuries) come back to us through different channels. Through manuscripts in which their songs were written down at a particular time (and copied by scribes later on); or through the transmission of a continuous oral tradition, which increased the number of songs and added variant lines even more generously than any scribal tradition; commentaries appeared and, finally, the poets came to life through their 'biographies.' These 'biographies' were voluminous *Bhaktamāls* with brief notes on a large number of *bhaktas*, or lengthy descriptions of a particular poet to which the *parcaīs* by Anantadās belong. The *parcaīs* were often scorned as mere legendary accounts, eulogizing and promoting a particular saint. We now know better. Even in the miraculous and quasi-historical accounts, a vivid picture of the times of the poet emerges, as is evident in the lengthy *Pīpā parcaī* discussed here.[10]

End Notes

1 Parśu Rām Chaturvedi, *Uttarī Bhārata kī santa-paramparā* (n.p.: [1964]).
2 For comparison, Anantadās wrote about Nāmdev in 46 double verses (2 chapters); Kabīr in 207 verses (12 to 13 chapters); Dhanā in 68 (7 chapters); Trilochan in 31 (1 chapter); and Angad in 144 (6 chapters).
3 He is of course not the Rāmacandra of the *Rāmāyaṇ* epic.
4 Winand M. Callewaert and Mukund Lath, *The Hindī Songs of Nāmdev* (Leuven: Departement Oriëntalistiek, 1989), 14–36.
5 See Winand M. Callewaert and Rupert Snell, eds., *According to Tradition: Hagiographical Writing in India* (Wiesbaden: Harrasowitz Verlag, 1994), 88.
6 Ibid., 99.
7 See Winand M. Callewaert, *The Hindī Biography of Dādū Dayāl* (Delhi: Motilal Banarsidass, 1988), 41.
8 For the appearance in many bodies, see the accounts of Dādū and Pīpā.
9 Deeds of past lives, good and bad ones, definitely influence human existence; see further in the *Pīpā parcaī* 4.2, 7; 8.1; 34.24.
10 For a critical edition and complete English translation of these parcaīs, see Winand M. Callewaert, *The Hagiographies of Anantadās: The Bhakti Poets of North India* (London: Curzon, 2000).

7

Dvārakā: The Making of a Sacred Place

ANDRÉ COUTURE

The *Harivaṃśa* (or *HV*)[1] is considered to be a later addition to that great Indian epic, the *Mahābhārata* (or *Mbh*). Evidence within the text, scant though it is, seems to suggest that this supplement was probably written early, in the second or the third century AD.[2] Naturally, the redactor of the *Mbh* knew that Dvārakā (or Dvāravatī)[3] was Kṛṣṇa's own city, even though he had not yet presented his hero's full lineage. Nor had he recounted how Kṛṣṇa had been born to Vasudeva and Devakī in the city of Mathurā in order to kill King Kaṃsa, or why he needed to remain hidden among the cowherds of that region, or how he decided to leave the city in order to oversee the construction of the wonderful city of Dvāravatī. In the *Harivaṃśa*, at Śaunaka's request, Ugraśravas resumes his account using the same narrative framework as the *Mbh*. He retells stories formerly told by the Brahmin Vaiśaṃpāyana to King Janamejaya, the latter having judged them necessary to complete his knowledge of Viṣṇu's manifestation as Kṛṣṇa.

Built at Kṛṣṇa's behest on the western coast of India after the fall of Mathurā, the city of Dvārakā was later destroyed due to strife among the Vṛṣṇis. Historians, archeologists, and specialists in mythology have written about this city.[4] But to my knowledge, this first detailed account of the city's foundation has never been studied in its own right

– as surprising as that may seem. Some of the introductory verses of *HV* 86 make it clear that this city was carefully built:

> Having threads in their hands, excellent Yādavas took the measurements (of the city). On this auspicious day, great king, they required (some Brahmins) to perform the rites for the deities of the site according to the rules (*vidhinā*). Then the very wise Govinda (Kṛṣṇa) told the architects: 'In this place [there] must be built for all of us a palace well-planned, with crossroads and well-ordered highways, in which our selected deities can be installed.' Having given their agreement to this long-armed Kṛṣṇa, the architects provided all the material necessary for the building of the fortress, according to the rules (*yathāvidhi*). They measured the gates and buildings properly (*yathānyāyam*), and laid the seats of Brahmā and so forth in the proper order (*yathākramam*). (*HV* 86.12–16)

These verses insist on a city having to be constructed according to proper rules, which is a good reason to take this text seriously, even if the description could at times be more explicit. Since it has not been done up to now, I think it is useful to fully discuss this episode of the foundation of Dvārakā and to consider it in its narrative setting, describing some of the problems encountered in the reading of the text and exploring ways in which its mythological and ritual context might be interpreted.

The Story of Dvāravatī's Foundation[5]

Kṛṣṇa kills King Kaṃsa after he and his elder brother, Saṃkarṣaṇa, have been asked to leave the Vṛndāvana forest to attend a great festival, which Kaṃsa himself has ordered to take place in the city of Mathurā. At the same time, Kṛṣṇa frees Ugrasena from the fetters Kaṃsa had placed upon him, restoring the erstwhile king to his throne. King Jarāsaṃdha dwells in the east in the huge city of Girivraja, the capital of the Māgadhas, which is encircled by five large mountains.[6] As a way of cementing their alliance, Kaṃsa had taken Jarāsaṃdha's daughters, Asti and Prāpti, in marriage (80.3). Determined to avenge Kaṃsa's death, Jarāsaṃdha, together with his friends Dantavaktra, Śiśupāla, Pauṇḍra, and Bhīṣmaka, surrounds the city of Mathurā and besieges it. Kṛṣṇa exults (*hṛṣṭamanāḥ*, 81.2) and tells his elder brother: 'Indeed the design of the gods is near at hand, since King Jarāsaṃdha has drawn near to us' (*tvarate khalu kāryārtho devatānāṃ na saṃśayaḥ // yathāyaṃ saṃnikṛṣṭo hi jarāsaṃdho narādhipaḥ /* 81.2cd–3ab). Jarāsaṃdha gives instructions to the kings and a long war breaks out. Saṃkarṣaṇa tries desperately to crush Jarāsaṃdha, but a celestial voice warns him that the hour of his enemy's death has not come yet (82.20–21). Even after eighteen battles, the Yādavas do not manage to kill him (82.27).

Finally convinced that the city of Mathurā has too many enemies, Kṛṣṇa decides to leave it and establish a new city designed especially for them (84.7–8) in the country of Ānarta (cf. 9.23). Kṛṣṇa's friends are still deliberating when they hear of King Kālayavana's approach (84.12, 35, 85). Knowing they must flee at once, the Vṛṣṇis make their way to the Western Ocean where they find a country of mangroves (*latā*) swept by coastal breezes. As soon as he reaches this area, Kṛṣṇa looks for a *puravāstu*, a site for a city (84.24), or a *durgasthāna*, a place for a fortress (86.2). The country is King Ocean's domain (*viṣayaṃ sindhurājasya*, 84.26). Mount Raivataka, a well-known landmark in the vicinity, stands as high as Mount Mandara (84.27; cf. *Mbh* 2.13.49). Raivataka is the residence of Ekalavya, the king of the Niṣādas, and has long been occupied (*adhyuṣita*) by Droṇa (84.28, 24, 27).[8] After a long investigation, Kṛṣṇa decides that this country fits their needs perfectly and sets up camp there for all the Yādavas.

Kṛṣṇa has already decided to call his fortress on the sea (*vāridurgā*, 85.4–5) Dvāravatī, a city 'having gates' (86.5–6), and is determined to make it as marvellous as Amarāvatī, the city of Indra, king of the gods. On the most auspicious day, under the asterism called Rohiṇī, he asks eminent Brahmins to celebrate the rites intended for the construction of a fortress (*durgasya ... kriyām*, 86.3) and invites the Yādavas to set to work. They choose the sites (*vāstuparigraha*, 86.11), take the measurements of the gates (*dvāra*), the buildings, the streets, and the squares. After rites are performed and the Brahmins are gratified (86.12), Kṛṣṇa suddenly has a truly divine idea (*daivā buddhi*, 86.19). Obviously, only Viśvakarman, the architect of the Gods, is powerful enough to build, out of his own mind (*svamatyā*, 86.20), a city likely to fulfill all the Yādavas' wishes. With this, he stands alone (*vivikte*) facing the Thirty Gods (*tridaśābhimukha*, 86.21) and immediately Viśvakarman appears before him inquiring as to which task he is to carry out. 'You heard what the Gods have decided,' says Kṛṣṇa to Viśvakarman. 'These Gods have accompanied me to earth. You alone can build a city worthy of my power' (86.27–30). The celestial architect promises to do all that he can but expresses the fear that the city may not be large enough for all of them. He believes that it will be possible to build a well-proportioned and auspicious city only if King Ocean withdraws his waters. Kṛṣṇa orders the ocean to yield twelve *yojanas*,[9] so that the whole city of Dvāravatī with its houses, doors, streets, places, women's apartments, shops, wells and tanks, moats, ramparts, and walls can be created by Viśvakarman.

Upon entering the city, Kṛṣṇa has another idea. He believes he should shower wealth on his friends, and summons Śaṅkha himself (Conch) to the city in order to carry out the task. Śaṅkha, the King of the Guhyakas, is presented as the source of all wealth and the abode of the God of wealth, Kubera (*vaiśravaṇavastavyam*, 86.55). He pours his wealth out on all the inhabitants of Dvāravatī and from that moment on there are no poor, starving, or dirty people left in the city (86.62). Then Kṛṣṇa calls God Vāyu, the universal source of life, and asks him to go to heaven and carry the famous Assembly Hall (*sabhā*) called Sudharmā (86.67) down to earth. When this is done, the Yādavas consider the *sabhā* as their own. Finally, Kṛṣṇa appoints Ugrasena as king of the city, (Sāndīpani) Kāśya as its chaplain, Anādhṛṣṭi as its general, Vikadru as its prime minister, and ten old men as its clan-guardians (*kulakara*). Dāruka becomes Kṛṣṇa's driver, Sātyaki (or Yuyudhāna) is judged to be the best of the warriors, and Saṃkarṣaṇa marries Revatī, the daughter of Revata (86.80).

The City of Dvāravatī as Described in the *HV*

A Marvellous City

The city of Dvāravatī is presented as a second Amaravatī (86.6, 30), thus comparing Kṛṣṇa to Indra (86.4). Measuring eight *yojanas* by twelve, with suburbs (*upaniveśa*) covering twice that area (93.27), the city is filled with golden-roofed palaces as tall as the peaks of Mount Meru (93.32). Of all the palaces, the one intended for Kṛṣṇa is described in great detail. In this huge, lavishly decorated building, measuring four *yojanas* by four (93.37), there are special pavilions (*prāsāda*) for his main wives[10] – the Kāñcana is for Rukmiṇī (93.39); the Bhogavant, for Satyabhāmā (93.40); there is one for Jāmbavatī, having no special name (93.41); the Meru is for Gāndhārī[11] (93.42–4); the Padmakūṭa is for Bhīmā (93.45); the Sūryaprabha is for Lakṣmaṇā (93.46); the Para is for Mitravindā (93.47–48); and the Ketumant is for Sudattā (93.49–50).

Kṛṣṇa's reception hall (*upasthānagṛha*) is named Viraja (93.52), a building measuring one half-*yojana* square (94.7). Guests can admire many beautiful views from here: Mount Vaijayanta (93.54); a peak named Haṃsakūṭa, measuring sixty *tālas* long and half a *yojana* high, and which is found close to Lake Indradyumna (93.54); the Meruśikhara, the golden peak of Mount Meru, located along the solar way, uprooted by Viśvakarman and brought there at Indra's request (93.56); the Pārijāta tree brought from Indra's paradise by Kṛṣṇa himself (93.57–8; 92.61-70); the Maṇiparvata, the mountain where Naraka Bhauma had confined the sixteen thousand women set free by Kṛṣṇa (94.22); many splendid trees taken from the city of Brahmā (*brahmasthala*) and others growing on Mounts Himālaya and Meru (93.59–60); many jewels, especially the Syamantaka which, although not mentioned in *HV* 93, was reputedly drawn out of the ocean by Prasena at the time the city was founded (cf. 28.12).

Dvāravatī is also surrounded by large mountains and beautiful forests similar to Indra's Nandana or Kubera's Caitraratha (93.13; cf. 93.20): to the east, Mount Raivataka (84.27; 93.14; 109.35) with three forests called Citrakambalavarṇa, Pāñcajanyavana, and Sarvartukavana (93.17); to the south, Mount Latāveṣṭa (93.15; 109.35) with three forests named Meruprabhavana, Bhārgavana, and Puṣpakavana (93.18); to the west, Mount Akṣaya (93.15) or Ṛkṣavant (109.35)[12] with two forests named Śatāvartavana and Karavīrakarambhi (93.19); and to the north, Mount Veṇumant (93.20; 109.35),[12] with two forests named Ramaṇa and Bhāvana. In addition to the buildings especially created by Viśvakarman, the *HV* repeatedly emphasizes the presence in this city of the Sudharmā *sabhā* carried from heaven by Vāyu (91.24; 95.15). Moreover, the Mandākinī, the celestial Gaṅgā, flows through the city, dividing itself into fifty branches and refreshing its air (93.21–3).

Even a cursory reading makes it clear that the *HV* provides a standard description of a celestial city, the oldest examples of which are perhaps the descriptions of the Brahmaloka contained in *Chāndogya Upaniṣad* (8.5.3)[13] and *Kauṣītaki Upaniṣad* (1.3–4).[14] The *Purāṇas* contain much more elaborate descriptions of the cities of the gods,–Bhogya, a city built by Viśvakarman for Śiva,[15] and Tripura, a city designed by Maya for the Asuras.[16] With its mountains, forests, palaces, assembly hall, and celestial river, Dvāravatī is designed to be a paradise on earth. Covered with gold and jewels, perfectly designed by the architect of the Gods, it is clearly a collection of the most precious things in the cosmos (cf. 93.5). When read by Kṛṣṇa's devotees, the descriptions of *HV* 86 and 93 must have sounded rather like a glittering account of the sensuous life of the immortals, a glimpse of what life might be like with Kṛṣṇa in his own celestial abode (*svasthāna*, 97.31). From this point of view, the implausibilities of the text (the presence of a mountain to the west of Dvāravatī, the peaks of huge mountains being carried into the reception hall) are of little importance. Dvāravatī seems to have a life of its own, as a space of celestial joy inside the human world.

Kṛṣṇa's (or Vāsudeva's) Abode

The existence of Dvāravatī should, of course, be analyzed as one element within a story. The city is presented within the story as an architectural construction. Dvāravatī is said to be dedicated to Viṣṇu (*vaiṣṇavī*, 86.44). It is a city meant to be a refuge for Kṛṣṇa (Viṣṇu's *avatāra*), his wives, and warriors.[17] Dvāravatī is the *avatāra's* city and it seems essential that he take up residence in this sort of city. Kṛṣṇa puts it bluntly to the Yādavas: 'Where we stand here, it is necessary to have a residence built for me' (*yatra vayaṃ sthitāḥ / avaśyaṃ tv iha kartavyaṃ sadanaṃ me*, 86.27). Kṛṣṇa does not manifest himself as a pure spirit or a disembodied entity that does not exist within the confines of space. As the gods have their own spatial environment in heavenly worlds, Kṛṣṇa also must be grounded, as it were, in an adequate *sadana* or abode. Like all living beings, he needs a foundation (*pratiṣṭhā*) to stand on, a divine world (*loka*) in which to manifest his radiance and force as a god, a stage (*raṅga*) to play on as a divine actor. This is the meaning of Kṛṣṇa's words to Viśvakarman:

> This site must be established for my benefit so that I can manifest myself, and must be covered all around with houses befitting my power ... You must build my abode as if it were in heaven, so that through this city people may see my prosperity and that of the Yadus' community.
>
> *tad iyaṃ bhūḥ prakāśārthaṃ niveśyā mayi suvrata /*
> *matprabhāvānurūpaiś ca gṛhaiś ceyaṃ samantataḥ //*
> *mama sthānam idaṃ kāryaṃ yathā vai tridive tathā /*
> *martyāḥ paśyantu me lakṣmīṃ puryā yadukulasya ca //* 86.28, 30.

A *sadana*, or *loka*, is something that looks like the physical embodiment of an agent (similar to the way in which Kṛṣṇa's divine weapons are his *tejasic* or energy body). Dvāravatī is the extension of Kṛṣṇa or Vāsudeva's own divine body. It partakes of his power and glory, and reifies or objectifies Kṛṣṇa's strength. It is, as it were, the hypostasis of his own splendour.[18]

A City Built in Accordance with the Rites

The first point to make is that the city that the Brahmins are about to build will not be built from scratch. Dvāravatī existed as a fully developed idea in Viśvakarman's mind (86.41) and was built by the Gods in heaven before being brought down to earth. It travelled to the earth as a bird (86.45). Like the bird-designed altar of the Vedic *agnicayana,* which is compared to a ship built to go to heaven and come back, the city of Dvāravatī is able to travel between the divine and human worlds, but begins its journey from the opposite side. In other words, before disappearing into the ocean, Dvāravatī follows the *avatāra's* trip from heaven to earth, rather than the sacrificer's trip from earth to heaven.

But in India, proper preparation of the site (*vāstu*) is necessary if construction is to be sound. Therefore, upon his arrival on the western coast, Kṛṣṇa looks for a suitable place for a dwelling. The region is covered with sand and red-copper soil (*sikatātāmramṛttakam,* 84.25), just the right colour of soil prescribed in the treatises for Kṣatriyas. The former name of Dvāravatī being Kuśasthalī, one may suppose that it is covered by *kuśa* grass.[19] According to the narrator Vaiśaṃpāyana, the place chosen by Kṛṣṇa 'has all the characteristics of a city, as if the Goddess Śrī had established her residence there' (*puralakṣaṇasaṃpannaṃ kṛtāspadam iva śriyā,* 84.25). Kṛṣṇa asks Brahmins to proceed with the rites on a favourable day. 'On a fortunate day, under Rohiṇī [asterism], having asked excellent Brahmins to utter the ritual 'svasti' with repeated acclamations of the auspiciousness of the day, he undertook the rites of a fortress building' (*rohiṇyām ahani śreṣṭhe svasti vācya dvijottamān / puṇyāhaghoṣair vipulair durgasyārabdhavān kriyān / /* 86.3).[20] Addressing the Yādavas, Kṛṣṇa adds that 'he has prepared the earth as a dwelling for Gods' (*kalpiteyaṃ mayā bhūmiḥ ... devasadmavat,* 86.5). This sentence may be seen as an allusion to the altars (*vedi*) built to receive the deities invited to Vedic sacrifices.

In fact, all construction must begin with the establishment of a set of deities on a specific site. As in a Vedic sacrifice, the soil must be adequately prepared to assure its purity and fertility. The building of Dvāravatī seems to have followed the rules known for ritual constructions. Even if it was not explicitly stated, it does not seem too risky to suggest that the soil of the future Dvāravatī would have been ploughed, levelled and sown. After this, the rituals used for building residences would have been followed.[21]

The *HV* says that Dvāravatī resembles a large chessboard with eight squares on each side (*svāyatāṣṭāpadopamā*, 84.29).[22] This rather strange notation becomes important when, two chapters later, one reads the following verses. The architects (*sthapati*) 'measured the gates and buildings properly, laid the seats of Brahmā and so forth in the proper order, those of the Waters (*āpaḥ*), of Agni, of Sureśa, and of Dṛṣadolūkhala, and assigned Gṛhakṣetra, Indra, Bhallāṭa, and Puṣpadanta to the four doors related to the four deities' (*yathānyāyaṃ nirmimire dvārāṇy āyatanāni ca / sthānāni vidadhuś cātra brahmādīnāṃ yathākramam // apām agneḥ sureśasya dṛṣadolūkhalasya ca / caturdaivāni catvāri dvārāṇi vidadhuś ca te / gṛhakṣetrendrabhallāṭaṃ puṣpadantaṃ tathaiva ca //* 86.16–17).

The only way to make sense of this apparently strange list of deities is to compare it with those of the *vāstupuruṣamaṇḍala* used in the ritual of the construction of temples or cities.[23] Actually all brahmanic construction begins with the descent of the body of 'the man of the site' (*vāstupuruṣa*) down to earth. This *puruṣa* is a reproduction of the celestial world and must be ritually brought to the site of the building to be erected. Whether the site plan is made of sixty-four or eighty-one squares, the four middle squares are always occupied by Brahman or Hiraṇyagarbha. The twelve Ādityas (Aryaman, Vivasvān, Mitra, Mahīdhara, and the couples Savitṛ and Sāvitra; Indra and Indrajaya; Rudra and Rudrajaya; Āpaḥ and Apavatsa) are laid out around the Brahmasthāna or the seat of Brahmā. The four names of Gods in verse 17ab seem to correspond to the main deity in each of the pairs of these deities: Āpaḥ is explicitly named; Agni may be the same as Savitṛ (the Sun); Sureśa, the Lord of the Gods, is Indra, of course; and Dṛṣadolūkhala, 'the one with grindstone and mortar,' may be a form of Rudra. If the four deities of verse 17ab correspond to these four Ādityas, the *-ādi* after Brahmā could refer to the first four Ādityas of the list, namely Āryaman, Vivasvān, Mitra, and Mahī- or Pṛthivīdhara, who occupy the four double *padas* around the Brahmasthāna.

The outer border of the *vāstumaṇḍala* is occupied by thirty-two deities. They correspond, explains Kramrisch, to the total effulgence of the Hiraṇyagarbha, radiating from the middle of the *maṇḍala* through the Ādityas (the suns) up to the limits of the figure. Four of them are named: Gṛhakṣetra,[24] which may be a variation of Gṛhakṣata or Bṛhatkṣatra of the regular *maṇḍala* ;[25] Indra[26] is, of course, Mahendra; Bhallāṭa is the moon and its rays;[27] and Puṣpadanta (or Kusumadanta) is Garuḍa.[28] These four deities seem to be assigned to the four doors corresponding to the four deities of the compass (the *dikpālas*), respectively Yama (south), Sūrya (east), Soma or Kubera (north), and Varuṇa (west). Normally, on the *vāstupuruṣamaṇḍala*, Gṛhakṣetra and Yama stand together in the south; Indra and Sūrya in the east; Bhallāṭa and Soma in the north, and Kusumadanta and Varuṇa in the west.

This analysis, if acceptable, means that the construction of Dvāravatī begins with the realization of a real *vāstupuruṣamaṇḍala* and that the *vāstudevatās* alluded to in 86.13 are the gods that constitute the body of the *vāstupuruṣa* known from more recent texts beginning with Varāhamihira's *Bṛhatsaṃhitā*. In other words, we may infer from these verses that the Brahmins constructed the city of Dvāravatī using the same procedures as they would have for a temple (cf. *devasadmavat* 86.5) and that the apparently more elementary procedure attested to in the *HV* is probably several centuries older than the *Bṛhatsaṃhitā*, which is usually dated from about the middle of the sixth century.

A City in Need of Space

As I have tried to show, the city of Dvāravatī is regarded as Vāsudeva's abode, but, according to Viśvakarman, there is not enough space available to accommodate it. The area set aside by Kṛṣṇa is too narrow to hold all the Yādavas and Kṛṣṇa's entire army. Viśvakarman asks King Ocean to withdraw his waters (*pratisaṃhṛ*, 86.36); he asks for extra land, a sort of *śeṣa* or supplement (even if the term is not used in this context). The ocean agrees to recede (*utsṛj*, 86.38, cf. 34) and uses a device (*yoga*) made of winds to push the sea far away from the coast (86.38). The space obtained from the receding ocean is said to be twelve *yojanas* (86.36). It is difficult to make this figure agree with the dimensions of the city, which is supposed to measure eight by twelve *yojanas*, even if the suburbs cover an area twice as large (93.27). But even if the details do not seem to fit together, what stands out, in my opinion, is that the surface available for the city on the land needs to be enlarged so it can accommodate all the Yādavas. In other words, the *sthāna*, which is part of Kṛṣṇa's total body, needs to be extended to suit the *avatāra's* greatness. At first glance, the episode seems quite strange and modern interpreters are quick to discard it or reduce the miracle involved to a mere account of a tidal wave. I am not at all convinced that ancient mythographers took the time to translate natural phenomena into mythological episodes. This narration must hint at some more essential characteristic of Kṛṣṇa's intervention on earth.

To understand the real import of this passage, it is best to study the episode within its own context. In the whole of the *HV*, Kṛṣṇa is rarely alone. In fact, his elder brother, Saṃkarṣaṇa, seems to function as his natural complement, his *śeṣa*. Without his presence, Kṛṣṇa does not even exist fully. Saṃkarṣaṇa is considered to be the incarnation of the serpent *Śeṣa* (a word meaning 'remainder,' 90.1. 4. 18). Viṣṇu asked the Goddess Ekānaṃśā or Yoganidrā to manage a special birth for him. Initially conceived in Devakī's womb, after seven months the fetal Saṃkarṣaṇa is mysteriously transported to Nandagopa's cow-station (*vraja*), where Rohiṇī, Vasudeva's eldest wife, lives (cf. 25.1; 47–8). Saṃkarṣaṇa completes his gestation period in Rohiṇī 's womb and he is always known as her son, while Kṛṣṇa is considered to be Devakī's son. During the whole of their stay in the Vṛndāvana forest, Saṃkarṣaṇa and Kṛṣṇa are said to be one person divided into two for the sake of the world (cf. 51.1–6). The brothers complement each other, like the Puruṣa and the Pradhāna, the soul and matter in the Sāṃkhya philosophy – or, to use the technical terminology of the Mīmāṃsā, like the *śeṣin* and the *śeṣa*. Kṛṣṇa is the one who needs a complement (*śeṣa*) to exist fully. In other words, it seems that the logic that requires Saṃkarṣaṇa to exist along with Kṛṣṇa extends to the architectural platform which is to be Kṛṣṇa's abode. If Kṛṣṇa cannot exist without a complement, namely his elder brother, Kṛṣṇa's earthly residence also requires a complement, presented by the ocean in this unusual episode.

A City Overflowing with Prosperity

Dvāravatī is repeatedly described as the resting place of Prosperity (Śrī or Lakṣmī). Not only is the city compared to a wife, it is filled with the pavilions of Kṛṣṇa's wives. The city accommodates Kṛṣṇa's spouses, the wives of the other Yādavas, as well as the sixteen thousand women who have been regarded as Kṛṣṇa's wives from the time he liberated them from Naraka's tyranny (96.1–3; cf. 91–2). Moreover, returning to Dvāravatī after Naraka's death, Kṛṣṇa and Saṃkarṣaṇa enter the *sabhā* filled with women – namely Devakī, Kṛṣṇa's mother, and Rohiṇī, Saṃkarṣaṇa's mother (96.9) – and join Ekānaṃśā (or Yoganidrā), another famous woman born from Yaśodā's womb in Kaṃsa's *vraja* (cow-station). Known as the sister of Saṃkarṣaṇa and Kṛṣṇa, she was moved into Mathurā at the time Kṛṣṇa left it, as a ruse intended to detract attention from her brother's departure. The description given by the *HV* runs as follows:

> Then both excellent men reached Devaki's daughter, a woman able to assume any shape at will and referred to by the name Ekānaṃśā. Lord [Kṛṣṇa] was born at the same hour and moment as she was. On account of that, Puruṣottama killed Kaṃsa and his troops. On Vāsudeva's order, this young woman was allowed to grow up there, protected as a son (*putravat*) and worshipped in the Vṛṣṇis' dwelling place (*sadman*). Because she appeared by herself (*ekām*) and for Keśava's protection, the people called this invincible *yogakanyā*, Ekānaṃśā. All the benevolent Yādavas worship this woman as the Goddess who protected Kṛṣṇa by using her divine form. Mādhava approached her and clasped her hand with the tip of his right hand as one reaches for a very dear friend. In the same way, the very mighty Rāma embraces this woman, smells her head and seizes her with his left hand. People admire the sister who stands between Rāma and Kṛṣṇa, [shining] like Śrī on her lotus holding a golden lotus in her hand. Having spread many grains of rice, an array of beautiful flowers and parched grain on her, the women left as they had come.

tataḥ prāptau narāgryau tu tasyā duhitaraṃ tadā /
ekānaṃśeti yām āhur narā vai kāmarūpiṇīm //
tathā kṣaṇamuhūrtābhyāṃ yayā jajñe saheśvarah. /
yatkṛte sagaṇaṃ kaṃsaṃ jaghāna puruṣottamaḥ //
sā kanyā vavṛdhe tatra vṛṣṇisadmani pūjitā /
putravat pālyamānā vai vāsudevājñayā tadā //
tām ekām āhur utpannām ekānaṃśeti mānavāḥ /
yogakanyāṃ durādharṣāṃ rakṣārthaṃ keśavasya ca //
tām vai sarve sumanasaḥ pūjayanti sma yādavāḥ /
devavad divyavapuṣā kṛṣṇaḥ saṃrakṣito yayā //
tāṃ ca tatropasaṃgamya priyām iva sakhīṃ sakhā /
dakṣiṇena karāgreṇa parijagrāha.mādhavaḥ //
tathaiva rāmo 'tibalas tāṃ pariṣvajya bhāvinīm /
mūrdhny upāghrāya savyena parijagrāha pāṇinā //
dadṛśus tāṃ priyāṃ madhye bhaginīṃ rāmakṛṣṇayoḥ /
rukmapadmakaravyagrāṃ śriyaṃ padmālayām iva //

athākṣatamahāvṛṣṇyā puṣpaiś ca vividhaiḥ śubhaiḥ /
avakīrya ca lājais tāṃ striyo jagmur yathāgatam // (96.11–19)

This sister, Ekānaṃśā by name, and also called Yoganidrā,[29] is certainly one of the most important characters in Kṛṣṇa's story. She is said to have grown in the Vṛṣṇi's dwelling place (i.e., Mathurā), whereas Saṃkarṣaṇa and Kṛṣṇa hide in the forests surrounding this city. Kṛṣṇa and his elder brother do not stand alone in the *sabhā* of Dvāravatī. In between them is this woman who embodies the *māyā* through which Kṛṣṇa achieves his ends. The celestial city of Dvāravatī does not therefore belong to Kṛṣṇa alone: it is the city of Kṛṣṇa, Saṃkarṣaṇa, and Ekānaṃśā, three deities who form a transcendent unity. They are present at Mathurā at the very beginning of the story and stand in Dvāravatī at its end. Ekānaṃśā is obviously an aspect of Prosperity which overflows in Dvāravatī. The relationship between Kṛṣṇa and Prosperity is clear for Indra: 'Where Modesty (*hrī*) is, Prosperity (*śrī*) is; where Prosperity is, Humility (*saṃnati*) is; Modesty, Prosperity, and Humility always stay in the great-souled Kṛṣṇa' (96.72).[30]

A City Dedicated to Dharma

When Kālanemi reigns over the world, five deities refuse to approach him: Veda, Dharma, Kṣamā, Satya, and Śrī (38.1) prefer to stay with Viṣṇu. In fact, Prosperity (Śrī) is rooted in *dharma,* and everyone knows that the *avatāra* Kṛṣṇa has come to earth to re-establish the laws of righteousness. 'For whenever the law of righteousness withers away and lawlessness arises, then do I generate Myself [on earth]. For the protection of the good, for the destruction of evil-doers, for the setting up of the law of righteousness I come into being age after age' (*Bhagavadgītā* 4.7–8).[31] In the *HV,* too, Kṛṣṇa is repeatedly linked to *dharma* (85.65; 96.29; 97.31, for example). Dharma also inhabits Dvāravatī, but its presence is mainly symbolized by the celestial *sabhā,* which is more precisely referred to as Sudharmā. 'Having informed all the Gods of Kṛṣṇa's words and begged them for permission, he [Vāyu] seized the Sudharmā hall and went down to earth. Once he had given the Sudharmā hall to the virtuous (*sudharma*) and unwearying Kṛṣṇa, God Vāyu disappeared' (86.71–2).

The relationship between the *sabhā* and the dharmic Kṛṣṇa is made explicit in this passage, although no explanation is given. In a later episode, relegated to Appendix I of the critical edition, a Brahmin named Janārdana goes to the city of Dvārakā and enters the *sabhā* Sudharmā. There he sees Kṛṣṇa, the lord of Indra, who has the same appearance as Sudharmā (*apaśyad devadeveśaṃ sudharmākṛtisaṃsthitam*, no. 31, l. 2763). The *sabhā* is, of course, a place where *dharma* is uttered before being realized. It is a place where the Goddess Vāc (Word) reigns. Kṛṣṇa is said to be the best of speakers (86.35). He addresses the Yādavas in 86.5–10, telling them of his decision to build the city. He tells the architects what to do (86.14), and so on. The construction of Dvāravatī is preceded and accompanied by Kṛṣṇa's speech. By asking Vāyu to bring this *sabhā* to the middle of Dvāravatī, Kṛṣṇa thereby confirms the need for a place to display Vāc in the city, a place for the expression of *dharma*. In this *sabhā* Kṛṣṇa, Saṃkarṣaṇa, and Ekānaṃśā appear together, as a compendium of the active forces of the cosmos. One may infer from the union of these three deities that the Vaiṣṇavas considered this celestial *sabhā* to be a true manifestation of the *dharma*, which Kṛṣṇa comes to restore.

Dvāravatī: A City Deserted and Destroyed

A City Perfectly Built and Totally Destroyed

It is well known that the marvellous city of Dvāravatī was completely destroyed. The magnificence of its construction was paralleled by the radical nature of its demise. The *avatāra* needs an abode in order to establish his presence on earth and when he disappears so also does his abode. The seer Nārada himself predicts the annihilation of the city:

> After restoring the laws among the mortals, offering sacrifices with abundant fees and realizing the goal aimed at by the Gods, [Kṛṣṇa] will go back to his own place (*svasthāna* = Vaikuṇṭha, N.). Having acquired Dvārakā, so sensuous, so delightful, and coveted by the seers, the most famous Kṛṣṇa will go to the ocean. Bedecked with various jewels, studded with hundreds of sacred trees (*caitya*) and sacrificial posts (*yūpa*), Dvārakā with all its forests will enter into Varuṇa's dwelling (= the ocean). The ocean, who knows the Archer's thoughts, will flood this [city] of Vāsudeva's creation having the brightness of the Sun's residence (*sūryasadanaprakhyām*). Nobody other than Madhusūdana, among the Gods, Asuras or humans, is able to live there. (97.31–5)

The *HV* reports nothing further about the destruction of Dvāravatī. But as a supplement to the *Mbh*, this text does not need to repeat an episode duly recounted there in Book 16 (*Mausalaparvan*). On the thirty-sixth year after the Bharata war, Vaiśaṃpāyana tells King Janamejaya that Yudhiṣṭhira heard that the Andhakas, Vṛṣṇis, and Bhojas have been destroyed and that only Vāsudeva (Kṛṣṇa) and Balarāma (Saṃkarṣaṇa) have escaped. How is it possible, asks Janamejaya, that all of these warriors were destroyed before the very eyes of Vāsudeva (16.2.1)? The Brahmin's answer refers to a curse placed upon the Yādavas. These proud warriors tried to fool a group of ascetics who were visiting Dvārakā. They disguised one of them, the great Sāmba, as a pregnant woman and asked these *munis* about the sex of the child to be born. The answer was scathing: 'Sāmba will bring forth a fierce iron pestle (*musala*), which will hasten the destruction of the Vṛṣṇis and Andhakas. Their entire lineage will be wiped out (*ucchettṛ*), except Vāsudeva who will be killed by Jaras, and Halāyudha (Saṃkarṣaṇa), who will go back to the ocean' (16.2.8–10). Informed about the curse, Kṛṣṇa, who knew that the end was near (*antajña*), accepted the words of the *munis* (16.2.13). Sāmba brought forth a *musala* and King Ugrasena had it reduced to fine powder (*sūkṣmaṃ cūrṇam* 16.2.16) and thrown into the sea. The embodied form of Time wandered about the houses of Dvāravatī and many bad omens appeared everywhere (16.3.1). The streets swarmed with rats and mice. The women dreamed about a black woman (*kālī strī*) pacing through the city at night (16.4.1). Kṛṣṇa's disk given by Agni returned to heaven (16.4.3). The Yādavas went on pilgrimage to Prabhāsa, became inebriated, and stroked themselves with blades of Ereka grass, which had come in contact with the *musala* dust, and were changed immediately into iron pestles. All of the Yādavas were then killed. Arjuna came from Indraprastha, bringing Kṛṣṇa's women with him, but, unable to summon his divine weapons, he was attacked by cowherds (*ābhīra*) and defeated.

In this text all the omens appearing in the city presage unstoppable destruction. Ultimately, the destruction of Dvāravatī is attributed to Kāla, Time, or Death. Kṛṣṇa had asked Prajāpati's son Viśvakarman to create this fabulous city, but the *munis*, specialists of *nivṛtti*, bring about its destruction. In some passages, Kṛṣṇa is also said to be the genuine builder of Dvāravatī; and according to *Mbh* 3.13.31, Kṛṣṇa himself is the one who casts Dvāravatī into the ocean. Even if Kāla and other causes are invoked, ultimately Kṛṣṇa himself is the only one who presides over the construction as well as the destruction of the city.

The *Brahmapurāṇa* suggests another version of the foundation and disappearance of Dvārakā. Seeing that the Yādava army was baffled by Kālayavana, Kṛṣṇa thought that Jarāsaṃdha would take advantage of the situation to bring the whole country under his rule. To counter Jarāsaṃdha's *coup de force,* Kṛṣṇa decided to build a fort which could be defended even by women. 'After thinking thus Govinda (Kṛṣṇa) requested twelve *yojanas* from the Great Ocean and built the city of Dvārakā there' (*iti saṃcintya govindo yojanāni mahodadhim / yayāce dvādaśa purīṃ dvārakāṃ tatra nirmame* / / 1.88.13). Later, after more than a hundred years (1.101.18–20), when it is obvious that Kṛṣṇa and Saṃkarṣaṇa have performed the task of annihilating the Asuras from the face of the earth and the burden of the earth has been reduced, Kṛṣṇa agrees that all the Devas must return to heaven. He answers the messenger sent to him by the Gods: 'I have only begun the destruction of Yādavas. If they remain unexterminated, they will constitute a great burden upon the earth. Hence I shall hurriedly remove (that burden) within seven nights. In the same manner as it had been taken from the ocean I shall put Dvārakā back into the ocean, exterminate the Yādavas and return to heaven' (*prārabdha eva hi mayā yādavānām api kṣayaḥ // bhuvo nāmātibhāro 'yaṃ yādavair anibarhitaiḥ / avatāraṃ karomy asya saptarātreṇa satvaraḥ // yathāgṛhītaṃ cāmbhodhau hṛtvā 'haṃ dvārakāṃ punaḥ / yādavān upasaṃhṛtya yāsyāmi tridaśālayam //* 1.101.22–24). In this version of the myth as well, Kṛṣṇa is entirely responsible for the command to destroy the Yādavas and their city. Since the creation of Dvārakā is conceived as the sudden appearance of an island out of the ocean, its destruction merely reverses the process.

The Relationship of Dvāravatī with Mathurā

When analyzing the mythology related to Dvāravatī, one might be inclined to consider the city in and of itself. Upon closer examination, the text reveals an impasse. The narration links Dvāravatī and Mathurā. The Yādavas were dwelling in Mathurā and had to leave this city to take up residence elsewhere. Let us examine what the text has to say more carefully. Mathurā was built at a place called Madhuvana, in honour of the great Dānava Madhu. His son Lavaṇa is a figure dreaded by all living beings. Proud of his army and his great power, Lavaṇa challenges Daśaratha's son, Rāma, who is ruler of the invincible city of Ayodhyā. To counter the haughty Dānava, Rāma merely sends his younger brother Śatrughna who quickly kills him. Śatrughna cuts the forest with his arrows (*astra*) and, being one who has a consummate knowledge of *dharma*, he decides, for the welfare of the region (*bhavāya tasya deśasya*, 44.52), to build the city of Mathurā there (44.22–53). The city is wonderful, comparable to a beautiful woman (44.54–66). Later all four of its gates are put under siege by the divisions of Jarāsaṃdha's army (81.38–47). Kaṃsa, a proud king who is a new Kālanemi served by the troops of Rākṣasas, succeeds Śūrasena and Ugrasena in the kingship of this city.

Mathurā is a thriving (*sphīta*, 44.28, 54) city constructed in a very fertile region (44.58; 80.17). Not far from it stands the mountain named Govardhana where young Kṛṣṇa tended cows (45.35). Jarāsaṃdha's intent is to destroy all the buildings which disturb the evenness of the city, levelling it to make a perfect site (*bhūmi*) for a new city (*adyaiva tu nagary eṣā viṣamoccayasamkaṭā / kāryā bhūmisamā sarvā bhavadbhir vasudhādhipaiḥ* // 81.50).[32] Kṛṣṇa is unable to kill Jarāsaṃdha, even after eighteen battles. Mathurā's small size and its vulnerability to attacks are two more reasons for leaving it (84.5). The Yādavas must leave Mathurā (84.11), and quickly, since Kālayavana is approaching. Even if the reasons given for such a move merit further investigation, it is already clear that the Yādavas abandon Mathurā, emptying the city.

A striking parallel between the trajectory followed by Madhuvana and Kuśasthalī is evident. Both residences are destroyed – Madhuvana is destroyed by Śatrughna, and Kuśasthalī is destroyed by the Puṇyajanas (Yakṣas) and Rākṣasas (9.32). Both places are transformed into cities – Mathurā is built by Śatrughna and Dvāravatī by Kṛṣṇa. Both cities are finally abandoned by the Yādavas. The destruction of Dvāravatī is more complete since the city disappears into the ocean, but the intent is the same[33] – the destruction of cities based on the following logic: a residence is built only to be later destroyed; rebuilt only to be later destroyed again; and so on. The city of the *avatāra* is a concrete example of the law of construction and destruction.

The Relationship of Dvāravatī to the Forests near Mathurā

Vṛndāvana is a marvellous forest that looks like Dvāravatī. Both places appear to be residences where people rejoice like the Gods in heaven. Indeed, Dvāravatī appears to be a copy of Vṛndāvana. Since Vṛndāvana is also meant to be a residence for Kṛṣṇa and Saṃkarṣaṇa, what we have said about the cities of Mathurā and Dvāravatī applies equally well to this forest.

Kṛṣṇa and his elder brother spend their childhood as cowherds in a forest-station called a *vraja* or *govraja*, or a *ghoṣa*. They tend Kaṃsa's cows in the forests surrounding Mathurā and live in a temporary dwelling especially constructed for their stays there. The *HV* describes two of these *vrajas*, the first one in a forest called Mahāvana and the other in the famous Vṛndāvana.[34]

Vasudeva carries young Kṛṣṇa into a first *govraja*, which is described fully in *HV* 49, 16–30. It is a most peaceful and pleasant place near Mount Govardhana, well protected against wild beasts, with very level pastures of tasty grass all around. Inside, are several enclosures and stables, numerous chariots, and of course *gopa* and *gopī* doing the chores. It is a forest centre especially designed for the cows and for the preparation of butter, and so on.

After seven years, this magnificent station is abandoned, as it is impossible for the cows and their cowherds to remain in this forest. 'It is the most disgraceful place for both of us,' says Kṛṣṇa to his elder brother. 'The cowherds have eaten everything edible, consumed wood and fodder, and destroyed the trees ... This forest has no delights and is unattractive; its winds are useless; no more birds live in it; it is as insipid as a rice dish without curry!' (52.9–14). As a result of all these devastations, concludes the text, 'this station looks like a city' (*ghoṣo 'yaṃ nagarāyate*, 52.15), comparing the forest to the desolation of a city governed by a king like Kaṃsa. Kṛṣṇa decides to move to a new forest, describing Vṛndāvana as another Indra's Nandana (52.21–7). By skillful means, Kṛṣṇa causes a pack of wolves to spring from all the hair of his body, killing cows and cowherds alike (52.29–36). The station being completely empty (53.19), the surviving cowherds and cows form a procession, quickly arriving at the forest of Vṛndāvana. 'They built the huge station which cows need as a dwelling' (*niveśaṃ vipulaṃ cakre niveśāya gavāṃ hitam* / / 53.20). This new station, measuring one *yojana* by two *yojanas*, is then fully described (53.21–35) in such a way that it is comparable only to heaven.

A few years later, on Kaṃsa's invitation, Kṛṣṇa and his brother leave Vṛndāvana for the city. When the brothers leave, the *bhāgavata* Akrūra, the old cowherds and all the inhabitants of the station also prepare to leave the forest (69.28-30). It is as if the whole station were abandoned, at least temporarily. Then Vṛndāvana forest seems to be completely forgotten in the narration, as if it had been wiped from the narrator's mind. Some time later, however, Saṃkarṣaṇa returns to memories of his childhood in the forest through a flashback, *smṛtvā gopeṣu yatkṛtam,* 'recalling his deeds among the cowherds' (83.1).

Looking carefully at what happens to the forest-stations, one sees a parallel between the events that take place there and those which take place in the cities of Dvāravatī and Mathurā. The *vraja* located in the first forest is completely destroyed by the cows, which in turn are eaten by the wolves which spring from Kṛṣṇa's body. The cowherds then build a second *vraja* in Vṛndāvana, which will in its turn be abandoned. Table 1 summarizes the series of parallels implied in Vaiśaṃpāyana's narration.

Obviously these parallels overlap and cannot be reduced to a linear sequence. But this cyclical changing of residences is surely a fact that merits further investigation.

Table 1

Madhuvana	Kuśasthalī	The *vraja* in Mahāvana
Madhuvana destroyed	Kuśasthalī destroyed	This *vraja* destroyed
Mathurā built	Dvāravatī built	A new *vraja* built in Vṛndāvana
Mathurā abandoned for Dvāravatī	Dvāravatī submerged; Yādavas' return to heaven	This *vraja* abandoned for the city of Mathurā

The Hypothesis of a Ritual Model

Why is it that these cities and forests are constantly being built and then destroyed? The first thing to understand is that all of these places, despite the sumptuous descriptions, are meant to be no more than temporary residences. They are *sadanas* for sovereigns who reign for a given period of time, or for an *avatāra* who comes down to earth and goes back to heaven. These royal seats are places from where the *avatāra* struggles against the upheaval of *dharma.*

Because of these factors, I suggest, at least as a hypothesis, that the construction of these cities follows a well-known ritual model – the Vedic construction of an altar and later, the building of a temple. The altar built for the *agnicayana,* for example, not only has to be built but must also disappear. The same altar cannot be used a second time for a similar purpose. In the same way, the cities which serve as seats for the *avatāra* are built and destroyed. They are as transient as the sacrifice itself. They are conceived as momentary constructions which must be rebuilt over and over again.[35]

Conclusion

Can I now bring this study to a close? No, I cannot, but I can suggest some directions for research based on these premises that may help us to understand the context of such an ageless text as the *HV*.

The Historical Existence of Dvāravatī

After reading the episode of the construction of Dvāravatī according to the *HV* carefully, further questions about the historical existence of such a city seem pointless. Of course, I do not want to suggest that the interesting archeological studies led by scholars like Dr S.R. Rao are futile.[36] Nevertheless, I think that the results that can be obtained through archeology about the existence of a very ancient harbour on this coast do not concern the same reality as the one which can be met in the reading of a text like the *HV*. The Dvārakā I presented in this chapter has, first of all, an existence in the mind of a narrator whose aim is to come to grips with the eternal problems of life. This imaginary city is an element of a narration that deals with men and women who face daily suffering and are trying to find ways of liberating themselves from it. The Dvāravatī, which devotees can visit nowadays, relies on the power of such mythological episodes dealing with Viṣṇu and Kṛṣṇa, as is also the case for Gokul and Vrindāban. These are places of the religious imagination, which have nothing to do with ancient cities that might be discovered through excavations or submarine archaeology.

The Urban Problem According to the HV

The difficulty of living in cities seems a much more important theme to the author of the *HV* than I suspected when I first read the text. From the beginning of this text, cities are a central concern. King Pṛthu makes the earth an inhabitable place. He levels the earth and divides it into villages and cities. The earth is overburdened because there are too many such constructions and its burden must be removed. Nevertheless, it is also true that the earth cannot exist without these cities (*HV* 5–6). 'The Mahātman Rāma Bhārgava killed the kings who are my husbands,' says Earth to Kaśyapa. 'I am a widow and my cities are empty' (42.44–5). With many desolate cities and kingdoms, the earth becomes weaker and weaker (*viviktapurarāṣṭraughā kṣitiḥ śaithilyam eṣyati*, 43.55), says Vaiśaṃpāyana, speaking about the great Bharata war.

Everything looks as though the city was the *Sitz im Leben* for the reflections found in the *HV*. It is as if the redactor of the *HV* was living at a time when the city with all its ambiguities had become a central theme for reflection. To be aware of the *dharma* can mean to build a city (cf. 44.52), but once constructed the city is also to be abandoned. The city seems to be essentially an ambiguous place. It is a residence for the king, but a residence which is bound to be deserted. Brahmanism seems to conclude that a city must be built according to the proper rituals for the reign of the ruler, just like the residences of the deities, but like any other ritual construction it too must be destroyed. Dvāravatī is such a dharmic city and may serve as an example for the construction of all other cities.[37]

From the Vedic Agrarian Cult to Urban Brahmanism

Charles Malamoud has shown the importance of the traditional opposition between village and forest.[38] The *HV* (and the *Mbh,* too) seems, however, to draw parallels between cities and forests. Forests can be as dreadful as they are wonderful; they are dwelling places for Rākṣasas as well as ascetics. In opposition to forests, Vedic villages symbolize order. But in the Purāṇic texts such as the *HV*, the ambiguity of the forests is used to reveal another ambiguity which the cities carry within their own being. Between the city of Mathurā, ruined by Kings Kaṃsa, Jarāsaṃdha, and Kālayavana, and the marvellous Dvāravatī, the narration draws a parallel: both cities are ultimately destroyed. Like the cows and cowherds who travel from one station to another, the inhabitants of cities and their kings must move from one city to another. Everything that is built is bound to be destroyed, before being reconstructed. This new 'theology' offers a vision of *dharma* that extends beyond a simple contrast of forests and cities, embracing the whole world in all its contradictions. Kṛṣṇa inaugurates a new space and a new time for people living in a new world.

Vāsudeva as the Lord of Dwellings?

The name of Viṣṇu's *avatāra* in the *HV* is Kṛṣṇa, but this Kṛṣṇa is also known as Vasudeva's son, and of course Vāsudeva is a very common designation for Kṛṣṇa. One of the traditional explanations for the name Vāsudeva refers to the episode of Kṛṣṇa's birth (cf. *Bhāgavata-Purāṇa* 10.8, 14; 26.17). But in the *Mbh* and the *HV*, another explanation is often given. Kṛṣṇa is named Vāsudeva because he dwells in all beings (*vasanāt sarvabhūtānām*, *Mbh* 5.68.3; *HV* App. 1, No. 31, 1189), or because he is the ultimate refuge for all beings (*sarvabhūtādhivāsaśca*, *Mbh* 12.328.36; cf. *Viṣṇu-Purāṇa* 6.5.80). In these glosses, the name Vāsudeva is obviously connected with the idea of dwelling (Sanskrit root *vas*). Vāsudeva not only needs dwellings for himself on earth, but is himself the true abode of all that is.[39] To continue this reflection, we would need to take the famous episode of Kṛṣṇa's childhood into account, wherein Kṛṣṇa is transformed into Mount Govardhana and transforms the mountain itself into a large house (*gṛha*) able to accommodate the cows, the cowherds, and even the three worlds – but that is the topic for another essay.

End Notes

1 Unless otherwise indicated, the *Harivaṃśa* (hereafter cited as *HV*) and the *Mahābhārata* (hereafter cited as *Mbh*) are quoted according to *Mahābhārata*, ed. Vishnu S. Sukthankar et al. (Poona: Bhandarkar Oriental Research Institute, 1927–66).

2 See André Couture, *L'enfance de Krishna. Traduction des chapitres 30 à 78 du Harivaṃśa* (*Éd. Cr.*) (Québec: Les Presses de l'Université Laval, 1991), praes., 72–77; 'Est-il possible de dater le *Harivaṃśa*?' in *Contacts Between Cultures: Selected Papers from the 33rd International Congress of Asian and North African Studies, Toronto, Aug. 15–25, 1990*, vol. 2, *South Asia*, ed. Kay Koppedrayer (Queenston, ON: E. Mellon Press, 1992), 156–60.

3 Dvāravatī is the proper name given by Kṛṣṇa to the city that he built on the western coast of India (86.6; cf. also 84.29). Nevertheless, in the *Mbh* and *HV*, the shorter form 'Dvārakā' is more often used. The *Mausalaparvan* of the *Mbh* uses Dvārakā seven times and Dvāravatī only twice; *HV*, 84–94, uses Dvārakā twenty-two times and Dvāravatī thirteen times.

4 A.D. Pusalker, 'Dvārakā,' in *B.C. Law Volume*, part I, ed. D.R. Bhandarkar et al. (Calcutta: The Indian Research Institute, 1945); H.D. Sankalia, 'Antiquity of Modern Dwarka or Dwarka in Literature and Archaeology,' *Journal of the Asiatic Society of Bombay* n.s., 38 *Dr. Bhau Daji Special Volume* (1963), 74–84; 'Dwarka in Literature and Archaelogy,'

Sarada Pitha Pradipa 11 (1971), 14–30; 'Vrishṇis, Sātvatas, Krishṇa, and Dvārakā,' *Journal of Ancient Indian History* (University of Calcutta) 11 (1977–78), 1–5; Z.D. Ansari and M.S. Mate, *Excavations at Dwarka (1963)* (Poona: Deccan College Postgraduate and Research Institute, 1966); V.B. Athavale, 'In Which of the Four Dvārakās Did Ekānaṃśā, the Daughter of Yaśodā Exchanged for Kṛṣṇa, Arrive for the Pārijāta Plantation Ceremony?' *Poona Orientalist* 19 (1954), 17–34; P.V. Kane, *History of Dharmaśāstra*, vol. 4 (1953; reprint, Poona: Bhandarkar Oriental Research Institute, 1971), 748–50; Bimanbehari Majumdar, *Kṛṣṇa in History and Legend* (Calcutta: University of Calcutta, 1969), chap. 4; R.N. Mehta, 'Migration of Yādavas from Mathurā to Dwārakā: Chronology of the Myth,' *Journal of the Oriental Institute* 46, nos. 1–2 (Sept.–Dec. 1996), 77–81; Haripriya Rangarajan, *Spread of Vaiṣṇavism in Gujarat up to 1600 A.D.* (Bombay: Somaiya Publications Pvt. Ltd., 1990), 1–3, 29–33, 49; S.R. Rao, 'Excavation of the Lost City of Dvārakā in the Arabian Sea,' *Contacts Between Cultures*, vol. 2, *South Asia*, ed. Koppedrayer, 225–28; 'Submergence of Dvārakā is a Fact,' *Purāṇa* 34, no. 2 (1992), 3–32.

5 The *Viṣṇupurāṇa* and the *Brahmapurāṇa* mention the departure of the Yādavas for Dvārakā, but in a few lines only. The *Bhāgavatapurāṇa* has a little more to say about Dvārakā (see 10.50, 50-55; also 1.11–12), but nothing similar to the very substantial narration of the *HV*.

6 The names of these mountains are Vaihāra, Varāha, Vṛṣabha, Ṛṣigiri, and Caityaka, *Mbh* 2.19.2. The *Mbh* (Book 2, Jarāsaṃdhavadhaparvan) does not report a siege of Mathurā by Jarāsaṃdha (cf. Majumdar, *Kṛṣṇa in History and Legend*, 111). The *HV* makes no mention either of the disguise used by the Pāṇḍavas as *snātakas* to enter the city of Girivraja nor the ensuing battle. Both traditions appear to be independent.

7 The northern part of the present Kāṭhiavād (Gujarat).

8 This Ekavalya is the son of Śrutadevā, one of Śūra's and queen Bhojyā's daughters and Vasudeva's sister. He is said to be a famous member of the Niṣāda tribe who was raised by the Niṣādas (*HV* 24.14–27).

9 A *yojana* is usually considered as equivalent to 9 miles or 14.4 kilometres.

10 The question of Kṛṣṇa's main wives is an intricate issue. There are eight of them in *HV* 88.34-42 (2.60.34–42), as well as here in *HV* 93.39–50. This list is also given in 98.2–4 (2.103) but with a few additions. These lists, and others occurring in the oldest *Purāṇas*, should be studied in their own right. Note that Nīlakaṇṭha's commentary on *HV* 2.60.41–2 only tries to match this list with the later and different version given in the *Bhāgavata-Purāṇa* 10.58. See S.N. Tadpatrikar, 'The Kṛṣṇa Problem,' *Annals of the Bhandarkar Oriental Research Institute* 10 (1929), 309–14; W. Ruben, *Krishṇa.*

Konkordanz und Kommentar der Motive seines Heldenlebens (Istanbul: n.p., 1943), 177–80; Majumdar, *Kṛṣṇa in History and Legend*, 125–26.

11 This name does not occur in the other lists of the *HV*. The *Mbh* mentions it in 7.10.10 and 16.8.71. Nīlakaṇṭha considers it as synonym for Satyā Nāgnajitī. See *Mahābhāratam* with Nīlakaṇṭha's commentary *Bhāratabhāvadīpa*, ed. Pandit Ramchandrashastri Kinjawadekar (Poona: Chitrashala Press, 1929–33), 7.11.10, 16.7.73.

12 In 109.35, Kṛṣṇa tells Ugrasena to search for Aniruddha in the peaks of Mounts Veṇumant, Latāveṣṭa, Raivakata, and Ṛkṣavant. This list appears roughly equivalent to the one found in 93.14–16, where the fourth mountain is named Akṣaya. The Calcutta edition gives the name Kṣupa for the name of a mountain standing to the west of Dvārakā (see Monier-Williams, *A Sanskrit-English Dictionary*, 331). Of course, the large mountain supposedly to be found to the west of Dvārakā poses a problem for those who consider this city to be a historical reality.

13 'Now, Ara and Nya are the two seas in the world of brahman, that is, in the third heaven from earth. In that world are also the lake Airaṃmadīya, the banyan tree Somasavana, the fort Aparājita and brahman's golden hall Prabhu.' *Upaniṣads*, trans. Patrick Olivelle (Oxford: Oxford University Press, 1996), 170.

14 'Now, in this world (of brahman) are located the lake Ara, the watchmen Muhūrta, the river Vijarā, the tree Ilya, the plaza Sālajya, the palace Aparājita, the doorkeepers Indra and Prajāpati, the hall Vibhu, the throne Vicakṣaṇa, and the couch Amitaujas.' Ibid., 203.

15 Cf. *Liṅgapurāṇa* 1, 80, quoted by Stella Kramrisch, *The Presence of Śiva* (Princeton: Princeton University Press, 1981), 333.

16 Kramrisch, *Presence of Śiva*, 406–407.

17 Madeleine Biardeau insists that Kṛṣṇa's warriors (Vṛṣṇis, Andhakas, and Bhojas) 'assurent sa présence combattante dans le camp où il faisait lui-même fonction de cocher. Tous étaient comme autant d'émanations de Kṛṣṇa lui-même. Ils n'ont pas d'être hors de Kṛṣṇa.' Jean-Michel Péterfalvi et M. Biardeau, *Le Mahābhārata*, tome 2, livres VI à XVIII, extraits traduits du sanscrit par Jean-Michel Péterfalvi, introduction et commentaires par Madeleine Biardeau (Paris: Flammarion, 1986), 340. The same can be said about Kṛṣṇa's wives. One of the points I want to make is that Dvāravatī itself is also a part of Kṛṣṇa's cosmic being.

18 See Jan Gonda, *Loka: World and Heaven in the Veda* (Amsterdam: N.V. Noord-Hollandsche Uitgevers Maatschappij, 1966). This passage looks like a commentary on the word *dhāman*: Dvāravatī is, as it were, Viṣṇu's *dhāman*, that is a manifestation of Viṣṇu's presence or brightness. Jan

Gonda, *The Meaning of the Sanskrit Term Dhāman* (Amsterdam: N.V. Noord-Hollandsche Uitgevers Maatschappij, 1966), chap. 5.

19 Cf. Sankalia, 'Antiquity of Modern Dwarka,' 78–79.

20 Cf. Mayamata 4.1–2.

21 The spirits of an old place must depart before a new habitation can be built. Cf. Stella Kramrisch, *The Hindu Temple*, vol. 1 (Delhi: Motilal Banarsidass, 1976), 13–14. New residents must first get rid of former ones. Nothing is said explicitly for Dvāravatī. But when *HV* summarizes what King Pṛthu did to make the earth inhabitable and thriving, he says: 'The Earth (*vasuṃdharā*) has been divided [into villages and cities] and cleaned (*śodhitā*) [from all its demons]' (*HV* 6.41). The rules applied by the Brahmins preparing the vedic altar seem also to be those followed by King Pṛthu when earth was transformed into a dwelling for living beings at the beginning of a cosmic period or *kalpa*. He uses the end of his bow as a plough to level the surface of the earth, praises its fecundity and divides it into villages and cities (*HV* 6). Kramrisch refers to the levelling of the surface of the earth by King Pṛthu as a sort of model followed by all builders of residences. Kramrich, *Hindu Temple*, vol. 1, 16-17.

22 *Rāmāyaṇa* 1.5.16 says that the city of Ayodhyā is laid out like a chessboard (*aṣṭāpadākārām*).

23 See the diagrams in Kramrisch, *Hindu Temple*, vol. 1, 32, 86–88, and Michael W. Meister, 'Fragments from a Divine Cosmology: Unfolding Forms on India's Temple Walls,' in *Gods, Guardians and Lovers: Temple Sculptures from North India (A.D. 700–1200)*, ed. Vishakha N. Desai and Darielle Mason (New York: The Asia Society, 1993), 97.

24 *HV* vulgate has Śuddhākṣa (2.58.18).

25 According to Kramrisch, Gṛhakṣata or Bṛhatkṣatra is a name for Budha or Mercury. Kramrich, *Hindu Temple*, vol. 1, 91.

26 *HV* vulgate has Aindra (2.58.18).

27 Kramrisch, *Hindu Temple*, vol. 1, 91.

28 Ibid., 93.

29 André Couture, 'The Problem of the Meaning of Yoganidrā's Name,' *Journal of Indian Philosophy* 27 (1997), 35–47.

30 See *HV* 47.26-59 and App. I, no. 8. The complementarity between Kṛṣṇa's and Saṃkarṣaṇa's sister as a fighting Goddess in Mathurā and a new Ekānaṃśā appearing in Dvāravatī rather as a spouse and associated with welfare is examined in André Couture and Charlotte Schmid, 'The Harivaṃśa, the Goddess Ekānaṃśā and the Iconography of the Vṛṣṇi Triads,' *Journal of the American Oriental Society* 121, no. 2 (2001), 173–92.

31 R.C. Zaehner, trans., *The Bhagavad-Gītā*, with a Commentary Based on the Original Sources (London: Oxford University Press, 1973), 184.

32 This is the way Pṛthu proceeded to make the earth a perfect residence for humanity, and the other builders did the same after him, cf. Kramrisch, *Hindu Temple*, vol. 1, 14–17.

33 The city of Vārāṇasī or Kāśī also was cursed by Nikumbha; it was consequently emptied of all its population for thousands of years and occupied by the *rākṣasa* Kṣemaka. King Alarka restored the royal lineage of the Kāśīs. Favoured by Lopāmudrā with an extremely long life, Alarka finally killed Kṣemaka and rebuilt the city (*HV* 23.58–68). According to other texts, Vārāṇasī was later once more destroyed by Kṛṣṇa to avenge the boldness of Pauṇḍraka, an ally of the king of this city who was pretending to be Vāsudeva (see *Viṣṇu-Purāṇa* 5.34; *Brahma-Purāṇa* 1.98).

34 André Couture, 'Campement de bouviers et forêts dans trois versions anciennes du mythe d'enfance de Kṛṣṇa,' *Journal Asiatique* 270, nos. 3–4 (1982), 385–400.

35 Paul Mus's monumental study on Barabudur should be studied with this question in mind. In it Mus speaks of the *stūpa* as Buddha's architectural body and compares it to the construction of altars in Vedic rituals. Paul Mus, *Barabudur: esquisse d'une histoire du bouddhisme fondée sur la critique archéologique des textes*, 2 vols. (Hanoi: Impr. d'Extrême-Orient, 1935).

36 Alok Tripathi firmly believes in the existence of a settlement named Dvārakā, not at the place of the modern Dwaraka, but somewhere near Mount Girnar (Junagadh). See his '*Dvārakā* in Literature and Archaeology,' *Man and Environment* 21, no. 2 (July–December 1996), 49–58, that I happened to read only after completing this essay.

37 Once the problem of cities is clearly brought to the fore in a text like the *HV*, archeological and historical works by Romila Thapar, F.R. Allchin, and so on, could certainly help their context to be better understood.

38 Charles Malamoud, *Cuire le monde* (Paris: Éditions La Découverte, 1989).

39 The *Viṣṇupurāṇa* 1.2.12 makes the point even more clearly: 'The wise men call him Vāsudeva, because he is said to be everywhere and everything dwells in him' (*sarvatrāsau samantaṃ ca vasaty atreti vai yataḥ*).

8

Place in the Sacred Biography at Borobudur

ROBERT L. BROWN

No other monument in the Buddhist world can match Borobudur in terms of the extent and detail of narrative scenes depicted in its several kilometres of relief carvings. Nor can any monument equal the close relationship between image and text that is found there. Indeed, these facts have not been lost on scholars of Buddhism and art history, with Borobudur being the focus of probably more scholarship for well over a century than any other Buddhist monument in the world.[1]

Yet, astoundingly, no consensus of what the monument is or what it means has been determined. In fact, an agreement has never been reached as to what kind of Buddhism it represents – Mahāyāna or Tantric.[2] No one knows how the monument was used, or even by whom.[3] And with its extensive and detailed relief carvings along its galleries, there is still debate as to the identification of many of the narratives depicted, why certain stories are told, and why they are being told in particular ways.[4] With so much material to work with, and so much scholarship written, it is difficult to understand why more of a consensus has not been reached.

One possible reason for our difficulty in determining answers to even fundamental questions regarding Borobudur is that the monument is in the centre of the island of Java, in what is today Indonesia, while the texts that were used there are Indian texts (including the *Karmavibhaṅga*, the *Jātakamālā*, the *Lalitavistara*, and the *Gaṇḍavyūha*). That is, we have a local artistic tradition used with imported Indian texts. While this is true for Buddhism everywhere outside India, it is rare for scholars to suggest that there is any disjuncture between the text and the image. The assumption is that the texts carried the same homogenized message and understandings wherever they appeared, and that they fit easily with the local visual tradition. I think, however, that the textual fit with the local culture was a place of tension, and Borobudur supplies visual evidence of one such disjuncture.

I am not saying – and this needs to be clear – that the Javanese artists, monks, and worshippers saw the Indian texts and the stories they told as foreign. There was one Buddhist world (as I argue below) and Borobudur was clearly one of its centres. But Java was not India, and the Buddhist texts and their narratives of sacred biography were not 'visualized' in the same way in Java as in India.

To demonstrate this I look at how sacred place was seen at Borobudur in the context of the sacred biographies being told in the texts. I focus on the actual seeing of the image, rather than, for example, on memory, or history, or on the words of the texts themselves. I argue that sacred place was depicted at Borobudur through local understandings of 'place,' understandings that reverberate with the texts to a greater or lesser degree but cannot be explained by the stories told by the texts.

Nor can they be explained by artistic conventions borrowed from Indian art, although conventions to identify certain figures as important, honoured, or sacred in narrative scenes are few in number and recur in many traditions. For example, a figure may be depicted as the most sacred in a scene by an iconographical trait, such as a halo, or by his/her relationship to the other figures – placed in the centre, made larger, raised up, and so on. These artistic conventions are so universally used and geographically widespread that it is difficult to separate them into influences and borrowings. Some Indian artistic conventions do not occur at Borobudur, such as making the most sacred or important figure in a scene larger than the others; everyone is the same size in the Borobudur reliefs. Other conventions, such as identifying a central figure by surrounding him/her by retainers and attendants, occur in Indian narrative scenes. The extent and number of attendants at Borobudur, however, are particular and indicate a unique convention.

One more point needs to be made before discussing the reliefs (which can be found at the end of this chapter). It is important to note who was looking at the images at Borobudur, and I think it was a very special group who did so – the elite. Let me suggest that we divide the ancient population of Southeast Asia into three groups – the elite, the common people, and the people of the forest – with each group seeing place in a different way. By using art, we can only see place in ancient Southeast Asia through the eyes of the elite. Elements of Hinduism and Buddhism are there, but so are local elite notions of what constructed place. It is difficult to know to what extent the common people and those who lived in forests (and thus the majority of the population) saw the places in which they lived through a Hindu and Buddhist interpretation. I don't think they saw their world in these strictly religious terms. It is much more probable that the elites' local understanding of place was shared. Further, I think that it was not until the thirteenth century and later, with the domination of Theravāda Buddhism and Islam, that most Southeast Asians (both elite and commoner) began to see their world in more unified ways.

Despite the enormous bibliography on Borobudur, I have yet to read any scholar who has asked how notions of sacred place can be found in the depictions of the textual narratives on the monument. I propose that sacred place is established in three ways: by hierarchy; by a great person and his/her followers; and by the depiction of monuments.

Hierarchy

A sense of hierarchy is everywhere in the reliefs. The position of the figures locates their importance. Those of more importance are placed higher: they are placed on a raised seat, or on an animal or cart, or have others bend before them. Those inside a structure are ranked higher than those outside. Gestures can indicate ranking as well.

Almost any relief can be used to demonstrate how hierarchy is ordered. Figure 1 is one of a series of twenty reliefs that illustrates the love story of Prince Sudhana and Manoharā.[5] In this scene, Sudhana is being told by his mother what has happened to the absent Manoharā, but nothing of the story needs to be known to determine the hierarchy of the figures. Sudhana and his mother sit facing one another inside a pavilion, his mother telling, Sudhana listening. That Sudhana's mother is the most honoured of all figures in the relief is indicated by her being raised the highest. She sits on a small platform that places her head above that of Sudhana and the others. Sudhana is next, placed a little lower, but still inside the pavilion. His subservience to his mother is further indicated by his lowered head and arms crossed in front of his chest. There are fourteen retainers. There are thirteen men in Sudhana's entourage, who wait outside seated on the ground, Sudhana's elephant mount beside them. Sudhana's mother has a single female servant, kneeling behind her holding a plate of food.

Vertical hierarchy is inherent in the organization of the reliefs themselves, with the *karma* reliefs at the bottom of the monument, moving through the *jātakas* or the life scenes, to the *Gaṇḍavyūha* reliefs, from the mundane to the ethereal.[6]

Hierarchy is constantly being judged in the Southeast Asian cultures I know, particularly with the body – its posture, the location of the head and feet, the hand gestures, use of the eyes. With each meeting, two people use their bodies to announce their relative hierarchy, who is above, who below. Power is seen in the movement, or usually lack of movement, of the body; powerful people do not need to move, gesture wildly, or threaten to accomplish their will.

Over and over again, the action of the reliefs stops for a summation of what has gone on before through two people having a dialogue; the figures sit or stand, gestures frozen, having an imagined talk, one superior, one inferior (as in fig. 1). In reality, however, this is less of a dialogue and more of a question-and-answer session, with one person (the questioner) ignorant and the other (the teacher) knowing everything, thus maintaining the strict hierarchical difference.

Great People

One of the most obvious elements of the reliefs is the need for each to show a great person and his/her retainers. It would be interesting to compute how many of the thousands of figures in the reliefs are there as companions and retainers to the main actors; my guess would be about 95 percent. Anyone who is important must have them. The great people and their retinues stand or sit in motionless groups, then move on in processions; no one of importance travels without them.

The hero of the *Gaṇḍavyūha,* the text depicted in a series of 488 reliefs that take up most of the upper three galleries, is a merchant's son (also named Sudhana) who visits a series of teachers. Figure 2 shows Sudhana on his way from his thirty-fifth teacher to the next, riding in an elaborate howdah on his elephant, accompanied by fifteen retainers,[7] some walking, some riding horses, and three adoring deities flying in the air. The text is silent on how Sudhana went from this teacher to the next. It simply says he 'left her.'[8] There are seven sequential reliefs that show Sudhana in stationary dialogue before the elephant scene, each with a different teacher that required his travelling from one to the next (although no travelling is shown). Three reliefs of meetings follow with three more teachers, before the artist again depicts Sudhana moving on.[9] It appears that the artist has put Sudhana on the elephant almost arbitrarily, perhaps to move the non-existent action along.

While geography is important, and we often know from the texts the names of the places represented in the reliefs, they are rarely if ever identified or differentiated visually. Important geography is defined by the presence of great people (and gods), or, as we shall see, by man-made monuments.

Two other features of great people and their retainers are their body type and their decorations. They are beautiful, young, and almost always heavily decorated and jewelled. One searches in vain for anything but these (literally) beautiful people, except, of course, in the *karma* reliefs. But here we find that it is only those who have bad *karma* who appear as common people. Those with good *karma* and thus good rebirths look like the beautiful figures in the other reliefs.[10]

The body types are so standardized that even in the scene, where a nun is represented, she looks almost naked (fig. 3).[11] She is read as yet another perfectly beautiful person, her glorious female body not masked by the opaque covering of an actual nun's robe.

Great people also spend much of their time preparing for events. The series of 120 reliefs depicting the Buddha Śākyamuni's life can be used as an example: it takes twelve reliefs to reach conception, and another sixteen until his birth is shown. Twenty-eight reliefs, or just under one-quarter of the total, are dedicated to the preparation of the birth. Such careful preparation for an event is seen in other relief sequences as well. Indeed, in some ways, the extensive *Gaṇḍavyūha* reliefs can be seen as a massive preparation for Sudhana's final vow of bodhisattvahood.

Monuments

There are hundreds of monuments depicted in the reliefs of Borobudur, and they have received considerable study. There are temples, *maṇḍapas, vihāras, stūpas,* and palaces which look very much like temples (fig 4). At times the structures appear to be represented in an X-ray view, so that the inhabitants (almost always great people) can be seen inside (fig 5). At other times the structures appear to be more *maṇḍapas,* platforms with a pillar-supported roof, as in figure 1. Some structures are mysterious, appearing without doors,[12] for example, and the *stūpas* (while fairly rare) show a variety of forms that do not occur in the extant archaeological and artistic remains we have from Java (fig 6). But many of them, both in their design and decoration, are reflected in the many stone temples built at the same time (in a very brief period of only about one hundred years) that dot central Java.[13] One can only imagine what the landscape would have looked like covered by the probably thousands of now-lost wooden structures. Building and constructing were of tremendous importance.

While nature is depicted in the reliefs, particularly trees and ponds, it appears very structured and constructed, much like the monuments themselves and decorated in a similar fashion. The trees are often celestial trees, or wish-fulfilling trees that produce jewels, gems, and cloth as well as fruits and flowers. When Sudhana visited his sixteenth teacher, a banker named Ratnacūḍa, the text describes at length his home and gardens:

> Sudhana saw that the house was radiant, made of gold, wide and high, surrounded by silver walls, adorned with crystal terraces, embellished with hundreds of thousands of lapis lazuli turrets, on coral pillars; there was a lion seat arrayed with red pearls ... covered with a canopy of radiant jewels, draped with a net of wish-fulfilling jewels, arrayed with countless gemstones. There was a lotus pond, with cool water, made of emeralds. Surrounded by trees of all kinds of jewels, the house was large.[14]

When the artist depicted the meeting (fig. 4), he seated Sudhana outside holding his hands together in honour while Ratnacūḍa sits inside his beautiful home, which looks very much like a temple. The jewel trees are a tour de force combining symbols of honour, wealth, and status – flowers (lotuses), fruits, chains, bells, jewels, umbrellas, and fly whisks. Where is the emerald pool? It is indicated by the enormous pot with flowers (*pūrṇaghaṭa*) placed between Sudhana and the house. In the depiction of nature, the Borobudur artists – as authors of the text – had no interest in what we call 'natural beauty,' tranforming natural objects like trees and pools into artificial constructions of power and plenty.

Borobudur itself is an artificially built and decorated mountain. It is curious that there is no other monument in Java like it, nor, in fact, is there a monument depicted like it among the hundreds of buildings shown in the reliefs. I don't know why this is, but it emphasizes just how unique a place Borobudur is.

Place in the Text

It is useful to look at how place is described in some of the texts used at Borobudur in order to contrast these descriptions with the ways sacred place is created visually in the reliefs. Sacred place is not uniformly described in the texts used at Borobudur. 'Sacred' place, for example, is not described in the *Jātakas* and the *karma* texts, but it does appear in the *Lalitavistara* and the *Gaṇḍavyūha,* which are pertinent to our discussion. The *Lalitavistara,* a biography of Śākyamuni, is illustrated in 120 reliefs in the first gallery. The *Gaṇḍavyūha,* which tells the pilgrimage of Sudhana towards bodhisattvahood, is depicted in 488 reliefs in the next three galleries. These two texts are very different. But however different, their sacred places are created in the same three ways in the reliefs: through hierarchy, great people, and monuments.

One passage from the *Lalitavistara,* which is presented visually by three reliefs (figures 7, 8, and 9) at Borobudur, reads as follows:

> As soon as the Bodhisattva was born, the gods sons Maheśvara turned to Śuddhāvāsakāyika gods sons and spake thus: 'The Bodhisattva, the Great Being, has appeared in the world and will in a short time attain the highest and most perfect Wisdom. Come, let us go and greet him, do him homage, honour and praise him.' Then the gods son Maheśvara surrounded and followed by twelve hundred thousand gods sons, after filling the whole great city of Kapilavastu with radiance, came to the place where Śuddhodana's palace stood ... and after saluting the Bodhisattva's feet with his head and throwing his upper garment over one shoulder, he walked around him some hundred thousand times, keeping his right side towards him, took the Bodhisattva in his arms, and spoke encouraging words to Śuddhodana. After the gods son Maheśvara with the Śuddhāvāsakāyika gods sons had thus performed the ceremony of the great homage, he returned to his own dwelling ...
>
> Then the oldest Śākyas, men and women, gathered together, came to king Śuddhodana and spake thus: 'O king, this thou should know, the prince must be brought to the temple.' And he answered and said: 'It is

> well, let the prince be brought there' ... Thus, while praise and rejoicing sounded everywhere and the streets, crossways, markets, and gateways were dressed with innumerable adornaments, King Śuddhodana set forth after decorating the carriage of the prince within the palace, accompanied and followed by brahmans, teachers of the veda's, chiefs of the guilds, heads of families, councillors, rulers of the frontier, guardians of the gateways, followers, friends and relations, with the prince along the road, that was sprinkled with perfumes, strewn with blossoms, filled with horses, elephants, carriages and troops on foot, where umbrellas, flags and banners were planted, and all kinds of music resounded. A hundred thousand gods drew the carriage of the Bodhisattva and many hundred thousand million of koṭi's of gods sons and apsaras scattered showers of blossoms in the air and made melody upon instruments of music.[15]

The text is filled with visual imagery (characteristics are even more exaggerated in the *Gaṇḍavyūha*) and stresses numbers: Maheśvara circumambulates the Bodhisattva 'some hundred thousand times'; there are 'many hundred thousand millions of koṭi's' of gods in the sky; and so forth. Such rich textual visualization both helps and hinders the artist – it is highly suggestive of what images to include, yet makes it impossible to include all but a tiny number of them, and it is completely impossible to approximate the enormous numbers described.

We can see that in each of the three panels the artist used the three ways to produce sacred place. The great people are placed above, either in a *maṇḍapa* or in a cart (figs. 7, 8, and 9). Within the raised space, there are slight modulations to raise the Bodhisattva and his father to the highest spot. The Bodhisattva himself is the only figure shown more or less frontally and without another figure overlapping his. He is clearly a chubby, healthy, and wealthy baby, accompanied by a great number of people and gods. But note that in the third panel (fig. 9), the artist did not attempt to include the many places, people, and gods described. In this panel, the hierarchical arrangement and the accompanying retinue create the sacred place. In other words, the artist ignored the text's description of places, gods, people, and animals.

Note also that in the first relief (fig. 7) the central action of circumambulation by Maheśvara of the Bodhisattva is not shown. As so often is the case at Borobudur, the focus is on a meeting frozen in time. Likewise, the second panel (fig. 8) illustrates nothing more than two simple lines of dialogue: 'O king, this thou should know, the prince must be brought to the temple,' and the answer, 'It is well, let the prince be brought there.' To devote an entire panel to this, an event completely lacking in narrative content, is surprising, but it gives the artist the opportunity to do what he/she likes best: show a frozen moment of inaction when an underling requests something from his superior while surrounded by a group of watching attendants.

Universal Laws

A fourth way in which sacred place is created at Borobudur is neither directly related to the texts nor to the local visual imagery, but to a shared notion of how the universe works in a Buddhist world. Or, to put it another way, it is a notion that appears in both the texts and the reliefs without the need to trace one to the other. For example, the laws that determine people's lives – whether one will live a long or short life, be healthy or ill, strong or weak, rich or poor, and so on – are clearly outlined in the texts as well as the reliefs. There are also laws that determine how a person moves through endless lives, each life cementing a grain of sand into the building of a gigantic dam of righteous actions, so that one eventually reaches enlightenment.

The way to be righteous is stated over and over again: one must enter the company of the enlightened. In the galleries of Borobudur, worshippers walk among the enlightened, those who are their companions, models, and teachers. The lessons the enlightened teach are righteous action: compassion, selflessness, giving, knowledge, purity, humility, and so forth. This use of the monument may be the best way to explain it as a sacred place.

These are the rules that control Borobudur and, presumably, the world of the worshippers. These are rules that apply everywhere, and bring the Borobudur worshippers into the shared world of Buddhism.

Conclusion

Borobudur is a place of the beautiful, the successful, the perfect in body and soul. It is a place of solemn, careful movement and actions, of stately processions and constant teaching. It is a place in which there are a few important people, and most everyone else is there for these few people's benefit: to point to their accomplishments, their significance, and their purity; to accompany them and carry gifts and food for them. It is a place of vast wealth and of all things that are extravagant and valuable: jewels and gems, gold and silver, cloth, mirrors, perfumes, lamps, flags, and music. The monuments – pavilions, temples, *stūpas*, and even nature itself – are elaborately and beautifully decorated. It is a place where the rules that govern life and its outcome, both the mundane and the spiritual, work without doubt and with consistency.

Certainly, one may point to the characteristics of the texts that were used that mandate such a place; or one could argue that it is an idealized space, never meant to reflect reality. Still, this is a place reserved for the great, for the elite, and for the perfected – in short, for the few. Are we to interpret this to mean that these few are paralleled by its worshippers, probably the Śailendra royalty, its court and monks? I think so. Nevertheless, the first three ways place is determined, through hierarchy, great people, and monuments, appear to be predominantly local in character, particularly in the way they take visual form in the reliefs. In other words, however strongly related Borobdur is to Indian texts, religion, and art , it reveals in its reliefs an identification with 'sacred place' that draws on local understanding and imagery.

Finally, let me return to what such local 'seeing' of sacred place in the Indian textual stories may mean in terms of our present-day understanding of Borobudur. I want to suggest that place in the Indian Buddhist texts used at Borobudur was visualized through local concepts of how space for important people (the elite) was conceived. Perhaps Buddhist texts, recorded in sacred words (here, Sanskrit) between covers or as memories within heads, can float across boundaries of culture and vernaculars. Art, on the other hand, as an object, or a concrete thing, is more inert and much less able to move easily across cultural boundaries. Local understanding always dominates in art. If so, the disjuncture between text and image at Borobudur may, in part, help to explain why our using the texts to understand the images has been such a battle with so few victories recorded.

Figure 1: Sudhana speaking to his mother.

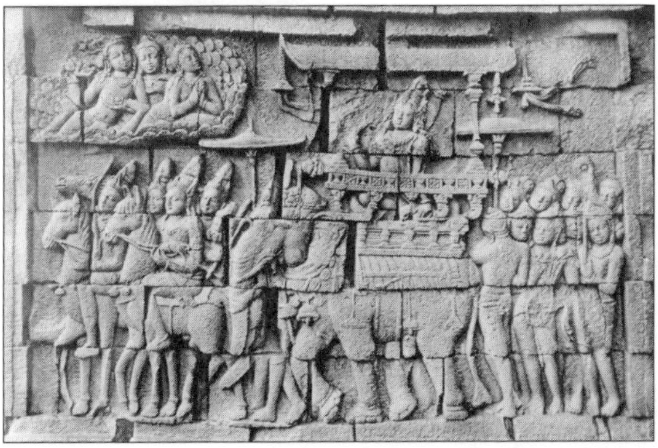

Figure 2: Sudhana travelling on an elephant to visit his next teacher.

Figure 3: A nun teaching Sudhana.

Figure 4: A merchant teaching Sudhana.

Figure 5: A goldsmith teaching Sudhana.

Figure 6: People worshipping a stūpa.

Figure 7: The gods honour the bodhisattva.

Figure 8: The Śākyas ask that Śākyamuni be brought to the temple.

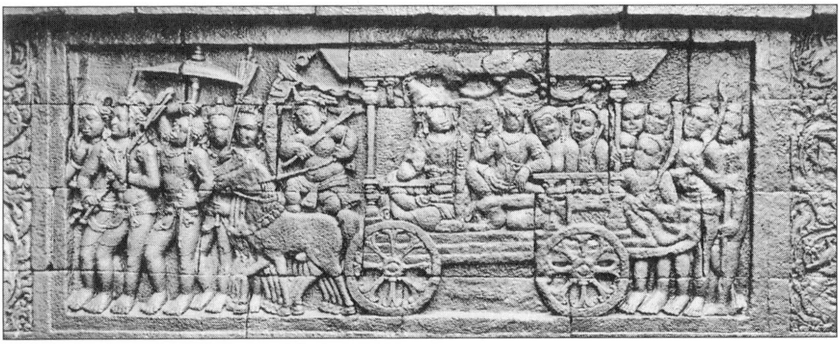

Figure 9: Śākyamuni being brought to the temple.

End Notes

1 There is no comprehensive bibliography published of Borobudur scholarship. The bibliography in *Borobudur: History and Significance of a Buddhist Monument,* ed. Luis Gomez and Hiram W. Woodward, Jr. (Berkeley: Asian Humanities Press, 1981) is a handy place to start looking for references. As a visual resource, the recently published book, Jean-Louis Nou and Louis Frédéric, *Borobudur* (New York: Abbeville Press, 1996), with an earlier 1994 French edition, is invaluable, as it republishes almost all of the photographs of the reliefs first published in a Dutch edition in 1920 and again in an English edition in 1927. The photographs were taken during the restoration of Borobudur between 1907–11, the only time that the series of covered *karma* reliefs were ever fully exposed and photographed. The photographs were published in three huge portfolios. N.J. Krom published *Archaeologische Beshrijving* in 1920. Th. van Erp published *Bouwkundige Beschrijving* in 1931. Both volumes, along with the three portfolios of illustrations, were published by Martinus Nijhoff at The Hague, and together were entitled *Beschrijving van Barabuḍur.* Krom then published in 1927, again with Martinus Nijhoff, a two-volume English translation of his Dutch volume, entitled *Barabuḍur: Archaeological Description,* along with three portfolios of illustrations with English captions using the same plates as the Dutch edition. All the illustrations in this article are photographed from the 1927 portfolios.

2 While Mahāyāna is the most likely, Tantric Buddhism has its adherents. See, for example, Lokesh Chandra, 'Borodudur: A New Interpretation,' in *The Stūpa: Its Religious, Historical and Architectural Significance,* ed. Anna Libera Dallapiccola (Wiesbaden: Franz Steiner Verlag, 1980), 301–19. Of course, the issue here is largely one of definition of the two categories.

3 There is more or less agreement that the monument was built over a period of some years, around AD800–840. We know the name of the dynasty under whom it was built (the Śailendras), but despite considerable, and often very interesting, speculation, little regarding who built it and why is known.

4 See Jan Fontein, *The Law of Cause and Effect in Ancient Java* (Amsterdam: n.p., 1989), and Robert L. Brown, 'Narrative as Icon: The Jātaka Stories in Ancient Indian and Southeast Asian Architecture,' in *Sacred Biography in the Buddhist Traditions of South and Southeast Asia,* ed. Juliane Schober (Honolulu: University of Hawaii Press, 1997), 64–109.

5 The story and its depiction at Borobudur are discussed in Jan Fontein,

'Notes on the Jātakas and Avadānas of Barabuḍur,' in *Borobudur,* ed Gomez and Woodward, 85–108, and Padmanabh S. Jaini, 'The Story of Sudhana and Manohara: An Analysis of the Texts and the Barabuḍur-Reliefs,' *Bulletin of the School of Oriental and African Studies* 29 (1966), 533–58.

6 The vertical and sequential organization of the reliefs is discussed by many scholars. See Brown, 'Narrative as Icon,' 78–84.

7 Or about fifteen, as it is not clear how many figures walk just in front of the elephant.

8 Thomas Cleary, trans., *The Flower Ornament Scripture: A Translation of the Avtamsaka Sutra,* vol. 3 (Boston: Shambhala, 1987), 205.

9 See the reliefs in either the portfolio of Krom, *Barabuḍur: Archaeological Description,* or in Nou and Frédéric, *Borobudur.* They are Second Gallery, reliefs 1147–1158.

10 Again, see illustrations in either of the sources mentioned in note 9. Also, Fontein, *Law of Cause and Effect.*

11 This is the nun (*bhikṣuṇī*) Siṃhavijṛṃbhitā, one of Sudhana's teachers. See Cleary, trans., *Flower Ornament Scripture,* 141–46, for the textual description of the visit.

12 For example, reliefs 11128 and 11137.

13 See Daigoro Chihara, *Hindu-Buddhist Architecture in Southeast Asia* (Leiden: Brill, 1996), 91–133 for a survey of Central Javanese architecture.

14 Cleary, trans., *Flower Ornament Scripture,* 114.

15 The translation is from N.J. Krom, *The Life of the Buddha on the Stūpa of Barabuḍur According to the Lalitavistara-Text* (1926; reprint, Varanasi: Bharatiya Publishing House, 1974), 38–40.

9

Ratannāth's Travels

VÉRONIQUE BOUILLIER

Space is a central concern in the biography as well as the cult of the Siddha Ratannāth.[1] One can even say that both are structured around a sacred geography, the main characteristic of which is to oppose the strictly local to the world outside. This tension appears as a factor of legitimacy and provides us with a clue to understanding one of the main themes in the story and ritual of Ratannāth, the intertwining of models of royal power and religious authority. This leads in turn to the figure of the Devī as a bestower of power. Before dealing with the relationships that Ratannāth's story establishes between these three paradigms – space, kingship, and goddess – let us look briefly at the religious and historical context of the Siddha's appearance.

Ratannāth is a prominent figure for the Yogīs of the Dang Valley in the western part of the Nepalese Terai. The Terai, the lowlands bordering India, was well known until the beginning of this century for its jungles filled with wild game and infested with malaria. The Dang Valley is a small part of the Terai included in the Mahabharat Hills. It was covered with forests and inhabited by the semi-nomadic ethnic group of the Dangaura Tharus. Until the end of the eighteenth century, the valley was politically autonomous, a small kingdom isolated from the main Nepalese political centres because of its geography, and probably paying tribute to the North Indian leaders, mainly from Oudh. But in the second half of the eighteenth century, Prithvi Narayan, the new king of Gorkha, a petty kingdom of Central Nepal, undertook to conquer and unify the whole of Nepal. He partially succeeded in doing so. The Dang Valley was conquered by Prithvi Narayan's successor in 1786, and the vanquished king, Nawal Sen, was forced to take refuge in India on the other side of the border, where he accepted the protection of the Balrampur Raja.

It is in this former kingdom of Dang and in close relationship with the kingship that a *maṭh* – a monastery – of the Gorakhnāthis or Kānphaṭā Yogīs was founded. Gorakhnāth was a saint in the eleventh or twelfth century known as a propagator of hatha yoga. His disciples wore large earrings and were named Kānphaṭā or 'split-ears.' They worshipped Śiva and Bhairav, practiced yoga, and were credited with having special powers known as *siddhis*. They often had close relationships with kings.[2] That was the case in Western Nepal. For Dang, it seems that their coming into the valley took place at the same time as the conquest of the Rajput kings, who dominated the local Tharu tribes around the fifteenth century. But this is not certain, as the first written documents date only from the end of the eighteenth century.

The Kānphaṭā monastery, situated in the hamlet of Caughera in the Dang Valley of Southwest Nepal, is named Ratannāth's monastery in many documents where it is mentioned that Siddha Ratannāth was the founder of the *maṭh* or the temple (*sthan*). This is said to have occurred 'in former times,' 'in the beginning,' 'before,' 'a long time ago.' Today the link with the Siddha Ratannāth is obvious. The oral tradition among the Yogīs or the local villagers, the small booklets published in the monastery, and the narrative paintings on the monastery, or on canvas, are constant reminders of the life of Ratannāth. Books and paintings both tell us an enigmatic story, the source of which may be the *Meghmālā*, a manuscript from eighteenth century. This manuscript is mentioned in the library of Raja Man Singh from Jodhpur, who was well known for his connections with the Nath gurus[3] and is credited with having written some Nath treatises.

Ratannāth's presence in the Caughera monastery is not only narrative. The ritual makes him come to life as the *pīr* or the head of the monastery. The head of the monastery is considered to be the incarnation of Ratannāth and as we shall see, during an annual pilgrimage, he travels through a specific territory to the town of Devi Patan in the Gonda district of Uttar Pradesh in India. The origin of this pilgrimage (*yātrā*) is probably quite ancient, perhaps dating to the period before the conquest of Dang and the escape of the last independent king. But its raison d'être, perhaps in the mythological world of the Tharus, remains an open question for me.

If we look at the places visited by Ratannāth in the legend and at the ones visited by the ritual Ratannāth, we find two opposing themes: an emphasis on the local sites and the importance of travelling outside, to a foreign land. These appear to be connected to issues of legitimacy for the Caughera Monastery.

The Hagiography

Ratannāth's life is narrated in locally published booklets and is depicted on canvasses or wall paintings for the obvious purposes of edifying those who come here. Visitors are invited to learn about the deeds of the saint by visiting a small art gallery especially arranged in front of the main sanctuary.

The hagiography, as it is presented in Caughera, is clearly divided into two cycles with two different parts: the first part concerns the appearance of Ratannāth, his birth, and his conversion by Gorakhnāth; the second part deals with his missionary activities.

The Initiation: Local Roots

In the first part of the hagiography, Ratannāth is shown rooted in the landscape of Dang and involved in the rise of the Dang kingdom as a political entity. Two different versions of the legend about the foundation of the Caughera monastery have a renouncer-king as a hero: Ratannāth is first known as Ratna Parīkṣaka, the son of the king of a land described as a jungle and called *savā lakh jhaṛkhaṇḍa* (one hundred and twenty five thousand bushes), as Dang was called. After the death of his father, Ratna Parīkṣaka becomes king, and is said to have been a virtuous one. According to the most popular version of the legend, his meeting with Gorakhnāth happened as he was going hunting, an activity proper to a king. It is in the kingdom of Ratna, in the jungle of the king, that the Siddha Gorakhnāth takes the appearance of a deer and provokes Ratna in order to convert him. Gorakhnāth wants the king to establish his cult in the kingdom of Dang, to dedicate his kingdom to him, and to make him the tutelary deity. Another version of the legend goes so far as to say that Gorakhnāth appears to Ratna in order to give him the kingdom of Dang, in exchange for the diffusion of his cult.

Both legends show us the hero Ratannāth deeply rooted in a specific territory and linked to the Dang kingdom, the growth and prosperity of which he secures through the protection of Gorakhnāth. In exchange for this, Ratannāth changes his role from king to devotee. The centre of the kingdom is now linked to the Caughera monastery, which houses the object symbolizing the initiation of Ratannāth, a vessel full of ambrosia, an *amritpātra* given by Gorakhnāth to his disciple for worship. In the past, the monastery was situated close to the palace and the *rājguru,* the guru of the king, lived there. The lands, the revenues of which were necessary for the cult, were also given to the monastery by the kings of Dang.

The Travels

After demonstrating the importance of the local in Ratannāth's story through his past and future links with Dang, the narratives in his hagiography go on to describe how Ratannāth spent the rest of his life travelling. He disappears from Dang, following Gorakhnāth's order, and travels throughout Northwest India teaching yoga – that is to say, Gorakhnāth's path – to the subjects of the 'Badshah.'[4] In his travels, he performs miracles and wins the allegiance of emperors and sovereigns as described in his biography:[5]

– He makes the emperor's garden bloom again and receives allegiance from the emperor who promises to protect the Hindus from then on.

– On the road to Kabul, he performs two miracles in Attock (a village located at the famous ford on the Indus River). First, he turns two boatmen who refuse to ferry him across into stone. His anger is still inscribed in the landscape: two rocks mark the spot and still bear the names of the boatmen, Jamal and Kamal. The second miracle is the only one in the hagiography dictated by compassion: Ratannāth restores to life a wedding party drowned in the river.

– He then goes to a place called Shamsher Gaha in the mountains of Khorasan, where there are seven lakes and a cave containing the *parasmaṇī,* the philosopher's stone.

– Afterwards, he travels to Jalalabad and stays in a fortress where, according to the wishes of the emperor, he leaves his shawl as an object of worship.

– Finally, he goes to Bhatinda, where he gives his blessing to Mahmud Ghori and secures his victory against Prithvi Raj Chauhan. The conqueror, Mahmud Ghori, expresses his gratitude by founding temples in Kabul, Jalalabad, and Peshawar (where until recently there was a temple dedicated to Gorakhnāth and Ratannāth).

The sanctity of the holy founder of Dang is thus established and recognized by the 'Badshah,' the Muslim overlord. The holy places linked to Ratannāth's story form a political and religious geography taking shape at the beginning of the Muslim domination. These holy places tell a story of a wonder-worker ascetic, supported by Muslim conquerors and, in turn, supporting their power. It is surprising that he is not a Sufi!

A Paradoxical Figure

The paradox of the Dang Ratannāth is multifold: he is worshipped as a local saint, known as a founder of the Dang Kingdom, yet he is rarely mentioned in the official Nath tradition. His reputation is built on his travels to the important places of Northwest India (the main centres of the Ghaznavids, independent from the Delhi Sultanate until the Mongol conquest around 1270), which were probably centres of Sufi teaching.

Ratannāth, the saint of Dang, was revered for miracles he performed in distant Muslim lands (Punjab and Khorasan). He is still better known under the name of Ratan Baba, a Sufi saint and disciple of Mohammad. His exceptional longevity of six hundred years allows him to be an important Sufi master of the twelfth century, whose last dwelling was in Bhatinda. But the Yogīs of Dang are not aware of this Sufi version of their founder's life. Rather, they recount another event; they link Ratannāth to a holy place nearer to Dang and make him an undisputed champion of Hinduism for his fight against Aurangzeb, an emperor who is described as a destroyer and persecutor of the Hindus. In the legends of Dang, the emperor submitted himself to Ratannāth and wanted to become his disciple, following him as far as the temple of Devī Bhagavatī in Devi Patan, where Ratannāth prayed to the goddess, 'Please, kill this insolent king.' When the Devī kills Aurangzeb, Ratannāth vows to express his gratitude and devotion to her by visiting her every year in her Devi Patan temple, coming from his abode in Dang. On one such pilgrimage, he ends his life, 'disappearing before his devotees' eyes.'

This legend explains the annual pilgrimage that the Yogīs of Dang make to this Devī sanctuary in the Gonda district in India, not far from the Nepalese border. In this legend, of which I have only oral versions (there is no mention of it in the booklets or paintings), we can see an attempt to unite the two sides of the Ratannāth's biography: one side as an amalgam of local traditions, rooted in the reality of life in the Dang monastery, and the other side as hagiography, which establishes Ratannāth's sanctity through a reference to a remote missionary enterprise of conversion.

The Ritual

This double centrifugal and centripetal orientation, which marks the hagiography of Ratannāth, also characterizes the organization of the ceremonial calendar in the Caughera monastery. The ritual cycle and therefore the whole life of the monastery are centred on two events that express an opposite relationship to space. The local link between Ratannāth and the monastery can be seen in the rite of *pīrsthāpanā*, or installation of the *pīr.*[6] This yearly festival celebrates the renewal of Ratannāth's incarnation in the *pīr.* The outside reference appears in the journey, the *yātrā* or the *savāri* (visit), that follows the *pīrsthāpanā* and during which almost all the Yogīs of Caughera travel for one month to Devi Patan.

Pīrsthāpanā

The Pīr or head of the monastery keeps his office only for one year. During the months of Phālgun (February–March,) on the eleventh day of the dark lunar fortnight, the Yogīs choose a new head and consecrate him during the festival of *pīrsthāpanā,* the public selection and acceptance of the new *pīr* as the embodiment of Ratannāth, especially in his capacity as the one who worships the vessel of ambrosia. The *pīr* re-enacts the performance of Ratannāth as it is depicted on the many paintings in the monastery: seated cross-legged, with his ritual paraphernalia, he makes *pūjā* to the glittering *amritpātra.*

The *pīrsthāpanā* takes place in the monastery of Caughera and is divided into the following sequences:

– First, the *amritpātra* is solemnly taken out of the sanctuary by the current *pīr* and brought to a kind of ceremonial hall where the *pūjā* will be performed in front of all the Yogīs and visitors. The *pīr* lays down the ritual objects and makes a first *pūjā* to this essence of Gorakhnāth.

– Then, all the Yogīs are gathered and consulted about the new nominations. Four offices have to be filled: the *pīr* and his assistant, the *pūjāri* of Bhairav and his assistant. After they have been chosen by common agreement, they take an oath in front of Bhairav and the *pīr*-to-be receives a special cap. This conical cap, made of red felt or velvet with a black string, is supposed to be the exact copy of the hat received by Ratannāth from the Muslim emperor after the miracle of the green garden. And indeed it looks much like a dervish cap. Ratannāth is always depicted with this hat, and the *pīr*, as soon as he receives it, is supposed to represent the Siddha.

– The third part consists in the progressive replacing of the last year's *pīr* by the newly selected one. The old *pīr* is still seated in front of the *amritpātra* in the ceremonial hall; the new *pīr*, after receiving his hat in the Bhairav temple a few yards away, climbs the stairs in a sitting position (in *padmāsana*), progressing in small jumps, and gradually takes the place of the former *pīr*. The seat of Ratannāth, the throne of the *pīr*, must never remain empty. When the new *pīr* has been installed, all the Yogīs and the important local people come to pay respect to him. They bow in front of him (blowing into their small *nād* or whistle received at the initiation) and give some rupees as a ceremonial offering. This is the official enthronement of the *pīr*.

– The new *pīr* then makes *pūjā* to the *amritpātra* for the first time. Helped by the former *pīr*, who teaches him all the gestures, he makes a series of *mudrās*, sometimes with his hands hidden under a huge ochre scarf. He waves the fly whisk one hundred and eight times in front of the *pātra* and mutters mantras. When he has finished the *pūjā*, all the objects are collected and the new *pīr*, carrying the *amritpātra*, leaves the hall and proceeds to the main temple where he puts the 'recipient-god' back on its throne.

After this ritual installation, the *pīr* is introduced to his new responsibility as an administrator of the *maṭh* property. The account books and the various objects which constitute the treasure of Caughera are taken out of the temple room, presented to the administration committee, and counted in front of the old and new *pīrs*.

The Yātrā

The consecration of the new *pīr* as the new Ratannāth in his local dimension, as the founder and head of Caughera, is not completed until the journey to Devi Patan has been made. This sanctuary in the Gonda district is dedicated to Durgā Bhagavatī and her *pūjā* is done by Kānphaṭā Yogīs. We do not know much about the origin of this place and still less about the Yogīs' pilgrimage. Local tradition says that a temple – the third one after the first erected by Karṇa and the second by Vikramāditya – was built there by Ratannāth, but that it was destroyed by Aurangzeb, or a captain from his army, who was killed by the Devī.

Ratannāth's biography tells us of a special relationship between him and the Devī. They were either disciples of the same guru, *guru-bhāi,* or she helped him and he promised to visit her once a year (as we have seen). But if we look at the history of the Dang Valley, we see that Devi Patan is just near the town of Tulsipur where the king of Dang, Nawal Sen, took refuge when he was driven out by Gorkha armies in 1786. One interpretation would be to link the origin of the pilgrimage to Devi Patan to this exile of the king, but there are problems with this theory. It seems, according to the documents we have, that the pilgrimage occurred prior to this event, particularly since one edict from 1789 (only three years after the conquest) enjoins 'not to give trouble to the Yogīs for the Patan Devī *yātrā*.' The tradition seems to have been already well established.

The *yātrā* takes altogether one month from Caughera to Devi Patan, but the journey itself requires five days – more exactly five nights – one way. The departure is on the first day of the month of Caitra (fifteen days after *pīrsthāpanā*); after a one-night walk through the Siwalik Chain, the procession stops for fifteen days in Deopur in the district of Deukhuri. Settled near a temple of Ratannāth, the Yogīs receive homage from the local people and gather their offerings – a tribute called *kaṭālā* that they have been entitled to collect from the houses of Deukhuri for at least two hundred years. They start their journey again on the night of the new moon and stop at three places (with Devī temples) before reaching Devi Patan on the fifth day of the bright half of Caitra, where they stay until the tenth day. Their stay falls on the main festival of the temple for the month of Caitra, or small Dasain. This festival commemorates the victory of the Devī over the Asura Mahiṣa and was, until recently, the occasion for thousands of animal sacrifices, in particular the sacrifice of pigs over the alleged grave of a Muslim invader. In Devi Patan, the Dang Yogīs make the *pūjā* of their *pātradevata* four times in front of the Devī temple, then take their leave and start the journey back to Caughera, stopping at the same places (but just two days at Deopur). The return to Caughera is celebrated with a public *pūjā* in the ceremonial hall, to show everybody that the god is really back.

The procession to the Devī temple is carefully organized: two Damāi musicians, who usually play for the *pūjās*, go first. One blows a *sahanai* (oboe), the other is carrying a *nagārā* drum.[7] Then come Yogīs carrying a silver mace (*āśā*), a pitcher, a braser that is used as *dhūnī* – the fire that the Yogīs keep constantly burning – and a red flag that represents Bhairav. Then comes the *pankha,* or *koṭval,* carrying a mace, followed by an assistant (the *sirāne*) who carries the carpets and cushions that will be the throne of the *amritpātra*. The *bhaṇḍari* or Bhairav's priest takes charge of the *rot,* the round flatbread which is the only food-offering to Gorakhnāth and must always precede the god during a ritual outing. Then come the two *pīrs,* each wearing a huge white shawl and the red cap which indicates their function. The former *pīr* carries a torch and the new *pīr* carries the *amritpātra,* wrapped in white cloth and flower garlands. He is followed by the *pūjāri* carrying a huge ceremonial umbrella. Then come other Yogīs with the ritual objects for the *pūjā,* the Brahmin officiant and, until a few years ago, about thirty Tharu carriers, tenants of the monastery on the *guṭhi* lands and thus required to provide this ritual service. They carry wood, food, and goods to be traded during the *melā,* the fair which follows the Devī festival.

What can be the reason for this long journey south, to India, to a Devī temple, through the former Dang kingdom? What is the meaning for the Caughera *maṭh,* of this reference to a sacred place dedicated to a Devī, to Durgā? I do not have a conclusive explanation, just some clues, some hypothetical interpretations.

First, there is a relationship of the pilgrimage to the general notion of wandering, which is part of ascetic life. The Yogīs of Caughera are part of a group of wandering Yogīs and, to quote R. Burghart writing about the Ramanandis, they appear as 'an autonomous itinerant monastery of liberated ascetics,' and 'as a moving centre which circulates within and pervades the Sacred Land of the Hindus.'[8] Carrying their *amritpātra*, the Yogīs of Caughera appear during this journey as 'a worshipping worshipful body which circulates within the sacred land,'[9] a land they are making sacred by their journey.

Second his journey is a royal procession. It is organized like a royal cortege: the *amritpātra* and the *pīrs* are surrounded by their court – formed by all the people having a ritual function – and their Tharu servants. They move forward with the royal paraphernalia: the *nagārā* drum, the umbrella, and the flags. The procession is like a royal tour of a king in his domain. And, as William Sax says, ' the linear order of procession is an icon of society.'[10] At every stop, the people – the subjects – come to bow and give offerings as they would pay their respects to their king.

But, in this case, there is an ambiguity: Who is really the king, the *amritpātra*, the *pīr*, or the king? And what is the estate of this king?

First, there is the *amritpātra* or *pātradev*. The *amritpātra* is supposed to be Gorakhnāth himself – or more exactly his *svarūp*, his essential form, given to Ratannāth – and it is carried with all the symbols of royalty: throne, umbrella, drum and so on.

Second, there is the *pīr*. He is assumed to be the embodiment of Ratannāth who was a king, Ratna Parīkṣaka, but during the procession we have two *pīrs*, each embodying Ratannāth but not totally; they still must go together to Devi Patan as if the god was divided in two or as if the transfer of the Ratannāth's divine quality to the new *pīr* was not yet fully carried out.

And third, there is the king of Dang. Before the conquest, his palace was next to the monastery, and he stayed there during the Yogīs' journey to Devi Patan; but after the conquest by the Gorkhas, the royal office was divided into two. The new Gorkha king stayed in Kathmandu but still patronized the monastery. The former king, the displaced king of Dang, was exiled near Devi Patan and was supposed to welcome the procession at its arrival there. (This role is now filled by the Balrampur Raja whose ancestor was victorious over the Tulsipur king after the mutiny.) There are clearly too many kings for any simple explanation.

Nonetheless, the territory through which the procession travels evokes the victorious journey made by a king through his conquered territories, 'like the victory processions in which medieval Hindu kings "took possession" of their realms by processing to their borders.'[11] There is also a connection between this part of the Dang kingdom and the estate of the monastery, especially in Deopur. The estate consists of the *guṭhi* lands given by the kings to Ratannāth. The tenure of the *guṭhi* lands gives the owner land rights but also administrative and legal rights and duties; to the owner is delegated some of the king's power.

This *yātrā* offers a model of kingship which unites spiritual and temporal power, or as Ronald Inden says, 'the transcendent variety of kingship in which the divine king, acting primarily as a ceremonialist, exercises ritual sovereignty.'[12] The legend tells us of a king-renouncer and the ritual tells us of a royal monastery or a monastic kingship. Perhaps, these give us a clue to understanding the past history of Dang.

Let us return to the Devī. The purpose of the journey for the Yogīs is to visit the temple of the Goddess when she is at the height of her power, during the annual festival that celebrates her victory over the Asuras. The Yogīs escort the *pīrs* and the *amritpātra,* as moving icons of the deity. Thus who is visiting the Devī? The legend tells us that Ratannāth made this promise; thus the important part is probably played by the *pīr,* as the embodiment of Ratannāth. As two *pīrs* are present, can we consider that the Devī's role is to confirm the choice of the new *pīr*? This is suggested by the traditional disappearance of the former *pīr* at the end of the ceremonies in Devi Patan. He is supposed to go somewhere else on pilgrimage and is forbidden to come to the monastery for the next year. On the return journey, there is only one *pīr.* The Devi Patan temple is the sacred place where the *pīr* has his legitimacy confirmed by an outside authority.

That this authority must be the Devī raises a problem.[13] The Kānphaṭās cannot be considered as true Śāktas. They worship the Goddess but not as a dominant figure. In Nepal, in every Nāth sanctuary, we have the divine triad of Gorakhnāth, Bhairav and the Goddess, but she is generally in a subordinate position. In Caughera, her temple is outside the main quarter and her priest is not chosen according to the same rotation as Bhairav's and Ratannāth's. But in the Devi Patan compound, the Devī is really in a dominant position, while Gorakhnāth is not even represented. Nevertheless the *pūjāris* are Kānphaṭā Yogīs. The connection of the Yogīs with the Goddess's temple is known in other places, for instance in Hing Laj, a very important Yogī pilgrimage site in Baluchistan. The place is a *pīṭh,* where the crown of Sati's head fell. According to Briggs, its origin myth is very similar to the one of Devi Patan: 'Formerly at Nagar Thatha Musalman faqirs in large numbers persecuted the followers of the Hindu faith. One day the Devī appeared to the Hindus riding on a lion and slew the faqirs. She then went to Hing Laj and made the place her abode.'[14] Briggs also thinks that some elements of Śiva-Parvatī mythology are added to an ancient cult to Śiva. But unlike the case of Hing Laj, Śiva is absent from Devi Patan and its cult.

Can we see in the journey and in the cult in Devi Patan a quest for *śakti*? Is the Patan Devī or Pāṭeśvari Devī the *śakti* of Ratannāth? Is their meeting a union of the two poles, masculine and feminine? Is the journey a way for the God to return to the source of his power? In this case, the travel made by Ratannāth from north to south, from the Himalayas to the southern plains of India, would be the opposite of the journey described by William Sax in his book *Mountain Goddess*, where Nanda Devī is taken from her southern, hot, fertile, and feminine abode to the ascetic, wild, frozen, and pure abode of Śiva, in order to be his wife. But the theory of a marital or complementary relationship between Ratannāth and Patan Devī is not expressed by the Yogīs. They prefer to insist on the celibate and chaste character of Gorakhnāth and generally of the Siddhas.[15] What they express is a link of brotherhood; Ratannāth and Devī were *guru-bhāi*, both disciples of Gorakhnāth.

But the Dangaura Tharus tell a different story. This local tribe, living in the Terai of Nepal on both sides of the Nepal–India border and used to the hard life in the jungle, has developed an original religious system, but one which includes elements of the Yogīs' world view. Their origin myth tells of the adventures of the first Tharu, called Guru Baba – a Yogic appellation – and his daughter Maiya.[16] The goddess is really the centre of their pantheon. She is an encompassing principle who changes form, characteristics, and ways of acting according to the three categories of space: household, village, forest. Her residence is at the centre of the world, which for the Tharus means Devi Patan. And Ratannāth is for the Tharus a kind of ancestral and local deity, whose travel with the Yogīs is viewed as a travel to meet his wife. He goes there to renew his power near the goddess. At the same time as the arrival of the Yogīs' procession at Devi Patan, the Tharu villagers celebrate a ritual they consider its equivalent: they take the ancestral deities out of the houses and carry them to the limits of the village where they meet the forest goddesses.[17] Thus, in the Tharu cosmogony, the link between Ratannāth and the Devī is explicitly a marital link, which unites the themes of the local male ancestrality with the outside female and encompassing power.

Tharu and Nath religious configurations intermingle. Occasionally, oppositions are represented and resolved, like the dichotomy between male and female, renunciation and kingship, as we see here.

Conclusion

Both the legends and the ritual show the same configuration, a to-and-fro motion between local status and outside consecration or confirmation. The legendary Ratannāth is a great local figure in Dang because he has been recognized and glorified abroad, and the actual Caughera *pīr* has to be confirmed, chosen again by the outside authority of the Devī. The autochthonous figure acquires pre-eminence through outside legitimation. Curiously, the Muslim sovereign and the Devī victorious over the Asuras share a common position with regard to Ratannāth and the *maṭh*: they bestow power.

Figure 1: Saint Ratannāth worshipping the amritpātra.

Figure 2: The pīr carrying the amritpātra during the Pīrsthāpanā.

End Notes

I would like to thank the participants in the 'Sacred Space and Sacred Biography' conference for their various comments. I am especially grateful to Phyllis Granoff for her acute and inspiring remarks.

1 For a more detailed presentation of the context and the references of the data given here, see V. Bouillier, *Ascètes et rois. Un monastère de Kanphata Yogis au Nepal* (Paris: CNRS Editions, Ethnologie, 1997).

2 See V. Bouillier, 'Des prêtres du pouvoir: les Yogis et la fonction royale,' in *Prêtrise, pouvoirs et autorité en Himalaya, puruṣārtha* 12 (1989), ed. V. Bouillier and G. Toffin, 193–214.

3 See D. Gold, 'The Instability of the King: Magical Insanity and the Yogi's Power in the Politics of Jodhpur, 1803–1843,' in *Bhakti Religion in North India: Community Identity and Political Action*, ed. D.N. Lorenzen (Albany: State University of New York Press, 1995).

4 This was the title of the Mughal emperors after Babur and was not supposed to be used in the time of Ratannāth!

5 For a detailed account of the many events of the Ratannāth's hagiography and for a study of some of their sources, see Bouillier, *Ascètes et rois*, chap. 3.

6 This Muslim title was often given to the head of the Yogis' *maṭh* Cf. G.W. Briggs, *Gorakhnāth and the Kānphaṭā Yogīs* (1938; reprint, Delhi: Motilal Banarsi-dass, 1973), 8, 81, 100, 119.

7 This drum, smaller than the huge ones played ordinarily for the *pūjā* at the temple, is connected with Tantric cult and kingship. It is always played at Gorakhnāth's temples.

8 R. Burghart, 'Wandering Ascetics of the Ramanandi Sect,' *History of Religions* 22 (1983), 370.

9 Ibid., 371.

10 W.S. Sax, *Mountain Goddess* (New York: Oxford University Press, 1991), 203.

11 R. Inden, 'Ritual, Authority and Cyclic Time in Hindu Kingship,' in *Kingship and Authority in South India*, South Asian Studies, University of Wisconsin–Madison 3, ed. J.F. Richards (Madison: South Asian Studies, University of Wisconsin--Madison, 1978).

12 Ibid., 29.

13 I am very grateful to Phyllis Granoff for the comparison she made with the Jain monasteries where it was common in medieval lineage histories to see a goddess confirming monastic heads. The idea that the goddess can and sometimes must protect the kingdom as well as the monastery,

that it is better for the prosperity of the kingdom if she is the tutelary deity of the king and of the monastery together, may be quite stimulating in the Hindu context as well.

14 Briggs, *Gorakhnāth*, 105.

15 They tell the myth of Gorakhnāth created by Śiva to demonstrate to Parvatī his capacity of being and creating alone: Śiva argues to Parvatī, 'Where you are, I am, is true, but the opposite, that where I am, you are, is not true.'

16 G. Krauskopff, *Maîtres et possédés. Les rites et l'ordre social chez les Tharu* (Paris: Editions du CNRS, 1989), 231-233.

17 Ibid., 52.

10

The Interweave of Place, Space, and Biographical Discourse at a South Indian Religious Centre

K.I. KOPPEDRAYER

This essay examines what a South Indian sectarian centre has to say about itself during one of its annual religious festivals. Insofar as it is possible for an institution – made up, after all, of a corporate group of diverse individuals with differing relations among themselves – to engage in a moment of self-reflection, and insofar as it is possible for a complement of ritual activities to articulate those self-reflections, the celebration provides us with a moment of institutional autobiographical reflection. Like much autobiography, that self-reflection conforms to certain conventions and derives some of its impetus (though certainly not all of its meaning) from authorial intention: an organized and choreographed event, the celebration has a main focus determined by the then head of the institution who organized the first one. That celebration and all subsequent ones follow a coherent set of activities, which in turn echo religious patterns common to South India. But, again, like most good autobiography, this autobiographical reflection manages to reveal more than might have been intended. As Bakhtin has observed, and others have now made commonplace, as much as an author attempts to control what is being said, there is an inevitable heteroglossia in any text – or life lived, or story told, or religious celebration undertaken.

The self-reflection that the celebration provides amounts to a dense narrative, filled with multi-vocalic images and gestures that involve interconnected layers of history, religious themes, and social relations. The celebration reflects on both the distant and recent past of the institution, acknowledges the web of relationships that make up the institution, and identifies, in the allusive language of ritual process, many of the relations and interconnections that inform its existence. One discourse that runs through the celebration concerns biographic/hagiographic narratives; two narratives in particular are played out against each other, one calling upon the other to express itself while in turn making meaning of the other. This dialogue helps locate the narratives and hence the institution in temporal, physical and conceptual space. Much meaning – acclaimed, contentious, hegemonic, and so on – emerges from this web of interconnections, only some of which can be taken up here. Place, space, and the weave of life history are what I discuss in the paragraphs that follow.

The Celebration: Āṭi Amāvācai

On the new moon day (*amāvācai*) of the month of Āṭi (July–August) the Dharmapuram Adhinam, a Śaiva sectarian centre (*maṭha*) located in the Tanjavur District of Tamilnadu, sponsors a festival celebrating one of the most important Śaiva pilgrimage sites in North India. The date of the celebration, Āṭi Amāvācai, marks the new moon of the first full month after the summer solstice, designating the lunar beginning of the dark half of the solar year. Further, it marks the completion of the sowing of new crops after the summer rains.[1] In the ritual calendar of South India, it is a traditional date to undertake ritual bathing and other purification ceremonies, and it is often celebrated by pilgrimage to sacred sites where ritual purification may take place.

The pilgrimage site celebrated at Dharmapuram is Mount Kailāsa, the very abode of Śiva. In early morning, the celebration begins when a large painting of Mount Kailāsa is taken from the hall where it is usually displayed and placed in the worship room of the institution. Later in the day, the head of the Adhinam conducts a special rite of worship to that image of Mount Kailāsa. Afterwards, it is taken on a night procession through the four streets that surround the institution and placed in a subsidiary shrine. There, in the presence of Mount Kailāsa, the head of the institution distributes sacralized offerings in the form of sweets (*prasādam*) to high-ranking guests and others, and rupee notes and coins to employees and lower-caste people in the service of the institution. When all the sweets and money have been distributed, Mount Kailāsa is returned to its customary place.

Though this celebration is unique to Dharmapuram, the sequence of events that outline the treatment given to the portrait of Mount Kailāsa is not; most temple festivals in South India follow the same basic pattern in which an image or icon is removed from its usual place, temporarily installed in another place, taken on one or more processions, and then reinstalled in its proper place. As well, this particular celebration is but one of many interludes of ritual activity at Dharmapuram. With the lineage of preceptors connected directly with Dharmapuram dating back to the sixteenth century, and with the antecedents of that lineage much older, the centre has a long and rich tradition. It follows a ritual calendar in which articulated patterns of activities, observances, and public statements occur on a daily, weekly, monthly, annual, and periodic basis. Life at Dharmapuram is centred on worship and ceremony; in the Śaiva Siddhānta tradition followed by the members of the lineage of this institution, knowledge and ritual activity are inseparable. Though there are common and expected patterns shared with other South Indian Śaivite centres that run through all of the rites undertaken at Dharmapuram, such as the patterning of worship around the preceptors of the institution, certain events highlight certain components or facets of the institution and its history. Taken together, the entire gamut of activities recites the multilayered history of Dharmapuram, rich with the tensions and competitive subnarratives of that history. One event might have as its main narrative one story within that history, yet, even then, others crowd in or are called upon to fill out the story being told.

In the case of Āṭi Amāvācai, the events of the day condense the complicated existence of the Adhinam into one succinct statement: Mount Kailāsa looms large in its workings. The point is obvious: one would expect a Śaivite centre that follows a religious tradition with devotional undertones to express a special reverence for the abode of Śiva. And indeed, veneration of Kailāsa is the central theme that runs through the celebration. Yet, unambiguous as this theme is, the full expression of the festival is far from simple; several stories fold into it and the stories told begin with the image of Mount Kailāsa.

The Image of Mount Kailāsa

The icon of Mount Kailāsa that is celebrated in this festival is a large painting of the mountain. It was made from a photograph taken in 1959 during a pilgrimage undertaken by the then head of the institution, Śrī-la-Śrī Cupiramaṇiyamtēcikar Ñāṉacampanta Paramācārya Cuvāmikaḷ, the twenty-fifth Gurumahāsannidhāṉam, or twenty-fifth preceptor in the institution's spiritual lineage. The visual concreteness of the image, based as it is on a reproduction of this preceptor's physical vision of Mount Kailāsa, calls to mind an observation Indira Peterson has made about the celebrated Tamil *nāyaṉmār* poetry of the seventh to ninth centuries. She comments upon the realism of the imagery used. Citing one example, she observes 'that, though rich in icongraphic and sensory detail, [the allusion to an icon or place] is devoid of fanciful figures of speech and poetic conceits. The iconography of the poem is thoroughly realistic,' corresponding with sculptural conceptions that help 'conjure up a precise "icon," a concrete image.'[2] Elsewhere, she suggests that in 'expressing a personal sentiment, praising a real God who manifests himself in particular places, and celebrating a particular community,' the Śaiva *nāyaṉmār* poets echo much earlier Tamil poetic conventions highlighting place and particularity.[3] Particularity, however, is not an end-in-itself, but a point of departure for devotional vision. That vision, grounded in a particular place, moves through the interconnectedness of place and presence to enable the sensation of intersubjective feeling and experience.

Dharmapuram's Āṭi Amāvācai celebration has intrinsic links to the *nāyaṉmār* poetry, as we will see shortly. The image of Mount Kailāsa recalls an interconnection of place and presence, but there are several layers to these interconnections. In its embrace of physical place the photograph then painting, the icon, with its recursiveness of life history and memory, weaves several images of Mount Kailāsa into one another. First, Mount Kailāsa is recalled as it is – not only as it rests in the Himalayas but also as it looms in the understanding of those associated with Dharmapuram. Second, there is testimony; the icon recalls a document – the photograph – of the pilgrimage in 1959 by the twenty-fifth preceptor of Dharmapuram's spiritual lineage. Finally, seen again and again on Āṭi Amāvācai, memories collapse in on each other – those of the vision and memory held by the twenty-fifth preceptor and the memories Dharmapuram has of that.

The Importance of Mount Kailāsa

It is important to understand the space, actual and conceptual, that the painting occupies in Dharmapuram's existence. Ordinarily the painting is found in *oṭukkam. Oṭukkam* is a site, a hall, in the Adhinam where Gurumahāsannidhāṉam takes seclusion and will see, or be seen by, only the most prominent or persistent visitors to the centre.

Glenn Yocum, in a field study of another Śaiva centre near Dharmapuram, which follows Śaiva Siddhānta traditions similar to Dharmapuram's, remarks that the protocols surrounding activities in *oṭukkam* 'are not unlike those associated with the *garbhagṛha* ("womb house," that is, sanctum) of a south Indian temple.'[4] At that Śaiva centre, as well as at Dharmapuram, *oṭukkam* was explicitly likened to 'a temple's *mūlastānam* ("root place," that is, sanctum).'[5]

At Dharmapuram, there are several areas of activity in *oṭukkam*. When the head of the centre, who is also the head of the lineage of preceptors of the Adhinam, receives visitors, he is seated behind a desk. When, however, the concerns are spiritual or when the history of the lineage is of importance, activity shifts to the *gurupīṭam* (the seat of the guru in the form of a low throne-like seat), a shift of orientation quite evident to outside observers.[6] The *gurupīṭam* signifies the authority of the Adhinam's spiritual lineage. Above that seat, the image of Mount Kailāsa hangs; it is removed from that location only on Āṭi Amāvācai. All other times Mount Kailāsa looms over the presence of the *gurupīṭam*, the site of authority of the preceptor and thus the lineage of the institution.

Given the centrality of Mount Kailāsa in the Adhinam's self-definition, it is no coincidence that an image of Mount Kailāsa is found here. Members of Adhinam's lineage call themselves the Kailāsaparamparai, the lineage of Mount Kailāsa. They trace the origin of their teachings and ritual practices back to Mount Kailāsa, where, according to their tradition, Nandi approached Śiva as Śiva's first disciple and asked to be initiated into his mysteries. Nandi, once initiated, transmitted these mysteries to his disciple, the celestial Sanatkumāramūṉivar who, in turn, passed them on to another disciple. According to this tradition, Parañjōti, the fourth of this celestial line took an earthly disciple, the child prodigy Meykaṇṭār, who is credited with producing the *Civañāṉapōtam*. Though not the earliest of the fourteen works known as the *Śaiva Siddhānta Śāstra*, this work is considered seminal by all Śaiva Siddhāntins. Meykaṇṭār, and the three in the line after him, Aruṇanti, Maṟaiñāṉacampantar and Umāpati, are considered the main preceptors (*santāṉācarya*) of Śaiva Siddhānta; their works make up the bulk of the Śaiva Siddhānta canon.

The chroniclers of the Dharmapuram Adhinam trace the lineage of the guru of the sixteenth-century Guruñāṉācampantar, the founder of the *maṭha*, back to this lineage, descending from one of the disciples of Umāpati, the last and most prolific of the *santāṉācarya*. The present Gurumahāsannidhāṉam is thus heir to this lineage and to the sacred wisdom that has been transmitted from guru to disciple through initiation. For the members of the Dharmapuram Adhinam, the seat of their guru is Mount Kailāsa; the wisdom that animates their guru, embodied in the present Gurumahāsannidhāṉam, is descended from Śiva himself.

The spiritual authority maintained by the Adhinam comes from Mount Kailāsa, but that authority can be realized only through the maintenance of the lineage of the Adhinam. All that makes up the Adhinam – rites, doctrine, membership, patronage, and so on – depend upon the centre's transmission of its wisdom and its vitality. In other words, the very existence of what Mount Kailāsa represents is vested in the head of the lineage, who embodies the potency of the Adhinam in his potential to transmit the wisdom of Śiva through the initiation of disciples. The most visible symbol of this potency is the *gurupīṭam*, over which looms Mount Kailāsa, an idea literally as well as figuratively that the members of the Adhinam never lose sight of. They say that the vision the twenty-fifth Gurumahāsannidhāṉam had during his pilgrimage gives meaning to the Kailāsaparamparai. An image reinforcing that association appears on the cover of a relatively recent work published by Dharmapuram that provides a history of the Adhinam, its previous heads, its contributions to Tamil Śaivism, and a history of its role as the manager of several temple centres and temple endowments. That work (*Tarumai Kaṉakāpikṣēka Viḻāmalar*),[7] released on the date when the Śiva temple at Dharmapuram was reconsecrated, shows a facsimile of the same painting celebrated on Āṭi Amāvācai, but here with an image of Śiva giving instruction to Nandidēvar drawn in. The image of Mount Kailāsa also recalls the source of the lineage.

The celebration on Āṭi Amāvācai is a reaffirmation of the source of vitality of the centre. Such reaffirmation opens the day, for on the morning of Āṭi Amāvācai, Gurumahāsannidhāṉam carefully cleans the image and replaces its *bindu*, charging it with divine energy through his *pūjā* rite. In that circular process, which draws upon his ritual authority and ritual ability to undertake the *pūjā*, he is revitalizing that which empowers himself and the Adhinam he represents. Later, in the night procession and during the installation of the image of Mount Kailāsa in the special shrine room, everything that fits in the interconnected workings of the centre is drawn into the celebration.

Patrons, devotees, caste affiliates, employees, all are brought before Kailāsa, where their connections with Dharmapuram are sealed with the ritual gestures of honouring, gifting, blessing, or paying. The different transactions – employees are symbolically paid, VIPs are honoured, devotees are blessed – made in the presence of Mount Kailāsa map out the Adhinam's place in the worldly cosmos of South India. By the time the image of Kailāsa is reinstalled over the *gurupīṭam*, the reality of Dharmapuram, and what is connected with its historical presence, is hegemonically secured. With the procession of Mount Kailāsa through the streets that mark out the centre's physical location, the Adhinam lays claim to its history, and to those parts of people's lives that have sustained its existence. With gestures that mask or mute any voices of contention, the Adhinam lays claim to its presence. Marked out by a looming image of Mount Kailāsa and the lineage derived from that seat of Śiva, authority is vested centrally; lateral extensions of that authority are derivative of its central claim.

Darśana of Kailāsa

The life histories of the heads of the lineage are tied to that central claim, but they also help shape and inform it. These life histories provide layers of meaning, the texture, to the central claim. A closer look at the image celebrated on Āṭi Amāvācai suggests how. One way of seeing this image is to look at it in comparison with others. Recall that this image was rendered from a photo taken during the twenty-fifth Gurumahāsannidhāṉam's 1959 pilgrimage to Mount Kailāsa. Other paintings, also made from photographs taken during the same pilgrimage, are displayed in the Adhinam. For example, a large painting of the twenty-fifth Gurumahāsannidhāṉam standing before Mount Kailāsa hangs prominently in the *gurumaṇṭapa*, or hall where portraits and photographs of the previous heads of the Adhinam are displayed. Another representation, a bas-relief based on the same photograph, adorns the eastern gateway to the Adhinam. Another painting of the same image of the twenty-fifth Gurumahāsannidhāṉam before Mount Kailāsa is the site of daily worship in the shrine built by the present head of the Adhinam to commemorate his predecessor and the pilgrimage he undertook. Not surprisingly, when one considers the layers of reflexivity at play, this shrine is the stopping place that has already been described. During the night procession it is here where *prasādam* is redistributed and where those in the service and employment of the Adhinam are reminded of that with the coins they are given.

These other paintings (and their collective reiteration of the connection between the twenty-fifth Gurumahāsannidhāṉam and Mount Kailāsa) occupy places of no small significance in the Adhinam. One, the painting in the *gurumaṇṭapa,* commands a place for the twenty-fifth Gurumahāsannidhāṉam in the iconic history of the lineage. Another, the bas-relief on the gateway, signals, like an auspicious emblem, the site of the institution. Another, the painting in the shrine, recalls the meaning expressed in the Śaiva initiations transmitted through the lineage. The shrine itself, built by the present Gurumahāsannidhāṉam in homage of his preceptor, the twenty-fifth Gurumahāsannidhāṉam, recalls the love or devotion expressed by a disciple of the lineage and that love which circulates between guru and disciple. These other images, powerful as they are, are different from the one celebrated on Āṭi Amāvācai. They show the twenty-fifth Gurumahāsannidhāṉam with Mount Kailāsa. What is celebrated here is an image of Mount Kailāsa alone, revealing the sacred site in the way it must have been revealed to the twenty-fifth Gurumahāsannidhāṉam while he stood in the Himalayas.

With this difference, more interwoven layers come into play. The festival was instituted as an annual celebration at the behest of the twenty-fifth Gurumahāsannidhāṉam himself in the year following his pilgrimage. He apparently initiated the celebration to commemorate his vision of Mount Kailāsa in much the same way that the earlier Śaiva saints, the *nāyaṉmār,* sang their hymns in response to the visions they had of the lord at the various temples they visited throughout South India. Aṭi Amāvācai, the day of the celebration, is the *same day* that the twenty-fifth Gurumahāsannidhāṉam stood before Mount Kailāsa and took *darśana* of it.

The image of Mount Kailāsa represented in the painting thus captures the vision the twenty-fifth Gurumahāsannidhāṉam himself had of the place where Śiva dwells, and anyone who looks at the portrait will share in that vision. Meriting a vision of the lord's abode is a recurrent theme in South India. Sight of the lord's dwelling place is a rare privilege associated with religious grace (*aruḷ*) and there are many examples in Tamil literature of struggling devotees yearning to be recipients of this grace. In the eyes of the Adhinam's followers, the vision allowed to the twenty-fifth Gurumahāsannidhāṉam during his pilgrimage is an indication of his greatness. On account of spiritual qualifications exemplified in the undertaking of the pilgrimage, he was a recipient of grace that entitled him to see Mount Kailāsa and the celebration on Āṭi Amāvācai pays homage to the spiritual merit he earned.

The pilgrimage and the vision of Mount Kailāsa signify more, however, than just spiritual merit. According to the Śaiva Siddhānta tradition, the guru is the perfectly realized soul; he has, upon receiving the anointment of guru (*ācāryābhiṣekam*), become of the nature of Śiva. When the guru acts, it is actually Śiva acting through the form of the guru.

This concept of guru is associated with the Adhinam's entire line of preceptors, but even now, the twenty-fifth Gurumahāsannidhāṉam is profoundly revered, even by those closely associated with Dharmapuram's present head. The twenty-fifth Gurumahāsannidhāṉam is especially remembered by many of the Adhinam's followers as an embodiment of grace, capable of transmitting it to others. The celebration of his pilgrimage provides the Adhinam's followers with an occasion to experience his grace. On Āṭi Amāvācai, anyone at Dharmapuram has the possibility of darśana of Mount Kailāsa through his grace; this possibility is reinforced by the reverence to the twenty-fifth Gurumahāsannidhāṉam. Those who participate in the Āṭi Amāvācai celebrations experience much more than a sharing in the spiritual merit earned by the twenty-fifth Gurumahāsannidhāṉam in the pilgrimage to Mount Kailāsa; they partake in a vision of Mount Kailāsa that is brought about by him. Hence the Āṭi Amāvācai festival is celebrated both in homage to the twenty-fifth Gurumahāsannidhāṉam whose greatness entitled him to such a vision and as a means of experiencing the spiritual merit he engendered.

Observations that Norman Cutler has made about early Tamil bhakti poetry are pertinent here. He observes that the poetry was performative, citing 'contact, participation, communion, and ultimately identification' as the leitmotifs of the poetry.[8] Calling the material hymns rather than poetry, Cutler suggests that aesthetic considerations informed the performance and reception of the material: 'The words are effective if and only if they trigger a psychological and emotional response.' The hymns' sacredness 'is located not so much in external, objective features of sound as in internal, subjective states of mind which are reflected in and transmitted by the hymns.'[9] Cutler establishes his argument on examining the links between the hagiographies of the poets, the relationship between poet and deity, and the relationship between poetry and audience.

Basing his discussion first on the *āḻvār* poetry of the Vaiṣṇava community, and then extending it to include the *nāyaṉmār* material of the Śaivites, Cutler cites several modes of interaction precipitated by the hymns and their performance. In the first mode, the primary actors are the poet and the deity, the poet the addresser and deity the addressee.[10] But, through the institution of public recitation and performance of the hymns, another mode of appreciation is effected. In that, the poet-saint is the first member of a series of individuals that expands to include the community as a whole; 'the series begins with the *āḻvār*, the principal performer of the sacred hymns, and extends to his "substitutes" – Maturkāvi, Naṭhamūni, Naṭhamūni's nephews [disciples of the poet-saint and redactors of the hymns and the saint's hagiography], the temple servant who holds the office of *araiyar* [temple servant who recites the hymns], and by association, the congregation of Śrīvaiṣṇavas who "support" the *araiyar's* recitation.'[11] The expansion is progressive: from poet to redactor, then to the institution of formal temple recitation of the hymns on the part of the temple servants, then on to the community.

Morevoer, the community who listens to the recitation is no mere passive participant; many have memorized and thus internalized the hymns. Implied here is that any devotee who recites the hymns or participates in the recitation not only follows the example of the poet-saint, 'but actually assumes the persona' of the poet-saint.[12] The modes of interaction include recreation of the original relationship between poet-saint and deity, the witnessing and appreciation of that relationship, its infusion and sharing among other members of the community, and finally the intersubjectivity of audience and poet-saint. Cutler stresses that these modes of appreciation 'involve not so much the *communication* of a message from author to audience as a profound *communion* between the two.'[13] He recognizes the conceptual linkages between the poet-saints and deity, and the sense that the poet-saints were infused with the deity's presence. He calls this a 'process of divination,'[14] whereby the experience of devotion engenders divinity in the devotee. Such identification is mediated by the intersubjectivity between audience and recalled poet-saint, enabling the audience to experience several modes of presence simultaneously.

Cutler cautions that there are some differences to be found in the treatment of the Śaiva hymns and the Śaiva saints, particularly as not all of the Śaiva saints or *nāyaṉmār* were poets or hymn-singers. The celebration of place appears more prominently in the Śaiva material. The emergence of the Tamil Śaiva community was, in part, tied into the pilgrimage map created by the poets' movement from place to place. Likewise, the Tamil Śaiva community's (or rather communities') traditions of collection and recall of the hymns and their introduction into temple settings have their own particular twists, different from the Śrīvaiṣṇavas' history. Notwithstanding these differences, however, Cutler suggests that the rhetorical modes he has identified in the Śrīvaiṣṇava material also found in the Śaiva material.

My examination of the series of interconnections at play during Dharmapuram's Āṭi Amāvācai celebration has found such involvements, particularly in those mediated by linkages between the actual and conceptual site of Mount Kailāsa and the connection that site has to the Adhinam's lineage, as well as the connections between Mount Kailāsa and the life story – lived, recalled, and enacted – of the twenty-fifth Gurumahāsannidhāṉam. These interconnections work themselves out while simultaneously conflating the interlocking subjective states specified by Dharmapuram's lineage tradition. Put another way, auto/bio/hagiography are conflated. The celebration, instituted by the twenty-fifth Gurumahāsannidhāṉam himself, is his inscription of an autobiographical moment; celebrated, it is his biography/hagiography that folds back into both the inner state of the Adhinam and the inner subjectivity of the participants. The participants are linked intersubjectively with the twenty-fifth Gurumahāsannidhāṉam. Further, these linkages explicitly draw upon and reconfigure the *nāyaṉmār* tradition for the present moment because Āṭi Amāvācai is not only the *same* date as the twenty-fifth Gurumahāsannidhāṉam stood before Mount Kailāsa, but also the same date that Tirunāvukkaracar, a beloved *nāyaṉmār*, had his vision of Mount Kailāsa. In other words, temporal space is added to the physical space, the conceptual space, and the life history that come together in this celebration.

The Date of the Celebration and the *Nāyaṉmār* Connection

Collected in the Tamil *Tirumuṟai,* the outpourings of the saints who wandered from temple to temple in South India during the seventh to ninth centuries singing of sites and devotion inform Śaiva religiosity perhaps more pointedly than any of the philosophical works of the Śaiva Siddhānta canon. Tamil vēḷāḷa Śaivites associated with Dharmapuram and the other Śaiva centres often punctuate their discussions with recitations from the *Tirumuṟai* or with retellings from the *Periyapurāṇam,* Cēkkiḻār's hagiographies of the sixty-three saints. As well, in conversation, the current Gurumahāsannidhāṉam of Dharmapuram cited the *Tirumuṟai* as the source of Dharmapuram's spirituality.

Of the sixty-three *nāyaṉmār,* Tirunāvukkaracar, or Appar as he is better known, is revered as an extraordinary combination of grace and piety. Stories from his life are recounted endlessly throughout Tamilnadu, and he is counted as one of the four *cāmayācārya* (preceptors of the faith). As Cutler puts it, as '*ācāryas,* or teachers, the four saints are assimilated to the prototype of all Śaiva *ācāryas,* Śiva in the form of Dakṣiṇamūrti, the teacher.'[15] Known for his conversion from Jainism and for his active propagation of Śaivism, many of his hymns offer intensely personal reflections on the religious journey that brought him to Śiva. Often laden with repentance for his time as a Jain monk, his hymns document a journey of the soul. The journey he sings of doesn't stop with his past, however. Other of his hymns walk his listeners through his travels to the many shrines of Śiva. According to tradition, his pilgrimages took him to North India. In his old age he was seized with intense desire to visit Mount Kailāsa.

The account of Appar's travels to Mount Kailāsa is related in Cēkkiḻār's *Periyapurāṇam.*[16] According to the *Periyapurāṇam,* Tirunāvukkaracar was at Kālahasti worshipping at the sacred feet of Kaṇṇappar, an earlier *nāyaṉār.* There he felt a desire to see the magnificent sight of Śiva on Mount Kailāsa. He went north, worshipping at Śrīśailam, and then to Kāśī where he worshipped Viśvanath. He continued northwards subsisting on roots and fruits, travelling day and night. As his feet became cracked and sore, he crawled on his hands, then on his elbows, and finally along the full length of his body, which began to bleed. Still he was determined to reach Kailāsa.

Then he encountered a sage engaged in austerities who challenged his determination. When Appar satisfactorily demonstrated his resolve, and a voice spoke from the sky telling him to rise up, he did and his wasted body was restored. Appar then recognized that the sage was Śiva himself, but protested that he had been denied his vision in Kailāsa. Śiva responded by telling Appar that he had to continue singing his praises (implying that it was not time yet for Appar's departure from the world), but that he would be granted the vision he so desired at Tiruvaiyāṟu, a temple located in the Tanjavur District. Śiva then told Appar to immerse himself in a nearby lake. Appar did and popped out of the small tank at Tiruvaiyāṟu. There he had a vision of Śiva seated majestically on Mount Kailāsa with Umā at his side and Nandi in attendance. In the vision, Appar saw the whole world pervaded with Śiva and Śakti, and felt their presence as he had never before. He was overcome with bliss. When the vision was withdrawn, he went into a delirium, but then realized that he had truly experienced grace. In the hymn he sings at Tiruvaiyāṟu, he sings that he saw the Lord's holy feet, he saw what he had never seen before.[17]

This story is one of many well-known episodes of Appar's hagiography. Anyone who is attending the Āṭi Amāvācai celebration is aware of the significance of the date and, indeed, when I attended it, many were quick to draw my attention to it.[18] Moreover, according to a biographical sketch of the twenty-fifth Gurumahāsannidhāṉam,[19] his inspiration for the pilgrimage came at the Tiruvaiyāṟu Śaiva temple complex, which is at present under the Adhinam's administration. The inspiration came when he was taking *darśana* of Teṉkailāya, or Southern Kailāsa, a shrine within the complex that houses an image of Appar. There, according to the account, Vaṭakayilāyanātaṉ, the deity of the shrine known as North Kailāsa gave a boon to the twenty-fifth Gurumahāsannidhāṉam that his desire to see Mount Kailāsa would be fulfilled.[20] So he undertook the pilgrimage, leaving Dharmapuram on June 19, 1959.

Commentators on the pilgrimage have said it was a religious miracle that the twenty-fifth Gurumahāsannidhāṉam's vision of Mount Kailāsa on August 4th 1959 coincided with the anniversary of Appar's vision.[21] They have found other connections between the twenty-fifth Gurumahāsannidhāṇam and Appar, such as the fact that when the twenty-fifth Gurumahāsannidhāṉam ascended to the *gurupīṭam* (April 20, 1945), it was the *nakṣatra* (asterism) of Appar.[22] These observations go beyond comparison; they suggest an identification of the twenty-fifth Gurumahāsannidhāṉam with Appar. For a South Indian Śaivite, the notion of spiritual kinship with a near-divine figure like Appar is a powerful claim indeed.

The story of the twenty-fifth Gurumahāsannidhāṉam and of his pilgrimage to Mount Kailāsa calls upon the presence of Appar to express itself. The memory of the twenty-fifth Gurumahāsannidhāṉam is inseparable from the knowledge of Appar and from what the date Āṭi Amāvācai means in Appar's hagiography. To borrow a phrase from Leigh Gilmore,[23] the simultaneous assembling and dissembling of autobiographical/biographical/hagiographic identities is significant, as they locate the presence of the twenty-fifth Gurumahāsannidhāṉam within living memory while reminding one just how much time, space, and identity are spanned in that memory. As present as the twenty-fifth Gurumahāsannidhāṉam is in this celebration, so also is Appar. The type of vision that Appar experienced of Mount Kailāsa has been brought to Dharmapuram by the twenty-fifth Gurumahāsannidhāṉam and continues to be there. Just as the story of Appar tells us that Kailāsa is not there, but here, so also the celebration on Āṭi Amāvācai tells us that the experience was not just then, but also now.

Finishing the Circle

Given the layers of interconnections we have seen thus far, it should not be surprising that there are more. Like a series of Chinese boxes, one sitting inside the other, there is another story that fits in here. The temple at Tiruvaiyāṟu, the temple where Appar had his vision of Mount Kailāsa, is at present owned by Dharmapuram. Its connections with this temple predate the actual founding of the Adhinam. A noted scholar of the sixteenth century, Kamalaiñāṉapirakācar, was the preceptor of Guruñāṉacampantar, the founder of the lineage at Dharmapuram. One of Kamalaiñāṉapirakācar's co-disciples, Ñāṉakuttār, was stationed at Tiruvaiyāṟu, and possibly served the temple in some capacity as an overseer of temple rituals or temple endowments, as did both Kamalaiñāṉapirakācar at Sikkil and Guruñāṉacampantar at Dharmapuram. Ñāṉakuttār produced a *talapurāṇam*, or temple chronicle, of Tiruvaiyāṟu, which includes an interesting episode that relates to the material in this chapter. It incorporates several elements that relate to the place, the *paramaparai* (or lineage), and Mount Kailāsa. The story is of Tirunandi Dēvar, who is presented as the same Nandi of the *Kailāsaparamparai*. The story is recounted in a publication from Dharmapuram that chronicles the stories of the temple site.[24] In summary, the story goes as follows.

> Sage Śilāda being without progeny desired a son. He worshipped the Lord who commanded him to perform the *putrakāmeṣṭi* sacrifice on the understanding that he would find a child placed in a box while he ploughed the sacred plot, but that the child would only live up to the age of sixteen years. Śilāda performed the sacrifice and discovered a box. He opened the box to find inside a divine form with four arms and three eyes with a moon on the crest. Immediately he was instructed to shut the box and reopen it. He did. Inside was a beautiful child. The sage named the boy Japeśvara.
>
> By the age of fourteen years he had mastered the Vedas, the Āgamas, and the Śāstras. His parents grew sad with the thought that he had only two more years to live. On learning the cause of their sadness, he went to the Ayyarappar (Tiruvaiyāṟu) temple to undertake a severe penance by posting himself in the Brahma-Viṣṇu tīrtha. The water reptiles and fish fed themselves on his flesh, reducing him to a mere skeleton. God then appeared before him, sprinkled on him the river waters, [Tiruvaiyāṟu represents five sacred rivers – Sūryapuṣkaraṇī, Gangātīrtha, Candrapuṣkarāṇī or Amṛtanadi, Paḻāṟu, and Nandivainoraitīrtha or Nanditīrtha, which are said to have been created for Nandi's abhiṣekam,] restored his body to its original unimpaired condition and blessed him with the traditional sixteen gifts. Japeśvara was then married to Svayamprakāśī, the granddaughter of Vaśiṣṭha and the daughter of Paṅguṉi when the *punarpūsa* constellation was ruling. Finally Japeśvara received the upadesam of the Lord, ascended to Mount Kailāsa, and became the head of the attendants of Śiva. He obtained the honour of guarding the main gate there and became the prime founder of the *santānācārya*, the line of Śaiva Siddhānta preceptors. He bears the name of Nandi Dēvar.

This story brings us back full circle to the creation of the *Kailāsaparamparai*. We started with the image a Śaiva lineage holds of Mount Kailāsa, and in our travels through the narratives that circulate around that image, we are taken to the waters that are the origins of that lineage. Like Appar, we started with a yearning to see Mount Kailāsa, but ended up at the *tīrtha* at Teṉkailāsa. Our travels have mimicked Appar's journey; the story told about the Nandi at Tiruvaiyāṟu does as well, except in reverse order. Appar sought Mount Kailāsa, only to find it at Tiruvaiyāṟu, while here the *tīrtha* enables the sage to ascend to Mount Kailāsa, where through his becoming the prime attendant of Śiva, the *Kailāsaparamparai* commences.

Like Nandi, the twenty-fifth preceptor of Dharmapuram – a preceptor of the *Kailāsaparamparai* – began his journey to Kailāsa at Tiruvaiyāṟu. But this story reminds us that as a member of the *Kailāsaparamaparai,* his journey had, in fact, begun long before that. Purportedly about beginnings, the story of Nandi from Tiruvaiyāṟu ends up saying more about circularity, how places of beginnings and places of endings are not so easily separated. These stories and journeys are embedded in each other, possibly because the use, production, and generation of them, in their different modes of performance, ritual, pilgrimage, autobiography, hagiography, temple legend, and so on, have been dictated by members of the Kailāsa lineage. Afterall, they have also produced the knowledge embedded in the vision of Mount Kailāsa that their lineage offers.

Conclusion

Dharmapuram's Śaiva Siddhānta tradition stems from several sources. One source, only touched upon in passing in this essay, is deeply rooted in the Sanskrit Āgamas, which offer instruction in the Śaiva rites of initiation and worship followed by the lineage. The way the worship of Mount Kailāsa is undertaken on Āṭi Amāvācai, for example, derives from Āgamic tradition; likewise, the rites that admit a member to Dharmapuram's Kailāsa lineage and those that bestow the qualifications of preceptor on one have come to Dharmapuram through knowledge found in Āgamic sources.

Though the Dharmapuram Adhinam pointedly acknowledges itself as heir to the Āgamic tradition in many of its ritual processes, it acknowledges other sources through the moods engendered by the elaboration of such rites. In its ritual evocation of shared identity and an immediacy of experience, the Āṭi Amāvācai celebration privileges an expression of religiosity found in the Tamil Śaiva *Tirumuṟai*. As shown by its decisive but near-subliminal invocation of Appar, who could experience Kailāsa only when standing on Tamil soil, the celebration delimits Dharmapuram's religious arena, and prescribes the nature of the experience for those who participate in it. By manipulating an image like Mount Kailāsa that conveys layers of significance for South Indian Śaivites, and by prompting the readings that result, the Dharmapuram Adhinam takes a moment on Āṭi Amāvācai to articulate its presence and claim its place in the complex world of the South Indian tradition.

A staged moment of self-reflection and self-presentation, the Āṭi Amāvācai celebration stakes out certain claims about the Dharmapuram Adhinam through an interweave of contemporary and earlier life history. This interweave embeds one history in another, offering intersubjective possibilities through these interwoven narrative discourses. The life of the institution, the life of its understanding of lineage, the life of its past preceptor, the life of a revered Śaiva saint, and the lives of the participants in the Āṭi Amāvācai celebration are woven together and fixed in place by their link to Mount Kailāsa. This site is both real and envisioned at Dharmapuram.

End Notes

1 Fred W. Clothey, 'Chronometry, Cosmology, and the Festival Calendar of the Tamil Cultus of Murukan,' in Fred W. Clothey, *Rhythm and Intent: Ritual Studies From South India* (Madras: Blackie & Son Publishers, 1983), 56.

2 Indira Peterson, *Poems to Śiva: The Hymns of the Tamil Saints* (Princeton: Princeton University Press, 1989), 29.

3 Ibid., 33.

4 Glenn E. Yocum, 'A Non-Brahman Tamil Saiva Mutt: A Field Study of the Thiravavaduthurai Adheenam,' in *Monastic Life in the Christian and Hindu Traditions: A Comparative Study*, Vol. 3, *Studies in Comparative Religion*, ed. Austin B. Creel and Vasudha Narayanan (Lewiston/Queenston/Lampeter: Edwin Mellon Press, 1990), 251.

5 Ibid., 252.

6 Marie-Louise Reiniche, 'Le temple dans la localité. Quatre exemples au Tamil-nadu,' in *L'espace du temple 1: espaces, itinéraires, méditations*, ed. Jean-Claude Galey (Paris: Éditions de l'École des Hautes Études en Sciences Sociales, *Puruṣārtha* 8: 1985), 95.

7 *Tarumai Kaṉakāpikṣēka Viḻāmalar*, ed. Kaṉakāpikṣēka Viḻākkuḻviṉar (Tarumapuram: Ñāṉacampantam accakam, 1961).

8 Norman Cutler, *Songs of Experience: The Poetics of Tamil Devotion* (Bloomington, IN: Indiana University Press, 1987), 39.

9 Ibid., 52.

10 Ibid., 46.

11 Ibid.

12 Ibid.

13 Ibid., 51.

14 Ibid.

15 Ibid., 49.

16 *St. Sekkizhar's Periya Puranam*, trans. T.N. Ramachandran, Part 1 (Thanjavur: Tamil University, 1990), 327–33; *Cēkkiḻār Cuvāmikaḷ Aruḷcceyt Tiruruttoṇṭarkaḷ Carittirameṉṉum Periyapurāṇam Vacaṉakāviyam* (Ceṉṉai: B. Irattiṉanāyakar and Sons, 1984), 164–212.

17 Peterson, *Poems to Śiva*, 300.

18 The Adhinam's almanac, *Irakākṣi Varusam* (Tarumapuram: Ñāṉacampantam accakam,1984), 59, draws attention to this connection. Members of the Adhinam's staff, such as Sri K. Ramakrishnan, the deputy schroff, structured their discussion of the celebration around this connection. Several articles in the twenty-fifth Gurumahasannidhāṉam's commemorative volume, *ŚrīlaŚrī Kayilai Kurumaṇi Niṉaivu Malar*, ed. Irāmaliṅkat Tampirāṉ (Ñāṉacampantam Patippakam, 1972), highlight the connection between Appar and the twenty-fifth Gurumahāsannidhāṉam.

19 Ciṅkāravēlaṉ, Cō, 'Paṇpunalaṉkal,' in *ŚrīlaŚrī Kayilai Kurumaṇi Niṉaivu Malar*, 58.

20 Ibid.

21 Taṇṭapāṇi Ṯēcikar, Ca, 'Aruḷ Aṉupavaṅkaḷiṟ Cila,' in *ŚrīlaŚrī Kayilai Kurumaṇi Niṉaivu Malar*, 42.

22 Vacantā Vaittiyanātaṉ, 'Tāyiṟ Ciṟanta Talaivaṉ!' in *ŚrīlaŚrī Kayilai Kurumaṇi Niṉaivu Malar*, 117.

23 Leigh Gilmore, 'The Mark of Autobiography: Postmodernism, Autobiography and Genre,' in *Autobiography and Postmodernism*, ed. Kathleen Ashley, Leigh Gilmore, and Gerald Peters (Amherst: University of Massachusetts, 1994), 7.

24 Visvalinga Thambiran, *Sri Panchanathiswaraswarni Temple, Tiruvaiyaru* (Tarumapuram: Gnanasambhandar Press, 1965), 8–9.

11

Portraiture and Jain Sacred Place: The Patronage of the Ministers Vastupāla and Tejaḥpāla

JACK C. LAUGHLIN

Biographies and Family Prominence

The thirteenth century Jain laymen Vastupāla and his brother Tejaḥpāla are credited with the patronage of numerous religious edifices within their own Jain community as well as within the Hindu community.[1] They are also remembered as exceptionally able ministers under the Caulukya-Vāghelā regime of Gujarat. As legendary statesmen and temple-builders, these two brothers are arguably Śvetāmbara Jainism's most famous historical laymen. Their fame has been propagated by the great tradition of biographical writing, which began with authors sponsored by Vastupāla and which, in fact, includes material written by Vastupāla himself. Vastupāla and Tejaḥpāla remained popular biography subjects for centuries after their deaths. Both the contemporary texts and later ones include tales of their heroic service to the state and elaborate accounts of their service to religion.

All medieval Indian biographies are far more 'bardic' than purely historical; they do not seek to report objective fact, but present their protagonists as historical heroes who accomplish great deeds in the secular or religious worlds. The glorification of certain events or persons may even be in the service of particular social or religious agendas. The biographies of Jain monks especially may have an avowed sectarian purpose: to demonstrate the superiority of Jainism over other religions or the superiority of particular monks and their lineages over other monks and lineages.[3] In the biographies of Vastupāla and Tejaḥpāla, we can recognize, in addition to the romanticization of history and reports of purely legendary events, the effort to create particular identities for the brothers. Since much of this material dates from the era of the brothers and since Vastupāla himself sponsored much of this literature, it is apparent that the creation of particular biographical personae served at least in part to further the brothers' own religious and political ambitions.

The biographies of Vastupāla and Tejaḥpāla contain two broad themes that speak to the brothers' identities as leaders of the Jain community and as ministers of the state. First, texts and even inscriptions consistently assert that the brothers were born into a noble lineage that had also served the state and Jain community with distinction. The importance of a high birth is proverbial in India, and social status among the castes and clans of 'Rajputana' is very much dependent upon public assent to a known lineage history. However, in the absence of any independent evidence for the history of Vastupāla's family, I am suspicious of the claims about it in the biographies.

Second, certain texts provide unusual accounts of how the brothers attained their pre-eminent political position. The political rise of the brothers was dependent upon the ascension of the Vāghelās to rulership over the Caulukyan kingdom of Gujarat. It is in the context of certain fantastic accounts of the assumption of sovereignty by the Vāghelās that appointment of the brothers to their respective ministerships is related. It is apparent that there was something irregular about the Vāghelā rise to power and hence something irregular about the rise of the brothers. Yet it is also apparent that the authority that the Vāghelās granted to the brothers did not go unchallenged even within the Vāghelā court; a number of other ministers undoubtedly coveted the positions enjoyed by the brothers. Thus, the stories about the origin of the power of the Vāghelās and the brothers provide occasion for the claim of intimacy between the Vāghelā kings and the brothers, in addition to justifying the authority of both.

A number of texts, including Vastupāla's own *Naranārāyaṇānanda*, claim that Vastupāla and his brother came from an illustrious Jain family of the Prāgvāṭa caste hailing from Patan.[4] The texts give the names of the brothers' ancestors back to their great-great-grandfather; the same degree of ancestry is also represented in the family portraits in Tejaḥpāla's Mt Abu temple. The texts say that each of the ministers' ancestors served the Caulukya court in one ministerial capacity or another. The texts also suggest that the ancestors were Jain temple patrons on the order of their famous descendants. However, I can find no references to any of these men in any source independent of those concerning Vastupāla and Tejaḥpāla. At the very least, none of these ancestors enjoyed the kind of influence that either Vastupāla or Tejaḥpāla did. And none ever demonstrated the kind of piety that their famous descendants did – to the best of my knowledge, there are no independent records of a donation made or building project undertaken by any of them. In the absence of any data to corroborate the claims made for the ancestors in the texts, I have to believe that Vastupāla and Tejaḥpāla were in fact self-made men.

The questionable fame of the brothers' ancestors aside, some very late stories indicate that the brothers were burdened with a social handicap that only their great influence and accomplishments could mask. It is said in these later stories that Kumāradevī, the mother of Vastupāla and Tejaḥpāla, was a widow when she married Āśvarāja, the brothers' father.[5] An Old Gujarati genealogical text adds that this fact split the the brothers' Prāgvāṭa caste into the Vṛddhaśākhā (the 'old' or 'superior branch,' the modern Vīsā branch) and the Laghuśākhā (the 'new' or 'inferior branch,' the modern Daśā branch), which was allied with Vastupāla. As Sandesera says, many scholars reject this tradition because it is found only in later sources, but it contains the kind of information that Vastupāla's contemporaries would undoubtedly have wished to suppress; therefore, we should give some currency to the idea that Vastupāla and Tejaḥpāla were the sons of a remarried widow. We can then recognize that the brothers' social ambitions, expressed through their public works, also required no less than the reinvention of their family history.

The brothers' reinvention of themselves or suppression of certain facts about their genealogy, or both, is apparent from the fact that many biographies of the brothers begin by stating that they and their family were very poor, and only later became rich and powerful, which many accounts say was due to the supernatural intervention of one deity or another. Accounts of the early life of the brothers say that they and their family lived in the village of Sumhālaka, which was a freeholding granted to Vastupāla's father Āśvarāja by a Caulukyan king. But following the death of Āśvarāja, the family moved to the village of Maṇḍalī. Sometime after that, the family moved again to the town of Dhavalakka. Some accounts report that the brothers first met the Vāghelās at Dhavalakka, apparently the Vāghelā capital, and from there they embarked upon their ministerial careers. However, the move to Dhavalakka and the family's poverty are also notable for they provide the context for Tejaḥpāla's most famous deed, the building of the Lūṇigavasahī at Mt Abu.[6] It is said that Lūṇiga, Vastupāla's eldest brother, was dying and bemoaned the fact that because of the family's poverty he could not donate even a small image to the Vimalavasahī, the oldest of the Delwara Jain temples on Mt Abu. In time Lūṇiga died, but sometime after that the family acquired much wealth by the miraculous favour of Śrīmātā, the patron goddess of Mt Abu, and with that wealth Tejaḥpāla was able to construct the Lūṇigavasahī in honour of his dead brother.[7]

Donations and Portrait Statues

It is apparent that, in one way or another, the family was undistinguished before Vastupāla and Tejaḥpāla became successful. But once they were successful, they made every effort to make their family prominent. Tejaḥpāla built the magnificent temple at Mt Abu in honour of his dead brother (according to popular legend) or his son and wife (according to the temple *praśastis*). In the years after the temple's initial consecration, Tejaḥpāla made a number of additions to it which became opportunities for the glorification of his entire immediate family. In the approximately thirty inscriptions from Mt Abu recording these additions, Tejaḥpāla transferred the merit of those donations to his immediate family as follows: one to his son; one each to his two wives; two to his older brother Malladeva; one each to his seven sisters; one each to the two wives of Vastupāla; one each to the two wives of Malladeva; one each to his two daughters-in-law; one each to the three wives of the son of Vastupāla; one to the daughter of Malladeva; and one to Vastupāla 's grandson, in addition to the original gift of the temple for the merit of his wife and son.[8] Epigraphical evidence of similar gifts by Vastupāla is almost entirely lacking. However, the longer *Vastupālapraśasti*, written by Vastupāla 's court poet Narendraprabhasūri,[9] tells us about Vastupāla's donations for the merit of Malladeva (v. 33, 71), offspring (v. 46), grandson (v. 59, 76), wife (v. 72), Tejaḥpāla's wife (v. 84), and assorted others not related to Vastupāla or whose relationship to him I cannot ascertain (v. 61, 64, 65).

The number of donations that the brothers made on behalf of the ancestors is rather small compared with the donations for the immediate family. Tejaḥpāla made only one addition to his Mt Abu temple for the merit of his ancestors. Vastupāla's gifts for the ancestors are similarly sparse. The *Vastupālapraśasti* says that he renovated a Jain temple in the village of Vyāgrapalli, which was originally built by the ancestors,[11] for their merit (v. 45), and he donated four Jina images, one on each of the four peaks of Mt Girnar (vs. 89–92), in the name of his father, grandfather, great-grandfather, and great-great-grandfather.[12]

It is not that Vastupāla and Tejaḥpāla showed little concern for the religious merit of their ancestors or that they were indifferent to their ancestors' fame (or lack of it), references to ancestry in the biographies notwithstanding. Rather, the brothers provided for the memory of their ancestors in a very special way. At a number of temples that either Vastupāla or Tejaḥpāla had built, they included portrait statues of immediate family members, but especially of their ancestors. These statues might have served to produce merit for the subjects, but they might also have served to assert a social status for the ancestors that they may or may not have otherwise possessed, and so too legitimate the brothers' status within the Jain community.

The donation of portrait statues was not an innovation by the brothers. Many lay people donated portrait statues, particularly of their parents, to temples that they themselves or others had built. Furthermore, the lineage portraits that Tejaḥpāla put in his Mt Abu temple clearly were inspired by similar portraits in Vimala's earlier temple there.[13] However, it is apparent from some of the other family portraits attributed to Tejaḥpāla and Vastupāla that the brothers expanded upon popular conceptions behind earlier portraits and imbued some of the portraits that they sponsored with meanings not known to earlier examples. Generally speaking, Vastupāla and Tejaḥpāla presented their ancestors, and perhaps themselves and immediate family as well, in sculpted form as gods and certain mythical personages. I cannot go so far as to say that they sought the deification of the portrait subjects, but at the least they compared the subjects to gods of a very special sort, either with respect to the function of those gods or their place in Jain myth. The aim must have been to give the subjects a very special status in the public eye, but more narrowly, I believe that the portrait statues were intended as an assertion of authority by the brothers and their family over their own

Jain community. The brothers required legitimacy for their growing wealth and power, since they apparently did not inherit the necessary social status from their ancestors. They might have especially required some special means to justify their authority if Kumāradevī was in fact a remarried widow, that is, if their parentage was socially suspect, and if this had led to some social strife within the lay Jain community.

While the legitimation of the brothers' authority over their religious community is apparent in some of their public works, the legitimation of their political authority, as well as that of their sovereigns, is apparent in others. Given the unusual circumstances under which Vastupāla and Tejaḥpāla attained their pre-eminent political position, and under which the Vāghelās gained authority over at least part of the Caulukyan empire, I think it is clear that elements of the brothers' public building activity were meant to legitimate Vāghelā rule, as exercised by the brothers. At the same time, Vastupāla and Tejaḥpāla had their own problems with legitimacy within the Vāghelā government. In their public works we see a claim of solidarity between them and the Vāghelā throne.

As I have pointed out, some biographies of Vastupāla and Tejaḥpāla say that the brothers were first presented to the Vāghelā court at Dhavalakka. However, other accounts describe this introduction differently. Thus it is uncertain when this contact was initiated. The exact circumstances under which the brothers went into the service of the Vāghelās are also obscure. Yet it is clear that the brothers' impressive ministerial careers were dependent upon the assumption of independent Vāghelā authority over parts of Gujarat.

Vastupāla's Mt Girnar inscriptions say that he and his brother were transferred into the service of the Vāghelās in 1220 from the service of Bhīma II, the Caulukyan king of Gujarat. Sources all agree that Bhīma was an ineffectual ruler. Gujarat was invaded several times by neighbouring kings and the Muslims; Bhīma even suffered a lengthy usurpation from about 1224. It appears that some kind of stability was restored to the kingdom by the actions of the Vāghelās, perhaps with the help of Vastupāla and Tejaḥpāla; extending this service to the Caulukyas seems to have given the Vāghelās a power base from which they eventually took the throne outright.[14]

The Vāghelās had a nominal claim to the throne of Gujarat, for they were a collateral branch of the Caulukyas: Ārṇorāja Vāghelā was the son of the sister of the mother of the famous Caulukyan king Kumārapāla.[15] Ārṇorāja's son was Lavaṇaprasāda and Lavaṇaprasāda's son was Vīradhavala. It was under Lavaṇaprasāda that the Vāghelās came into their own. He apparently served as regent under Bhīma II. Vīradhavala was eventually supposed to become king but he died before Bhīma. When Bhīma died, and after the very brief reign of Tribhuvanapāla Caulukya, Vīsaladeva, the son of Vīradhavala, became the first Vāghelā king of the former Caulukyan empire.

The myths about the shift of power from the Caulukyas to the Vāghelās began with contemporary authors and were repeated in later decades. The most important account was penned by Someśvara and is notable because Someśvara was a court poet and the *purohita* of Bhīma II, but he appears to have shifted his loyalty to Lavaṇaprasāda and Vastupāla as well.[16] Someśvara relates that the Caulukyan empire had been divided between some of the royal ministers and vassals because of the weakness of Bhīma II.[17] The Goddess of the Royal Fortune of the Kingdom of Gujarat appeared to Lavaṇaprasāda asking him and his son to save her. Lavaṇaprasda asked Someśvara himself what to do and the poet advised him to bring Vastupāla and Tejaḥpāla into his service, hence the rise of the Vāghelās and the brothers.

Other authors provide interesting variations on this supernatural call to action. In the *Vasantavilāsa* of Bālacandra, written shortly after the death of Vastupāla and at the behest of Vastupāla's son Jaitrasiṃha,[18] the Goddess of Royal Fortune appears to Vīradhavala in a dream, not to his father, telling him to appoint Vastupāla and Tejaḥpāla as ministers. Arisiṃha, another poet in the service of Vastupāla, provides the most unusual account in his *Sukṛtasaṃkīrtana*. In it, Kumārapāla, the famous Caulukyan king, who had been reborn as a powerful god because of his great faith in the Jain religion, appears to Bhīma II in a dream. He commands Bhīma to save the crumbling kingdom. The solution to the kingdom's woes is the appointment of Lavaṇaprasāda as the Lord of All (*sarveśvara*) and the naming of his son Vīradhavala as crown-prince (*yuvarāja*). In the morning after the dream, Bhīma reports his vision to Lavaṇaprasāda and fulfills the god's demands. Vīradhvala for his part asks the king to give him a minister who is able enough to restore the kingdom to its former glory. Bhīma, singing the praises of the ancestors of Vastupāla, transfers Vastupāla and his brother Tejaḥpāla into the service of Vīradhavala.

The justification of Vāghelā rule by the introduction of the divine sanction of the Rājalakṣmī and especially the deified Kumārapāla suggests that the Vāghelās claimed an authority to which they were not really entitled and for which they did not have universal support.

The historical evidence for early Vāghelā rule shows that they confidently asserted paramount authority in parts of Gujarat, in keeping with Someśvara's and Arisiṃha's claims for them, but elsewhere they had to be content with a more modest status.[19] In the Mt Abu and Mt Girnar inscriptions (1231 and 1232), the former written by Someśvara himself, Lavaṇaprasāda is called by the most regal title 'Mahārājādhirāja.' Bhīma II was still ruling at this time and only to him should this title have been applied; in other inscriptions from Mt Abu and in other sources, Lavaṇaprasāda is called merely 'Mahāmaṇḍaleśvara Rāṇaka' under the authority of Bhīma.[20]

The accounts legitimizing Vāghelā rule also served to legitimize the ministerial authority of Vastupāla and Tejaḥpāla: if Vāghelā sovereignty was open to question then so was the ministerial authority of Vastupāla and Tejaḥpāla because of their allegiance to the Vāghelās and their part in the apparent coup. At the same time, the stories about how the brothers became servants to Lavaṇaprasāda and Vīradhavala must have also been intended to show that the Vāghelās were, in some way, beholden to the brothers for their acquisition of the kingdom. The brothers' need for legitimacy in Vāghelā courtly circles is apparent from later anecdotes that say Vastupāla found himself on the outs at court when Vīsaladeva, the son of Vīradhavala, became king.[21] Some stories go so far as to say that Vastupāla was replaced as chief minister by one Nāgaḍa, a Nāgara brahmin. In truth, though, it seems that Vastupāla held the ministership until his death, at which time he was succeeded by Tejaḥpāla, and only upon the latter's death did Nāgaḍa assume the chief ministership. Other stories about the conflict between Vastupāla and Vīsaladeva say that the minister's position was salvaged by the timely intercession of the poet Someśvara who, as we have seen, was a great propagandist for the Vāghelās and the brothers.

While these stories about Vastupāla's particular courtly difficulties might not be historically true, they might be true at least in spirit. For though Someśvara would have us believe that the Vāghelā kings, at least Vīradhavala, never wavered in their support of the ministers, it is apparent that the authority of the ministers did not go unchallenged (perhaps even by Nāgaḍa). In Someśvara's Mt Abu *praśasti* (1231) it is said that 'the wise Caulukya Vīradhavala did not even lend his ears to the whispers of the slanderers when they were talking about those two ministers.'[22] Furthermore, a Mt Girnar inscription of the next year, in the middle of a panegyric upon Vastupāla's generosity, asks, 'What is the use of talking about sinful and wicked ministers who have nothing in their mind but malice against the people?'[23]

In addition to the family portraits sponsored by Vastupāla and Tejaḥpāla, we also find a number of portrait statues of the Caulukya and Vāghelā kings. I believe that some of these images were erected to further the kingdom-wide political agenda of the brothers and their sovereigns, while others were meant to to serve the brothers' interests in narrower Vāghelā circles. Tejaḥpāla is credited with a set of portraits of the former Caulukyan kings at Dabhoi, southeast of Baroda in Gujarat. Additionally, Vastupāla is said to have erected a number of statues of the Vāghelās in conjunction with his good works at several sites. The statues of the Caulukyas appear to have been an element in the effort to reconsolidate the Caulukyan empire and to justify the authority of Tejaḥpāla (and Vastupāla) and the Vāghelā chiefs. The Vāghelā statues appear to have promoted Vāghelā rule throughout Gujarat. But additionally, they must have promoted the idea of the intimacy between the brothers and the Vāghelā throne, because many of them were erected in conjunction with portrait statues of the brothers or include figures of the brothers.

While the literature about Vastupāla and Tejaḥpāla projects the unique identities of these exceptional men and has been closely studied, portraiture also informs us about the kind of image or images the two ministers tried to create for themselves, in their Jain community and in the kingdom at large. However, the evidence of these, or any other medieval Western Indian portraits for that matter, has been little scrutinized by scholars. In this chapter, I discuss three groups of statues sponsored by the brothers at Dabhoi, Mt Girnar and Mt Abu. Groups of statues set up at these sites were understood to be the Guardians of the Quarters (*lokapālas* or *dignāyakas*), implicitly in the Dabhoi and Mt Girnar cases, but explicitly at Mt Abu.

The Guardians of the Quarters are pan-Indic deities who may number four, eight, or ten, and occupy a number of places in Indic myth. They are most commonly associated with kingship and protection. Indra is their most prominent member. The Indian king is regularly identified with Indra since Indra is the king of the gods but also one of the *lokapālas*.[24] In the *Arthaśastra,* the king is said to be Indra's representative on earth (9.10) and as such is responsible for holding festivals, especially those promoting fertility (the Indra Festival being one of the most important). The *Nāradasmṛti* says the king is Indra in visible form and in the *Mahābhārata* kings are called 'companions of Indra' (2.31.63). Quite commonly the king is thought to embody the essence of Indra along with that of the other *lokapālas*, a conception that is common to *Manusmṛti, Rāghuvaṃśa* and other works. In *Rāghuvaṃśa* (6.1) the king is actually called *naralokapāla,* as he is in the *Rājataraṅginī* of Kalhaṇa (1.344). In Jain myth, the gods led by Indra are central to narratives about the lives of the Jinas. They serve as the model of Jain lay devotion and temple patronage.

The fact that the portraits of the Caulukyan kings, which Tejaḥpāla set up in the rampart around Dabhoi, seem to have numbered ten, makes me believe that the images were meant to appear as the Guardians of the Quarters. The intention must have been to evoke the supernatural protective power of the *lokapālas* and hence to enhance royal power over the region. I also believe that at least four if not all eight portraits, which Vastupāla is said to have erected on the peaks of Mt Girnar, and which represented himself, his brothers, and four of his ancestors, were also intended to evoke the most basic function of the *lokapālas* in order to present Vastupāla or his kinsmen as very special leaders and protectors of the Jain community. The inference that the Mt Girnar and Dabhoi portraits represent the Guardians of the Quarters, based on the fact that they occur in numbers associated with those gods, is further supported by evidence from Tejaḥpāla's temple at Mt Abu. Tejaḥpāla included in the temple ten portraits representing his lineage, which were explicitly intended to appear as 'the Guradians of the Quarters perpetually coming to see the Jina,' according to one of the main temple inscriptions.[25] The allusion to the Guardians of the Quarters in this case does not refer to the protective power of these gods, but appears to evoke narratives about the enlightenment of the Jinas. When a Jina attains omniscience, the stories report, the gods descend to earth and build a special pavilion for him, called the *samavasaraṇa,* in which gods and humans then gather to listen to the Jina's first sermon. The Mt Abu portraits imply a homology between the Jain temple and the *samavasaraṇa,* and Jain temple patrons are like the gods who build the *samavasaraṇa.* Thus Tejaḥpāla presented himself (and his family) as patrons of an extraordinary sort.

I first discuss the portrait statues at Dabhoi; in this context I also discuss the statues of the Vāghelā kings that are credited to Vastupāla. I then discuss statues at Mt Girnar and conclude with those at Mt Abu, which are the only extant portrait statues made by either brother. Medieval Jain literature often exaggerates the patronage of famous temple-builders. There are few extant remains of temples built by the brothers; the large number of public works sponsored by Vastupāla and Tejaḥpāla may well be exaggerated in some textual accounts. The number of statues attributed to the brothers in some texts might also be exaggerated. However, for the sake of argument, I assume that all the statues I describe and which are known only from texts, did exist at one time. The statues credited to Vastupāla and Tejaḥpāla were elements in a biographical tradition exclusively devoted to these two men that began with their own court poets, and were used and manipulated to create sacred space, particularly in the case of the famous centres of Jain pilgrimages. The statues, then, were used by the brothers to create for themselves a social, political, and religious identity in their own time and for posterity.

Vastupāla's and Tejaḥpāla's Royal Portraiture

The Dabhoi Rampart

According to Jinaharṣa's *Vastupālacarita* (1441), Tejaḥpāla saw that the people of Dabhoi lived in constant fear of predatory invasions and so he had built around the town 'a cloud-licking rampart rising even up to the sun (upon which were placed) images of the (Caulukyan) kings beginning with Mūlarāja.'[26] If we count the deceased Caulukyan kings up to the time the wall was built, the total is exactly ten.[27] Since these images were the same in number as the portraits in Tejaḥpāla's Mt Abu temple, I believe that the Dabhoi portraits were intended to represent the Guardians of the Quarters. It is possible to conclude that the representations of the Caulukyan kings as the *lokapālas* in image form was intended to indicate that the kings had literally become those gods. I have cited a number of Hindu texts that describe an intimacy between earthly kings and the *lokapālas*, and, as we have seen, Arisiṃha did not hesitate to describe Kumārapāla Caulukya as reborn as a god in his account of the rise of the Vāghelās. If the Dabhoi portraits were supposed to represent the *lokapālas* and the Caulukyan kings were supposed to have been reborn as those gods, then the portraits must have been meant to serve as the supernatural protectors of Dabhoi. That is to say, the portraits were meant to evoke the most basic function of the *lokapālas*, as guardians of place.

We cannot ignore the context of political events involving Vastupāla and Tejaḥpāla when we interpret the statues at the Dabhoi rampart. As I noted above, the stories about the brothers' entry into royal service belie their precarious political position with their Vāghelā lords.

However, it is difficult to locate these images in an exact historical context because it is not entirely certain if and when Tejaḥpāla ordered a rampart to be built. There is a fragmentary inscription at Dabhoi dated 1253 and written by Someśvara, but it does not refer to this fortification. If Tejaḥpāla did order the rampart, he could not have done so any earlier than 1229, the date of Arisiṃha's *Sukṛtakīrtana*, which mentions patronage by Vastupāla and Tejaḥpāla at Dahboi but does not mention the rampart.

The fate of Dabhoi in the years before it was fortified by Tejaḥpāla is important, though this history is also not entirely clear. Dabhoi had been part of the Caulukyan empire, but in the course of the usurpation of Bhīma II and the invasion by the Paramāras (c. 1210), Dabhoi fell into Paramāra hands for some time, and the Cāhamānas, the Yādavas, and the Muslims fought over all of Lāṭa, the region which included Dabhoi.[28] At some point, Dabhoi was rescued by Lavaṇaprasāda, perhaps through the efforts of Vastupāla and Tejaḥpāla, and Caulukya-Vāghelā control over it was maintained for many years after.[29] Either the Vāghelās or the brothers took Dabhoi from the Paramāras, for Narendraprabha's *Vastupālapraśasti* says that Vastupāla replaced the gold pitchers atop the Vaidyanātha temple, which Subhaṭavarman Paramāra had destroyed.[30]

Once Dabhoi was reclaimed, defending it was an ongoing struggle as is clear from Vastupāla's most famous deed in the region, the defeat of the Muslim merchant Saïd of Broach and his general Śaṅkha at the port of Cambay.[31] Sources say that Vastupāla was made governor of Cambay in order to put an end to the piracy and corruption occurring there as a result of Bhīma II's weak rule.[32] The death of Vastupāla's general Bhuvanapāla (also called Lūṇapāla) in the battle with Śaṅkha is also significant – on the spot where Bhuvanapāla fell in battle, Vastupāla erected a Śiva temple called Bhuvanapāleśvara,[33] which may have signalled the deification of Bhuvanapāla. At the very least, the temple was a glorified hero-stone, examples of which may be found throughout Gujarat and Rajasthan and in parts of the south, where hero-stones often served as boundary markers.[34] Assuming the temple of Bhuvanapāleśvara did once exist, it could have served to mark the reclamation of Lāṭa by the Caulukya-Vāghelā crown. Furthermore, the rampart of Dabhoi with its portrait statues of the Caulukyan kings, presuming that it was built close to or after the battle at Cambay, could have served the same purpose.[35]

Whether or not the statues at Dabhoi are related to the battle with

Śaṅkha, it is still curious that Tejaḥpāla chose to portray the Caulukyas rather than the Vāghelās, to whom he owed a greater loyalty and who appear to have been more responsible for the rescue of Dabhoi. Inscriptions which refer to the Vāghelās, some of which I have already mentioned, indicate that before the mid-thirteenth century, the Vāghelās had only limited power in parts of Gujarat, but were bold enough to claim paramount power in others. The Vaghelās continued to owe allegiance to the Caulukyas through the end of the thirteenth century in some parts of Gujarat, so perhaps they could not claim rule over Dabhoi when it was saved and had to claim it on behalf of the Caulukyas. While the Caulukyas seem to have lost much of their authority over north Gujarat, the memory of their rule in the south may still have had a certain power.

At the time that Tejaḥpāla built a rampart at Dabhoi, the Vāghelās and their ministers legitimated their authority with reference to the Caulukyas, pursuing their ambitions as loyal servants. The restoration of the boundaries of the Caulukyan empire, however, must have enhanced Vāghelā political power, later permitting them to claim the throne outright. It is important to note that when Vīsaladeva became king he asserted his exclusive authority over Dabhoi by performing Vedic sacrifices and patronizing the Nāgara Brahmins of the region.[36]

The Vāghelā Portrait Statues

Tejaḥpāla placed the statues of the Caulukyas on the rampart at Dabhoi in an attempt to solidify Caulukya-Vāghelā authority in south Gujarat, indirectly affirming the Vāghelās' own authority as exercised through their ministers. The legitimacy of Vāghelā rule, and the position of Vastupāla and Tejaḥpāla under it, were depicted through several portrait statues of the Vāghelās and of the brothers themselves, which Vastupāla included in his patronage at several sites.

At Dabhoi, Vastupāla set up images of Vīradhavala Vaghela, his Queen Jayantadevī, his own brothers Tejaḥpāla and Malladeva, and himself in the new Jain temple he built there.[37] At Mt Girnar, he made an image of Vīradhavala and himself mounted on the same elephant.[38] According to Arisiṃha, images of Vīradhavala, Tejaḥpāla, and Vastupāla mounted on elephants were set up at Śatruñjaya.[39] Later sources describe these particular images a little differently. The *Prabandhacintāmaṇi* says there were three images at Śatruñjaya: one each of Lavaṇaprasāda and one each of Lavaṇaprasāda Vīradhavala on elephants and one at Vastupāla on horseback.[40] Jinaharṣa says that Vastupāla erected images of his lord, his wife, his guru, his brother, and himself in the temple of the Lord of Stambhanakatīrtha (Pārśvanātha), and images of himself and brother on horses – 'furthermore, he had portrayed his lord King Vīra [dhavala] with Queen Jayantadevī in an image mounted on an elephant like Indra with his companion Śacī.'[41]

It is difficult to date precisely when any of these portrait statues would have been made. However, Vastupāla's patronage at Dabhoi must have predated Tejaḥpāla's, which dated to before 1229, the date of Arisiṃha's *Sukṛtakīrtana,* which does not know the Dabhoi rampart but does know the works of Vastupāla. Thus the Vāghelā statues made by Vastupāla at Śatruñjaya must have been made before 1229 since they are mentioned by Arisiṃha. Inscriptions from Mt Girnar describe Vastupāla's works there in the period around 1232 and presumably portrait statues there were made around the same time. The Vāghelā statues then, all seem to date from the time when the Vāghelās were still trying to stake their claim to the sovereignty of Gujarat. These images might have been intended to further such a claim.[42]

Portraying the kings on elephants certainly evokes kingship since the elephant is one of the most obvious Indian symbols of royal power. The elephant is also the mount of Indra. Since Jinaharṣa thought that the statues of Vīradhavala and his queen at Śatruñjaya appeared as Indra and Śacī, that might have been how the other statues of the kings were supposed to appear. The statues of Vastupāla and family that accompanied some of those royal portrait statues may have suggested some of Indra's retinue. Hence, the statues presented the Vāghelās and the brothers by extension as the very model of royalty, a not very subtle claim to political authority.

In addition, the proximity of statues of the brothers to statues of their sovereigns may have stressed the close relationship between the brothers and the Vāghelās. Such a claim would have been particularly useful to the brothers, especially if the animosity that was directed towards Vastupāla within the Vāghelā court had a long history, predating the coronation of Vīsaladeva. As noted above, Dabhoi was liberated by the Vāghelās and probably through the actions of Vastupāla and Tejaḥpāla, who maintained control of the area. If we look at the Dabhoi statues of the Vāghelās and the statues of the brothers in this light, we might imagine that Dabhoi was a good location for the brothers to assert the interdependence of the Vāghelās and themselves. The statue group might have even implied that the

Vāghelās were deeply beholden to the brothers for improving their political position.

Other statues commissioned by the two ministers could be considered in the context of political authority, but since they appear in Jain temples, they could be considered exclusively in Jain terms. I first discuss statues from Mt Girnar to demonstrate how they represented a certain kind of religious or political authority which the ministers exerted over their Jain community, and then turn to the ten mounted statues at Mt Abu to show the ways in which the ministers claimed a special status among Jain temple patrons.

The Girnar Portrait Statues and the Religious Authority of Vastupāla and Tejaḥpāla

Written sources say that Vastupāla sponsored many works on Mt Girnar (Saurashtra). However, little remains except the much renovated Neminātha temple. It is in this temple and elsewhere on the mountain that Vastupāla is said to have erected a number of significant portrait statues. I am particularly interested in eight of these statues that may be considered as the Guardians of the Quarters or as the *kṣetrapālas*. Other statues and conceptions are briefly touched on, but fuller explication of them is reserved for my discussion of the Mt Abu portrait statues.

According to Narendraprabhasūri's *Vastupālapraśasti*, Vastupāla erected on Mt Girnar images of Caṇḍapa and Malladeva on the Ambikā Peak; Caṇḍaprasāda and himself on the Avalokanā Peak; Soma and Tejaḥpāla on the Pradyumna Peak; and Āśarāja and another whose name is missing from the text on the Śāmba Peak.[43] Based on the pattern of the first three pairs, the unknown subject of the fourth might have been Lūṇiga, the fourth and youngest son of Āśarāja and Kumāradevī, the parents of Vastupāla, Tejaḥpāla, and Malladeva. These statues consisted of the four males of Vastupāla's generation paired respectively with their great-great-grandfather, great-grandfather, grandfather, and father.

A number of potential meanings lie behind these eight images. On the one hand, Narendraprabha says that on each of the four peaks with each of the four pairs of portrait statues Vastupāla donated a Jina image for the merit of the ancestor portrayed. The statues of the ancestors might have augmented the merit from the initial gifts of the Jina images; by standing in proximity or devotion to these Jina images, the statues garnered for their subjects the same merit as the subjects would have obtained from actually standing before the Jina images.[44] Such a purpose might have been intended for some or all of the statues erected by Vastupāla and Tejaḥpāla, especially for the ancestor portraits: the brothers must have felt as much a sense of filial obligation as the numerous other patrons who sponsored portrait statues of their parents and loved ones (presumably for the merit of the subjects).

On the other hand, the total of eight suggests that the statues were meant to appear as the Guardians of the Quarters who may number ten, as in Tejaḥpāla's Mt Abu and Dabhoi portraits, but also eight. Or perhaps just the ancestor portraits were meant to appear as the Guardians of the Quarters since those gods may also number four. I argue below that behind the comparison of the Mt Abu portraits to Guardians of the Quarters is the homology of the Jain temple to the *samavasaraṇa*; by this homology, Tejaḥpāla declared himself and his family to be extraordinary temple patrons comparable to the gods who built the *samavasaraṇa*. Above I argued that the ten portrait statues at Dabhoi protected that town as the Guardians of the Quarters, fulfilling the most basic function of those deities. The Mt Girnar statues could have been erected with either of these conceptions in mind.

However, I wish to consider another possible meaning – that the statuess might have represented the more generic protector-gods, the *kṣetrapālas,*[45] which alluded to the Jain mythology about Mt Girnar. When Jinaharṣa came to write about the portrait statues on the peaks of Mt Girnar more than two hundred years after the fact, he repeated Narendraprabha verbatim with respect to the first three pairs; but where the identity of one of the subjects is missing in Narendraprabha's text, Jinaharṣa wrote that the subject was Vastupāla's mother.[46] According to Jinaharṣa, the Mt Girnar statues consisted of seven males and one female. In chapter 2 of Jinaprabha's *Vividhatīrthakalpa,* seven members of the Yādava clan, to which belonged Neminātha, the twenty-third Tīrthaṇkara, and Kṛṣṇa, who figures into the story of Neminātha according to the Jains, became *kṣetrapālas* on Mt Girnar due to their great asceticism.[47] In Jinaprabha's description of Mt Girnar in the same account, an image of one of those *kṣetrapālas* was to be found on the Ambikā peak (on which Vastupāla is said to have placed images of his brother Malladeva and his great-great-grandfather Caṇḍapa). In chapter 4 of the *Vividhatīrthakalpa,* Jinaprabha says that the *kṣetrapāla* manifests himself at numerous places on Mt Girnar.[48] Jinaharṣa then might have thought that the Mt Girnar statues in question were meant to represent seven *kṣetrapālas*. This might have been the case, given the legend reported by Jinaprabha. To my mind, it is not important which deities the statues were intended to represent, *kṣetrapālas* or *lokapālas*, Guardians of Place or Guardians of the Quarters. What is important is that, one way or the other, Vastupāla claimed a very special relationship between himself and his family and Mt Girnar.

Jinaprabha's *Vividhatīrthakalpa* is not the only text to report that certain laymen were reborn on Mt Girnar as Guardian Deities. In Merutuṅga's *Prabandhacintāmaṇi*[49] (1304), a Jain merchant named Dhāra along with his five sons made a pilgrimage to Mt Girnar. They were Śvetāmbaras, while the king who ruled over Mt Girnar was a Digambara. When a battle for control of the mountain broke out between the two sects, Dhāra's five sons were killed and because of their zeal for the faith were reborn on Mt Girnar as *kṣetrapatis*.[50] The story of Dhāra does not say that there were ever images of Dhāra's sons as Protector Gods at Mt Girnar, but other sources report that portraits of historical people served as guardians of place. A sixteenth century inscription from Ekaliṅgajī says that the Sisodia king Rājamalla placed four images on the peaks of Mt Citrakūṭa representing four warriors who died in battle there; the inscription describes the images as 'ready ... with their strong arms to put down the hardy and robust warriors of the other side.'[51] Another story from the *Prabandhacintāmaṇi* relates that when the Caulukyan king Jayasiṃha Siddharāja[52] completed his massive Rudramahālaya Śiva temple, he added to it images of distinguished kings, generals of the cavalry, generals of the infantry, and an image of himself as a devotee, 'and so entreated that, even if the country were laid waste, this temple might not be destroyed.'[53] Both the Ekaliṅgajī inscription and this story from the *Prabandhacintāmaṇi* imply that portrait statues were used as supernatural protectors of their respective locales.[54] It is possible that a similar conception lay behind the four statue pairs sponsored by Vastupāla at Mt Girnar.

If this was the case, we might wonder why Vastupāla took the unusual step of setting up his ancestors (along with himself and his brothers) as the protectors of Mt Girnar in image form. The story of Dhāra informs us that possession of Mt Girnar was hotly contested; other stories say that not only did the Śvetāmbaras and Digambaras fight over the mount, but the Jains as a whole fought for the site, especially with the Buddhists.[55] With these facts in mind I imagine that Vastupāla wanted to bring some stability not only to Mt Girnar but to Jainism in Western India as a whole, and offered himself and his brother (and his lineage by extension) as paramount lay authorities over the Jain congregation. I have been attempting to demonstrate throughout this discussion that Vastupāla and Tejaḥpāla were donors of a very unusual sort. I add to this argument some details about their donations to further confirm this and to show the ways in which the two men tried to create a certain cohesiveness within Jainism.

First, Vastupāla's Mt Girnar temple is known as the 'Temple of the Three Auspicious Moments,'[56] honouring the fact that Neminātha's enlightenment, first sermon, and final liberation occurred on the mountain.[57] The temple has an unusual plan that consists of three shrines in a triangular relationship: the two flanking shrines represent Mt Sammetaśikhara, a mountain in Bihar where Pārśvanātha attained liberation, and Mt Aṣṭāpada, identified with Mt Kailāṣa where Ādinātha attained enlightenment and where his son Bharata constructed the first Jain temple.[58] Inside the two shrines are images of Mt Meru and the *samavasaraṇa*, both representing places where the gods honour auspicious moments (*kalyāṇaka*) in the career of the Jina. The Mt Girnar temple implies that worship in it or pilgrimage to it is equivalent to worship at or pilgrimage to Mt Sammetaśikhara and Mt Aṣṭāpada.

Other sources indicate that this was not the only equivalence Vastupāla set up at Mt Girnar. Jinaprabha says that Vastupāla also constructed there the Śatruñjayāvatārabhavana (Prakrit *sittujjāvayārabhavaṇa*), 'the temple of the Śatruñjaya incarnation.'[59] Vastupāla's inscriptions from Mt Girnar say that he also built shrines of Pārśvanātha's Stambhanaka-incarnation,[60] Mahāvīra's Satyapura-incarnation and Sarasvatī's Kaśmīra-incarnation. Such equivalences applied to some of the ministers' other temples as well. After Tejaḥpāla's Neminātha temple at Mt Abu was built, it and Vimala's earlier Ādinātha temple there became known respectively as the Girnāratīrthāvatāra and the Śatruñjayatīrthāvatāra, since Neminātha is closely associated with Mt Girnar and Ādinātha with Mt Śatruñjaya.[61] But more importantly, Jinaharṣa says that Vastupāla commissioned on Mt Śatruñjaya 'the temple of the Lord of Raivatatīrtha [Neminātha of Mt Girnar] with (images of) the Ambikā, Avalokana, Śāmba and Pradyumna summits.'[62] By the addition of the portrait statues to the actual summits of Mt Girnar, combined with the images of the summits at Mt Śatruñjaya, Vastupāla might have implied that the (supernatural) protection afforded by the portraits extended to Mt Śatruñjaya through the images on Mt Girnar's peaks.

Vastupāla and Tejaḥpāla were exceptional patrons insofar that they, like no others, sponsored temples at numerous sites in Western India. As part of their good works, they interlinked sites not only in Western India but also in Jainism's original heartland, Mt Sammetaśikhara. Through their statues at the Western Indian sites, especially the 'guardian' images at Mt Girnar, the brothers and their ancestors stood guard over the entire circuit of Jain pilgrimage. The two ministers' ability to extend such a great quantity of patronage to Jain holy sites must have given them a great deal of authority within Jain circles. Certainly they exerted due influence over their own temples: one of the Mt Abu *praśastis* informs us that the trust governing Tejaḥpāla's Mt Abu temple consisted of Vastupāla, Tejaḥpāla, their brother Malladeva, four of Tejaḥpāla's brothers-in-law, and their descendants.[63] Presumably the other temples built by the brothers were similarly governed and given the number of temples they apparently built, their actual control over the sacred geography of Jainism in Gujarat must have been extensive. With the portraits, in conjunction with other objects, they expanded their very visible influence.

A written record of 1242 further suggests the kind of influence the two ministers must have had over even the day-to-day affairs of the whole Jain community.[64] Though the record comes down to us only as a paper manuscript, it reports that it was originally engraved in stone at Mt Śatruñjaya. In the record is a resolution, passed by a conclave consisting of temple-dwelling and wandering Jain monks and important laymen, declaring that monks who father children and any such children who may have become ascetics retroactive to a date four years previous are to be considered anathemas by the community. Tejaḥpāla, his son, and Vastupāla's son were just three of the laymen in attendance; however, none of the others is known to us. Tejaḥpāla had the resolution entered into the state record (*śāsanapaṭṭika*), preserving it in his capacity as a state minister. Therefore, I presume, that the record assumed the nature of law and its enforcement was within Tejaḥpāla's power, even though the record never says that the conclave was convened at Tejaḥpāla's request or that the resolution was his idea. Despite the fact that the conference occurred after the death of Vastupāla (but within the year of it), I assume that while Vastupāla lived he had the same influence in the Jain community.

If the eight images on the four peaks of Mt Girnar represent

Guardians of the Mountain and if that site is interchangeable with every other, then those statues stood guard over the entire Jain sacred geography. They might have been meant to protect Jainism from external enemies; they might also have been meant to protect Jainism from its own internal enemies, from internal conflicts and laxity, and from its own traditional lack of cohesiveness.[65]

The Mt Abu Portraits and the Jain Temple as Samavasaraṇa

I hoped to demonstrate above the exceptional influence Vastupāla and Tejaḥpāla exerted over the Jain community in the kingdom of Gujarat. The evidence from at least one of the sets of portraits from Tejaḥpāla's Lūṇigavasahī at Mt Abu points to a uniquely Jain manner by which the two brothers claimed a pre-eminent status among Jains. I believe that these portrait statues imply a homology between the Jain temple and the *samavasaraṇa*, or pavilion of the Jina's first sermon. If the two brothers constructed their temples as conscious allusions to the *samavasaraṇa*, then they were comparing themselves to the gods who built those pavilions or to the original congregation of gods and humans who heard the Jina's sermon in it. In this context, I consider other statues from Mt Girnar which also suggest a comparison between the brothers and family as temple patrons to the gods who built the *samavasaraṇa*. I also consider evidence from Mt Girnar, Mt Śatruñjaya, and Dabhoi that implies a comparison between Vastupāla and his family and certain mythological personalities in the narratives of the building of the *samavasaraṇas* of particular Jinas.

The statues in Tejaḥpāla's Mt Abu temple were originally set up in two separate sets at the back of the temple. The first set, which is extant, consists of ten reliefs showing near-life-size figures of the men of Tejaḥpāla's line with their wives all standing in an attitude of devotion. In front of these reliefs are ten elephants upon which Tejaḥpāla and nine males in his line were once mounted, though all those figures are now missing. One of the main temple inscriptions says of these men that 'their ten images, mounted on the shoulders of she-elephants, give them the appearance of the *Guardians of the Quarters* perpetually coming in order to see the Jina.'[66] The simile of the gods approaching the (enlightened) Jina applied to these statues in a temple complex implies the comparison between the temple and the *samavasaraṇa*, where the gods first honour the newly enlightened Jina.

The presence of the elephants in the pavilion housing the statues at the back of the temple has given it its name, *hastiśālā*.[67] Tejaḥpāla's *hastiśālā* was not a new development in Jain temple architecture, but took its inspiration from the earlier *hastiśālā* in front of Vimala's Mt Abu temple. That structure, which was not part of the original temple program, was built in stages by some of Vimala's descendants between 1147 and 1181, long before Tejaḥpāla's temple was built. Within it are large images of Vimala on horseback and ten elephants, which were once mounted by members of Vimala's family: the seven elephants at the front were erected by Pṛthvīdeva in 1147–48, and I presume that the figure of Vimala on horseback was also installed at this time; the three elephants at the rear were set up by Dhanapāla in 1180–81.[68] In the midst of these images is a sparsely adorned *samavasaraṇa,* erected in 1156 by a minister named Dhādhuka.[69] Dhādhuka's decision to place the *samavasaraṇa* in the middle of the *hastiśālā* suggests that he at least recognized a connection between the *samavasaraṇa* and the portrait statues and the Jain temple. I believe that Tejaḥpāla later exploited this connection and recognized the significance of the ten elephants in the Vimalavasa-hī *hastiśālā* when he had the *hastiśālā* added to his Mt Abu temple.

In textual descriptions of it, the *samavasaraṇa* is a circular or square pavilion consisting of three terraced ramparts each with four gates at the cardinal points. At the top, four lion-thrones face the gates and are shaded by a mythical tree. Descriptions of the *samavasaraṇa* occur in several texts, but it did not become an important subject of iconography until the later medieval period. Hemacandra's *Triśaṣṭiśalākāpuruṣacarita* contains a long description of Ādinātha's *samavasaraṇa* and abbreviated accounts of those for the other twenty-three Jinas. Although the *Samavasaraṇastavana* agrees with Hemacandra's description on most points, it does provide some interesting variations on the details.[70]

The stories of the construction of the *samavasaraṇa* follow a basic pattern from the Jina's enlightenment to his sermon. When the Jina attains omniscience, the gods' thrones shake and they descend to earth. Various gods prepare the ground for the pavilion in the way a site is prepared for the construction of a temple. Then the structure itself is erected, and the *Samavasaraṇastavana* says, '[I] if there be a god possessed of high supernatural powers, that is, Indra, he alone does all this; if not, the other gods may or may not do it.'[71] Hemacandra says that the *vyantaras*[72] 'are the functionaries in the case of all *samavasaraṇas*.'[73] When the Jina enters the pavilion and sits on the eastern throne, the gods make three images of him for the other three thrones. Hence, the *samavasaraṇa* represents in a sense the first Jain temple and the first occasion upon which the Jina is represented in image form; in this sense the gods, and sometimes Indra in particular, are the paradigm of Jain temple patronage.

Since Indra is reckoned among the *lokapālas* in pan-Indic mythology and since a set of *lokapālas* is assigned to each of the Indras of the different heavens in Jain cosmology,[74] we might suppose that the ten Mt Abu portrait statues were meant to equate the patron and his family with some Jain heavenly host led by Indra. The temple patron is exceptional among the faithful; the wherewithal to have a temple constructed demonstrates that he is very meritorious and that merit has provided him with the wealth to undertake such an extraordinary act of piety. The temple patron stands among the rest of the faithful virtually (if not literally) as Indra, the paradigm of patronage and devotion. This identity is not exclusively Jain; the architectural manual *Aparājitapṛcchā* says that in the construction of Hindu temples, the *ācārya* is Brahmā, the architect is Viṣṇu, and the patron (*yajamāna*) is Śakra or Indra.[76]

Some of the elements of the completed *samavasaraṇa* found in the texts are interesting as they remind us of the portraits styled as *lokapālas*. As just described, the *samavasaraṇa* consists of three terraced concentric ramparts rising to thrones upon which the Jina and his images sit. Each rampart has a gate at each of the four cardinal points and each gate is guarded by a pair of deities. The *Samavasaraṇastavana* says that the gates of the top rampart are each guarded by a pair of gods from one of the four major classifications of gods in the Jain pantheon, the Suras (or Vaimāṇikas), Vāṇa-Vyantaras, Jyotiṣkas, and Bhavanapatis for a total of eight.[76] These pairs have the proper names Soma, Yama, Varuṇa, and Dhanada (which is another name for Kubera); in one list or another these four gods are Guardians of the Quarters. These four pairs of guardians put us in mind of the four pairs of portraits that Vastupāla placed upon the four peaks of Mt Girnar. They might also remind us of the elephant-mounted portraits at Mt Abu, despite their number of ten.

Hemacandra says that at the gates of the first or uppermost rampart are pairs of Vaimāṇikas, Vyantaras, Bhavanapatis, and Jyotiṣkas gods standing as door-guardians (*dvārapālas*) and adds that the Jyotiṣkas[77] look like 'the sun and the moon, at evening time.'[78] I mention this because in Merutuṅga's account of the birth of Vastupāla and

Tejaḥpāla, the sun and the moon descended into the womb of Kumāradevī 'and were conceived in her, as the two ministers, named Vastupāla and Tejaḥpāla, like two chiefs of the Jyotiṣka gods.'[79] The identification of Vastupāla and Tejaḥpāla with the sun and the moon, chiefs of the Jyotiṣka gods, which are known to be guardians of the *samavasaraṇa,* provides us with one more allusion to the *samavasaraṇa* and divinity in the statues.

Jinaharṣa tells us about the statues within Vastupāla's Mt Girnar Neminātha temple that present Vastupāla, Tejaḥpāla, and their father and grandfather as the door-guardians of the temple/*samvasaraṇa* in a very obvious way. According to the *Vastupālacarita,* on the right and left sides of the *trikamaṇḍapa,* Vastupāla placed images of his father and grandfather mounted on horses;[80] he placed images of his father and grandfather in the *gūḍhamaṇḍapa;*[81] and on the right and left sides of the door to the *garbhagṛha,* he placed images of himself and Tejaḥpāla mounted on elephants.[82] The principal structure of Vastupāla's Mt Girnar temple, like the typical medieval Jain temple, consists of exactly these three galleries. Thus, the Mt Girnar temple, with portraits on either side of the entrance to each of its aligned galleries, represents both horizontally and from the perspective of the gates of a single cardinal point what the *samavasaraṇa* represents in three tiers and with gates at all four cardinal points.[83]

By evoking the idea of the *samavasaraṇa* for their temples, Vastupāla and Tejaḥpāla presented themselves as exceptional patrons: they were not merely pious laymen but veritable gods (Merutuṅga claims without hesitation that the brothers were Jyotiṣka gods incarnate). At the same time, they claimed that they were paragons of devotion just as the gods were. The stories about the *samavasaraṇa* provide an archetype for temple patronage and for temple worship. The Jina's enlightenment is also one of the five auspicious moments in the career of the Jina. When the Jina reaches each moment, as in the case of his enlightenment, the gods' thrones shake and they descend to earth to worship him. At the birth of the Jina, the gods take the baby Jina-to-be to Mt Meru for his bathing ceremony. The ritual re-enactment of the Five Auspicious Moments is an important aspect of Jain temple devotions. In it, as Lawrence A. Babb says,

> those who worship the Tīrthankars are, paradigmatically, the deities ... When human beings engage in acts of worship, they take on the roles of gods and goddesses. Moreover, Indra and Indrāṇīs, the kings and

queens of the gods, are the principal figures emulated by human worshippers. In many important *pūjās* worshippers wear tinsel crowns to symbolize this identity.[84]

Vastupāla evoked this very homology between the gods (especially Indra) and devotees, in a way entirely unique to the medieval Jain temple, through something called the Indramaṇḍapa. This temple hall is unknown to Sanskrit architectural manuals and so we cannot be certain what its purpose was.[85] Its name hints that it might have been connected to the ritual of the Five Auspicious Moments, bearing Babb's description of that ritual in mind; Jinaprabha, with reference to the Mt Girnar Indramaṇḍapa, says, '[people] who enter the Indramaṇḍapa containing the image of the Lord of Jinas to perform the ablutions of Blessed Nemi appear like the Indras.'[86]

Vastupāla also invoked this greater mythological context at Mt Girnar, for as I have said, the Sammetaśikhara and Aṣṭāpada shrines on either side of the main temple contain exceptionally large images of the *samavasaraṇa* and Mt Meru respectively; in myth, these are sites at which the gods led by Indra honoured the Jina's enlightenment and birth. Additionally, according to Jinahara, Vastupāla placed statues of his ancestors in the Sammeta shrine, which contains the *samavasaraṇa*, and statues of his mother and sisters(s) in the Aṣṭāpada shrine, which contains the image of Mt Meru.[87] Vastupāla's and Tejaḥpāla's comparison of themselves and their family to the gods may not have been original in Jain ritual life, but the expression of it, through the carefully contrived installation of portraits, certainly was.

To conclude this part of my discussion, I wish to note how Vastupāla invoked the *samavasaraṇa* in certain aspects of his temple patronage and compared himself and his family not to the gods who built it, but to familiar characters from the lives of the Jinas. Vastupāla compared himself to Kṛṣṇa, known among the Jains as the kinsman of Neminātha and important to the mythology of Mt Girnar, and to Bharata, son of Ādinātha and the first (human) temple-builder.

Vastupāla's patronage at Mt Girnar clearly connects him to Kṛṣṇa and the story of Neminātha. According to one of Jinaprabha's hymns on Mt Girnar, Kṛṣṇa first honoured with images the three auspicious moments in Nemi's life, which occurred on the mountain, and he also built an Ambikā temple there.[88] Vastupāla also built an Ambikā temple on Mt Girnar,[89] but more importantly, he built his Mt Girnar temple as 'the Temple of the Three Auspicious Moments' (*kalyāṇatrayamandira*) in which worship was thought to produce miracles (*camatkāritabhavya[kṛt]*).[90] Furthermore, the *Triśaṣṭiśalākāpuruṣacarita* version of the story of Neminātha says that Kṛṣṇa approaches Neminātha's *samavasaraṇa* on an elephant along with his whole family, and upon arriving he dismounts and takes his place inside with the assembly that consists of gods and men.[91] Vastupāla may have been attempting to evoke this very episode by the statues of himself and family mounted on elephants at Mt Girnar.

Still another association is evoked at Dabhoi where Vastupāla is said to have erected an image of his mother Kumāradevī mounted on an elephant in the gate-house (*balānaka*) of the Pārśvanātha temple he built, *appearing like the mother of Ādinātha* with a silver garland in her hand.[92] Vastupāla erected another image of his mother mounted on an elephant in a temple of Marudevī, the mother of Ādinātha, behind his Mt Girnar temple.[93] In Hemacandra's version of the story of Ādinātha, Marudevī proceeds on an elephant to her son's *samavasaraṇa* with Bharata, the son of Ādinātha, after learning of Ādinātha's enlightenment. When she sees her son, she is immediately enlightened herself and then promptly dies. Marudevī is a popular subject of iconography, being portrayed on an elephant at sites like Mt Śatruñjaya and Ranakpur. Vastupāla's intent was no doubt to honour his mother and hold her up as a paragon in the community.

I cannot help but recall the theory that Kumāradevī was a remarried widow and that this was a point of serious friction within the Prāgvāṭa caste; the comparison of Vastupāla's mother to a madona-like figure from Jain mythology was perhaps an attempt to mask or offset the social stigma that was attached to Kumāradevī's widowhood. The comparison could also imply a comparison between Vastupāla and Bharata, the first temple-builder. Upon Ādinātha's fast unto death on Mt Aṣṭāpada, Bharata builds the first Jain temple there.[94] In it he places images of his father and the monks who died with him, including Bharata's own ninety-nine brothers. He also includes an image of himself as a worshipper.[95] Medieval Jain portraiture could be connected to this reference as could the numerous portrait statues attributed to Vastupāla and Tejaḥpāla. I know of no other portrait statues which, in any way, evoke this mythological connection as closely as do these portraits by Vastupāla.

Conclusion

Vastupāla and Tejaḥpāla are remembered as exceptional Jain patrons and politicians. The construction of numerous religious edifices is attributed to them and several accounts probably exaggerate the extent of their patronage. Therefore, the number of portrait statues attributed to them might also be exaggerated. However, even the scant remains of their patronage, particularly the Mt Abu and Mt Girnar temples, show that they were patrons on par with medieval kings. Similarly, the Mt Abu statues are exceptional among medieval Jain portraits, for almost nowhere else do we find such large portrait images, and the images of individuals mounted on elephants are almost without precedent. Therefore, it is possible that many of the statues attributed to the brothers in texts did in fact exist. Certainly, the fact that authors recorded the details I have discussed shows that in some way, at least, the brothers succeeded in creating for themselves unique and exalted identities through the idea of the portrait statues.

My discussion has not been exhaustive, for I have left out a few stray references to portrait statues associated with Vastupāla and Tejaḥpāla. I have focused on the most unusual images and attempted to show some of the unique allusions and circumstances that lie behind them. I have considered portrait statues that reflect the roles of the two men as senior ministers in the changing Caulukya-Vaghela sovereignty, and I have thoroughly explored the Jain contexts for many of the images. I am not suggesting that any statue or group of statues evoked any single meaning; I believe that the images were, for the most part, laden with multiple meanings in order to evoke in the mind of any viewer at least one extraordinary comparison of the subjects with the gods or mythological archetypes. Each of these ideas shows the attempt by Vastupāla and Tejaḥpāla to present themselves as the most exceptional of donors in one way or another.

End Notes

Some of the research resulting in this essay was conducted in India with the support of a doctoral fellowship from the Shastri Indo-Canadian Institute 1995–96.

1 See Rājaśekhara, *Prabandhakośa,* Singhi Jaina Series 6, ed. Jina Vijaya

(Śāntiniketan: The Adhiṣṭhātā-Siṅghī Jaina Jñānapīṭha, 1935), section 156 for a list of Jain and Hindu donations by Vastupāla and Tejaḥpāla. According to this list the brothers also patronized mosques for their Muslim subjects, but I do not believe that any archaeological evidence verifies this.

2 See the sources cited in Bhogilal J. Sandesara, *Literary Circle of Mahāmātya Vastupāla and Its Contribution to Sanskrit Literature* (Bombay: Bharatiya Vidhya Bhavan, 1953).

3 See P. Granoff's essay in P. Granoff and Koichi Shinohara, *Speaking of Monks* (Oakville, ON: Mosaic Press, 1992).

4 Rājaśekhara, *Prabandhakośa*, 101.

5 See Sandesera, *Literary Circle*, 26–27, and the sources cited there.

6 Jinavijaya Muni, ed., *Purātanaprabandhasaṃgraha* 34, Singhi Jaina Series 2 (Śāntiniketan: The Adhiṣṭātā-Siṅghī Jaina Jñānapīṭha, 1936).

7 Although the temple is commonly known by this designation, the temple *praśastis* are clear that Tejaḥpāla had the temple built for the merit of his wife Anupamādevī and his son Lūṇasiṃha or Lāvaṇyasiṃha. See *Arbudācalapradakṣiṇā Jaina Lekha Saṃdoha*, ed. Muni Jayantavijayajī (Bhavnagar: n.p., V.S. 2005 [1948–49]), inscriptions 250–51 (hereafter cited as *Abu II*). One of the inscriptions for an addition to the temple by Tejaḥpāla refers to the temple as the 'Lūṇavasahikā' (*Abu II*, 260). Since the temple was built for the merit of Lūṇasiṃha (as well as Anupamādevī) the temple's proper name might refer, not to the minister's dead brother Lūṇiga, but actually to his son, despite the fact that all later accounts of the building of the temple say that it was built in the name of Lūṇiga.

8 *Abu II*, 250 and following.

9 Narendraprabhasūri, *Vastupālapraśasti*, in Muni Śrī Puṇyavijaya Sūri, ed., *Sukṛtakīrtikallolinyādi Vastupālapraśastisaṃgraha*, Singhi Jaina Series 5 (Bombay: Bharatiya Vidya Bhavan, 1961), 24–29.

10 *Abu II*, 256. I must note that later sources report that Tejaḥpāla had constructed on Mt Girnar a temple to Pārśvanātha, which he named the Aśvarājavihāra after his father, and a water tank named the Kumārasāra after his mother. See Jinaprabhasūri, *Vividhatīrthakalpa*, trans. John Cort, in The Clever Adulteress, ed. P. Granoff (Oakville, ON: Mosaic Press, 1990), 257; Merutuṅga, *The Prabandhacintāmaṇi or Wishing-Stone of Narratives*, trans. C.H. Tawney (Delhi: Indian Book Gallery, 1987), 159.

11 This is one of the rare references I have found to any donation by the ancestors of Vastupāla and Tejaḥpāla, but there is no other evidence corroborating it. Incidentally, Vyāgrapallī or Vāghelā (10 miles

southwest of Patan in Gujarat) is said to have been a village granted to Ārṇorāja Vāghelā by Kumārapāla Caulukya, although all literary accounts imply that Dhavalakka or Dholka (southwest of Ahmedabad) was the Vāghelā capital at least from the time of Lavaṇaprasāda). See Sandesera, *Literary Circle*, 28.

12 These were accompanied by portraits of those beneficiaries and are discussed below; this fact makes these gifts no ordinary merit transfers. There are other stray references to donations by Vastupāla for the merit of the ancestors. See, for example, Jinaharṣa, *Vastupālacarita*, ed. Muni Kirtivijaya (Ahmedabad: n.p., 1941), VI. 702 (hereafter cited as *VC*). However, I still think that there are just not as many as we would expect.

13 These are discussed in detail below.

14 See Sandesera, *Literary Circle*, 29–32.

15 Ibid., 28. Jain accounts of the succession of Kumārapāla make it clear that his sovereignty was unusual also for he was not the direct heir to his predecessor Jayasiṃha Siddharāja, but came from a collateral lineage. See A.K. Majumdar, *Chaulukyas of Gujarat* (Bombay: Bharatiya Vidya Bhavan, 1956), chap. 7.

16 The work in question, the *Kīrtikaumudī* of Someśvara, was written about 1232 and is a panegyric of Vastupāla. See Sandesera, *Literary Circle*, 44–47.

17 Someśvara, *Kīrtikaumudī*, Singhi Jaina Series 32, ed. Śrī Puṇyavijayajī (Bombay: Bharatiya Vidya Bhavan, 1961), II.83–115.

18 Sandesera, *Literary Circle*, 77–78.

19 See Majumdar, *Chaulukyas of Gujarat*, 163–64, and sources cited there.

20 See ibid., 164, and sources cited there.

21 See ibid., 175–78, and Sandesera, *Literary Circle*, 32, and the sources cited there.

22 *Epigraphia Indica* VII, 215, v. 28.

23 James Burgess, *Revised Lists of Antiquarian Remains in the Bombay Presidency*, Archaeological Survey of India Reports, New Imperial Series 16, rev. Henry Cousens (Bombay: Government Central Press, 1897), 328.

24 See Jan Gonda, *Ancient Indian Kingship from the Religious Point of View* (Leiden: E.J. Brill, 1969), 'The Indra Festival According to the Atharvavedins,' 'A Note on Indra in Purāṇic Literature,' 'The Sacred Character of Indian Kingship,' in *Selected Studies* IV (Leiden: E.J. Brill, 1975), and the primary sources cited in those works.

25 *Abu II*, 250, v. 63; *Epigraphia Indica* VIII, 218; see also *VC* VIII, 229.

26 Translated from *mūlarājādibhūpālamūrttibhiḥ sphuritodayam, nagarāḥ parito vapramabhraṃliham* ... (III.364).

27 Someśvara's *Kīrtikaumudī* and Arisiṃha's *Sukṛtasaṃkīrtana* both give the

number of kings up to Bhīma II as ten, and this number is confirmed by inscriptions. I note that Someśvara tells us in his *Surathotsava* that his own ancestors, who he says served as *purohitas* to the Caulukyan kings, also numbered ten. See Sandesera, *Literary Circle*, 44.

28 See Majumdar, *Chaulukyas of Gujarat*, chap. 9.

29 Ibid.

30 V. 48.

31 Many of Vastupāla's biographies discuss this event in detail and it is the subject of the one act military drama the *Śaṅkhaparābhava*, ed. B.J. Sandesera (Baroda: The Oriental Institute, 1965).

32 See Sandesera, *Literary Circle*, 29–30.

33 Merutuṅga, *Prabandhacintāmaṇi*, trans. Tawney, 163; Narendraprabhasūri, *Vastupālapraśasti*, in Puṇyavijaya, ed., *Sukṛtakīrtikallolinī*, v. 61. There is no archaeological evidence for the existence of this temple.

34 See S. Settar and Günther-Dietz Sontheimer, eds., *Memorial Stones* (Dharwad: Institute of Indian Art History, 1982).

35 The use of portraiture to mark the borders of Indian kingdoms appears to have a long history; Giovanni Verardi speculates that the images of the Sātavahana kings which once adorned the Nāṇaghāṭ cave in Maharashtra (c. first century AD) marked the frontier of the Sātavāhana domains. Giovanni Verardi, with a note by Alessandro Grossato, 'The Kuṣāṇa Emperors as Cakravartins Dynastic Art and Cults in India and Central Asia: History of a Theory, Clarifications and Refutations,' *East and West* 33 (1983), 249–50.

36 Majumdar, *Chaulukyas of Gujarat*, 178.

37 Narendraprabhasūri, *Vastupālapraśasti*, in Puṇyavijaya, ed., *Sukṛtakīrtikallolinī*, v. 48; *VC* III.372.

38 Narendraprabhasūri, *Vastupālapraśasti*, in Puṇyavijaya, ed., *Sukṛtakīrtikallolinī*, v. 81.

39 Arisiṃha, *Sukṛtasaṃīkrtana*, XI.18. Someśvara, writing at the same time, says they were mounted on horses (Someśvara, *Kīrtikaumudī*, IX.35).

40 Merutuṅga, *Prabandhacintāmaṇi*, trans. Tawney, 159.

41 *VC* VI.638-640.

42 With reference to the Vāghelā portraits that Vastupāla is said to have erected at Dabhoi, this statement appears to contradict my explanation of the Caulukyan portraits in the Dabhoi rampart, which I have said demonstrate that the brothers could not claim Dabhoi for the Vāghelās. However, I think that the portraits of the Vāghelā king and queen, within a Jain temple, did not immediately or directly make a strong claim to paramount sovereignty over Dabhoi by the Vāghelās in the way

that the Caulukyan portraits in the very public rampart surrounding the entire town did.

43 Translated from Narendraprabhasūri, *Vastupālapraśasti*, in Puṇyavijaya, ed., *Sukṛtakīrtikallolī*, v. 89–92:

tadīye śikhare nemiṃ caṇḍapaśreyase ca yaḥ /
mūrtiṃ ramyāṃ tadīyāṃ ca malladevasya ca vyadhāt //
caṇḍaprasādapuṇyaṃ varddhayituṃ yo 'valokanāśikhare /
sthāpitavān nemijinaṃ tanmūrtiṃ svasya mūrtiṃ ca //
pradyumnaśikhare somaśreyase neminaṃ jinam /
somamūrtiṃ tathā tejaḥpālamūrtiṃ ca yo 'tanot //
yaḥ śāmbaśikhare nemijinendraṃ śreyase pituḥ
... tanmūrtiṃ ca kārayāmāsa bhaktitaḥ //

In the non-Jain (Hindu) topography of Mt Girnar these peaks are called Ambikā, Gorakhnāth, Kālikā Mātā, and Dattātreya. See Jinaprabhasūri, *Vividhatīrthakalpa*, trans. Cort, in *Clever Adulteress*, ed. Granoff, 256–90, and G. Bühler, introduction to the *Sukṛtasaṃkīrtana*, by Arisiṃha, 79.

44 Certainly this was the intent behind the image of the Jain monk Guṇasena, which was donated by a disciple for the subject's merit, Acharya Kanchansagarsuri, *Shri Shatrunjay Giriraj Darshan in Sculptures and Architecture*, Aagamoddharak Granthamala 59 (Kapadwanj: Aagamoddharak Granthamala, 1982), insc. 152; as well as the image of King Pṛthvīdeva which was donated by his wife for the king's increased merit, S.P. Tewari, 'No. 7–National Museum Inscription of Kelachchadevī V.S. 1239,' *Epigraphia Indica* 41 (1975–6), 58–60. How a portrait could produce merit for its subject is explained by an inscription referring to the portrait of the Cāhamāna prince Meghanāda, which says that the prince worshipped Śiva by his portrait for the increase of his own lifespan, progeny, fortune, and so on. Ram Sharma, 'No. 27–Menal Inscription of the Chahamana Prince Meghanada, Vikrama 1312,' *Epigraphia Indica* 37, pt. iv (October 1967), v. 3.

45 The *kṣetrapālas* are generic protectors of place.

46 Compare the following to *Vastupālapraśasti* 92 cited above: / *tanmūrttiṃ mātṛmūrttiṃ ca kārayāmsa bhaktitaḥ* / / VC VI.729. Since Jinaharṣa changes the syntax of Narendraprabha's verse in supplying the otherwise missing information, I believe that he, too, had before him a text with a lacuna in it and then guessed that the other portrait represented Vastupāla's mother.

47 Jinaprabhasūri, *Vividhatīrthakalpa*, trans. Cort, in *Clever Adulteress*, ed. Granoff, 251–52.

48 Ibid., 254.

49 Merutuṅga, *Prabandhacintāmaṇi*, trans. Tawney, 200–201.

50 The term *Kṣetrapati* is, of course, synonymous with *kṣetrapāla*. I note that the names of two of the sons of Dhāra are the same as two of the Yādavas in Jinaprabha's account. Thus it may very well be that both stories confound some common source or one was the source for the other. For my purposes this is not really important, as I am only interested in the claim that certain personalities are believed to have been reborn as Gods of Place at Mt Girnar.

51 'A stone inscription of Ekalingaji near Udeypore in Meywar. Dated Saṃvat 1545,' in *A Collection of Prakrit and Sanskrit Inscriptions* v. 70 (Bhavnagar: Bhavnagar Archaeological Department n.d.).

52 The predecessor of Kumārapāla who reigned c. 1100–50.

53 Merutuṅga, *Prabandhacintāmaṇi*, trans. Tawney, 90.

54 I must add the unique case of Jaymal, and Pata, Hindu warriors of Chittor, who died in a confrontation with the Mughal Emperor Akbar. Akbar was so impressed with the courage of these two men that he placed images of them mounted on elephants at the main gate of his fort at Agra. Later Shah Jahan moved the images to the fort at Delhi, where Francis Bernier saw them sometime in the middle of the seventeenth century. Bernier writes 'These two large elephants, mounted by the two heroes, have an air of grandeur, and inspire me with an awe and respect which I cannot describe.' See Muniraj Vidyavijayaji, *A Monk and a Monarch*, Shree Vijayadharmasuri, Jain Book Series 59 (n.p., 1944), 20–21. Nowhere is it claimed that these images served as protectors of the Mughal forts; however, as unusual a Muslim emperor as Akbar was, I cannot believe that he would take the extraordinary step of erecting anthropomorphic images out of mere tribute to those soldiers, or even from some aesthetic sense, especially in light of the stronger cases I have presented where such images were erected as Protectors of Place. See also P. Granoff, 'Worship as Commemoration: Pilgrimage, Death and Dying in Medieval Jainism,' *Bulletin d'études Indiennes* 10 (1992), 191–92, for the very interesting story of the tigress who starved herself to death at the gate to Śatruñjaya and was honoured by the people with a stone image to the right of the gateway.

55 For that matter, other sites, particularly Śatruñjaya, have been disputed even up to the present. A large portion of the seventeenth century *Bhānucandragaṇicarita* by Siddhicandra, Singhi Jain Series 15, ed. Mohanalal Dalichand Desai (Ahmedabad: The Sañchālaka-Siṅghī Jaina Granthamālā, 1941), is taken up with the dispute over Śatruñjaya

between the two Śvetāmbara monastic lineages, the Kharataragaccha and the Tapāgaccha.

56 Jinaprabhasūri, *Vividhatīrthakalpa*, chap. 3, v. 9, trans. Cort, in *Clever Adulteress*, ed. Granoff, 253.

57 Ibid.

58 See M.A. Dhaky, 'The Chronology of the Solanki Temples of Gujarat,' *Journal of the Madhya Pradesh Itihasa Parishad* 3 (1961), 67; James Fergusson, *History of Indian and Eastern Architecture* 1 (1876; reprint, Delhi: Munshiram Manoharlal, 1967), 33; Jinaprabhasūri, *Vividhatīrthakalpa*, chap. 5, trans. Cort, in *Clever Adulteress*, ed. Granoff, 257.

59 Jinaprabhasūri, Vividhatīrthakalpa, chap. 5, trans. Cort, in *Clever Adulteress*, ed. Granoff, 257. Jinaharṣa calls it 'the temple of the Lord of Śatruñjaya' (*Śatruñjayapateścaityam*), *VC* VI.699.

60 See Puṇyavijaya, ed., *Sukṛtakīrtikallolinī*, chap. 9.

61 Muni Shrī Jayantavijayaji, *Holy Abu*, trans. U.P. Shah (Bhavnagar: Shri Yashovijaya Jaina Granthamālā, 1954), 126.

62 Translated from: *tatrāmbikāvalokanaśambapradyumnasanubhiḥ /saha raivatatīrthendorasau caityamasūtrayat / / VC* VI.637. Such 'delocalization' of sacred space, as in the examples I have described, is not unique in Jainisṃ. Almost every Jain temple complex in Western India contains some representations of other famous pilgrimage places. The great Ranakpur Jain temple in Rajasthan contains a fifteenth century stone plaque schematically illustrating Śatruñjaya and Mt Girnar. In his description of the plaque, U.P Shah says that 'such representations, technically called *uddhāra* or *avatāra*, have been popular in Western India from c. fourteenth century onwards. The practice could have started earlier but no earlier representations in stone or paintings are yet discovered. Such representations on cloth are preserved in the Calico Museum, Ahmedabad, and in the National Museum, New Delhi, etc. Such modern Representations on walls of maṇḍapas of Jaina temples are quite common in Gujarat.' U.P. Shah, *Jaina-Rūpa-Maṇḍana* (New Delhi: Abhinav Publications, 1987), 340, and fig. 186. However, the interconnection of sites and their representations, such as associated with Vastupāla, is unprecedented as far as I know.

63 *Abu II*, 251; *Epigraphia Indica* VIII, 219–22.

64 U.P. Shah, 'A Forgotten Chapter in the History of Śvetāmbara Jaina Church or A Documentary Epigraph from the Mount Śatruñjaya,' *Journal of the Asiatic Society Bombay* 30 (1955), 100–13.

65 I note that one of Jinaprabha's hymns to Mt Aṣṭāpada says that Bharata, the son of Ādinātha, when he built the first Jain temple also had set up

'protector-men made of iron' (*lohajaṃtamayā ārakkhagapurisā*) to keep pilgrims from committing the religious offense called *āśātanā*. See Jinaprabhasūri, *Vividhatīrthakalpa*, 92, trans. Cort, in *Clever Adulteress*, ed. Granoff, 271. Sandesera and Thakur define *āśātanā* as 'insult or contempt (of a religious teacher or the scriptures or an image).' See Bhogilal J. Sandesara and J.P. Thakur, *Lexicographical Studies in 'Jaina Sanskrit,' The M.S. University Oriental Series* 5 (1962), 45, with reference to its occurrence in the *Prabandhakośa*. P. Granoff tells me (personal communication) that it refers to destroying or pillaging temples, defacing images and the like, exactly the kinds of things from which the Rudramahālaya was to be protected by the portraits.

66 *Abu II*, 250, v. 63; *Epigraphia Indica* VIII, p. 218; also, *VC* VIII.229.

67 Legend says that Vastupāla invited his friend Yaśovīra, a minister of a neighbouring kingdom, to describe the virtues and the faults of the Lūṇigavasahī. With respect to the portraits, Yaśovīra said that 'raising the (images of) the ancestors behind the Jina destroys the fortune of their descendants,' and that 'raising the images of Jain monks in an out of the way place renders fruitless the darśana received in the temple by you [that is, Vastupāla or Tejaḥpāla].' See Rājaśekhara, *Prabandhakośa*, 124, and *Purātanaprabandhasamgraha*, 53 and notes for variations on these criticisms.

68 The figures mounted on Pṛthvīdeva's elephants represented Nīnā, Vimala's chief ancestor; Lahara; Vīra, 'in the line of Lahara'; Neḍha, chief minister to Bhīma I of the Caulukya dynasty, son of Vīra, and brother of Vimala; Dhavala, son of Neḍha; Ānanda, son of Dhavala; and Pṛthvīdeva; son of Ānanda. The figures on Dhanapāla s elephants represented Jagadeva, elder son of Pṛthvīdeva; Dhanapāla, younger son of Pṛthvīdeva, and some unknown subject. See Jayantavijayaji, *Holy Abu*, 81, and *Abu II*, 233 for the labels on the elephants. It is notable that the lineage represented in the *hastiśālā* is collateral to Vimala's; another set of portraits, in cell 10 within the Vimalavasahī, represents another collateral line which branches off from Dhavala's brother Lāliga and was erected by his grandsons Hemaratha and Daśaratha who undertook renovations to the temple around the time that Pṛthvīdeva erected the *hastiśālā*. See Jayantavijayaji, *Holy Abu*, 42, and *Abu II*, 51 for an inscription concerning that renovation. These tandem renovation efforts may very well have been carried out peacefully, but at the same time I wonder if there was not a degree of rivalry in them; perhaps such a rivalry revolved around the issue of proprietorship of the temple.
Few of the figures that once adorned the elephants remain today, and

those that do are four-armed. U.P. Shah says that the figures must have been given this feature in order for them to carry their objects of worship. I find it hard to believe, however, that the sculptor, at the behest of even his patron, would resort to this device, usually reserved for the gods, for so mundane a purpose. Rather, I have to believe that the images were meant to appear as gods. See Jayantavijayaji, *Holy Abu,* 80n.

69 *Abu II,* 229.

70 D.R. Bhandarkar, 'Jaina Iconography,' *Indian Antiquary* 40 (May–June 1911), 125–30; 153–61 presents the *Samavasaraṇastavana* and *Triśaṣṭiśalākāpuruṣacarita* accounts side by side.

71 Ibid., 159.

72 The *vyantaras* and female *vyantarīs* are among the lowest gods in the Jain pantheon. Many Jain stories are told of humans who are reborn among this class of deities due to their great merit. Vastupāla and Tejaḥpāla had a special relationship with particular *vyantarīs* according to later stories about them. In particular, they owed much of their fortune to a former princess of Kanyākubja who died fleeing the Muslims and was reborn as a goddess. See Granoff, 'Worship as Commemoration,' 181–202, and sources cited there.

73 Hemacandra, *Triśaṣṭiśalākāpuruṣacarita,* 6 vols., Gaekwad's Oriental Series 51, 77, 108, 125, 139, 140, trans. Helen Moore Johnson (Baroda: Oriental Institute, 1931–62), I, 192.

74 Shah, *Jaina-Rupa-Maṇḍana,* 63.

75 Bhuvanadeva, *Aparājitapṛcchā,* Gaekwad's Oriental Series 115, ed. A. Mankad (Baroda: The Oriental Institute, 1950), 51.5.

76 Bhandarkar, 'Jaina Iconography,' 158.

77 The Jyotiṣka gods are of five classes: suns, moons, planets, asterisms, and stars. See Shah, *Jaina-Rupa-Maṇḍana,* 59.

78 Ibid.

79 Merutuṅga, *Prabandhacintāmaṇi,* trans. Tawney, 155–6.

80 *VC* VI.713.

81 M.A. Dhaky, 'The Western Indian Jaina Temple,' in *Aspects of Jaina Art and Architecture,* ed. U.P. Shah and M.A. Dhaky (Ahmedabad: L.D. Institute of Indology, 1975), 341.

82 *VC* VI.705. If we presume that these images, closest to the Jina, represent the guardians of the upper most rampart of the *samavasaraṇa,* then I must note that Merutuṅga s comparison of the brothers with the Jyotiṣka gods does not accord with Hemacandra's account of the *samavasaraṇa,* for he says that the Bhavanapatis guard the uppermost rampart. See

Ann Wood Norton, 'The Jaina Samavasaraṇa' (PhD diss., Harvard University, 1981), 34, citing Hemacandra, *Triśaṣṭiśalākāpuruṣacarita*, trans. Johnson, II, 93–94.

83 A less complete use of portraits to evoke the *samavasaraṇa* appears in *VC* VI.654, which says that Vastupāla placed images of his older brothers Lūṇiga and Malladeva on either side of the entrance to the Ādinātha temple at Śatruñjaya.

84 Lawrence A. Babb, *Absent Lord: Ascetics and Kings in a Jain Ritual Culture* (Berkeley: University of California Press, 1996), 77–79.

85 See Dhaky, 'The Western Indian Jaina Temple,' 354, for some speculation about it.

86 John Cort in his translation of the passage misses the fact that the verse refers to the Indramaṇḍapa calling it only 'the best of pavilions.' Jinaprabhasūri, *Vividhatīrthakalpa*, chap. 3, v. 10, trans. Cort, in *Clever Adulteress*, ed. Granoff, 253.

87 *VC* VI.706-7.

88 Jinaprabhasūri, *Vividhatīrthakalpa*, chap. 2, trans. Cort, in *Clever Adulteress*, ed. Granoff, 251–53.

89 *VC* VI.700ff.

90 Jinaprabhasūri, *Vividhatīrthakalpa*, chap. 3, trans. Cort, in *Clever Adulteress*, ed. Granoff, 253. Chapter 5 attributes the '*kallāṇattayaceia*' to Tejaḥpāla. Ibid., 257.

91 Hemacandra, *Triśaṣṭiśalākāpuruṣacarita*, trans. Johnson, V, 265–60.

92 *VC* III.369.

93 *VC* VI.710.

94 See Granoff, 'Worship as Commemoration,' 189–91, for sources reporting this story.

95 This is one of the few references to plastic portraiture in Jain mythology, excluding Jain mythico-historical literature such as *Vastupālacarita*, for example, of which I have made extensive use here.

12

Saints and Sacred Places in Saurashtra and Kutch: The Cases of the Naklaṃki Cult and the Jakhs

FRANÇOISE MALLISON

Saurashtra is the peninsula adjoining the Arabian Sea and forming the western province of Gujarat State. It is also called Kathiawad (Kāṭhiyāvāḍa), after the tribe of the *Kāṭhī,* peasant gentry who assimilated to the Rajputs and immigrated from Sind into the peninsula during the fourteenth and fifteenth centuries. Repeated waves of immigration have made Saurashtra different from the rest of the country not only in its features of physical and human geography but also in its socio-historic background. It is often compared with Rajasthan because of the pattern of its Rajput or pseudo-Rajput feudalism, but its social spectrum is much more complex and diversified.[1]

Another distinctive feature of Saurashtra is the wealth and the originality of its religious traditions. It provides sanctuaries that are known throughout India – Dwarka, Jain holy places like Girnar and Palitana, and Somnath and Nageśvar, two of the twelve jyotirlings (*jyotirliṅga*). The *Purāṇas* speak eloquently about the antiquity of this province and its place in classical Hinduism. Much less well known is its extraordinary wealth of holy men and women, and local cults, and its dense network of small popular sanctuaries covering the country. These smaller sanctuaries all belong to what the local authors call *loka-dharma*, popular religion.

Loka-dharma and Sant-*vāṇī* in Saurashtra

Among the authors who devoted their lives to collecting details about and describing this popular religious culture is Jayamall Parmar. In the 548 pages of one of his last works, *Sevādharamanā amaradhāma*,[2] 'Timeless Places in the Service of Religion,' he gives an account of the many different religious currents in Saurashtra: the Śaivite sanctuaries, be they big or small; the Samādhis, or tombs, of Hindu or Muslim saints or holy men; the worship of the Devī and Śakti; the Sun temples; the centres of various *sampradāyas* (such as the Svāmī Nārāyaṇīs, the Pranāmīs, or the Rāmānandīs); and community fairs like Tarṇetar, Madhavpur, and Bhavanāth at Mt Girnar. He also describes the vernacular literature and hymns, which speak of these groups and places. In addition to his book publications, he collected an abundance of details in the 732 issues of his magazine *Ūrmi Navaracanā*, published monthly from 1930 until 1991.

These popular religious currents are not mutually exclusive but often share common features. For instance, the *Sant-vāṇī*, a corpus of hymns shaped by Tantric influence, is the common property of different faith groups. Indeed, the *Sant-vāṇī* is held in high esteem by the entire Gujarati public despite its use of dialectal features that are particular to Saurashtra or Kacchī. The *Sant-vāṇī* originated from the combined activities of different groups of *loka-dharma* such as the Mahāpanth, Ravibhaṇpanth, Nāthpanth, Kabīrpanth, and – although at present its followers are no longer conscious of the fact – the Satpanth, the old name of the converted Nizārī Isma'īlīs in Gujarat and Kutch.

The Mahāpanthīs, also called by the names Mahāmārgīs, Bījamārgīs, and Nijārpanthīs, are a movement older and more numerous than the others, and are one of the secret Tantric sects of Gujarat. Theoretically open to all castes and all religions, the Mahāpanthīs are controlled by the caste of the untouchable Meghvāḷs. Only those who have received initiation from the guru may take part in the secret rites, the principal of which is the *pāṭa-pūjā*, celebrated by couples chosen according to their state of spiritual advancement (*jati-satī*). It is held on the second day of each lunar month (*bīja*), in honour of the Supreme Principle worshipped as *jyota-agni-nūr*, light and sun, the equivalent of Primeval Energy. In addition to Śiva Ādināth, the mythological founders of the movement are Ramdeopir,[3] Sahadev Jośī, and Devāyat Paṇḍit, the latter two belonging to both the Mahāmārgīs and the Isma'īlīs Nizārīs, called Satpanthīs.

Only the Mahāmārgī *bhajanas* or communal hymn-singing are accessible without initiation; they are preferably held on *bīja* days and may last the whole night (divided into two-hour-vigils). The *pada* or *Sant-vāṇī* (the verses) were composed by the founders and saints of the movement, men and women in equal proportion; since they do not distinguish between *jati* and *satī*, the gurus are often untouchables and women. Certain hymns are attributed to the divine authors Śiva or Śakti, or to the mythological heroes, Dhruv, Prahlād, Draupadī, Kuntī, and Markaṇḍ Ṛṣi.

Certain characteristics of the Mahāmārgī *bhajana* distinguish the *Sant-vāṇī* of Saurashtra:[4]

– *Guru-mahimā* (the greatness of the guru) means a total submission to the will of the guru, be he a Harijan or a woman (like Toral to Jesal). The guru alone is capable of leading the disciple towards the abolition of his or her self and passion. There is no worse sin than to be *naguru*, without a guru.

– *Raveṇī* (alluding to the churning of the milk ocean) describes the creation of the world, often as a dialogue between Śiva and Pārvatī (*Śiva śakti saṃvād*) where Śiva reveals the secret of both the creation of the world and of the Mahāpanth. Sometimes the *Raveṇī* are called *Sṛṣṭinī utpatti*.

– *Pyālo* or *Kaṭārī* (the cup) celebrates the joy of spiritual meeting when the *śiṣya* receives from the guru the *mantra* of salvation, thanks to which he accedes to Supreme Bliss, often described as the drinking of *amṛtarasa* (the liquor of immortality).

– Another type of *vāṇī* tells, or alludes to, the legends of Mahāpanthī saints, the stories of which have outgrown the limits of the *Sampradāya* and belong to the common culture of Saurashtra, and ultimately of Gujarat and Rajasthan. They often deal with unmarried couples such as the spiritual lovers Jesal and Toral or Lakho and Loyan, or married couples like the Rajputs Rupaṇḍe and Malde, or the untouchables Khimro and Dāḍalde.

– The *Ārādha* (adoration) is a prayer, which is used almost like a ritual *mantra* for the rites of the Mahāpanth, such as the complex and elaborate rite of the *pāṭa-pūjā*.[5] One of the most famous is the *Delamī-ārādha* by Devāyat Paṇḍit, part of which shows similarities with elements of the *āgama*.

– The *āgama* may be the most surprising of the *vāṇī*, describing the end of the Kaliyug and the accompanying events: the undoing of the dharmic order, the upsetting of natural phenomena, and so on. These *vāṇī* announce the arrival of the saving *avatāra*, Naklaṃka-Naklaṃki (or Niṣkalaṃka), corresponding to the tenth *avatāra* of Viṣṇu, Kalki, who will abolish untouchability and restore a new golden age in the Mahāpanthī context, or to Ali, the son-in-law of the Prophet, announcing the final resurrection (*Qiyama*), in the Nizārī Isma'īlī context.[6]

The structure, themes, and texts of the Mahāmārgī *bhajana* are also common to the other communities, or *loka-dharma*, mentioned above:

– The Nāths are always associated with the Mahāpanthīs, for instance in their ritual texts such as the *Delamī-ārādha* of Devāyat Paṇḍit, which includes Ādināth (Śiva), Cauraṅgīnāth, Matsyendranāth, and Gorakhnāth;[7] the *bhajana* as well as the *pāṭa-pūjā* are often led either by a Mahāpanthī guru or a Nāth; the Mahāpanthī-Nāth confraternity may also express itself through the choice of places for an *āśrama*. For instance Devīdās, a Mahāpanthī saint whose guru Loha-Laṅgarī was a Ramānandī, received from his spiritual master the order to settle on the site of an abandoned Nāth shrine at Vāvdī.
– The Ravibhāṇapanthīs are named after two of their gurus: Bhāṇa (1698–1755), a disciple of Kabīr and a rather late propagator in Gujarat of the Kabīrian message, and his disciple Ravi (1727–1804). Their successors Khīmsāheb, Trikāmsāheb, and Dāsījīvana are famous authors of *vāṇī* sung in every *bhajana*. The Ravibhāṇapanthīs are untouchables, as is often the case with the Kabīrpanthīs, who will take part in any *Sant-vāṇī-bhajana* even if Mahāpanthīs dominate the gathering. On the other hand a local group of ascetics, the Kāpaḍīs renouncers whose mission it is to sing the Nāth cycles of Gopīcand and Bhatṛhari as well as to be in the service of the living (*prāṇī-sevā*), takes its inspiration from the teaching of Kabīr. Kāpaḍīs wear the traditional pointed cap of Kabīr.
– It seems that at one stage the Nizārī Isma'īlī Satpanthīs of the region belonged to the same nucleus of religions. Of course, nowadays this is no longer acknowledged. The Khojas, as the Nizārī Isma'īlī are now called, form a closed community of middle rank in society; they are unaware of all they have in common with the *santa-vāṇī* tradition. However, their *gināna*, religious songs in the vernacular and secretly preserved, have characteristics of style, choice of metaphors, literary forms, and teaching in common with the *Sant-vāṇī*. The

āgama-vāṇī and the *dāsa-avatāra gināna* announcing the arrival of Naklaṃka, have authors in common as well as texts. Besides that, the Nizārī ritual of the *ghaṭa-pāṭa* may be considered to be a variant of the *pāṭa-pūjā*, as the same ritual *mantras* were recited on the occasion.[8]

Although, as elsewhere in India, there are examples of ascetic exploits and the outward renunciation of the saints, for instance in the case of the founder of the Nāth community in Kutch, Dharmanāth at Dhinodhar,[9] very special importance was given to the notions of compassion for living beings and of devotion to their service in order to attain the state of perfection.[10] Examples are numerous: for instance, the saint Kāpaḍī Mekaṇ Dādā who, accompanied by his dog Motiyā and his donkey Lālīyā, criss-crosses the Rann of Kutch on the lookout for anyone having lost his or her way in the desert in order to provide him or her with water and food (see fig. 1); or Saint Devīdās who transforms his *āśrama* at Parab-Vāvdī into a leper-house, thus attracting the wrath of his neighbours. Animals receive equal attention: the shrines belonging to the *Sant Vāṇī* group will have a *gośālā*. These shrines are also provided with all that is necessary for the *sadāvrata* (the vow to feed poor visitors every day), where the visitor will always be told that commensality is compulsory and that caste rules will not be observed. One cannot but be reminded of the presence of Buddhism in Saurashtra until the thirteenth century,[11] more precisely in the two regions concerned with the cult of Naklaṃki and the Jakhs: Pancal and Kutch.

The region of Pancal (Pāñcāḷa) borders the District of Surendranagar in the east and, the District of Rajkot in the south. Believed to be the country of Draupadī-Pāñcāḷī, or the refuge of the Pāṇḍavas, it is composed of small Kaṭhī kingdoms, some of them protected by Gebināth (near Soṅgadh, *tālukā* Chotila). Near Avaliya Thakkar are natural caves that have been reoccupied by Nāths. (See fig. 2.) There are also Buddhist architectural remains covered over by Kṛṣṇa temples or Sufi *dargahs*. Pancal, together with Sorath and the Barda Hills, is rich in popular religious traditions. The cult of Naklaṃki, with which we are concerned here, came into being in the area located between Morvi, Rajkot, and Wankaner.

Kutch is located in the northwestern-most district of Saurashtra, situated between the Arabian Sea to the south and Pakistan to the northeast. It is physically separated from Pakistan by the Great Rann and from India by the Little Rann. Thus it is as much connected to the province of Sind as to Kathiawad. Historical circumstances may have linked it to Saurashtra, yet Kacchī is a dialect of Sindhi. The preservation of socio-religious traditions in Kutch is in astonishing contrast to its openness to the outside world and the resulting migrations of peoples and ideas into the region. The cult of the Jakhs belongs to Kutch alone.

The Naklaṃki Cult in Saurashtra

The advent of the tenth *avatāra* of Viṣṇu, Kalki, either under the name of Naklaṃka-Naklaṃki (Niṣkalaṃka-Niṣkalaṃki)[12] in the *āgama pada* of the *Sant-vāṇī,* or of Naklaṃka in the *ginās* of the Nizārī Isma'īlīs, who await their saviour, the Imām Ali, is of fundamental importance to both.

At first sight it might seem surprising that the followers of Sakti, the Primeval Energy in the Form of Light (*Jyota-Agni-Nur*), should turn to an incarnation (*avatāra*) provided with qualities (*saguṇa*). However, this is exactly what happened. There are numerous *āgamas* describing the arrival of the saviour astride his white horse, surrounded by his allies Prahlād or Hariścandra, the Pāṇḍavas or Hanumān, and their armies. In a *pada* attributed to Toral, the consort of Jesal, she says she will recognize her Lord among all the sādhus and the deer because of his yellow garment and the unique golden horn on his forehead.[13] He is often called 'Kayam deva,' undoubtedly after the Arabic *Qāim*, the Lord of the Resurrection. The *āgama* says that he comes from the country of Dailam (*Delama deśa*), from Alamut (in Iran), that he will kill the demon Kaliṅga (who personifies the Kali-yuga), and that he will marry Meghaḍī Rāṇī, the young untouchable, or elsewhere Viśva Kumārī, the 'Virgin Universe' or the 'Virgin Earth.'

Dominique-Sila Khan concludes that the very concept of Naklaṃka could not have developed without the contribution of the Isma'īlīs missionaries and preachers, even if in their missionary efforts they had to borrow features offered by Hindu mythology. She suggests that some of the groups they converted later returned to Hinduism, although they continued to adhere to the hope of future delivery from their social condition.[14] That hope was shaped by beliefs and expressed in a language that they inherited from their former Muslim spiritual masters. The *āgamas* of the *Sant-vāṇī* of Saurashtra appear to confirm her hypothesis entirely.

There remains, however, a feature she could not take into account and which might have nuanced her conclusion: the existence of a cult of the God Naklaṃki in three sanctuaries located in Pancal or at its frontiers. One is located at Kerāḷā near Wankaner, and is said to have been established by a Bharwad woman (*bharavāḍa*, a cattle rearing caste) by the name of Rūḍīmāṃ, the sister of the great saint Rāṇīmāṃ, who herself had founded the second temple at Rajkot; a third temple is at Bhagathaḷā near Morvi, said to have been given to Mīṭhā bhagat, a disciple of Rāṇīmāṃ. These foundations are not very old. Rāṇīmāṃ lived from 1743 until 1847.[15] Born into a rather well-to-do Krishnite Bharwad Bhagat family who owned cattle herds, she and her sister are said to have miraculously found several *mūrtīs* of Kalki and worked for the establishment of the cult of Naklaṃki by obtaining land gifts from the local sovereigns as well as money for the construction of the temples.

The temple in the old town of Rajkot in the area of Naklaṃk (*Naklaṃka śerī*) is a simple structure on a platform. The *garbhagṛha* contains several small horse idols, each under a little umbrella, but the main one, Naklaṃki, has been put aside, to be replaced by a *mūrti* of Kṛṣṇa called Śyām-Bansidhar, which Rāṇīmāṃ is said to have miraculously received at the end of her life at Maliya (to the north of Morvi). The *garbhagṛha* is surrounded by a corridor so that the faithful may pursue uninterruptedly the *parikramā* of the idol while the long and elaborate *ārtī* goes on. (See fig. 4.) The attendants are from the lineage of Rāṇīmāṃ. The offerings are candy and coconuts. Rāṇīmāṃ had come to Rajkot after her marriage and established the temple by giving judicious advice to the king not to raise taxes on cattle, especially on cows. Her *pādukā* is venerated in the temple and her nearby dwelling is a sanctuary. Her main miracles are depicted on the walls of the temple, such as the resurrection of a child who had died from cholera and the dialogue with a sādhu who had entered into *samādhi*. The compound includes a kitchen to provide meals according to the *sadāvrata* rule. Caste is not taken into consideration in temple worship. As far as I can tell, Bharwad and Lohana are the main faithful, together with a few Brahmans from the surrounding area, but no Khojas (Nizārī Isma'īlīs) worship there.

The temple at Bhagathaḷā is slightly different. Its *mahants* (or heads) are renouncers succeeding each other from guru to disciple. The original idol of Naklaṃki is still *in situ* and is accompanied by Garuḍa as in the other shrines; the portraits of Thakurs of Morvi indicate their royal patronage. The arrangement of the temple is similar to the one at Rajkot: there is a prosperous *gośāḷā* and a kitchen for the *sadāvrata*.

The most important holiday is *aṣāḍa bīja*, which is a Mahāmārgī holiday. *Ārtī* and *bhajana* of the *Sant-vāṇī* are the main features of the cult. According to Dayārām Bhagat, the current *mahant*, the place was chosen simply because Naklaṃki will come to Bagathaḷā upon his advent. Two of the details concerning the temple structure are interesting. (See fig. 3.) First, there is the green triangular flag decorated with the crescent of the moon of the size on the second day (*bīja*) of its waxing; according to Dayārām Bhagat, Naklaṃki is a '*Pīr*,' a term used in the Islamic traditions and borrowed for the gurus in the regional sant tradition. This is said to be the reason for the flag. Second, the pinnacle of the temple is decorated with statuettes representing sādhus of the four *sampradāya* of the *Sant-vāṇī bhajana*: a Nāth in the position of meditation; a Ravibhāṇpanthī singing a *bhajan*; a Kabīrpanth with his cap; and a Mahāmārgī smoking opium. However, there is no obvious suggestion of an Isma'īlī presence.

Considering that the cult and the sanctuaries only developed in the nineteenth century, it would seem logical that the links once existing between the Mahāmārgī and the Khoja Isma'īlīs would be totally forgotten and that the two communities would have gone their separate ways. The situation, however, is a bit different. Professor Jani reported to one that, together with Mohanpuri Goswami and Praṅgiribapu, specialists of popular religious culture of Kutch, he will be researching the existence of ten more Naklaṃki temples in Saurashtra and Kutch that were once prosperous but now are forgotten. According to the informants of Professor Jani, the Naklaṃki cult flourished during the nineteenth century, particularly in the period between 1850 and 1900, due to increasing brahmanical rigidity against low castes and especially outcastes. A certain brahmanization of Saurashtrian society had been achieved under British rule. The Naklaṃki cult might have been encouraged by the Isma'īlī Khojas themselves, who were trusted by the depressed classes.[16] Until there is further proof, it remains difficult to decide,[17] but it seems a fact that, in spite of the re-Islamization of the Nizārī movement in India after the arrival of the Aga Khan in Bombay in 1850 and the reforms of the 3rd Aga Khan, Sultan Muhammad Shah (1877–1957), Naklaṃki has continued to be important among the Khojā. Two Isma'īlī texts from the 1920s, *Śrī Nakalaṃka Bhajana-saṃgraha* and *Śrī Nakalaṃka Sāstrā*,[18] suggest that a missionary movement dedicated to the cult of Naklaṃka at the end of the nineteenth and the beginning of the twentieth century existed among the Gujarati Isma'īlī Khojas, maybe among those called *Gupta Khojā* who are Hindus outwardly but secretly follow Isma'īlīsm. In any case, the cult of Naklaṃka bears witness to the confraternity of different *sampradāyas* in Saurashtra.

The Jakhs in Kutch

In the Kutch district there are many small sanctuaries, more or less abandoned, that display an alignment of statuettes representing seventy-two horseback riders, each holding a manuscript in one hand. (See figs. 5–7.) These are the Jakhs,[19] who are said to have come from overseas to alleviate the misery of the poor, to look after the sick, and to deliver the country from the tyrant king Puṃvrao. They are treated like gods. Their legend is known through heroic tales, whic describe how they defeated Puṃvrao, nephew of Kākhā Phulāṇī (at the end of the tenth century) and thereby thwarted the first attempt of the Samma Rajputs to control Kutch. Several versions of the legend exist; they were first brought to light by Alexander Burns in 1826, and L.F. Rushbrook Williams gave an exhaustive account of what is known about the Jakhs and their stories in 1958.[20]

According to the legends seven holy men, called Rikhis (Ṛṣis) or Saṃghars, came from somewhere near Byzantium. They worshipped their god Jakh on a hill not far from the fort of Puṃvrao, called Padhargadh. Their reputation for being able to make barren women bear children soon brought them to the attention of the queen. In some versions of the legend she is said to have given them access to the palace through an underground passage; in others, she is said to have been offended by them when they did not offer her the respect she felt was her due. In both accounts, the king becomes furious, in the one because they have violated the sanctity of his harem, and in the other, because they have insulted his wife. He has them arrested and condemns them to winnowing grain on a ground covered with nails. A compassionate barber freed one of them, who, from the top of a hill, called for the help of his god. Jakh is said to have arrived from Byzantium in the company of his seventy brothers and one sister. When Puṃvrao refused to liberate the prisoners, Jakh and his company killed Puṃvrao and cursed Padhargadh, which was ruined and abandoned only two years after it was built. Later on, the seventy-two Jakhs were deified and worshipped astride their horses.

Another tale was required in the eighteenth century to convince the ruler of Kutch, Rao Desalji (1716–51), of the fact that the Jakhs actually existed. In this tale, they appeared from the sky on their horses near the gold market (*sonī bazār*) at Bhuj, where a shrine, called Jakh Jar or Jakh Mandir, commemorates the event. (See fig. 8.) Although it is not visited much today, it is still well kept: twenty-four whitewashed niches are aligned on a platform surrounded by small structures, each providing shelter to three manuscript scrolls, doubtlessly standing for the seventy-two Jakhs; two Jakh statues stand in front of the niches along with two white flags. There was no trace of any recent *pūjā* (as of December 12, 1997), although Desaljī and his successors are supposed to come here to celebrate the arrival of the Jakhs once a year.

Rushbrook Williams quotes a more prosaic tale about the arrival of the Jakhs in Kutch which he attributes to the last royal bard.[21] Seventy-one shipwrecked men and a woman are said to have reached Jakhau on rafts (on the West Coast, Abaḍāsā *tālukā*, an ancient harbour, the name of which recalls the event).[22] They were supposed to have come from Byzantium and had clear skin, were tall in stature, and spoke a foreign language that was incomprehensible to the Kutchis. They travelled throughout the country and taught their art of medicine and other sciences; in exchange they were rewarded with horses. Their popularity provoked the jealousy of the cruel Puṃvrao, who imprisoned some of them. Their brother and sister, in order to free them, built a ballistic machine on a nearby hill, bombarding a part of the palace and killing the king. The queen organized a massacre of all the Jakhs in revenge. The people, grateful for their kindnesses, worshipped them as saints and even demigods in hilltop temples.

At Jakhau, where there once were many Jakh images, the cult is in recession. The recent silting-up of the harbour put an end to the commercial activities of the Bhanuśālī, who emigrated to Bombay, following the independence of India. Their arable land was taken over by Muslims. However, a small shrine was built between the small town and the sea as recently as twelve years ago; seven small images of the Jakhs on their horses, standing 30 to 50 cm high, can be seen there. Incense and coconuts bear witness to the existence of a cult. (See fig. 9.)

The liveliest temple is located at the village bearing the name Jakh, near the Padhargadh ruins (Nakhatrāṇā *tālukā*), and near the ruins of a large Śiva temple called Puṃvreśvar. The shrine on the top of a hill can be reached by a flight of steps. It is an open terrace, partially covered by a dome under which stand in a row the seventy-two whitewashed statuettes of the Jakhs on their horses, freshly painted, with their characteristic orange turbans and their moustaches, and with manuscript scrolls under their arms (see figs. 5–6); the image of their sister Sāyarī is different only by virtue of her smaller size. An earlier series of statuettes has been removed and put aside but not destroyed, because when a series is replaced, the preceding one is kept nearby and continues to receive garlands and honours (see fig. 7). An oil lamp is continuously lighted and hung on a pillar at the temple's entrance. *Darśana* is always available, and visitors are numerous.

Local writers as well as English scholars have tried to find a plausible explanation for the origin of these strange benefactors from a foreign land. Many theories have been put forward, some of them quite fanciful: some scholars argue that their name, Jakh, is derived from *yakṣa*, Hindu or Buddhist celestial beings; others argue that they were Greeks or Romans, Śākas or White Huns,[23] and even the Varangian (Scandinavian) Guards of the emperor of Byzantium! Somewhat more convincingly, Rushbrook Williams proposes an Iranian identity: they might have been Zoroastrians who, fleeing Islamization from northern Iran (as did the present day Parsis, who reached the coast of Gujarat as early as the ninth century), were shipwrecked and sought refuge on the coast of Kutch. Their peaceful ways and their knowledge would be in accordance with those attributed to the Jakhs. For Dalpat Shrimali, a specialist of the religious folklore of the untouchables in Saurashtra and Gujarat, the god Jakh might be an *avatāra* of Matang or Mataiṃ Dev, one of the great gurus of the Mahāmārgī mythology, born from a Brahmin father and an untouchable mother, and famous for his astrological science.[24] To others he is one of the great Hindu preachers of Nizārī Isma'īlīsm.[25] None of these theories can be proven, and the legend of the Jakhs does not seem to have crossed the Ranns of Kutch.

The popular religions of Saurashtra are not unique in their exclusive religious non-conformity nor their taste for obscure religious cults. The sants of Kathiawad have been compared with the Bauls of Bengal by Jayantilal Acharya;[26] so too the *Sant-vāṇī*, and the Jakh legends might be compared with the writings of Tamil Siddhas.[27] What probably renders these religious groups of Saurashtra different from Bauls and the Siddhas is the fact that they are accepted by the entire population. It is true that a Saurashtrian Brahmin does not seem to be troubled when visiting a shrine that practices the *sadāvrata* and that the spiritual authority of the saint overrules the dharmic social order; the saints who are of very low caste or an untouchable command esteem from all. Might these be features left over from the Buddhism of the past or from the Jainism which still exists, since both religions disregard caste hierarchy?

Paradoxically, this area, although it has traditionally been a conservatory of religious traditions, with its lively commerce and its ports on the Arabian Sea, has also been open-minded enough to receive new peoples and ideas. The worship of Naklaṃk Ali and the Jakhs illustrates both of these attitudes. The double capacity for preservation and assimilation gives the saints of Saurashtra a personality all their own. This same spirit of independence is encountered on the political level as well, as Saurashtra has remained semi-autonomous in spite of its successive Hindu, Muslim, Maratha, and English suzerains. Gandhi, hailing from Porbandar near the Barda Hills, certainly was one of the ultimate heirs of the sants of Saurashtra.

Figure 1: The Kapaḍī Mekaṇ Dādā (Kutch) from the shrine at Dhrang.

Figure 2: A Nāth-yogī in a cave near Avaliya Thakkar (Pancal).

Figure 3: Bagathḷa: Naklaṃki Mandirs.

Figure 4: Rajkot: The ārtī.

Figure 5: The 72 Jakhs.

Figure 6: The Jakhs.

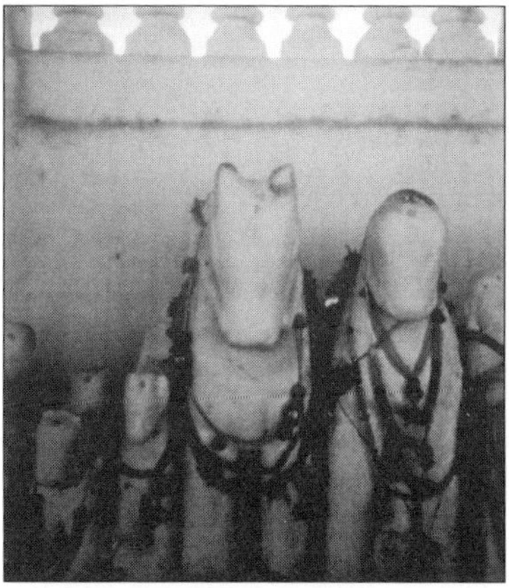

Figure 7: The Jakhs.

Figure 8: Bhuj: Jhakh Mandir.

Figure 9: Jakhau: The small shrine with seven Jakhs.

End Notes

1 See Harald Tambs-Lyche, *Power, Profit and Poetry; Traditional Society in Kathiawar, Western India* (New Delhi: Manohar, 1997).

2 Jayamall Parmar and Rajul Dave, *Sevādharamanā amaradhāma* (Amreli: Dr Jivaram Mahetā Smarak Trust, 1990).

3 Rāmdev (Rāmdeo, Rāmde) Pīr, a semi-legendary Rajput hero of the end of the fourteenth century who became the religious head of the untouchables in Rajasthan where today he is considered an *avatāra* of Kṛṣṇa, nevertheless gets a composite cult, in constant progress. See Dominique-Sila Khan, *Conversions and Shifting Identities, Ramdev Pir and the Ismailis in Rajasthan* (New Delhi: Manohar and Centre de Sciences Humaines, 1997), 60 ff.

4 On *Sant-vāṇī,* see Balvant Jani, ed., *Santa-vāṇī, tattva ane tantra* (Gandhinagar: Gujarat Sahitya Akadami, 1996); Nathalal Gohil, Niranjan Rajyaguru, and Manoj Raval, *Santa-vāṇīnuṃ sattva ane sauṃdarya* (Rajkot: Praviṇ Prakāśan, 1994); and Nathalal Gohil, *Saurāṣṭranā harijana bhaktakavio* (Keshod: N. Gohil, 1987).

5 See Niranjan Rajyaguru, *Bījamārgī gupta pāṭa-upāsanā ane Mahāpanthī-santonī bhajanavāṇī* (Gandhinagar: Gujarati Sahitya Akademi, 1995).

6 See Nathalal Gohil, *Āgama vāṇī* (Ahmedabad: Navabhārat Sāhitya Mandir, 1994).

7 See Rajyaguru, *Bījamārgī gupta pāṭa-upāsanā*, 59–60.

8 From this one might like to conclude that the ritual of the *pāṭa-pūjā* as well as the *sant-vāṇī* are part of the common origin shared by the Tāntrikas, the Nāths, and the Isma'īlīs, the three groups in Saurashtra from as early as the fourteenth-fifteenth centuries. This situation is different from the one in Rajasthan, where only ritual and textual evidence of an Isma'īlī presence remains. Dominique-Sila Khan has established the medieval presence of Isma'īlīism in Rajasthan and even further in Northern India. This Isma'īlī presence later disappeared and the disciples then returned to their original Tantric Hindu movements. See Khan, *Conversions and Shifting Identities*. A similar study has not yet been finished for Saurashtra where the simultaneous presence of the three groups as well as of the many little known texts they share do not allow the investigator to reach definite conclusions.

9 Dalpatrām P. Khakhar, 'History of of the Kamphatas of Kacch,' *Indian Antiquary* 7 (February 1878), 45–53; *Report on the Architectural and Archaeological Remains in the Province of Kacch, with five papers by the late Sir Alex Burnes* (1879; reprint, Patna: Indian India, 1978), 3–13.

10 One ought to remember that the reputation of the saints and the admiration they inspire must be shared in the eyes of the public with another hero figure, a negative one so to speak, that of the outlaw *bahārvaṭiyā*. The *bahārvaṭiyā* is a Kāṭhī unlawfully deprived of his lands who protests through becoming an honourary bandit and who protects the poor and might occasionally avenge their grievances. See Javerchand Meghani, *Soraṭhī bahārvaṭiyā* (Bhavnagar: Prasar, 1997).

11 See M.S. Moray, *History of Buddhism in Gujarat* (Ahmedabad: Saraswati Pustak Bhandar, 1965) and A.S. Gadre, 'Buddhist Influence in Gujarat and Kathiawar,' *Journal of the Gujarat Research Society* 1–4 (1939), 61–70.

12 On the etymology of Kalki and Niṣkalaṃkī, see Dominique-Sila Khan, 'The Coming of Nikalank Avatar: A Messianic Theme in Some Sectarian Traditions in North-Western India,' *Journal of Indian Philosophy* 25 (1997), 411 and n10. According to Professor H. Bhayani (interview by author, Ahmedabad, November 26, 1997), 'Nakalaṃki' is the result of a popular etymology, in reaction against the misinterpretation of *Kalki* as *Kalaṃki* (one who has a mark or a stigma); thus Na- or Niṣkalaṃki was understood to mean 'One without stain,' 'Pure.'

13 See B. Jani, 'The Contribution of Women Saints to the Santa Literature of Saurashtra' (paper presented at the École pratique des Hautes Études, Paris, May 19, 1998), 47, *pada* 5 vs. 2–6.

14 Khan, 'Coming of Nikalank Avatar.'

15 On Rāṇīmāṃ and her family, see Kalidās Mahārāj, *Rāṇīmāṃ*, 3rd ed. (Rajkot: Nakalaṃka Mandira Trust 1994); *Soraṭhī Strīsanto* (Ahmedabad: Sastu Sāhitya Vardhaka Kāryālaya, 1972), 95–105; Parmar and Dave, *Sevādharamanā amaradhāma*, 233–39.

16 Interview by author at Les Montèzes, Monoblet, May 12, 1998.

17 According to another informant, M. Madhubhai Bhaṭṭ of Rajkot (interview by author, December 7, 1997), near Nadiad (Kaira Dt., North Gujarat) there is a complex of three Naklaṃk *mandira* – one for Patils, one for untouchables, and the third one for Muslims!

18 Ahmedabad: 'Śrī Nakalaṃka Jñānaprasaraka Maṇḍala.' [The Circle for the Advancement of the Knowledge of Nakalaṃka], 1921 Bombay: 'Śrī Nakalaṃka Jñānaprasaraka Maṇḍala' [The Circle for the Advancement of the Knowledge of Nakalaṃka], 1922.

19 The etymology of Jakh can only lead to Sanskrit *yakṣa*, the guardian demigods or servants of Kubera, the god of wealth.

20 Alexander Burnes, 'An Account of the Ruins near Mujjul or Munjul in Cutch,' in Khakhar, *Report on the Architectural and Archaeological Remains*, app. 4, n8; L.F. Rushbrook Williams, *The Black Hills, Kutch in History and*

Legend: A Study in Indian Local Loyalties (London: Weidenfeld and Nicolson, 1958), 83–88, and ills.

21 Ibid., 86–87.

22 On Jakhau, see G.D. Patel, ed., *Gujarat State Gazetteers, Kutch District* (Ahmedabad: Government Press, Gujarat State, 1971), 598.

23 See Williams, *Black Hills*, 85.

24 Dalpat Shrimali, *Harijana santa ane lokasāhitya [kaṃthasthathi granthastha]* (Ahmedabad: Gujarāta Grantharatna Kāryālaya, 1993), 223.

25 See S. Nanjiani, *Khojā vṛttānta*, 2nd ed. (Ahmedabad: n.p., 1892), 133–36.

26 Jayantilal Acharya, *Gujarātanā santa kavio ane Bāulapantha (bāulagāno sāthe)* (Bombay: Forbes Gujarātī Sabhā, 1973).

27 K. Kailasapathy, 'The Writings of the Tamil Siddhas,' in *The Sants: Studies in a Devotional Tradition of India*, ed. K. Schomer and W.H. McLeod (Delhi: Motilal Banarsidas, 1987).

Bibliography

Ambāprasād 'Sumaṇ,' *Kṛṣak-jīvan-sambandhī Brajbhāṣā-Śabdāvalī.* 2 vols. Allahabad: Hindustānī Academy, 1960–61.

Ananya Modinī tathā Cāhvelī (Priyādās viracit). Edited by Śyāmsundar Śarmā. Bhelsā [Gwalior]: n.p., V.S. 1991 (1934).

Ansari, Z.D., and M.S. Mate. *Excavations at Dwarka* (1963). Poona: Deccan College Post-Graduate and Research Institute, 1966.

Arbudācalapradakṣiṇā Jaina Lekha Saṃdoha. Edited by Muni Shrī Jayantavijayajī. Bhavnagar: n.p., V.S. 2005 (1948–49).

Athavale, V.B. 'In Which of the Four Dvārakās Did Ekānaṃśā, the Daughter of Yaśodā Exchanged for Kṛṣṇa, Arrive for the Pārijāta Plantation Ceremony?' *Poona Orientalist* 19 (1954): 17–34.

Babb, Lawrence A. *Absent Lord: Ascetics and Kings in a Jain Ritual Culture.* Berkeley: University of California Press, 1996.

Ballalasena. *Dānasāgara.* Bibliotheca Indica 274. Edited by Bhabatosh Bhattacharya. Calcutta: Asiatic Society, 1953.

Banniyuan jing 般泥洹經 *Taishō shinshū daizōkyō,* edited by Takakusu Junjirō and Watanabe Kaigyoku. Tokyo: Taishō Issaikyō Kankōkai, 1924–32. Vol. 1, no. 6, 176–91.

Barrett, T.H. 'Exploratory Observations on Some Weeping Pilgrims.' *The Buddhist Forum* 1 (1990): 99–110.

———. 'The Emergence of the Taoist Papacy in the T'ang Dynasty.' *Asia*

Major, 3rd ser., 7, no. 1 (1994): 89–106.

Barz, Richard K. *The Bhakti Sect of Vallabhācārya*. Faridabad: Thomson Press, 1976.

Bhakt Māl Granth. Edited by Durgadās Lahilī. Calcutta: Bangladāśī Electric Machine Press, B.E. 1312 (1905).

Bhaktmāl: Pāṭhānuśīlan evaṃ vivecanā. Vol. 2. Edited by Narendra Jhā. Patna: Anūpam Prakāśan, 1978.

Bhandarkar, D. R. 'Jaina Iconography.' *Indian Antiquary* 40 (May–June 1911): 125–30, 153–61.

Bhumiratana, Amara. *Four Charismatic Monks in Thailand*. Master's thesis, University of Washington, 1969.

Bhuvanadeva. *Aparājitaparipṛcchā*. Gaekwad's Oriental Series 115. Edited by A. Mankaḍ. Baroda: The Oriental Institute, 1950.

Bielenstein, Hans. 'The Institutions of Later Han.' In *The Cambridge History of China 1: The Ch'in and Han Empires, 221 B.C.–A.D. 220*, vol. 1, edited by D. Twitchett and M. Loewe. Cambridge: Cambridge University Press, 1986.

Bizot, François. *Le figuier à cinq branches*. Paris: École Française d'Extrême-Orient, 1976.

———. *Le don de soi-même*. Paris: École Française d'Extrême-Orient, 1976.

———. *Les traditions de la pabbajjā en Asie du Sud-Est*. Göttingen: Vandenhoeck and Ruprecht, 1988.

Bizot, François, and François Lagirarde. *La pureté par les mots (Saddavimala)*. Paris: École Française d'Extrême-Orient, 1996.

Bokencamp, Stephen R. *Early Daoist Scriptures*. Berkeley: University of California Press, 1997.

Bouillier, V. 'Des prêtres du pouvoir: les Yogis et la fonction royale.' *Prêtrise, pouvoirs et autorité en Himalaya, puruṣārtha* 12 (1989). Edited by V. Bouillier and G. Toffin, 193–214.

———. *Ascètes et rois. Un monastère de Kānphaṭā Yogīs au Nepal*. Paris: CNRS Editions (Ethnologie), 1997.

Briggs, G.W. *Gorakhnāth and the Kānphaṭā Yogīs*. 1938. Reprint, Delhi: Motilal Banarsidass, 1973.

Brown, Robert L. 'Narrative as Icon: The Jātaka Stories in Ancient Indian and Southeast Asian Architecture.' In *Sacred Biography in the Buddhist Traditions of South and Southeast Asia*, edited by Juliane Schober. Honolulu: University of Hawaii Press, 1997.

Burgess, James. *Revised Lists of Antiquarian Remains in the Bombay Presidency*. Archaeological Survey of India Reports, New Imperial Series 16, revised by Henry Cousens. Bombay: Government Central Press, 1897.

Burghart, R. 'Wandering Ascetics of the Ramanandi Sect.' *History of Religions* 22 (1983): 361–83.

Burnes, Alexander. 'An Account of the Ruins near Mujjul or Munjul in Cutch.' In Dalpatrām P. Khakhar. *Report on the Architectural and Archaeological Remains in the Province of Kacch, with five papers by the late Sir Alex Burnes*. 1879. Reprint, Patna: Indian India, 1978.

Caitanyacaritāmrta. Edited by Śrīmadbhaktikevala Auḍulomi Mahārāj. Calcutta: Gauḍīya Mission, 1957.

Callewaert, Winand M. *The Hindī Biography of Dādū Dayāl*. Delhi: Motilal Banarsidass, 1988.

———. *The Hagiographies of Anantadās: The Bhakti Poets of North India*. London: Curzon, 2000.

Callewaert, Winand M., and Mukund Lath. *The Hindī Songs of Nāmdev*. Leuven: Departement Oriëntalistiek, 1989.

Callewaert, Winand M., and Rupert Snell, eds. *According to Tradition: Hagiographical Writing in India*. Wiesbaden: Harrasowitz Verlag, 1994.

Caurāsī baiṭhak caritra. Edited by N. Śarmā. Mathurā: Śri Govarddhan Granthmālā, V.S. 2024 (1967).

Cedzich, Ursula-Angelika. 'Das Ritual der Himmelsmeister im Spiegel früher Quellen: Übersetzung und Untersuchung des liturgischen Materials im 3. *chüan* des *Teng-chen yin-chüeh*.' Doctoral thesis, Würzburg University, 1987.

———. 'Ghosts and Demons, Law and Order: Grave Quelling Texts and Early Taoist Liturgy.' *Taoist Resources* 4, no. 2 (1993): 23–35.

Cēkkiḻār Cuvāmikal Aruḷcceyt Tiruruttoṇṭarkal Carittirameṉṉum Periyapurāṇaṃ Vacaṉakāviyaṃ. Eḍīṭēḍ by Irattiṇa Nāyakar Ceṇnai: B. Irattiṇanāyakar and Sons, 1984.

Chandra, Lokesh. 'Borodudur: A New Interpretation.' In *The Stūpa: Its Religious, Historical and Architectural Significance*, edited by Anna Libera Dallapiccola. Wiesbaden: Franz Steiner Verlag, 1980.

Chang Qu 常璩. *Huayang guo zhi* 華陽國志.. In *Huayang guo zhi jiaobu tuzhu* 華陽國志校補圖注. Edited by Ren Naiqiang 任乃強. Shanghai: Guji, 1987.

Chaturvedi, Parśu Rām. *Uttarī Bhārata kī santa-paramparā*. N.p., 1964.

Chen Guofu 陳國符. 'Shezhi 設治' and 'Shuzhi 署職'. In *Daozang yuanliu kao* 道藏源流考, Rev. ed. Peking: Zhonghua shuju, 1963.

Chen Meidong 陳美東, ed. *Zhongguo gu xingtu* 中國古星圖. Shenyang: Liaoning jiaoyu chuban she, 1996.

Chen Shou 陳壽. *Sanguo zhi* 三國志. Peking: Zhonghua shuju, 1985.

Chihara, Daigoro. *Hindu-Buddhist Architecture in Southeast Asia*. Leiden: Brill, 1996.

Ching-lang, Hou. *Monnaies d'offrandes et la notion de trésorerie dans la religion chinoise*. Paris: Collège de France, 1975.

Chisong zi zhangli 赤松子章曆. 335–36, no. 615.

Ciṇkāravēlaṉ, Cō, 'Paṇpunalaṉkal.' In *Śrīlaśrī Kayilaik Kurumaṇi Niṉaivu Malar*.

Ed. Irāmaliṇkat Tampirāṉ Tarumapuram: Ñāṉacampantam Patipakam, 1972, 50–61.

Cleary, Thomas, trans. *The Flower Ornament Scripture: A Translation of the Avatamsaka Sutra*. Vol. 3. Boston: Shambhala, 1987.

Clothey, Fred W. 'Chronometry, Cosmology, and the Festival Calendar of the Tamil Cultus of Murukaṇ' In *Rhythm and Intent: Ritual Studies From South India*. Madras: Blackie and Son Publishers, 1983.

A Collection of Prakrit and Sanskrit Inscriptions. Bhavnagar: Bhavnagar Archaeological Department, n.d.

Couture, André. 'Campement de bouviers et forêts dans trois versions anciennes du mythe d'enfance de Kṛṣṇa.' *Journal Asiatique* 270, nos. 3–4 (1982): 385–400.

———. *L'enfance de Krishna. Traduction des chapitres 30 à 78 du Harivaṃśa (Éd. Cr.)*. Québec: Les Presses de l'Université Laval, 1991.

———. 'Est-il possible de dater le Harivaṃśa?' In *Contacts Between Cultures. Selected papers from the 33rd International Congress of Asian and North African Studies, Toronto, August 15–25, 1990*, vol. 2, *South Asia*, edited by Kay Koppedrayer. Queenston, ON: E. Mellon Press, 1992.

——. 'The Problem of the Meaning of Yoganidrā's Name.' *Journal of Indian Philosophy* 27 (1997): 35–47.

Couture, André, and Charlotte Schmid. 'The Harivamsa, the Goddess Ekānaṃśā and the Iconography of the Vṛṣṇi Triads.' *Journal of the American Oriental Society* 121, no. 2 (2001): 173–92.

Cutler, Norman. *Songs of Experience: The Poetics of Tamil Devotion*. Bloomington, IN: Indiana University Press, 1987.

Dabanniepan jing 大般涅槃經, translated by Faxian 法顯 . In *Taishō shinshū daizōkyō*. Vol. 1, no. 7, 191–202.

Dadao jialing jie 大道家令戒. In *Zhengyi fawen tianshi jiaojie kejing* 正一法文天師教戒科經 12a–19b. *Zhengtong Daozang* 563, no. 789.

Daityāri. *Śaṅkaradeva-Mādhvadevar Jīvan Carita*. Edited by Haribilas Gupta. Tezpur: n.p., 1990.

Daoxuan lüshi gantong lu 道宣律師感通錄. In *Taishō shinshū daizōkyō*, Vol. 52, no. 2107, 435–42.

Davis, Richard. *Ritual in an Oscillating Universe: Worshipping Śiva in Medieval India*. Princeton: Princeton University Press, 1991.

De, S.K. *Early History of the Vaiṣṇava Faith and Movement in Bengal*. Calcutta: Firma K.L. Mukhopadhyay, 1961.

Delahaye, Hubert. *Les premières peintures de paysage en Chine: aspects religieux*. Paris: École Française d'Extrême-Orient, 1981.

Demiéville, Paul. 'Philosophy and Religion from Han to Sui.' In *The*

Cambridge History of China 1: The Ch'in and Han Empires, 221 B.C.–A.D. 220, vol. 1, edited by D. Twitchett and M. Loewe. Cambridge: Cambridge University Press, 1986.

Dengzhen yinjue 登眞隱訣. Compiled by Tao Hongjing 陶弘景. *Zhengtong Daozang* 193, no. 421.

Dhaky, M.A. 'The Chronology of the Solanki Temples of Gujarat.' *Journal of the Madhya Pradesh Itihasa Parishad* 3 (1961): 1–83.

———. 'The Western Indian Jaina Temple.' In *Aspects of Jaina Art and Architecture*, edited by U.P. Shah and M.A. Dhaky. Ahmedabad: L.D. Institute of Indology, 1975.

Dongxuan lingbao ershisi sheng tujing 洞玄靈寶二十四生圖經. *Zhengtong Daozang* 1051, no. 1407.

Du Guangting 杜光庭. *Shenxian ganyu zhuan* 神仙感遇傳. *Zhengtong Daozang* 328, no. 592.

Dudink, Adrianus. 'The Poem *Laojun Bianhua Wuji Jing*: Introduction, Summary, Text and Translation.' In *Linked Faiths: Essays on Chinese Religions and Traditional Culture in Honour of Kristofer Schipper*, edited by J.A.M. de Meyer and P.M. Engelfriet. Leiden: E.J. Brill, 1999.

Entwistle, Alan W. *Braj: Centre of Krishna Pilgrimage*. Groningen: Egbert Forsten, 1987.

Ershisi zhi 二十四治 (7th–10th c.). In *Yunji qiqian* 雲笈七籤 28. *Zhengtong Daozang* 677–702, no. 1032.

Fan Ye 范曄. *Hou Han Shu* 後漢書. Peking: Zhonghua shuju, 1963.

Fang Xuanling 房玄齡. *Jin shu* 晉書. Peking: Zhonghua shuju, 1974.

Fayuan zhulin 法苑珠林. Compiled by Daoshi 道世. In *Taishō shinshū daizōkyō*. Vol. 53.

Fergusson, James. *History of Indian and Eastern Architecture*. 2 vols. 1876. Reprint, Delhi: Munshiram Manoharlal, 1967.

Fobenxing ji jing 佛本行集經. In *Taishō shinshū daizōkyō*. Vol. 3, no. 190, 665–932.

Fontein, Jan. 'Notes on the Jātakas and Avadānas of *Barabuḍur.' In Borobudur: History and Significance of a Buddhist Monument*, edited by Luis Gomez and Hiram W. Woodward, Jr. Berkeley: Asian Humanities Press, 1981.

———. *The Law of Cause and Effect in Ancient Java*. Amsterdam: n.p., 1989.

Foucher, A. *La vie du Bouddha: d'après les textes et les monuments de l'Inde*. Paris: Payot, 1949.

Fracasso, Riccardo. *Libro dei monti e dei mari (Shanhai jing): Cosmografia e mitologia nella Cina Antica*. Venice: Marsilio, 1996.

Fufazang yinyuan zhuan 付法藏因緣傳. In *Taishō shinshū daizōkyō*. Vol. 50, no. 2058, 297–322.

Gabaude, L. 'Institution et réforme religieuse. Le cas de Man (1870–1949) et de Buddhadasa (1906).' In *Bicentenaire de Bankok*, edited by Thida Boontharm et al. Bangkok: Ambassade de France, 1982.
———. 'La triple crise du bouddhisme en Thaïlande.' *Bulletin de l'École Française d'Extrême-Orient* 83 (1996): 241–57.
Gadre, A.S. 'Buddhist Influence in Gujarat and Kathiawar.' *Journal of the Gujarat Research Society* 1–4 (1939): 61–70.
Gao Wen 高文, ed. *Sichuan Handai huaxiang zhuan* 四川漢代畫像磚. Shanghai: Shanghai renmin meishu chuban she, 1987.
Gernet, Jacques. *Buddhism in Chinese Society: An Economic History from the Fifth to the Tenth Centuries*. Translated by F. Verellen. New York: Columbia University Press, 1995.
Giles, H.A. *The Travels of Fa-hsien (399–414 A.D), or Record of the Buddhistic Kingdoms*. London: Routledge and Paul, 1959.
Gilmore, Leigh. 'The Mark of Autobiography: Postmodernism, Autobiography and Genre.' In *Autobiography and Postmodernism*, edited by Kathleen Ashley, Leigh Gilmore, and Gerald Peters. Amherst: University of Massachusetts, 1994.
Gohil, Nathalal. *Āgama vāṇī*. Ahmedabad: Navabhārat Sāhitya Mandir, 1994.
———. *Saurāṣṭranā harijana bhaktakavio*. Keshod: N. Gohil, 1987.
Gohil, Nathalal, Niranjan Rajyaguru, and Manoj Raval. *Santa-vāṇīnuṃ sattva ane sauṃdarya*. Rajkot: Praviṇ Prakāśan, 1994.
Gold, D. 'The Instability of the King: Magical Insanity and the Yogi's Power in the Politics of Jodhpur, 1803–1843.' In *Bhakti Religion in North India: Community Identity and Political Action*, edited by D.N. Lorenzen. Albany: State University of New York Press, 1995.
Gomez, Luis, and Hiram W. Woodward, Jr., eds. *Borobudur: History and Significance of a Buddhist Monument*. Berkeley: Asian Humanities Press, 1981.
Gonda, Jaṇ. *Loka: World and Heaven in the Veda*. Amsterdam: N.V. Noord-Hollandsche Uitgevers Maatschappij, 1966.
———. *The Meaning of the Sanskrit Term Dhāman*. Amsterdam: N.V. Noord-Hollandsche Uitgevers Maatschappij, 1966.
———. *Ancient Indian Kingship from the Religious Point of View*. Leiden: E.J. Brill, 1969.
———. 'The Indra Festival According to the Atharvavedins.' In *Selected Studies*. Vol. 4. Leiden: E.J. Brill, 1975.
———. 'A Note on Indra in Purāṇic Literature.' In *Selected Studies*. Vol. 4. Leiden: E.J. Brill, 1975.
———. 'The Sacred Character of Indian Kingship.' In *Selected Studies*. Vol. 4. Leiden: E.J. Brill, 1975.

Gosvāmī, Vāsudev. *Bhakt kavi Vyāsjī*. Mathurā: Agravāl Press, V.S. 2009 (1952).

Granoff, P. 'Scholars and Wonder-Workers: Some Remarks on the Role of the Supernatural in Philosophical Contests in Vedānta Hagiographies.' *Journal of the American Oriental Society* 105, no. 3 (1985): 459–67.

———. 'Worship as Commemoration: Pilgrimage, Death and Dying in Medieval Jainism.' *Bulletin d'Études Indiennes* 10 (1992): 181–202.

———. 'Defining Sacred Place: Contest, Compromise and Priestly Control in Some Māhātmya Texts.' *Annals of the Bhandarkar Oriental Institute* 79 (1998): 1–28.

———. 'Rāma's Bridge: Some Notes on Journeys Real and Envisioned.' *East and West* 48, nos. 1–2 (1998): 93–117.

———. 'Medieval Jain Accounts of Mt. Girnar and Śatruñjaya: Visible and Invisible Sacred Realms.' *Journal of the Oriental Institute.* Forthcoming.

Granoff, P., ed. *The Clever Adulteress and Other Stories: A Treasury of Jain Literature*. Oakville, ON: Mosaic Press, 1990.

Granoff, P,. and Koichi Shinohara. *Speaking of Monks*. Oakville, ON: Mosaic Press, 1992.

Guanzhong chuangli jietan tujing bingxu 關中創立戒壇圖經并序. Compiled by Daoxuan 道宣. Vol. 45, no. 1892, 807–19.

Gupta, Dīndayāl, and Premnarāyaṇ Ṭaṇḍaṇ. *Brajbhāṣā Sūrkoś*. Lucknow: Viśvavidyālay Hindī Prakāśan, V.S. 2031 (1974).

Gupta, Kiśorīlāl. *Nāgrīdās granthāvalī*. Vol. 2. Ākar Granthmālā 9. Benares: Nāgarīpracāriṇī Sabhā, 1965.

Haar, Barend ter. *The White Lotus Teachings in Chinese Religious History*. Leiden: E.J. Brill, 1992.

Hachiya Kunio 蜂屋邦夫. *Chūgoku dōkyō no genjō* 中國道教の現狀. Tokyo: Kyūko shoin, 1990.

Hanzhong ruzhi chaojing fa 漢中入治朝靜法. Cited and annotated in *Dengzhen yinjue* 3.

Hargūlāl. *Sarvopari nityavihāriṇī ras-sār (Aṣṭācāryoṃ kī Vāṇī)*. Vrindāban: Śrī Prem Hari Press, V.S. 2028 (1971).

Harper, Donald. 'Warring States: Natural Philosophy and Occult Thought.' In *The Cambridge History of Ancient China: From the Origins of Civilization to 221 B.C.*, edited by M. Loewe and E. Shaughnessy. Cambridge: Cambridge University Press, 1999.

Hawley, John Stratton. 'Author and Authority in the Bhakti Poetry of North India.' *Journal of Asian Studies* 47, no. 2 (1988): 269–90.

Hemacandra. *Triśaṣṭiśalākāpuruṣacarita*. 6 vols. Gaekwad's Oriental Series 51, 77, 108, 125, 139, 140. Translated by Helen Moore Johnson. Baroda: Oriental Institute, 1931–62.

Henderson, John B. 'Chinese Cosmographical Thought: The High Intellectual

Tradition.' In *History of Cartography*, Vol. 2, Book 2: *Cartography in the Traditional East and Southeast Asian Societies*, edited by J.B. Harley and David Woodward. Chicago: The University of Chicago Press, 1994.

Hendrischke, Barbara, and Benjamin Penny. '*The 180 Precepts Spoken by Lord Lao*: A Translation and Textual Study.' *Taoist Resources* 6, no. 2 (1996): 17–29.

Huangdi longshou jing 黃帝龍首經 *Zhengtong Daozang* 135, no. 283.

Inden, R. 'Ritual, Authority and Cyclic Time in Hindu Kingship.' In *Kingship and Authority in South India*, South Asian Studies, University of Wisconsin-Madison 3, edited by J.F. Richards. Madison: South Asian Studies, University of Wisconsin-Madison, 1978.

Irakāktāṣi Varuṣaṃ. Tarumapuram: Nāṉacampantam accakam, 1984.

Jaini, Padmanabh S. 'The Story of Sudhana and Manohara: An Analysis of the Texts and the Barabuḍur-Reliefs.' *Bulletin of the School of Oriental and African Studies* 29 (1966): 533–58.

Jani, Balvant, ed. *Santa-vāṇī, tattva ane tantra*. Gandhi-nagar: Gujarat Sahitya Akadami, 1996.

———. 'The Contribution of Women Saints to the Santa Literature of Saurashtra.' Paper presented at the École pratique des Hautes Études, Paris, May 19, 1998.

Jayantavijayaji Muni Shrī, *Holy Abu*. Translated by U.P. Shaḥ Bhavnagar: Shri Yashovijaya Jaina Granthamālā, 1954.

Jayantilal Acharya. *Gujarātanā santa kavio ane Bāulapantha (bāulagāno sāthe)*. Bombay: Forbes Gujarātī Sabhā, 1973.

Ji shenzhou sanbao gantong lu 集神州三寶感通錄. In *Taishō shinshū daizōkyō*. Vol. 52, no. 2106, 404–35.

Jinaharṣa, *Vastupālacarita*. Edited by Muni Kirtivijaya. Ahmedabad: n.p., 1941.

Jinavijaya, Muni, ed. *Purātanaprabandhasaṃgraha*. Singhi Jaina Series 2. Śāntiniketan: The Adhiṣṭātā-Siṅghī Jaina Jñānapīṭha, 1936.

Kailasapathy, K. 'The Writings of the Tamil Siddhas.' In *The Sants: Studies in a Devotional Tradition of India*, edited by K. Schomer and W.H. McLeod. Delhi: Motilal Banarsidas, 1987.

Kalinowski, Marc. *Cosmologie et divination dans la Chine ancienne: le compendium des cinq agents (Wuxing dayi, VIe siècle)*. Paris: École Française d'Extrême-Orient, 1991.

———. 'The Use of the Twenty-eight Xiu as a Day-count in Early China.' *Chinese Science* 13 (1996): 55–81.

Kanchansagarsuri, Acharya. *Shri Shatrunjay Giriraj Darshan in Sculptures and Architecture*. Aagamoddharak Granthamala 59. Kapadwanj: Aagamoddharak Granthamala, 1982.

Kane, P. V. *History of Dharmaśastra*. Vol. 4. 1953. Reprint, Poona: Bhandarkar

Oriental Research Institute, 1971.

Karṇapūra, *Caitanyacandrodaya Nāṭaka*. Calcutta: Sarasvati Press, 1885.

Keyes, Charles F. 'Death of Two Buddhist Saints in Thailand.' In *Charisma and Sacred Biography*, edited by Michael Williams. *Journal of the American Academy of Religion, Thematic Studies* 98, pts. 3 & 4 (1982): 149–80.

Khakhar, Dalpatrām P. *Report on the Architectural and Archaeological Remains in the Province of Kacch, with five papers by the late Sir Alex. Burnes*. 1879. Reprint, Patna: Indian India, 1978.

Khan, Dominique-Sila. 'The Coming of Nikalank Avatar: A Messianic Theme in Some Sectarian Traditions in North-Western India.' *Journal of Indian Philosophy* 25 (1997): 401–26.

______. *Conversions and Shifting Identities: Ramdev Pir and the Ismailis in Rajasthan*. New Delhi: Manohar, 1997.

Kornfield, J. *Living Buddhist Masters*. Santa Cruz: Unity Press, 1997.

Kou Qianzhi 寇謙之 (365–448). *Laojun yinsong jiejing* 老君音誦誡經. *Zhengtong Daozang* 562, no. 785.

Kramrisch, Stella. *The Hindu Temple*. 2 vols. Delhi: Motilal Banarsidass, 1976.

______. *The Presence of Śiva*. Princeton: Princeton University Press, 1981.

Krauskopff, G. *Maîtres et Possédés. Les rites et l'ordre social chez les Tharu*. Paris: Éditions du CNRS, 1989.

Krom, N.J. *The Life of the Buddha on the Stūpa of Barabuḍur According to the Lalitavistara-Text*. 1926. Reprint, Varanasi: Bharatiya Publishing House, 1974.

———. *Barabuḍur: Archaeological Description*. The Hague: Martinus Nijhoff, 1927.

Krom, N.J., and T. van Erp. *Beschrijving van Barabuḍur*. The Hague: Martinus Nijhoff, 1931.

Kṛṣṇadāsa. *Caitanyacaritāmrta*. Edited by Śrīmadbhaktikevala Auḍulomi Mahārāj. Calcutta: Gauḍīya Mission, 1957.

Kuwayama Shōshin. 'Keihin to Bappatsu.' 罽賓と佛鉢 In *Tenbō Ajia no Kōkogaku: Higuchi Takayasu Kyōju Taikan Kinen Ronshū*. 展望　アジアの考古学：樋口隆康教授退官記念論集. Tokyo: Shinchōsha, 1983.

———. 'The Buddha's Bowl in Gandhāra and Relevant Problems.' *South Asian Archaeology* 9, pt. 2 (1987): 946–74.

———. *Gandāra-kāpishī shi kenkyū* ガンダーラ　カーピシー姸究. Kyoto: Kyōtodaigaku Jimbunkagaku kenkyūsho, 1990.

Lalit Prakāś. Edited by Caturvedī, Banmālīlāl. Lucknow: Tālukdār Press, 1931.

Laojun bianhua wuji jing 老君變化無極經 (4th c.). *Zhengtong Daozang* 875, no. 1195.

Legge, James. *A Record of Buddhistic Kingdoms: Being an Account by the Chinese Monk Fa-Hsien of his Travels in India and Ceylong* (A.D. 399–414) *in Search of the Buddhist Books of Discipline*. New York: Pargon Book Reprint, 1965.

Lamotte, Étienne. *Histoire du Buddhisme Indien*. Louvain: Publications

Universitaires, Institut Orientaliste, 1958.
Li Houqiang 李后強, ed. *Wawu shan daojiao wenhua* 瓦屋山道教文化. Chengdu: Sichuan minzu chuban she, 2000.
Li Junming 李駿名. 'Qingcheng shan yu Heming shan 青城山與鶴鳴山.' *Zongjiao xue yanjiu* 宗教學研究 3–4 (1989): 15–16.
Lianhua mian jing. 蓮華面經 In *Taishō shinshū daizōkyō.* Vol. 12, no. 386, 1070–77.
Linghua ershisi 靈化二十四. In Du Guang-ting 杜光庭. *Dongtian fudi yuedu mingshan ji* 洞天福地嶽瀆名山記, 11a–15a. *Zhengtong Daozang* 331, no. 599.
Liu Shufen, 'Art, Ritual, and Society: Buddhist Practice in Rural China During the Northern Dynasties.' *Asia Major*, 3rd ser., 8, no. 1 (1995): 19–49.
Liu Weiyong 劉惟永 and Ding Yidong 丁易東. *Daode zhenjing jiyi dazhi* 道德眞經集義大旨. *Zhengtong Daozang* 431, no. 723.
Luxiang gangton lu 律相感通錄, attributed to Daoxuan. In *Taishō shinshū daizōkyō.* Vol. 45, no. 1898, 874–82.
Lu Xiujing 陸修靜. *Lu xiansheng daomen kelüe* 陸先生道門科略. *Zhengtong Daozang* 761, no. 1127.
Luo Kaiyu. 羅開玉. *Zhongguo kexue shenhua zongjiao di xiehe: yi Li Bing wei zhongxin* 中國科學神話宗教的協合—以李冰爲中心. Chengdu: Shu Ba shushe, 1990.
Mahābhārata, The. Edited by V.S. Sukthankar, S.K. Belvalkar, et al. 19 vols. Poona: Bhandarkar Oriental Research Institute, 1927–66.
Mahābhāratam with Nīlakaṇṭha's commentary *Bhāratabhāvadīpa*. Edited by Pandit Ramchandrashastri Kinjawadekar. Poona: Chitrashala Press, 1929–33.
Mahārāj , Kalidās .*Rāṇīmāṃ*, 3rd ed. Rajkot: Nakalaṃka Mandira Trust, 1994.
———. *Soraṭhī Strīsanto.* Ahmedabad: Sastu Sāhitya Vardhaka Kāryālaya, 1972.
Mahīśāsaka Vinaya. In *Taishō shinshū daizōkyō*, edited by Takakusu Junjirō and Watanabe Kaigyoku. Tokyo: Taishō Issaikyō Kankōkai, 1924–32.
Majumdar, A. K. *Chaulukyas of Gujarat.* Bombay: Bharatiya Vidya Bhavan, 1956.
Majumdar, Bimanbibihari. *Śrīcaitanyacariter Upādān.* Calcutta: Calcutta University, 1959.
———. *Kṛṣṇa in History and Legend.* Calcutta, University of Calcutta, 1969.
Malamoud, Charles. *Cuire le monde.* Paris: Éditions La Découverte, 1989.
Maspero, Henri. *Taoism and Chinese Religion.* Translated by Frank Kierman. Amherst: University of Massachusetts Press, 1981.
McMahan, David. 'Orality, Writing, and Authority in South Asian Buddhism: Visionary Literature and the Struggle for Legitimacy in the Mahayana.' *History of Religions* 37 (1998): 249–74.
Meghani, Javerchand. *Soraṭhī bahārvaṭiyā.* Bhavnagar: Prasar, 1997.
Mehta, R. N. 'Migration of Yadavas from Mathurā to Dwārakā: Chronology of the Myth.' *Journal of the Oriental Institute* 46, nos. 1–2 (Sept.–Dec. 1996): 77–81.

Meister, Michael W. 'Fragments from a Divine Cosmology: Unfolding Forms on India's Temple Walls.' In *Gods, Guardians and Lovers: Temple Sculptures from North India (A.D. 700-1200),* edited by Vishakha N. Desai and Darielle Mason. New York: The Asia Society, 1993.

Merutuṅga. *The Prabandhacintāmaṇi or Wishing-Stone of Narratives.*Translated by C.H. Tawney. Delhi: Indian Book Gallery, 1987.

Michaud, Paul. 'The Yellow Turbans.' *Monumenta Serica* 17 (1958): 47–127.

Miśra, Vidyānivās. *Sāhityik Brajbhāṣā koś.* 3 vols. Lucknow: Uttar Prades Hindī Samsthān, 1985–90.

Moray, M.S. *History of Buddhism in Gujarat.* Ahmedabad: Saraswati Pustak Bhandar, 1965.

Morinis, Alan. *Pilgrimage in the Hindu Tradition: A Case Study of West Bengal.* Delhi: Oxford University Press, 1984.

Mus, Paul. *Barabudur.* 1935. Reprint, New York: Arno Press, 1978.

Nābhādās Bhaktmāl. Edited by Sītārām Śaran. and Bhagavānprasād Rūpkalā. 1910. Reprint, Lucknow: Tejkumār Book Depot, 1969.

Nābhājī krt Śrī Bhakt Māl, Bhakti Ras Bodhinī ṭīkā evaṃ Bhakti Rasāyanī vyākhyā sahit. Edited by Rāmkrsṇadās Garge. Vrindāban: Viyogī Viśveśvar Nimbārkācārya Pīṭh, 1960.

Nagasawa Kazutoshi 長沢和俊. *Hokkenden Sōunkōki* 法顕伝宋雲後紀. Tokyo: Heibonsha, 1984.

Nāhaṭā, Agarchand. *Rāghavdās kṛt Bhaktmāl: Caturdās kṛt ṭīkā sahit.* Rājasthān Purātan Granthmālā 78. Jodhpur: Rājasthān Prācyavidyā Pratiṣṭhān, 1965.

Nanjiani, S. *Khojā vṛttānta.* 2nd ed. Ahmedabad: n.p., 1892.

Nārāyaṇdās, Svāmī. Śrī *Svāmī Rāghavdāsjī viracit Bhaktmāl: Svāmī Caturdāsjī kṛt padya ṭīkā tathā bhakti-caritra prakāśikā gadya ṭīkā sahit.* Pushkar: Dādādayālū Mahāsabhā, 1969.

Needham, Joseph. 'Astronomy.' In *Science and Civilization in China,* vol. 3. Cambridge: Cambridge University Press, 1959.

Neog, Maheshvar. *Early History of the Vaiṣṇava Faith and Movement in Assam Śāṅkaradeva and His Times.* Delhi: Motilal Banarsidass, 1965.

Nickerson, Peter. 'Abridged Codes of Master Lu for the Daoist Community.' In *Religions of China in Practice,* edited by D.S. Lopez. Princeton: Princeton University Press, 1996.

Nijmat Siddhānt: Śrī Mahant Kiśordāsjī kṛt. Vol. 2 (*Madhya Khaṇḍ*). Edited by Caraṇsevak Lālā (Vaiśya) Kedarnāth. Lucknow: Anglo-Oriental Press, V.S. 1971 (1915).

Norton, Ann Wood. 'The Jaina Samavasaraṇa.' PhD diss., Harvard University, 1981.

Nou, Jean-Louis, and Louis Frédéric. *Borobudur.* New York: Abbeville Press, 1996.

Nüqing guilü 女青鬼律. *Zhengtong Daozang* 563, no. 790.
Nyanatiloka. *Buddhist Dictionary: Manual of Buddhist Terms and Doctrines.* 4th rev. ed. Kandy: Buddhist Publication Society, 1980.
Ogawa Kan'ichi 小川貫弌. *Bukkyō bunkashi kenkyū* 仏教文化史研究. Kyoto: Nagata Bunshōdō, 1973.
Olivelle, Patrick, trans. *Upaniṣads.* Oxford: Oxford University Press, 1996.
Pauwels, Heidi Rika Maria. 'Harirām Vyās and the Early Bhakti-Milieu.' In *Studies in South Asian Devotional Literature: Research Papers 1988–1991, Presented at the Fifth Conference on Devotional Literature in New Indo-Aryan Languages, Held at Paris – École française d'Extrême-Orient, 9–12 July 1991,* edited by Françoise Mallison and Alan W. Entwistle. New Delhi: Manohar; Paris: École Française d'Extrême-orient, 1994.
———. 'Harirām Vyās's *Rās-pañcādhyāyī* and *Mān kī śr̥ṇkhalā*: A Critical Interpretation.' PhD diss., University of Washington, 1994.
———. *Kr̥ṣṇa's Round Dance Reconsidered: Harirām Vyās's* Hindī *Rās-pañcādhyāyī.* London Studies on South Asia, 12. London: Curzon Press, 1996.
Peltier, Anatole-Roger. *Introduction à la connaisance des hlvnṅ ba1 de Thaïlande.* Paris: École Française d'Extrême-Orient, 1977.
Péterfalvi, Jean-Michel, et M. Biardeau. *Mahābhārata* (Le). Tome 2. Livres VI à XVIII. Extraits traduits du sanscrit par Jean-Michel Péterfalvi. Introduction et commentaires par Madeleine Biardeau. Paris: Flammarion, 1986.
Peterson, Indira. *Poems to Siva: The Hymns of the Tamil Saints.* Princeton: Princeton University Press, 1989.
Pregadio, Fabrizio. 'The Book of the Nine Elixirs and its Tradition.' In *Chūgoku kodai kagakushi ron* 中國古代科學論. vol. 2. Edited by Yamada Keiji 山田慶兒 and Tanaka Tan 田中淡. Kyoto: Kyōto daigaku jimbun kagaku kenkyūjo, 1991.
Priyādāsjī kī granthāvalī. Edited by Bābā Kr̥ṣṇadās. Kusum Sarovar: Bābā Kr̥ṣṇadās, V.S. 2007 [1950].
Puṇyavijaya Sūri, Muni Śrī, ed. *Sukrtakīrtikallolinyādi Vastupālapraśastisaṃgraha.* Singhi Jaina Series 5. Bombay: Bharatiya Vidya Bhavan, 1961.
Purohit, Lalit Prasāḍ. *Rasik Ananya Māl: Māl evaṃ gadya rūpāntaraṇ.* Vol. 2. 1960. Reprint, Vrindāban: Veṇu Prakāśan, 1986.
Pusalker, A. D. 'Dvārakā.' In *B.C. Law Volume,* part I, edited by D.R. Bhandarkar et al. Calcutta: The Indian Research Institute, 1945.
Puvārāma Mahanta. *Bardowōgurucarita.* Edited by Maheśvara Neog. Guwahati: Guwahati Book Stall, 1977.
Puyao jing 普曜經. In *Taishō shinshū daizōkyō.* Vol. 3, no. 186, 483–539.
Raghurājsiṃh. *Bhakt Māl arthāt Rām Rasikāvalī.* Edited by Khemrāj Kr̥ṣṇadās.

Bombay: Lakṣmī Veṅkateśvar Steam Press, 1915 (V.S. 1971).
Rajanubhab, Damrong. *Monuments of the Buddha in Siam.* 2nd rev. ed. Translated by Sulak Sivaraksha and A.B. Griswolḍ. Bangkok: The Siam Society, 1973.
Rājaśekhara. *Prabandhakośa.* Singhi Jaina Series 6. Edited by Jina Vijaya. Śāntiniketan: The Adhiṣṭātā-Siṅghī Jaina Jñānapīṭha, 1935.
Rajyaguru, Niranjan. *Bījamārgī gupta pāṭa-upāsanā ane Mahāpanthīsantonī bhajanavāṇī.* Gandhinagar: Gujarati Sahitya Akademi, 1995.
Rāmacaraṇa. *Śaṅkaracarita.* Edited by Harinārāyan Dattabarua. Nalbārī: Dattabarua Publishing Company, 1996.
Rao, S. R. 'Excavation of the Lost City of Dvārakā in the Arabian Sea.' In *Contacts Between Cultures. Selected papers from the 33rd International Congress of Asian and North African Studies, Toronto, Aug. 15–25, 1990,* vol. 2, *South Asia,* edited by Kay Koppedrayer. Queenston, ON: E. Mellon Press, 1992.
———. 'Submergence of Dvārakā is a Fact.' *Purāṇa* 34, no. 2 (1992): 3–32.
Ray, R.A. *Buddhist Saints in India: A Study in Buddhist Values and Orientations.* New York: Oxford University Press, 1994.
Reiniche, Marie-Louise. 'Le Temple dans la localité. Quatre exemples au Tamilnadu.' In *L'espace du temple 1: espaces, itinéraires, méditations.* Ed. Jean-Claude Galey. Paris: Editions de l'École des Hautes Études et Sciences Sociales, 1982.
Robinet, Isabelle. 'Metamorphosis and Deliverance from the Corpse in Taoism.' *History of Religions* 19 (1979): 37–70.
———. 'The Taoist Immortal: Jesters of Light and Shadow.' *Journal of Chinese Religions* 13/14 (1986): 87–105.
Ruben, W. *Krishṇa: Konkordanz und Kommentar der Motive seines Heldenlebens.* Istanbul: n.p., 1943.
Rushbrook Williams, L.F. *The Black Hills, Kutch in History and Legend: A Study in Indian Local Loyalties.* London: Weidenfeld and Nicolson, 1958.
(Śabdārth evaṃ pramukh viṣayoṃ ke śīrṣak yukt) Śrī Bayālīs Lālā tathā padyā-valī: Racayitā: Śrī Hit Dhruvdāsjī Mahārāj. Edited by Lalitācaraṇ Gosvāmī. Vrindāban: Bābā Tulsīdās, V.S. 2028 (1971).
St. Sekkizhar's Periya Puranaṃ Pt. 1. Translated by T.N. Ramachandran. Thanjavur: Tamil University, 1990.
Saksenā, Nirmalā. *Sūrsāgar Śabdāvalī: Ek sāṃskritik adhyayan.* Allahabad: Hindustānī Academy, 1962.
Sandesara, Bhogilal J. *Literary Circle of Mahāmātya Vastupāla and Its Contribution to Sanskrit Literature.* Bombay: Bharatiya Vidhya Bhavan, 1953.
Sandesara, Bhogilal J., and J.P. Thakur. 'Lexicographical Studies in 'Jaina Sanskrit,' *The M.S. University Oriental Series* 5 (1962).

Sankalia, H.D. 'Antiquity of Modern Dwarka or Dwarka in Literature and Archaeology.' *Journal of the Asiatic Society of Bombay* 38 (n.s.), Dr. Bhau Daji Special Volume (1963): 74–84.

———. 'Dwarka in Literature and Archaelogy.' *Sarada Pitha Pradipa* 11 (1971): 14–30.

———. 'Vrishṇis, Sātvatas, Krishṇa and Dvārakā.' *Journal of Ancient Indian History* (University of Calcutta) 11 (1977–8): 1–5.

Śāṅkhaparābhava. Edited by B.J. Sandesera. Baroda: The Oriental Institute, 1965.

Sawa Akitoshi 澤章敏. 'Gotōbeidō seiken no shiki kōzō 五斗米道政權の組織構造.' In *Dōkyō bunka e no tenbō* 道教文化への展望. Edited by Dōkyō bunka kenkyū kai 道教文化研究會. Tokyo: Hirakawa shuppan, 1994.

Sax, W. S. *Mountain Goddess*. New York: Oxford University Press, 1991.

Schafer, Edward H. *Pacing the Void: T'ang Apporaches to the Stars*. Berkeley: University of California Press, 1977.

Schipper, Kristofer. 'Taoist Ordination Ranks in the Tunhuang Manuscripts.' In *Religion und Philosophie in Ostasien. Festschrift für Hans Steininger*, edited by Gert Naundorf et al. Würzburg: Königshausen and Neumann, 1985.

———. *The Taoist Body*. Translated by Karen C. Duval. Berkeley: University of California Press, 1993.

———. 'The Inner World of the *Lao-tzu chung-ching*.' In *Time and Space in Chinese Culture*, edited by Chun-chieh Huang and E. Zürcher. Leiden: E.J. Brill, 1995.

———. 'The True Form: Reflections on the Liturgical Basis of Taoist Art.' Forthcoming.

Settar, S., and Günther-Dietz Sontheimer, eds. *Memorial Stones*. Dharwad: Institute of Indian Art History, 1982.

Shah, U.P. 'A Forgotten Chapter in the History of Śvetāmbara Jaina Church or A Documentary Epigraph from the Mount Śatruñjaya.' *Journal of the Asiatic Society Bombay* 30 (1955): 100–13.

———. Jaina-Rūpa-Maṇḍana. New Delhi: Abhinav Publications, 1987.

Shangqing huangshu guodu yi 上清黃書過度儀. *Zhengtong Daozang* 1009, no. 1294.

Shangqing taishang dijun jiuzhen zhongjing 上清太上帝君九眞中經. *Zhengtong Daozang* 1042, no. 1376.

Sharma, Raṃ 'No. 27–Menal Inscription of the Chahamana Prince Meghanada, Vikrama 1312.' *Epigraphia Indica* 37, pt. iv (October 1967): 155–58.

Shi Zhijing 史志經, (attri) *Laojun bashiyi hua tushuo* 老君八十一化圖說. Ming ed. Reprinted in Florian Reiter, *Leben und Wirken Lao-tzu's in Schrift und Bild:*

Lao-chün pa-shih-i hua t'u-shuo. Würzburg: Königshausen und Neumann, 1990.

Shi Zhouren 施舟人 (Kristofer Schipper), ed. *Daozang suoyin: wuzhong banben Daozang tongjian* 道藏索引一五種版本道藏通檢. Revised edition by Chen Yaoting 陳耀庭. Shanghai: Shanghai shudian chuban she, 1996.

Shinohara, Koichi. 'Two Sources of Chinese Buddhist Biographies: *Stūpa* Inscriptions and Miracle Stories.' In *Monks and Magicians: Religious Biographies in Asia*, edited by P. Granoff and Koichi Shinohara. Oakville, ON: Mosaic Press, 1988.

———. 'The *Kāṣāya* Robe of the Past Buddha Kāśyapa in the Miraculous Instruction Given to the Vinaya Master Daoxuan (596–667).' *Chung-Hwa Buddhist Journal* 13 (2000): 299–367.

Shrimali, Dalpat. *Harijana santa ane lokasāhitya (kaṃthasthathi granthastha)*. Ahmedabad: Gujarāta Grantharatna Kāryālaya, 1993.

Siddhicandra. *Bhānucandragaṇicarita*. Singhi Jain Series 15. Edited by Mohanalal Dalichand Desai. Ahmedabad: The Sañchālaka-Siṅghī Jaina Granthamālā, 1941.

Sima Chengzhen 司馬承禎. *Tiandi gongfu tu* 天地宮府圖. In *Yunji qiqian* 雲笈七籤 27. *Zhengtong Daozang* 677–702, no. 1032.

Siṃha, Pratītrāy Laksmaṇ. *Lokendra Brajotsava*. Lucknow: Naval Kiśor Press, 1892.

Smith, Brian. *Classifying the Universe: The Ancient Indian* Varṇa *System and the Origins of Caste*. New York: Oxford University Press, 1994.

Snell, Rupert. *The Eighty-Four Hymns of Hita Harivaṃśa: An Edition of the Caurāsī Pada*. Delhi: Motilal Banarsidass, 1991.

Someśvara *Kīrtikaumudī*. Singhi Jaina Series 32. Edited by Śrī Puṇyavijayajiī Bombay: Bharatiya Vidya Bhavan, 1961.

Śrī Bhagavat Rasik Devjī kī Vāṇī. Edited by Vrajvallabh Śaraṇ. Vrindāban: Śrījī Mandir, V.S. 2044 (1987).

ŚrīlaŚrī Kayilai Kurumaṇi Niṉaivu Malar. Edited by Irāmaliṅkat Tampirāṉ Tarumapuram: Nāṉacampantam Patipakkam, 1972.

Śrīmad Bhāgavata Mahāpurāṇa: With Sanskrit Text and English Translation. 2 vols. 2nd ed. Edited and translated by Chimman Lal Goswami and M.A. Śāstrā. Gorakhpur: Gita Press, 1981.

Śrīmad Gosvāmī Śrī Nābhājī kṛt Śrī Bhaktmāl, Śrī Priyādāsjī kṛt kavittamayī Bhakti Ras Bodhinī ṭīkā sahit. Vol. 3. 3rd ed. Edited by Bhaktmālī Gaṇeśdās and Rāmāyaṇī Rāmeśvardās. Vrindāban: Rāmānand Pustakālay, V.S. 2039 (1982).

Śrī Nakalaṃka Bhajana-saṃgraha. Ahmedabad: 'Śrī Nakalaṃka Jñānaprasaraka Maṇḍala' (The Circle for the Advancement of the Knowledge of Nakalaṃka), 1921.

Śrī Nakalaṃka Sāstrā. Bombay: 'Śrī Nakalaṃka Jñānaprasaraka Maṇḍala'

(The Circle for the Advancement of the Knowledge of Nakalaṃka), 1922.
Śrīskanda Mahāpurāṇaṃ Vol. 2. Delhi: Nag Publishers, 1986.
Stein, Rolf A. 'Remarques sur quelques mouvements du taoïsme politico-religieux au 2e siècle ap. J.-C.' *T'oung Pao* 50 (1963): 1–78.
———. 'Spéculations mystiques et thèmes relatifs aux "cuisines" du taoïsme.' *Annuaire du Collège de France* 72e année (1972–3): 489–99.
Stephenson, Richard. 'Chinese and Korean Star Maps and Catalogs.' In *History of Cartography*, Vol. 2, Book 2: *Cartography in the Traditional East and Southeast Asian Societies*, edited by J.B. Harley and D. Woodward. Chicago: The University of Chicago Press, 1994.
Stewart, Tony K. 'Biographical Images of Kṛṣṇa-Caitanya: A Study in the Perception of Divinity.' PhD diss., University of Chicago, 1985.
Strickmann, Michel. *Le taoïsme du Mao Chan: Chronique d'une révélation*. Paris: Collège de France, 1981.
———. 'Therapeutische Rituale und das Problem des Bösen im frühen Taoismus.' *In Religion und Philosophie in Ostasien. Festschrift für Hans Steininger*, edited by G. Naundorf et al. Würzburg: Königshausen and Neumann, 1985.
Sūrasāgara. Vol. 1. 4th ed. Nāgarīpracāriṇī Granthmālā 35. Edited by Nanddulāre Vājpeyī et al. Benares: Nāgarīpracāriṇī Sabhā, V.S. 2021 (1964).
Tadpatrikar, S.N. 'The Kṛṣṇa Problem.' *Annals of the Bhandarkar Oriental Research Institute* 10 (1929): 269–344.
*Taiping guangji*太平廣記. Compiled by Li Fang 李昉 et al. Peking: Zhonghua shuju, 1961.
Taishang laojun jinglü 太上老君經律. *Zhengtong Daozang* 562, no. 786.
Taishang laojun zhongjing 太上老君中經. *Zhengtong Daozang* 839, no. 1168.
Taishang miaoshi jing 太上妙始經. *Zhengtong Daozang* 344, no. 658.
Taishō shinshū daizōkyō. Edited by Takakusu Junjirō and Watanabe Kaigyoku. 100 vols. Tokyo: Taishō Issaikyō Kankōkai, 1924–32.
Taizhen yudi siji mingke jing 太眞玉帝四極明科, *Zhengtong Daozang* 77–8, no. 184.
Taizhen ke 太眞科. Reference to the evolving Shangqing code *Taizhen yudi siji mingke* 太眞玉帝四極明科, cited in numerous sources close to the Heavenly Master liturgical tradition. Cf. *Taizhen yudi siji mingke jing* 太眞玉帝四極明科經, D 77–8, no. 184.
*Taizi ruiying benjijing*太子瑞應本起經. In *Taishō shinshū daizōkyō*. Vol 3, no. 185, 472–83.
Tambiah, S. J. *The Buddhist Saints of the Forest and the Cult of Amulets: A Study in Charisma, Hagiography, Sectarianism, and Millennial Buddhism*. Cambridge: Cambridge University Press, 1984.
Tambs-Lyche, Harald. *Power, Profit and Poetry: Traditional Society in Kathiawar,*

Western India. New Delhi: Manohar, 1997.
Tampirāṉ, Cuvāminātaṭ *Tiruvaruṭceyti*. Tarumapuram: Nāṉacampantam accakam, 1974.
Taṇṭapāṇi Tēcikar, Ca. 'Aruḷ Aṅupavaṅkaḷiṟ Cila.' In *ŚrīlaśrīKayilaiṉ Kurumaṇi Niṉaivu Malar*. Ed. Irāmaliṅkat Tampirān. Tarumapuram: Ñāṉacampantam Patipakam, 1972, 37–45.
Tarumai Kaṉakāpikṣēka Viḻamalar. Edited by 'Kaṇakāpikṣēka Viḻakkuḻuviṇar.' Tarumapuram: Ñāṉacampantam accakam, 1961.
Tatang neidian lu 大唐內典錄. Compiled by Daoxuan 道宣. In *Taishī shinshū daizōkyō*. Vol. 55. no. 2149. 219–342.
Taylor, J.L. 'From Wandering to Monastic Domestication.' *Journal of the Siam Society* 76 (1988): 64–88.
———. *Forest Monks and the Nation-State. An Anthropological and Historical Study in Northeastern Thailand*. Singapore: Institute of Southeast Asian Studies, 1993.
Tewari, S.P. 'No. 7–National Museum Inscription of Kelachchadevī V.S. 1239,' *Epigraphia Indica* 41 (1975–6): 58–60.
Thambiran, Visvalinga. *Sri Panchanathiswaraswarni Temple, Tiruvaiyaru*. Tarumapuram: Gnanagambhandar Press, 1965.
Tiyavanich, Kamala. *Forest Recollections: Wandering Monks in Twentieth-century Thailand*. Chiang Mai: Silkworm Books, 1997.
Tripathi, Alok. '*Dvārakā* in Literature and Archaeology.' *Man and Environment* 21, no. 2 (July–December 1996): 49–58.
Vaittiyanāṭan , Vacantā. 'Tāyir Cianta Talaivaṉl. In *ŚrīlaŚrī Kayilai Kurumaṇi Niṉaivu Malar*. Edited by Irāmaliṅkat Tampirāṉ. Nāṉacampantam Patippakam, 1972.
Varāha Purāṇa: Text with English Translation. Edited by Anand Swarup Gupta. Edited and translated by Ahibhushan Bhattacharya. Varanasi: All-India Kashiraj Trust, 1981.
Verardi, Giovanni, with a Note by Alessandro Grossato. 'The Kuṣāṇa Emperors as *Cakravartins* Dynastic Art and Cults in India and Central Asia: History of a Theory, Clarifications and Refutations.' *East and West* 33 (1983): 225–94.
Verellen, F. '"Evidential Miracles in Support of Taoism": The Inversion of a Buddhist Apologetic Tradition in Late T'ang China.' *T'oung Pao* 78 (1992): 217–63.
———. 'The Beyond Within: Grotto-Heavens (*Dongtian*) in Taoist Ritual and Cosmology.' *Cahiers d'Extrême-Asie* 8 (1995): 265–90.
———. 'Zhang Ling and the Lingjing Salt Well.' In *En suivant la voie royale: mélanges en hommage à Léon Vandermeersch*, edited by Jacques Gernet and

Marc Kalinowski. Paris: École Française d'Extrême-Orient, 1997.
(Vidyāraṇya). *Śaṅkaradigvijaya*. Ānandāśrama Saṃskrta Granthāvali 22. Edited by Vināyak Gaṇeśa Āpaṭe. Puṇe: Ānanda āśrama, 1932.
Vidyavijayaji, Muniraj. *A Monk and a Monarch*. Shree Vijayadharmasuri Jain Book Series 59. N.p., 1944.
Viṣṇu Purāṇa, The. Edited and translated by H.H. Wilson. Delhi: Nag Publishers, 1989.
Vṛndāvan-dhām-anurāgāvalī. Microfilm, Vrindāban Research Institute. Reel 666, acc. no. H5(3).
Vṛndāvanadāsa. *Caitanya Bhāgavata*. Edited by Śrīmadbhaktikevala Auḍulomi Mahārāj. Calcutta: Gauḍīya Mission, 1961.
Vyās, Harirām *Śrī Vyās-vāṇī*. 2 vols. Edited by Akhila Bhāratavarṣīya Śrī Hita Rādhāvallabhīya Vaiṣṇava Mahāsabhā. Vrindāban: Śri Vrajendra MachinePress, V.S. 1991 (1934).
———. *Śrī Vyās Vāṇī: Siddhānt aur Ras sahit*. Edited by Rādhākiśor Gosvāmī. Mathurā: Agravāl Press, V.S. 1994 (1937).
Wang Chunwu 王純五. *Tianshi dao ershisi zhi kao* 天師道二十四治考. Chengdu: Sichuan daxue chuban she, 1996.
———. *Dongtian fudi yuedu mingshan ji quanyi* 洞天福地嶽瀆名山記全譯. Guiyang: Guizhou renmin chuban she, 1999.
Wang Jianmin 王健民, Liang Zhu 梁柱 and Wang Shengli 王勝利. 'Zeng Houyi mu chutu ershiba xiu, bohu, qinglong tuxiang 曾侯乙墓出土的二十八宿青龍白虎圖象.' *Wenwu* 文物 (1979.7): 40–45.
Wang-Toutain, Françoise. 'Le bol du Bouddha: propagation du bouddhisme et légitimité politique.' *Bulletin de L'école Française d'extrême-orient* 81 (1994): 59–82.
Wei Fuhua. 衛复華. 'Zhongguo daojiao Wudoumi dao fayuan de Heming shan 中國道教五斗米道發源地鶴鳴山.' *Zongjiao xue yanjiu* 宗教學研究 (1989.1–2): 6–11.
White, D. G. *The Alchemical Body: Siddha Traditions in Medieval India*. Chicago: The University of Chicago Press, 1996.
Xiao Dengfu 蕭登福. '*Taishang xuanling beidou benming yansheng zhenjing* tanshu (1–2) 太上玄靈北斗本命延生眞經探述.' *Zongjiao xue yanjiu* 宗教學研究 (1997.3), 49–65; (1997.4), 30–39.
———. '*Taishang shuo nandou liusi yanshou duren miaojing* tanshu 太上說南斗六司延壽度人妙經探述.' *Zongjiao xue yanjiu* 宗教學研究 (1998.2), 1–7.
Xiaochun, Sun, and Jacob Kistemaker. *The Chinese Sky under the Han: Constellating Stars and Society*. Leiden: E.J. Brill, 1997.
Xu, Master 徐氏. *Santian neijie jing* 三天內解經 (5th c.). *Zhengtong Daozang* 876, no. 1205.

Xu Wenbin 徐文彬 et al., eds. *Sichuan Handai shique* 四川漢代石闕. Peking: Wenwu chuban she, 1992.

Xuandu lüwen 玄都律文. *Zhengtong Daozang* 78, no. 188.

Yan Kaiming 顏開明. 'Choujing zhi suozai di: Choujing shan Laozi miao 稠稉治所在地–稠稉山老子廟.' *Zongjiao xue yanjiu* 宗教學研究 1–2 (1990): 15, 67.

———. 'Daojiao Pinggai zhi yu Xinjin Guanyin si 道教平蓋治與新津觀音寺.' *Zongjiao xue yanjiu* 宗教學研究 1–2 (1993): 21–23.

Yangping zhi 陽平治. In *Zhengyi fawen tianshi jiaojie kejing* 正一法文天師教戒科經 20a–21b.

Yocum, Glenn E. 'A Non-Brahman Tamil Saiva Mutt: A Field Study of the Thiravavaduthurai Adheenam.' In *Monastic Life in the Christian and Hindu Traditions: A Comparative Study. Studies in Comparative Religion*, vol. 3, edited by Austin Creel and Vasudha Narayanan. Queenston, ON: Edwin Mellon Press, 1990.

Yoe, Shway. *The Burman: His Life and Notions*. Arran, Scotland: Kiscadale, 1989.

Yoshikawa, Tadao 吉川忠夫. 'Seishitsu kō「静室」考.' *Tōhō gakuhō* 東方學報 59 (1987): 125–62.

Yuanchen zhangjiao licheng li 元辰章醮立成曆. *Zhengtong Daozang* 1008, no. 1288.

Yunji qiqian 雲笈七籤. Compiled by Zhang Junfang 張君房. *Zhengtong Daozang* 677–702, no. 1032.

Zaehner, R.C., trans. *The Bhagavad-gītā, with a Commentary Based on the Original Sources*. London: Oxford University Press, 1973.

Zhang Bian 張辯. *Tianshi zhi yi* 天師治儀. First part 上. Preserved in *Shoulu cidi faxin yi* 受籙次第法信儀, 19b–30a. *Zhengtong Daozang* 991, no. 1244. Cf. *Zhengyi xiuzhen lüeyi* 正一修眞略儀. *Zhengtong Daozang* 990, no. 1239.

Zhang tianshi ershisi zhi tu 張天師二十四治圖 ap. *Sandong zhunang* 三洞珠囊, 7.6a–15a. Compiled by Wang Xuanhe 王懸河. *Zhengtong Daozang* 780–2, no. 1139.

Zhang Zehong 張澤洪. 'Wudou mi dao mingming de youlai 五斗米道命名的由來.' *Zongjiao xue yanjiu* 宗教學研究 (1988.4): 12–17.

Zhao Daoyi 趙道一. *Lishi zhenxian tidao tongjian* 歷世眞仙體道通鑑 (pref. 1294). *Zhengtong Daozang* 139–48, no. 296.

Zhao Zongcheng 趙宗誠. 'Du Guangting *Linghua ershisi* de yixie tedian 杜光庭《靈化二十四化》一些特點.' *Zongjiao xue yanjiu* 宗教學研究 (1990.1–2): 10–12.

Zhen'gao 眞告. Compiled by Tao Hongjing 陶弘景. *Zhengtong Daozang* 637–40, no. 1016.

Zhengtong Daozang 正統道藏. 1120 vols. Shanghai: Commercial Press, 1923–6.

Reprint. 60 vols. Taibei: Yiwen yingshuguan, 1962. Fascicule and work numbers according to Shi Zhouren 施舟人 (Kristofer Schipper) ed., 道藏索引一五種版本道藏通檢.

Zhengyi fawen jing zhangguan pin 正一法文經章官品. *Zhengtong Daozang* 880, no. 1218.

Zhengyi fawen taishang wailu yi 正一法文太上外籙儀. *Zhengtong Daozang* 991, no. 1243.

Zhengyi qizhi tu 正一氣治圖 ap. *Wushang biyao* 無上秘要, 23.4a–9a. *Zhengtong Daozang* 768–79, no. 1138.

Zhengyi tianshi gao Zhao Sheng koujue 正一天師告趙昇口訣. *Zhengtong Daozang* 1003, no. 1273.

Zhu Faman 朱法滿. *Yaoxiu keyi jielü chao* 要修科儀戒律鈔. *Zhengtong Daozang* 204–207, no. 463.

Zhuanji boyuan jing 撰集白緣經. Compiled by Zhiqian 支謙. In *Taishō shinshū daizōkyō*. Vol. 4, no. 200, 203–57.

Index

Q

R

S